THE COMMISSION OF THE EUROPEAN COMMUNITIES
DIRECTORATE GENERAL XII FOR SCIENCE RESEARCH AND DEVELOPMENT

PASSIVE SOLAR ARCHITECTURE IN EUROPE 2

D1741933

THE COMMISSION OF THE EUROPEAN COMMUNITIES
DIRECTORATE GENERAL XII FOR SCIENCE RESEARCH AND DEVELOPMENT

PASSIVE SOLAR ARCHITECTURE IN EUROPE 2

THE RESULTS OF THE
'SECOND EUROPEAN PASSIVE SOLAR COMPETITION 1982'

EDITED BY RALPH M LEBENS

THE ARCHITECTURAL PRESS LTD LONDON

*Mr. H. Davies, Deputy Director General of DGXII,
congratulates a competitor at the prize-giving
ceremony in Cannes.*

PREFACE

The Western world has, in this century, been negligent in its use of fossil fuels, which Nature has prepared for us over many millions of years. One can find evidence of this carelessness in all branches of industry and not least in the building industry. The world's store of fossil fuels is limited and it is urgent that we move towards other sources of energy, preferably those which do not necessitate our depending on materials imported from outside the European Community. In order to develop these sources a huge programme of research and development is required.

The Commission of the European Communities is encouraging and pursuing this programme and has indeed funded one tenth of all public energy research in the Community. In some areas its contribution has been much higher and in research into solar energy it has provided no less than 40% of the finance employed.

By the beginning of the next century, it has been foreseen, solar energy will be providing from 5 to 7% of Europe's energy needs and an even greater share will be accounted for by use of energy-conserving policies. The Commission regards Passive Solar Design as of great importance in the pursuit of these two means of reducing Europe's dependence on oil.

The European Passive Solar Design Competition is one of the ways the Commission has adopted to stress the importance of this source of energy.

The effect of climate on building design was early realised and for centuries builders were influenced by it, but the skills they had developed were largely forgotten after the Industrial Revolution. These skills must now be re-learnt and disseminated. The European climate demands that designers concentrate on conserving solar gains and minimizing heat losses in the winter months. The construction materials must be used in such a way as to absorb and store the heat gained from the sun and the rooms must be arranged so that they use this stored heat with little recourse to artificial and expensive means of distribution.

To encourage the use of passive solar energy the Commission funded a study in August 1979 to identify the centres of skill in the use of such design in Europe. This was followed by a meeting of experts later in the year which recommended that the Commission's programme should pursue two courses:

      (i) to develop and assess the necessary technology
     (ii) to disseminate the principles of passive solar design
           among those in the profession of building design in
           the EC countries.

This Second European Passive Solar Design Competition, like the first in 1980, is part of the policy of dissemination of the principles of passive solar design and it is hoped and expected that it will result in much greater interest in and wider use of these principles. Members of the panel of judges have assured us that our aim has been achieved to a considerable degree by both the competitions.

The excellence of the winning designs and the high standard of work submitted indicate that the passive solar approach to architecture is being very well received by the building design profession.

The Commission looks forward with confidence to the continued growth of interest and the consequent wide application of Passive Solar Energy in building design in Europe.

Dr W Palz
Head of the Division
"Solar Energy Research"
Commission of the European Communities

ACKNOWLEDGEMENTS

The editor would like to thank the supervisor of this contract at the Commission of the European Communities, Theo Steemers, for his constant guidance and close contact throughout the competition, the exhibition and the preparation of this book. Thanks for their involvement and support are also due to the technical assessors and judges (listed below) without whose expertise the competition would not have been successful. Finally, we are grateful to all those who have put so much time and effort into the organization of the competition, the exhibition and this book.

BOOK:

Sub-editing, organization and verification of calculations:	Simon Walter
Design:	Robert Budwig
Artwork and Planning:	Paul Rowley
Typing:	Diane Pearson
Proof reading:	Geoffrey Lebens and Claudia Bloom
Translation of drawings and photographs of models:	Competition award winning entrants
Printing advice:	Maritz Vandenberg and Keith Kneebone The Architectural Press, London
Additional photography:	Morley von Sternberg
Typesetting:	Galley Typesetting, London

EXHIBITION:

Simon Walter, Paul Rowley, Claudia Bloom and Geoffrey Dale

COMPETITION:

Competition entry documents:

Design and Artwork:	Paul and Esther Rowley and Andrew Myer
Technical supervision:	Andrew Myer
Technical assistance:	Professor John Page, University of Sheffield, UK Hans Lund, Technical University of Denmark Erotokritos Tsingas, Engineer, Public Utility Company, Thessaloniki, Greece
Organization of Registration and submissions:	Diane Pearson

Translation of documents:

Danish:	Lars Olsen, Technical University of Denmark, Lyngby, Denmark
Dutch:	Martin de Wit, Technische Hogeschool, Eindhoven, The Netherlands
French:	Christian Queffelec, Centre Scientifique et Technique du Batiment, Paris, France
German:	Christian Kupke, Fraunhofer Institut für Bauphysik, Stuttgart, F R Germany
Greek:	Erotokritos Tsingas, Thessaloniki, Greece
Italian:	Sergio Los, Bassano del Grappa, Italy

Technical assessment of entries:

Nick Baker	Energy Conscious Design, London, UK
Francois Penz	Martin Centre, Cambridge University, UK
Orazio Barra	University of Calabria, Cosenza, Italy
Francois Guyon	Centre Scientifique et Technique de la Construction, Brussels, Belgium
Albert Dupagne	University of Liege, Belgium
Federico Butera	Istituto di Fisica Tecnica, University of Palermo, Italy
Christian Kupke	Fraunhofer Institut für Bauphysik, Stuttgart, F R Germany
J Owen Lewis*	University College, Dublin, Ireland
Michel Raoust*	Consulting Engineer, Paris, France
Michel Schneider	CNRS, Nice, France
Wolfgang Ehlers	Technische Universitat, Berlin, F R Germany
Alexandros Tombazis	Architect, Athens, Greece
Martin de Wit	Technische Hogeschool, Eindhoven, The Netherlands

Competition direction and judging of entries:

James Barrett	Architect, Dublin, Ireland
Edward Cullinan*	Architect, London, UK
Michel Gerber	Architect, Perpignan, France
Sergio Los	Architect and Professor, Venice, Italy
Jaques Michel	Architect, Paris, France

* *Chairmen*

First published in 1983 by
The Architectural Press: London

© ECSC, EEC, EAEC,
Brussels and Luxembourg, 1983

ISBN 0 85139 957 6

Publication arranged by:
Commission of the European Communities
Directorate-General Information Market
and Innovation Luxembourg

EUR 8564

Printed in Great Britain by Biddles Ltd, Guildford

CONTENTS

INTRODUCTION
AND
ORGANIZER'S REPORT

This book presents the award winning schemes of the second architectural ideas competition held by the Commission of the European Communities, Directorate-General XII, for Science, Research and Development.

The aims of both competitions were similar: to disseminate information on the principles of climate sensitive design.

The purpose of this publication is threefold: to spread the ideas and principles of passive solar design to a wider audience, to document the competition so that some of the excellent designs submitted will have a wider influence, and to give a voice to the pioneering work being undertaken by a few innovative architects and designers in Europe.

This book will present the award winning schemes with verified performance calculations and a copy in English of all the entry documents sent out to competitors except the brief. The main requirements of the brief are outlined within this introduction.

The First European Passive Solar Competition — 1980

At the end of 1979 the Commission asked Ralph Lebens Associates, an architectural practice in London which specialises in passive solar design, to organize the 'First European Passive Solar Competition — 1980'. The competition was announced in early April of 1980, when the documents became available to the general public. The submission date for entries was 29 August 1980. The judging was in two stages: the first by technical assessors from all over Europe, and the second by a panel of international architects with experience in the field of passive solar design.

The prizes, totalling 30,000 ECU*, were awarded in November 1980, at a ceremony in the offices of the European Commission in Brussels.

The competition was open to architects and students of architecture resident in any of the EC countries, and entries were encouraged from multi-disciplinary groups. It was an 'Ideas Competition', for the application of passive solar design principles either to a new construction or to the rehabilitation of an existing building. Entries were invited in three separate categories:-

Category A: Multi-Storey Housing
Category B: Clustered Housing
Category C: Single Dwellings

There were 1000 registrants and 223 entries to the competition resulting in 11 prizes, 11 commendations and 3 special mentions. An exhibition of the winner's drawings and models has travelled throughout Europe. A book of the competition results entitled 'Passive Solar Architecture in Europe' has been published by the Architectural Press, London.

The Second European Passive Solar Competition — 1982

The general response to the first competition and the interest shown in the winning schemes prompted the Commission to hold a second competition. Ralph Lebens Associates were again asked to be the organizers. The aims of this second competition were to shift the emphasis of the competition to include design questions which are more pertinent to the needs of Europe.

An initial meeting of the judges in Brussels resulted in the definition of two categories:-

Category A: High Density, Low Rise Housing
Category B: Retrofit and Rehabilitation of Dwellings

These categories were chosen because they were thought to represent the more pressing problems in housing in Europe. The 'single house' category was omitted since this had been fully tackled in the first competition and it was not thought to be of such wide importance.

Entrants were asked to select real sites for their schemes within the EC countries. No cost limits for the passive components or the buildings were set but competitors were asked to bear cost in mind and advised that the judges would consider the economy of the schemes in their selection. It was also stated in the competition brief that within the category of retrofit and rehabilitation, "An area of particular concern is the large existing building stock of high-density high-rise housing stock (built between 1945 and 1970)".

The competition was launched in October 1981 and the final entry date was 27 August 1982.

It was decided to encourage schools of architecture to include the competition in their design studio work. The early launch date was essential if schools of architecture were to include the competition in their curricula. They were allowed to register for a fee of UK£25 (single registration was UK£5) for which they would recieve 40 sets of documents and could submit the 5 best schemes. Students were also permitted to register individually. The involvement of the schools in this way meant that the information within the competition documents would be distributed to many more designers and that the technical assessors and judges would not be over-burdened by increased numbers of submissions.

Another departure from the procedures in the first competition was that all competition entry documents were produced in the seven major European languages (Danish, Dutch, English, French, German, Greek and Italian) and submissions could be made in any one of these languages.

The following applications for the competition documents were received:

	Individuals	Schools of Architecture
Belgium	84	3 x 40
Denmark	75	—
France	366	1 x 40
Germany	376	4 x 40
Greece	27	1 x 40
Ireland	35	2 x 40
Italy	170	1 x 40
Netherlands	140	—
UK	119	9 x 40
Total	1395	20 x 40

The number of submissions for the competition were as follows:

	Category A	Category B	TOTAL
Belgium	8	8	16
Denmark	13	1	14
France	43	14	57
Germany	54	18	72
Greece	5	3	8
Ireland	5	1	6
Italy	28	3	31
Netherlands	18	4	22
UK	20	3	23
Total	194	55	249

The number of submissions from professional architects, architectural students and schools of architecture were as follows:

	A	B	TOTAL
Architects	133	42	175
Students	61	13	74
			249

An international technical assessment team of 13 experts within this field conducted the first stage of the competition assessment in September 1982.

The members of this team were:

Nick Baker	Energy Conscious Design, London, UK
Francois Penz	Martin Centre, Cambridge University, UK
Orazio Barra	University of Calabria, Cosenza, Italy
Francois Guyon	Centre Scientifique et Technique de la Construction, Brussels, Belgium
Albert Dupagne	University of Liege, Belgium
Federico Butera	Istituto di Fisica Tecnica, University of Palermo, Italy
Christian Kupke	Fraunhofer Institut für Bauphysik Stuttgart, F R Germany
J Owen Lewis†	University College, Dublin, Ireland
Michel Raoust †	Consulting Engineer, Paris, France
Michel Schneider	CNRS, Nice, France
Wolfgang Ehlers	Technische Universitat, Berlin, F R Germany
Alexandros Tombazis	Architect, Athens, Greece
Martin de Wit	Technische Hogeschool, Eindhoven, The Netherlands

The technical assessment process took one week and was followed by a 3-day final assessment by the following five international architects, all with experience of passive solar design:

James Barrett	Architect, Dublin, Ireland
Edward Cullinan †	Architect, London, UK
Michel Gerber	Architect, Perpignan, France
Sergio Los	Architect and Professor, Venice, Italy
Jaques Michel	Architect, Paris, France

Four prizes were awarded in each category with a total prize money of 30,000 ECU. Nineteen commendations and 3 special mentions were also awarded. These schemes are presented in full within this book.

The winning entrants received their prizes on 13 December 1982 at a ceremony held at the Palais des Festivals in Cannes at the opening of the Conference Internationale sur l'Architecture Solaire. The best entries were on display there for the duration of the conference — the first stop of their European tour.

*1 ECU (European Currency Unit) = 45.24 BFR, 8.13 DKR, 2.30 DM, 68.55 DRA, 6.53 FF, IRL £0.69, 1325.66 LIT, 2.55 HFL, UK£0.60.

† Chairmen

TECHNICAL COMMENT

In the first competition it was necessary to use the Los Alamos SLR calculation method and our comments at that time were that we needed "A universally applicable and generally comprehensible method ... for quantitatively evaluating the designs. There was none that was both reliable and easy to use. Such a design method still appears unavailable although the Balcomb SLR method, used for the competition, comes closest to this requirement. However, it does have its shortcomings ...", and continued to list a few of these shortcomings. It was hoped at that time that a future competition could have a simpler calculation method and one which could evaluate systems other than the simplest ones, a major drawback of the first competition method. But we found ourselves in precisely the same situation when it came to the second competition, and the only method available at that time was the second Los Alamos SLR method. It at least met one of our ambitions: it could evaluate mixed passive systems and with greater accuracy. Although it was adapted to suit the needs of the competition it was, unfortunately, still far too complex and, like the first competition method, showed few signs of being used as a design tool — iteration of such a complex method is too much to expect. Also the method is so opaque in its construction that there were few entrants who managed to complete their calculations correctly, and the difficulty of technical assessment was considerably increased. There are now two other manual calculation methods available to the designer: The Method 5000* and the third Los Alamos Method†. Both show signs of being simpler to use than the method used in this competition. The Los Alamos method is still very opaque but the Method 5000, although not less time-consuming, is far more transparent and so has much to teach the designer in terms of the benefits of different possible design strategies and systems used.

Because of the above mentioned problems with the calculation method we have had to correct most of the calculations for the schemes presented within this book. It was not possible to check the heat loss coefficients of the building elements or of the overall building other than to notice if there were any unbelievable values, but apart from that, all other values were checked and, where necessary, recalculated. It is therefore felt that the results here are reasonably accurate and should be able to indicate trends.

In the book on the first competition results we conducted some analysis of the performance results and presented the graphs shown in Figs. 1,2 and 3. It was pointed out at that time that we were unable to check the results and therefore the conclusions drawn were to be taken with some caution. The results seemed to show that there was a peak in the annual useful solar energy per m³ of heated volume which occurred between latitudes 44 and 48°N (Fig. 2). It was also noticed that a latitude-determined fan shaped graph was being produced (Fig.1) indicating the same type of trend when annual useful solar gain was plotted against solar aperture area. With reference to these diagrams it was stated that "At lower latitudes, progressively less heating is required and the

* Method 5000: the CEC selected manual calculation method was developed in Paris by M. Raoust et al. and is to be shortly published in the seven major European languages in "The CEC Passive Solar Handbook". French Method 5000: Methode 5000, by P Claux, J P Franca, R Gilles, A Pesso, A Pouget, M Raoust, Pyc. Edition, December 1982.

† "Passive Solar Design Handbook — Volume Three" Edited by R W Jones, US Department of Energy: DOE/CS-0127/3, July 1982

graph drops off rapidly. The steady fall in Useful Solar Gain towards the higher latitudes was not expected, as these have a longer heating season and should be able to make more use of incident solar energy. This could possibly be explained by the less than ideal typical solar radiation conditions in most of Northern Europe. The points below the curve are generally schemes with low aperture/heated volume ratios (0.1m²/m³ or less)".

Our first instinct was to attempt to validate or otherwise the conclusion which we had arrived at with the uncertain data from the first competition. With the checked results from the second competition we plotted the same graph as in Figure 2 (see Figure 5). The schemes were divided into 3 groups of aperture to volume ratio: less than 0.05, 0.05 to 0.15, and 0.15 to 0.36. Contrary to the graph in Figure 2, the results in Figure 5 show no conclusive diminishing of useful solar in the higher latitiudes, and the trend in the three groups is indistinct in the higher latitudes because there is insufficient data.

We plotted the Figures of Merit (kWh/m³DD – the annual auxiliary heating requirement per unit volume per degree day — 18.3°C base) against latitude (Figure 6). This Figure of Merit was recommended by some of the technical assessors of the first competition and is proposed as a method of normalizing the performance of building at different latitudes so that they can be directly compared. The higher the Figure of Merit, the worse is the performance of the building, i.e. the higher its auxiliary heating demand per unit volume and per degree day. In our calculation booklet we recommended that a Figure of Merit of approximately 0.0025 should be achievable in well insulated buildings. In Figure 6 it is mainly the schemes with high aperture to volume ratio which have high Figures of Merit.

We then plotted the new data onto a graph similar to Figure 1. The outcome of this is shown in Figure 4. The result shows such a random position of latitude that no demarcation lines could be possible.

The results were therefore proving to be rather inconclusive. It was decided to take several projects (including one from each aperture-to-volume-ratio category) and to subject them to the climate at varying latitudes throughout Europe. From the plots on Figure 6, those lying between 0.0025 and 0.0075 were chosen for the experimental runs. The climates chosen were Nice 43°40′N, Paris 48°49′N, London 51°28′N, Eskdalemuir 55°19′N and Lerwick 60°09′N. The weather data from these 5 locations is shown in Figure 7.

The graph in Figure 5 was then attempted using the experimental runs data. The result is shown in Figure 9 which seems to indicate that the 44 to 48°N latitude peak is not correct. A fan shape is clearly indicated although the sensitivity to local climatic conditions is also clear from the dips and rises. It is difficult to say whether or not the dip from Eskdalemuir to Lerwick is due to local climatic conditions rather than general latitude-dependent trends.

Such conclusions do not take account of the complex interaction between useful solar gain, the aperture-area-to-heated-volume ratio, and the Figure of Merit (as defined above).

A plot of Figure of Merit against latitude was made using the experimental runs data (Figure 10). One would expect that if the Figure of Merit is a true normalized measure of the way that the building performs, it would remain almost constant when the building is moved from one climate to the next. This would certainly be true if the auxiliary heating requirement was dependent on the external temperature only. The only other factor which could be responsible for this lack of flatness, other than

internal gains (which remain constant in the schemes and are subtracted before solar gains are dealt with, therefore having no effect) is the useful solar gains. It is very difficult to rely too heavily on slight changes in these two graphs (Figures 9 and 10) but it is highly likely that because of the increasing length of the heating season with increase in latitude above 48°N the annual total of useful solar energy remains at worst constant and at best increases slightly. When the latitude decreases below approximately 48°N solar energy is becoming responsible for a greater proportion of the total heating load (i.e. percent solar heated is higher) but because of the small load of the building anyway, the quantity of useful solar gains per unit volume or per unit area of glazing is reducing. Figure 8 (annual useful solar to aperture area) illustrates the same thing in a slightly different way and is directly comparable with Figure 1. Here again something quite the contrary to the unverified results of the first competition is being shown. The higher values of useful solar energy to aperture area are those of the higher latitudes.

The above seems to be indicating that the solar energy contribution of one square metre of south-facing vertical glazing in Nice will be able to contribute less useful solar energy per year than one in London. It is suspected that if the building were designed with the correct aperture to volume ratio for Nice then the quantity of useful solar per unit area of glazing would be approximately the same as the useful solar energy per unit area of a "correctly" sized passive solar system in London or in Lerwick (with some minor differences due to non-latitude-dependent different weather characteristics of these locations). Given the size of the sample and the possible fallibility of the calculation method for European climates, this can be seen essentially as guesswork but it is clear from these studies that much more European parametric work is needed to include such factors as "conservation to passive solar cost optimisation" and the relationship of these to "aperture area to heated volume ratio", "annual useful solar energy to latitude", and "Figure of Merit". It is also clear that, because of the many responsibilities of the design solution other than energy saving, designers must be closely involved in such studies.

It is hoped that the design solutions and performance predictions included in this book will inspire more designers to incorporate the principles of passive solar design in their buildings and that such a technical analysis will encourage individual governments and the European Commission to sponsor further European research to investigate the correct perspective on climate sensitive design in relation to other energy conservation techniques within buildings.

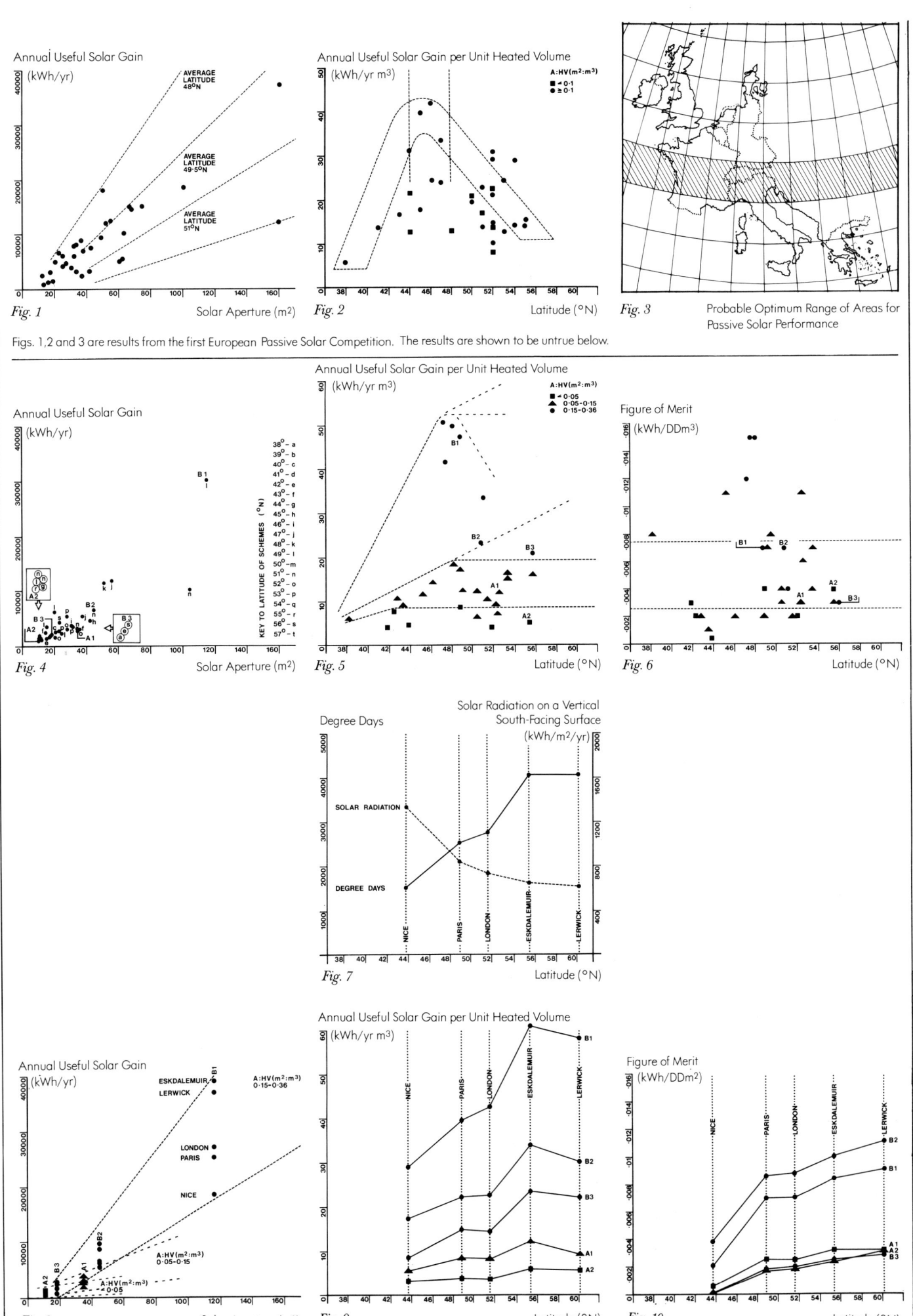

Fig. 1 — Annual Useful Solar Gain (kWh/yr) vs Solar Aperture (m²)

Fig. 2 — Annual Useful Solar Gain per Unit Heated Volume (kWh/yr m³) vs Latitude (°N)

Fig. 3 — Probable Optimum Range of Areas for Passive Solar Performance

Figs. 1, 2 and 3 are results from the first European Passive Solar Competition. The results are shown to be untrue below.

Fig. 4 — Annual Useful Solar Gain (kWh/yr) vs Solar Aperture (m²)

Fig. 5 — Annual Useful Solar Gain per Unit Heated Volume (kWh/yr m³) vs Latitude (°N)

Fig. 6 — Figure of Merit (kWh/DDm³) vs Latitude (°N)

Fig. 7 — Degree Days / Solar Radiation on a Vertical South-Facing Surface (kWh/m²/yr) vs Latitude (°N)

Fig. 8 — Annual Useful Solar Gain (kWh/yr) vs Solar Aperture (m²)

Fig. 9 — Annual Useful Solar Gain per Unit Heated Volume (kWh/yr m³) vs Latitude (°N)

Fig. 10 — Figure of Merit (kWh/DDm²) vs Latitude (°N)

JUDGES' REPORT

A major aim of this Second competition was to bring the design of solar buildings into the debate concerning a future architecture for our cities and towns; and we were well rewarded in this aim by receiving 192 entries for Category A and 54 entries for Category B, many of which tackled urban and suburban problems with much understanding and commitment.

In the recent past, houses which were designed to use the sun to aid in heating and ventilation have usually been either individual, and more or less experimental, or, at best, in small groups. Under those circumstances the house can concentrate on the effectiveness of the solar system and its own architectural expression as an autonomous object relating only to the hill, the clearing in the forest, the field, the seashore upon which it lies. The house is an object in the context of its semi-natural surroundings and its peculiarities, especially its tendency to face one way only, can be resolved in a composition suitable to itself within that context.

If we are to move forward from this position, we will need to examine ways in which solar houses can form groups, can contain major buildings among them and can create and present elevations to those open space elements which go to make up our towns and cities, the street, the boulevard, the piazza, the avenue, the park, the passage, the court; those spaces between buildings that need meaning and connection in order to become tolerable places in which to be.

So among the schemes for newly built houses at a density above 180p.p.ha. (Category A), we looked for schemes which not only made satisfactory houses themselves but contributed to the spaces between and beyond them. Among the schemes which proposed to alter and rebuild existing buildings (Category B) we looked for both an improvement in the performance of the buildings and evidence that they now sat more logically, less disruptively, more prettily into the town or the city that surrounds them.

The schemes were also assessed for their solar performance. In the final assessment we were interested not only in technical efficiency but we also looked for suitability to the type of building proposed and capacity to contribute positively to the quality of the place, both inside and out, and to the aesthetics of necessity. We were interested in the economy of the means employed in its widest sense, simplicity of construction and ease and comprehensibility of operation. We enjoyed those schemes that were clearly and simply explained by means of drawing and writing and, since Architecture before building is graphically represented, we also found it easiest to like those schemes that were most beautifully drawn.

So good was the general standard of entry from all our points of view that by halfway through the judging process we were still considering 48 schemes in Category A and 20 schemes in Category B and our final choices were made only after much hard work and discussion. It also became clear to us that Category B was considerably harder for the entrants to handle than Category A, as the number of entries testify.

So our final choices for the four prizes in each section are those that we agree to be the best in each Category. Our commended schemes name the runners up and at the same time represent a number of specific tendencies that interested groups of competitors.

In Category A the First, Second and Third prizewinners are all schemes which largely succeed in dealing with the most difficult issue that faced competitors: the creation of linked and multi-directional urban spaces formed by grouped houses which are also required to be oriented south.

The Commended schemes in Category A represent a number of further issues that clearly interested competitors as much as they did the judges, and the Commended schemes are grouped loosely in accordance with the issues they raise — this does not, of course, constitute an order of merit.

In Category B the First and both the Third prizewinners are schemes for the transformation of post-war housing blocks, the problem which the conditions of the competition stressed; the Second prize goes to the best of the schemes produced for the rehabilitation of historic buildings for use as houses. We award two third prizes, both for schemes that remodelled housing schemes.

As with Category A, the Category B Commendations and Special Mentions are not in order of merit but we have used an order loosely based on the issues raised.

We wish to thank the competitors for their hard work and for their commitment to the undoubted future of energy conscious design. We should also like to thank the organisers for their highly efficient arrangements.

Edward Cullinan, Chairman

TECHNICAL ASSESSORS' REPORT

Encouragement may be taken from this second competition that, in the last two years, the essential principles of passive solar design have become better known in Europe. While there seemed to be fewer proposals with gross design misconceptions than in the earlier competition, the assessors were disappointed that outstanding design concepts were few in number and that vigorous technical economic consideration and development of the classic passive approaches were seen in very few entries.

Many schemes suffered from over-complexity, with an excessive variety of techniques incorporated into one design. There was good use of shading devices to minimise overheating and some interesting proposals for summer cooling. The importance of thermal mass is well established, but practical considerations such as the implications for finishes and the acoustic environment were not dealt with. Of particular importance is the poor quantitative appreciation of the comparative performances of the various passive techniques in different European climates, perhaps reflecting the influence of inappropriate design publications, especially from North America, or reflecting the lack of European measured data. This emphasises the need for data gathering from test buildings to be incorporated into design guidelines and other professional support specifically suited to European conditions.

Many designs made good use of mechanical ventilation, often combined with auxiliary air heating systems. Heat emission devices were however generally poorly integrated and controls rarely considered. Some competitors ingeniously modified the section to increase solar penetration, but conflicts may be observed between attempts to increase the solar aperture while maintaining an efficient ratio between external envelope and enclosed space. In the new housing category, site planning and layout were generally disappointing, too many schemes being either built into south facing hillsides in special circumstances, or alternatively set out in somewhat crude terrace layouts. Much more work is needed on retrofit possibilities. In both categories, the graphic presentation of the concepts and technical proposals could in most cases have been much clearer.

The assessors identified certain misconceptions or unrealistic expectations which recurred. Large shared sunspaces and atria were proposed without consideration of practical difficulties such as fire safety, ventilation and so on, and the solar liability of horizontal glazing under winter and summer conditions was largely overlooked. The effectiveness with which remote rock bed heat stores may be charged by air drawn from sunspaces is suspect in northern Europe. Glazing areas and insulation standards were considered only rarely to be optimised and it is thought that in some cases overheating would occur. There was concern on the part of the assessors that certain proposals for internal insulating shutters might add substantially to the fire hazards of a building's interior.

It is clear from many entries that further work is needed in detailed design and product development for highly insulated building construction, shutters and blinds. Phase-change materials are needed with the melt points appropriate to passive solar applications. In planning the building, there are opportunities for improving the thermal zoning of the interior spaces in relation to diurnal variation in solar gain and occupancy — though it is necessary to be realistic about the temperature differences which can be maintained within a well-insulated envelope. The controls needed to operate passive systems efficiently and in conjunction with various auxiliary heating systems are not yet developed.

The calculations forming part of each entry provided many difficulties for the assessors as well as they clearly did for most competitors. Firstly, though, the competition organisers must be congratulated on the manner in which they tackled what is an extremely difficult objective, to provide a method through which competitors from all over Europe might predict the performance of their design proposals. It must be observed that the modelling of passive solar system performance is as yet at an early stage of development, and it is too early for any general agreement on calculation method. The value of the method used in this competition is shown in that most competitors succeeded in completing the calculations booklet and obtaining some performance predictions. The assessors, however, thought the method's lack of "transparency" a disadvantage, in that it seemed that many competitors did not have a physical understanding of the method and so could not use it creatively. Its complexity was off-putting and made iteration unlikely; simpler methods without unacceptable reduction in accuracy should soon become available. Problems also arose because competitors did not understand the limitations of the method, in particular its reduced reliability for superinsulated buildings. Among the errors seen most frequently in the entrants' calculations were optimistically low ventilation and infiltration rates, thermal transmittance, and overestimation of useful internal gains. Several competitors misunderstood the use of the shading diagrams, and calculation of effects of buffer spaces did not include allowance for the preheating of ventilation air, which was commonly utilized. Distinctions were blurred between primary, secondary and remote thermal storage mass, and excessive thicknesses of mass were assumed to be useful and so included in the calculations.

In conclusion the assessors would emphasise that these comments are not intended to reflect upon the competitors who took such trouble to present their ideas in this important competition, but rather to suggest areas of further study and development so that passive solar techniques may be widely and cost effectively used in European buildings. The opportunities presented by the huge stock of existing buildings requires special attention, and there is a need to gain experience through building and to increase the concern with realisation.

Owen Lewis, Chairman
12 September 1982.

DATA

EXPLANATION OF TECHNICAL DATA

GUIDELINES FOR
PASSIVE SOLAR HEATING
DESIGN

DATA BOOKLET

EXPLANATION OF TECHNICAL DATA

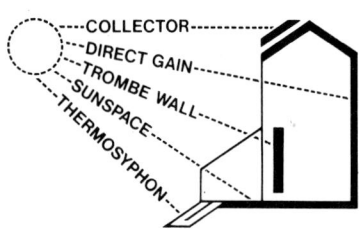

TECHNICAL DATA

1. Latitude: °   'N
2. Altitude: m
3. Data Point:

DWELLING DESCRIPTION (Typical Unit)
4. Heated Volume: m³

APERTURE   A   B   C   D

5. System Type
6. Net Area m²
7. Glazing Layers
8. Night Insulation
9. τ
10. Comment

11. Aperture/Heated Volume: m2/m3
12. Primary Mass/
       Related Aperture: Wh/m²°C
13. Remote Mass/
       Related Aperture: Wh/m²°C
14. Air Change Rate: ac/h m.v.
15. Building Loss Coeff.:   kWh/DD
       :   W/°C

DWELLING PERFORMANCE (Typical Unit)
16. % Internal Gains:
17. % Auxiliary Heating:
18. % Useful Solar Gains:
19. Annual Solar Gains Fraction:
20. Figure of Merit: kWh/DDm²
21. Useful Solar Gains/
       m² of Aperture: kWh/m²yr
22. Min. Temp. without Heating: °C
23. Min. Outdoor Temperature: °C

ENERGY CHARACTERISTICS

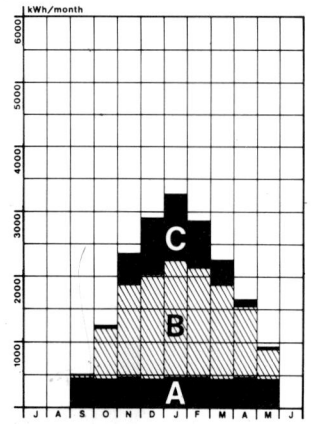

DESCRIPTION OF TERMS USED IN THE TECHNICAL DATA LISTINGS

DIAGRAM: The diagram at the top of each listing is used to represent the types of systems employed within the scheme.
1. : The latitude of the site
2. : The altitude of the site
3. : The meteorological station from which climatic data was obtained.

DWELLING DESCRIPTION (Typical Unit)
4. : The total heated volume of the dwelling.

APERTURE: A,B,C or D
5. : The solar systems employed in the scheme are abbreviated as follows:

C: Active Collector — used in hybrid systems	TS: Thermosyphon
DG: Direct Gain	TW: Mass or Trombe Wall
SS: Sunspace	WW: Water Wall

For explanation of system types see the reprinted 'Guidelines for Passive Solar Heating Design'.

6. : The total glazed aperture area of each system (after reduction in area due to window frames).
7. : Indicates whether the collector is single, double or triple glazed.
8. : Indicates whether or not the collection areas are insulated at night.
9. : This is a lumped factor describing transmitted solar radiation compared with that incident on a south orientated vertical surface. The reduction or increase is as a result of orientation, tilt of the aperture, the ground reflectance, the transmittance of the glazings, the shading due to site obstructions, and the presence of specular reflectors or overhangs in front of the aperture.
   The factor is an approximate annual average of those values which appear in Column 8.17 of the Calculations Booklet (pages 139 - 155 in Appendix).
10. : This describes which of the factors outlined above were instrumental in shaping the value of τ
   The following abbreviations are used:

O : Obstruction	T : Tilted Aperture
O/H : Overhang	R : Specular Reflector

N,S,E,W etc. : indicate the orientation of the aperture
off S : indicates that the aperture does not face directly south

11. : The proportion of the net solar aperture area to the total heated volume of the dwelling.
12. : The total primary thermal storage capacity per square metre of related aperture area.
   The meaning of and guidance to the values of primary thermal mass are given in the 'Design Guidelines' Booklet (pp 17-19).
13. : The remote thermal storage capacity per square metre of related aperture area.
14. : The design air change rate due to infiltration and ventilation. If a heat exchanger is used the air change rate shown is the adjusted value as used in the calculations. In this case "m.v." appears after the value.
15. : The total heat loss from the building per day per °C temperature difference between the inside and outside. This figure is the fabric losses of the building, (including those through the solar components) plus the infiltration and ventilation heat losses. It is expressed in both kWh/DD and W/°C.

DWELLING PERFORMANCE (Typical Unit)
   The information provided under this heading is useful for comparing the performance of the different schemes and systems:
16. : The total annual internal gains as a percentage of the gross annual heat loss
   (the gross annual heat loss = auxiliary heating requirement + useful solar gains + internal gains).
17. : The total annual auxiliary heating requirement as a percentage of the gross annual heat loss.
18. : The total useful solar gains as a percentage of the gross annual heat loss.
19. : The annual solar savings fraction is calculated from the ratio of the annual auxiliary heating requirement to the annual net thermal load. This effectively compares the auxiliary heating requirement with that of the same building with no solar or internal gains.
   It is given by: $1 - \dfrac{\text{total auxiliary heating requirement}}{\text{total net thermal load}}$
20. : The figure of merit is suggested as a comparison figure for schemes located in different climates. It normalizes the building performances by taking into account the thermal load of the building arising from the climatic conditions of the site.
   It is given by: $\dfrac{\text{total auxiliary heating requirement}}{\text{heated volume x degree days (18.3°C base temp.)}}$
21. : The total annual solar gains used for space heating per unit aperture area.
22. : The annual minimum internal temperature without auxiliary heating is calculated using the average annual minimum outdoor temperature, the nightly internal gains (usually around 1.5kW) and the night-time building loss coefficient.
23. : The annual minimum external temperature was obtained from the Data Booklet or from local sources.

GRAPH : For each scheme a histogram of gross heat loss for each month has been plotted. This shows for a typical unit, proportions of internal gains (lower portion of graph, A) of useful solar gains (middle shaded portion, B) and of the auxiliary heating requirement (upper portion of graph, C).

GUIDELINES FOR PASSIVE SOLAR HEATING DESIGN

COMMISSION OF THE EUROPEAN COMMUNITIES
Directorate General XII for Research, Science and Education

By: Ralph M. Lebens, 4 Tottenham Mews, London W.1, UK
Graphics: Paul and Esther Rowley, 56 High Street, Upwood, Hunts, UK
Printing: Albry Printing Company, Wallingford, Oxon, UK   © Ralph Lebens 1980

CONTENTS

1 INTRODUCTION

This booklet has been produced for the Commission of the European Communities DG XII (for Research, Science and Education). It is aimed at building designers and attempts to give guidelines for passive solar design. It is important to stress that a good design will result from a balanced approach to both the guidelines presented within this booklet and the other client-specified design constraints — none of the guidelines is of such overriding importance that it should be adhered to at the expense of the resulting design.

THE PASSIVE SOLAR HOME makes use of the materials from which the dwelling is constructed to directly capture, store and distribute the solar heat to its occupants. High heat capacity material (such as brick, concrete, stone or water) absorbs this solar energy as it enters the house and stores it in the form of heat. The living spaces of the home are carefully arranged so that they are in direct thermal contact with this store, allowing these spaces to be heated directly without the expense of special plumbing or forced hot air distribution systems.

PASSIVE DESIGNS require considerations of solar and heat flow, in every detail and component. Floor plan layout, circulation patterns, window location and the selection of wall and floor materials all affect how well a passive design will work. The entire house *is* a solar energy system with many of its components now having dual functions: both the traditional function of providing an enclosure and the solar function of collecting, storing and distributing heat. Windows not only let in light and allow a view, but collect heat as well. Walls which subdivide and enclose space can also store and radiate heat. Components whose functions were primarily structural, spatial or aesthetic may double as solar heating components. Often a traditional building component can be replaced by one with dual solar function enabling real savings in solar heating and at minimum risk.

Passive solar design is not a new concept, it has been used by almost all indigenous builders for centuries and it is only the short time-span since the Industrial Revolution in which, due to cheap energy, building designers have lost the skills of designing in harmony with the climate. Such skills offer great potential in cost effective energy saving within buildings.

The Commission of the European Communities is sponsoring the production of this booklet with the intention of spreading the philosophy and principles of solar design to as many members of the building design profession as possible.

2 CATEGORIES: DESIGN CONSIDERATIONS & CONFLICTS

PASSIVE SOLAR SYSTEMS

DIRECT GAIN

a. **DIFFUSING** — south-facing window is solar collector; insulation; optional moveable insulation; thermal mass

b. **NON-DIFFUSING** — optional moveable insulation; thermal mass

INDIRECT GAIN

a. **MASS TROMBE WALL** — optional moveable insulation; solid, dark-coloured storage mass

b. **WATER TROMBE WALL** — optional moveable insulation; water heat-storage tank

c. **ROOF POND** — moveable insulation; metal ceiling

ISOLATED GAIN

a. **SUNSPACE** — optional moveable insulation & shading; glazing; thermal mass

b. **THERMOSYPHON** — heated air; rock bed thermal mass

COOLING — not defined here include:

1. DIRECT GAIN
   a. DIFFUSING
   b. NON-DIFFUSING

Features: a & b.
Most commonly applied passive solar systems. The sun enters the living space and its energy is stored in thermal mass within this space. The thermal mass is externally insulated from the climate.
Moveable insulation may be considered on the south windows.

Considerations: a & b.
Heat loss from large areas of glazing.
Shading devices for summer.
Glare.
Size of windows and overheating.

Conflicts: a. View.
          b. Furnishings and energy store.

2. INDIRECT GAIN
   a. MASS TROMBE WALL
Named after Dr Felix Trombe's and Jacques Michel's work in Odeillo, France. The wall is dark coloured on its south face and massive. It is placed behind glazing. Behind both glazing and wall is the living space.
The wall stores solar energy during the day and transmits it, by means of conduction, to the living space several hours later. The time taken for this energy to travel through the wall is related to the thickness of the wall. For immediate transfer of heat, it is possible to open the space between the wall and glass to the room air.

Considerations: Overheating.

Conflicts: View, access and system sizing.

   b. WATER TROMBE WALL
In principle the same as a mass Trombe wall system except that contained water replaces the solid wall. Water has greater heat capacity per volume than does concrete or brick and, because it is a liquid, will distribute the heat evenly throughout the mass. Collection efficiency is increased, because of reduced outer surface temperatures, but there is the problem of containment to contend with.

   c. ROOF POND
Principle same as the water Trombe wall but placed on the roof. The only means of heat distribution is by radiation through a metal ceiling. Moveable insulation is necessary to reduce unwanted heat loss in winter and heat gain in summer.

Conflicts: Structural requirements to carry water.
          Snow or low altitude winter sun will hamper collection   thus may not be practical for high latitudes.

3. ISOLATED GAIN
   a. SUNSPACE
Atrium, greenhouse or conservatory. South orientated glazed space which is isolated from the living areas. It is used for extension to the living space but only seasonally. The storage mass can be in the form of a Trombe wall or may be placed in the floor or ceiling of the living spaces, and linked to this by means of a small fan. Such isolated thermal storage with forced air connection produces a hybrid rather than a passive system, but the difference between the two, unless large mechanical equipment is used, is only academic.

   b. THERMOSYPHON
This employs the change in density of the collection fluid to create circulation through heat storage mass. This thermal mass may be placed in the living room floor or ceiling.

Considerations: The collector must be placed below the storage mass.

RADIANT COOLING TO THE NIGHT SKY
EVAPORATIVE COOLING
DEHUMIDIFICATION
UNDERGROUND BUILDING

3 ISOLATED DESIGN FACETS & PRINCIPLES

3.1 SITE and MICROCLIMATE

Site investigation is a major factor in passive solar design - the building must respond to its site and micro-climate in much the same way as a plant does.
During site investigation look for sheltering and shading land forms and vegetation.

A The Sun: Maximize the Benefits

Summer sun: heats domestic water and possible induced ventilation

Winter sun: heats house and domestic hot water

Sun pathfinder[1, 2] is used to project the path of the sun throughout the year on the site.

This will tell if trees or buildings will block out the sun at any time of year.

B The Wind: Protect the Building

from COLD PREVAILING WINTER WINDS and also create protected external areas by means of:-

a) Evergreen trees as a shelter belt

b) Earth berms

c) Building shapes: small protected area

Shaped roof deflects winds: larger protected area

3.2 THERMAL COMFORT

should be the starting point for ENERGY CONSCIOUS DESIGN

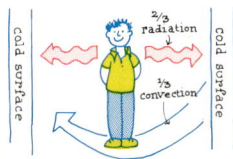  

a) PRINCIPLES OF HEAT LOSS — 2/3 radiation; 1/3 convection

b) THE PROBLEM: In a poorly insulated building—no convection loss but still discomfort — room temp 22°C; cold surface; radiation

c) THE SOLUTION: with efficient use of insulation a room temperature of 18°C will provide a comfortable THERMAL ENVIRONMENT because the external surfaces are insulated and therefore warmer — 18°C

But SUCCESSFUL insulation can lead to problems of OVERHEATING

thermostat can be set this low and comfort achieved

insulation over window at night

3·3 OVERHEATING

It is necessary to prevent overheating during Spring and Autumn for 2 reasons:
1. THERMAL COMFORT - but one may argue that venting & shading are then possible.
2. TO MAXIMISE THE SOLAR ENERGY COLLECTED - if area of glazing is too large some of the energy collected will have to be thrown away by venting

Thus it would be more economical to reduce overheating by means of additional storage mass (thermal mass) or by reduced glazing area. There are rules of thumb guidelines for thermal mass (see 4·5) and design method for testing against over-heating (see 8·3).

SOLUTIONS — either reduce glass area   or increase thermal mass

Summer overheating can be dealt with by ventilation.

3·4 VISUAL COMFORT is important.
It is often a problem in DIRECT GAIN SYSTEMS

Large areas of glass can cause GLARE

REDUCE GLARE by means of windows giving light to rear of room to increase lighting levels there by:

clerestory   side windows

And REDUCE CONTRAST by: splayed reveals   light coloured window walls

RULE OF THUMB

y should not exceed 2-2½ x in a room with only one window wall

4 ISOLATED COMPONENTS

4·1 VEGETATION

A WINTER: SHELTER from the prevailing winds - Trees must be EVERGREEN

B SUMMER: SHADING and EVAPORATIVE COOLING - Trees must be DECIDUOUS

Different types of trees have different shading factors in WINTER [3]

Types of trees compatible with climate, local soil conditions and exposure must be researched by designer.

4·2 WINDOWS
Look at this in conjunction with Section 3·1
Objectives: A. MAXIMIZE Winter heat gain
B. MINIMIZE Summer heat gain
C. MINIMIZE Winter heat losses
D. MAXIMIZE Summer ventilation

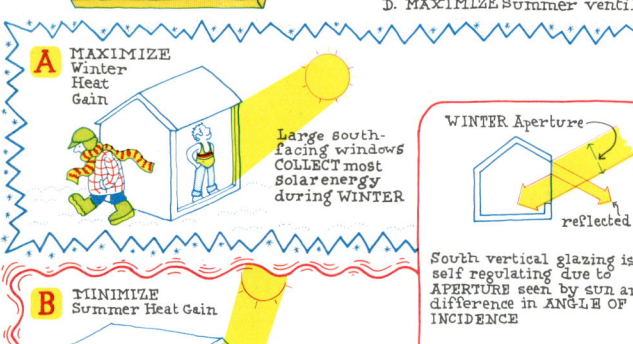

A MAXIMIZE Winter Heat Gain

Large south-facing windows COLLECT most solar energy during WINTER

WINTER Aperture — reflected

South vertical glazing is self regulating due to difference in APERTURE seen by sun and ANGLE of INCIDENCE

SUMMER Aperture — reflected

B MINIMIZE Summer Heat Gain

Large windows on East, West or on South slope may cause SUMMER OVERHEATING

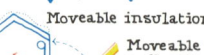

C MINIMIZE Winter Heat Losses

Moveable insulation

Moveable insulation with reflective surface to increase energy collection

Large RADIATIVE HEAT LOSS to clear night sky in WINTER from sloping glazing

Many different types of MOVEABLE INSULATION now available but does not insulate while collecting. PROBLEM also of good edge seals.

GLASS now being produced [4] which reflects INFRA-RED RADIATION without significant reduction in solar transmission

D MAXIMIZE Summer Ventilation

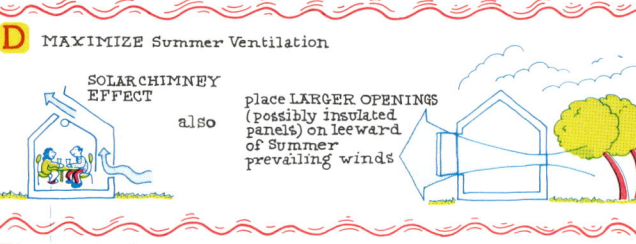

SOLAR CHIMNEY EFFECT   also   place LARGER OPENINGS (possibly insulated panels) on leeward of Summer prevailing winds

4·3 HEAT LOSSES

INSULATION & INFILTRATION

By means of careful attention to insulation and infiltration it is possible to reduce economically the energy losses of houses built to present standards by 60%. Of the remaining 40% ⅔ can be picked up by solar energy. It is important not to look at cost effectiveness on each modification but to look at the cost effectiveness of total package.

A Insulation

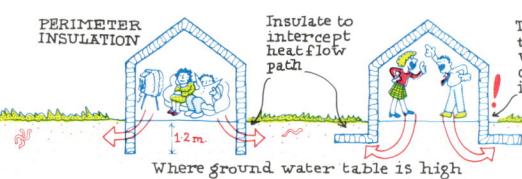

PERIMETER INSULATION   Insulate to intercept heat flow path   The detailing of this insulation where the building contacts the ground is DIFFICULT

1·2 m.

Where ground water table is high insulate under entire floor.

EXTERNAL INSULATION   If the house is to be used continuously INSULATE EXTERNALLY to allow massive walls to moderate the extremes of room temperature

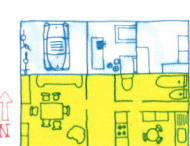

INSULATING BUFFER   Place utility rooms, garages and other non-living spaces on North side of dwelling to act as INSULATING BUFFER

B INFILTRATION AND VENTILATION

Infiltration is responsible for from 50% (well insulated houses) to 38% (poorly insulated) of total space heating loads in housing.

SOLUTION: Weatherstrip all doors and windows. Caulk all construction joints and gaps. Use air locks for external doors. Possibly have mechanically controlled ventilation

By use of weatherstripping and careful attention to reduce infiltration, it is possible to minimise the air change rate within a dwelling to about 0·5 air changes/hour. At this level comfort can still be maintained.

4·4 THERMAL MASS
is employed to tame the indoor air temperature fluctuations by storing solar energy for later release.

CONCRETE   BRICK   STONE   WATER

Any material with HIGH HEAT CAPACITY may be used. ← Most common

The darker the surface the more solar energy will be absorbed and therefore the more energy potentially stored within the thermal mass.

OBJECTIVE OF THERMAL MASS: to maintain a low surface temperature.
Thus WATER which spreads its heat quickly by convection currents is GOOD - but containment is a problem.

SECONDARY THERMAL MASS has a strong moderating influence [2] on room air temperatures.

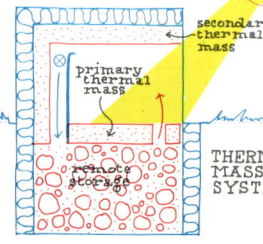

primary thermal mass   secondary thermal mass   remote storage

THERMAL MASS SYSTEMS

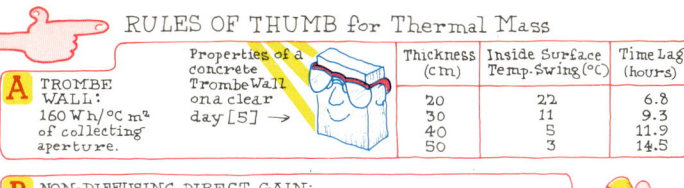

RULES OF THUMB for Thermal Mass

A TROMBE WALL: 160 Wh/°C m² of collecting aperture.

Properties of a concrete Trombe Wall on a clear day [5] →

Thickness (cm)	Inside Surface Temp. Swing (°C)	Time Lag (hours)
20	22	6.8
30	11	9.3
40	5	11.9
50	3	14.5

B NON-DIFFUSING DIRECT GAIN:
Primary Thermal Mass: 160-240 Wh/°C m² of collecting aperture
(Rule of Thumb for direct gain is noon on 21st December)

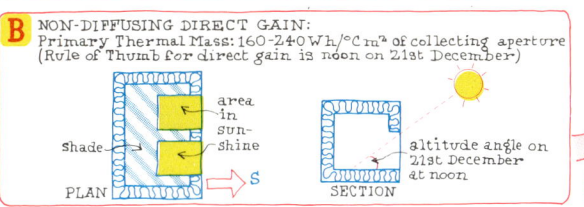

PLAN — shade, area in sun-shine
SECTION — altitude angle on 21st December at noon

C DIFFUSING DIRECT GAIN: 290 Wh/°C m² of floor area [6]

D REMOTE STORAGE: 80-120 Wh/°C m² of collecting aperture for fan-forced rock beds. For sizing see Ref [7]

4·5 INCIDENTAL HEAT GAINS

4 PERSON 3 BEDROOM HOUSE [8]

Incidental heat gains in the heating season for a 3 bedroom house [8].

Occupants	= 4 kWh/day
Lighting	= 1·4 "
Cooking	= 3·4 "
Appliances	= 3·4 "
Hot Water	= 3·4 "
TOTAL	= 15·6 kWh/day

Almost all energy used by lighting and appliances is transformed into heat.
Heat loss to the house from domestic hot water discharged into drains varies with equipment used because this determines water volume & temperature.

4·6 SHADING DEVICES

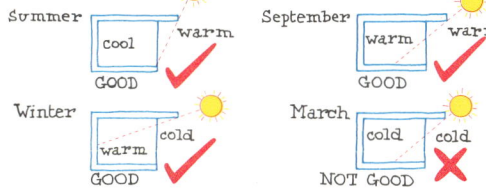

A Fixed — Fixed shading devices do not allow for lack of synchronisation of solar altitude and season.

Summer: cool / warm GOOD ✓
Winter: warm / cold GOOD ✓
September: warm / warm GOOD ✓
March: cold / cold NOT GOOD ✗

March and September solar altitudes are the same: but it may be much colder in March than in September.

B Moveable — Moveable shading devices with dual or triple function can be used but this may be expensive

Moveable blind
SUMMER: shade + solar chimney
WINTER: night insulation

C Trees — Small-branched DECIDUOUS trees can be used for shading (see Section 4·1)

4·7 AUXILLIARY HEATING

Unless building can heat itself without solar gains (i.e. by internal heat gains only) it must have some form of BACK-UP HEATING DEVICE.

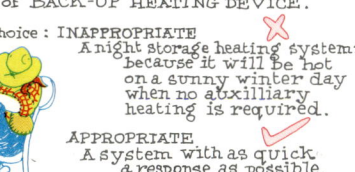

Choice : INAPPROPRIATE ✗
A night storage heating system: because it will be hot on a sunny winter day when no auxilliary heating is required.

APPROPRIATE
A system with as quick a response as possible.
Sizing:
The auxilliary system should be sized for:-
- night conditions,
- no internal heat gains,
- outdoor winter design temperature.

5 CALCULATION METHODS

Several different calculation methods have been developed for passive and low energy buildings. They each have their advantages and disadvantages.
The better known methods are given here to provide an overview.

5·1 Annual Heating Load Calculations

There is no accurate method of heating load calculation.
This is because with RANDOM SAMPLE FIELD TESTS of identical houses there are ratios of 4.1 in annual energy consumption [9]
INHABITANT BEHAVIOUR PATTERNS cause such differences and they cannot be accurately predicted by a calculation method.

A. TRADITIONAL METHOD
Published degree day figures X Total building heat loss per day °C.
Disadvantages: The degree day base temperature is arbitrarily set and does not allow for low energy design.

B. THE 'BIN' METHOD [2]
An adjusted degree day figure X Total building heat loss per day °C.
Disadvantages: Data for various degree day base temperatures are not universally available.
Assumption: There is no overheating (ie. to be used after method 5.3 B.a.)

C. THE LOS ALAMOS SOLAR LOAD RATIO [10, 11] AND SOLAR HEATING FRACTION METHODS [19] These are universally applicable because the data exists for all countries.
Disadvantages: It is produced for a situation where overheating is allowed to happen and thus there are no means of sizing the solar heating system in terms of comfort.

D. FINITE DIFFERENCE THERMAL NETWORK PROGRAMMES
Hourly time-step and yearly calculation capability [12, 13].
Most accurate but still has the limitation imposed by the difficulty of predicting occupant behaviour.

5·2 Cost Analysis

DISCOUNTED CASH FLOW   OR   LIFE-CYCLE COSTING ANALYSIS [16]
"Cost/Load" is a calculator programme with the 'bin' method of annual heating load analysis coupled to a Life-Cycle Costing sequence [2].
Allows for: Increase in fuel prices
Effects of inflation
Loss of potential revenue from capital.

5·3 Overheating Analysis

The methods are various:

A. STEADY STATE FOURIER CURVE ANALYSIS [17]

B. FINITE DIFFERENCE:
a. Calculator methods: 1. TEANET [18]
2. Passive simulation program (PSP) [2].
b. Computer methods: 1. DEROB [13]   3. BLAST 3.0 (14)
2. PASOLE [12]. 4. ESP (15)

5·4 Condensation

The UK Building Research Establishment Digest no. 110 on Condensation is available by post from HMSO books, PO Box 569, London SE1 9NH.
Price UK£0.50 + £0.14 (UK and Ireland), £0.31 (Europe) postage.
Condensation calculations are also well documented in such books as:
Markus, TA and Morris, EN, "Buildings, Climate and Energy", Pitman Publishing Ltd. 1980

6 RECOMMENDED LITERATURE

1. Anderson, B. and Riordan, M. "The Solar Home Book", 1976, Brick House Publishing Company. 3 Main Street Andover, Massachusetts 01810, USA. Telephone: (617) 475-9568. ($9.50 + postage).
2. Lebens, R.M. "Passive Solar Heating Design", Applied Science Publishers, Rippleside Commercial Estate. Barking. Essex, England. Telephone: (01) 595-2121. (£16 for U.K., £21 for overseas, postage included).
3. Mazria, E. "Passive Solar Energy Book", Rodale Press, Emmans, Pennsylvania, USA.($10.95 + postage)
4. "Solar Age Ref. 7". Solar Age, Church Hill, Harrisville, New Hampshire 03450, USA. Telephone: (603) 827 3347 ($2.50 + postage).
5. "Archi de Soleil" par B. Bardou et V. Arzoumanian, editions Parentheses.
6. "Archi Bio" par J.L. Izard, editions Parentheses.
7. Wright, D "Natural Solar Architecture", Van Nostrand Reinhold Co., New York, N.Y., USA.
   "Soleil, Nature, Architecture" par D. Wright, editions Parentheses, 13360 Roquevaire, France.
8. Sergio Los and Natasha Pulitzer, L'Architettura dell'Evoluzione", 1977, Luigi Parma, Bologna, Italia.
9. "Le Scienze dell'Artificiale" series edited by Sergio Los, published by Franco Muzio, Via Bonporti, 36, Padova, Italia.
10. "Architektur und Energie" von Peter Steiger, Von Prof. Steiger, Technische Universitat, Darmstadt, Bundesrepublik Deutschland.
11. Lebens, R.M. "Passive Solar Architecture in Europe – Results of the First European Passive Solar Competition 1980", Architectural Press, London, 1981.
12. U.S. Department of Energy, "Passive Solar Design Handbook", Volumes 1 and 2, 1980, NTIS, U.S. Department of Commerce, 5285 Port Royal Road, Springfield, VA 22161, ($14.00 plus postage).

7 REFERENCES

[1] Mazria, E. "The Passive Solar Energy Book", Rodale Press, USA. 1979
[2] Lebens, R.M. "Passive Solar Heating Design", Applied Science Publishers, UK. 1980
[3] Holzberlin, T.M. "Don't let the Trees Make a Monkey of You", Proceedings of the 4th National Passive Solar Conference, October 1979, Kansas City, Missouri, USA. (p.416)
[4] Thermoplus by Flachglass A.G., West Germany.
[5] Balcomb, J.D. "Designing Passive Solar Buildings to Reduce Temperature Swings", LASL paper LA UR-78 1316 Los Alamos, USA. 5th May 1978.
[6] Morgan, F.A. "Patent Specification 1022411, 29 March 1962". Patent application No. 12351/61. Published 16 March 1966. UK.
[7] Balcomb, J.D. "Designing Fan Forced Rock Beds", Solar Age, November 1979. USA.
[8] Heap, R.D. Data assembled at Electricity Council Research Centre, UK, from MR 415 and Electricity Supply Industry Statistics.
[9] Cornish, J.P. "The Effect of Thermal Insulation On Energy Consumption in Houses". British Building Research Establishment, East Kilbride, UK. 1976
[10] Balcombe, J.D.; McFarland, R. "A Simple Empirical Method for Estimating the Performance of a Passive Solar Heated Building of the Thermal Storage Wall Type." "Proceedings of the 2nd National Passive Solar Conference March 1978. Philadelphia, Pennsylvania, USA.
[11] Wray, W.O., Balcomb, J.D., McFarland, R.D. "A Semi Empirical Method for Estimating the Performance of Direct Gain Passive Solar Heated Buildings", Proceedings of the 3rd National Passive Conference. San Jose USA. January 1979.
[12] McFarland, R.D. "PASOLE: A General Simulation Program for Passive Solar Energy", Los Alamos Scientific Laboratory. LA 7433 MS. October 1978
[13] Arumi Noe, F., Northrop, D. "A Field Validation of the Thermal Performance of a Passively Heated Building as Simulated by the DEROB System." Energy and Buildings, Vol. 2, No. 1, January, 1979. p. 65.
[14] Kammerud, R. Lawerence Berkeley Laboratories, University of California, Berkeley, U.S.A.
[15] Clark, J. ABACUS, University of Strathclyde, Glasgow, Scotland, UK.
[16] Chapman, P.F. "The Economic Evaluation of Solar Energy Schemes", UK Section of I.S.E.S., Conference (C12) The Royal Institute, London, July 1977.
[17] Niles, P.W.B. "A Simple Direct Gain Passive House Performance Prediction Model", Proceedings of the 2nd National Passive Solar Conference, March 1978. Philadelphia, Pennsylvania, USA.
[18] Kohler, J.T. and Sullivan, P.W. "TEANET: A Numerical Thermal Network Algorithm for Simulating the Performance of Passive Systems on a TI 59 Programmable Calculator". T.E.A. Inc. Harrisville, New Hampshire USA.
[19] U.S. Department of Energy, "Passive Solar Design Handbook", Volume 2 of 2, 1980.

The Commission of the European Communities Directorate General XII for Science Research & Development

Second European Passive Solar Competition 1982

DATA BOOKLET

The Commission of the European Communities Directorate General XII for Science Research & Development

Second European Passive Solar Competition 1982

DATA BOOKLET

The Commission of the European Communities Directorate General XII for Science Research & Development

Second European Passive Solar Competition 1982

DATA BOOKLET

The Commission of the European Communities Directorate General XII for Science Research & Development

Second European Passive Solar Competition 1982

DATA BOOKLET

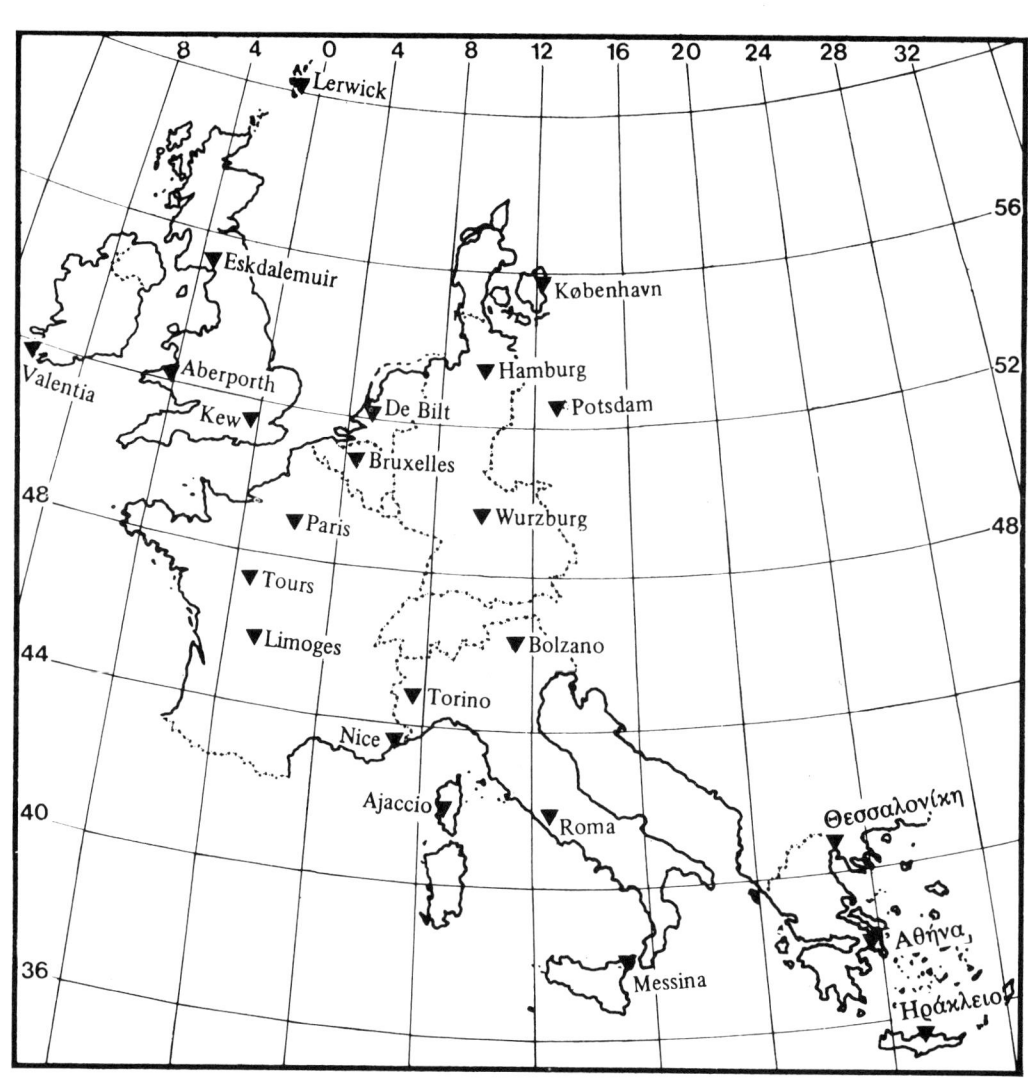

1

Figs. 1-6 are taken from

"The Passive Solar Energy Book", Mazria, E., Rodale Press, U.S.A.

with the kind permission of the author.

Figs. 7, 9-32 are taken or derived from

"Passive Solar Design Handbook, Volume 2", Balcomb, J.D., U.S. Dept. of Energy.

Details of Solar Radiation (except for Greece) have been adapted from the following sources, using the graphs of vertical/horizontal ratios derived for this booklet from measured European data:

'Solar Radiation and Radiation Balance Data 1964-68', Hydrometeorological Publishing House, Leningrad, 1970.
'World Survey of Climatology', Elsevier Scientific Publishing Co., 1977.

Monthly average air temperatures (except for Greece) are taken from:

'Tables of Temperature, Relative Humidity, Precipitation and Sunshine', Pt. III, Europe and the Azores, Met. 0.856c, HMSO London.

Annual Degree Days (Base 18.3°C) have been calculated from the monthly average air temperatures, by the method in the calculation booklet.

We would like to thank the following for help in preparing the data

Professor J. Page, Dept. of Building Science, University of Sheffield
Dr. H. Lund, Thermal Insulation Laboratory, Technical University of Denmark
E.P. Tsingas, Passive Solar Design Group, University of Thessaloniki

2

SUN CHARTS

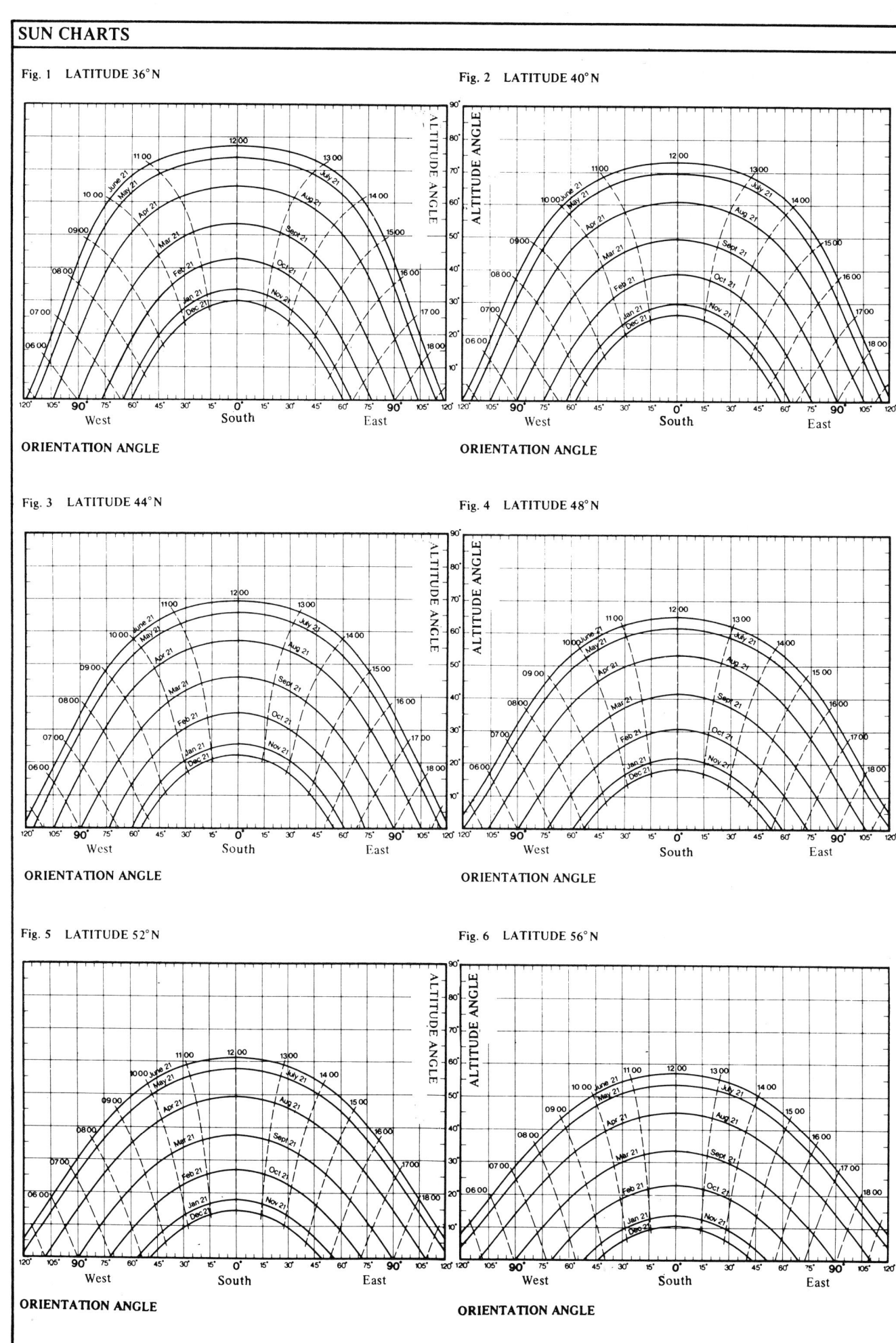

Fig. 1   LATITUDE 36°N

Fig. 2   LATITUDE 40°N

Fig. 3   LATITUDE 44°N

Fig. 4   LATITUDE 48°N

Fig. 5   LATITUDE 52°N

Fig. 6   LATITUDE 56°N

COMMENTS ON EUROPEAN WEATHER

1. Solar Radiation. Broadly speaking the monthly totals of horizontal solar radiation are almost identical for sites with the same latitude. There is little difference between the monthly totals for Valentia, Aberporth, London, Brussels or Wurzburg. This phenomenon can be seen very easily in the solar radiation maps drawn up by B. de Jong*.

2. Air Temperatures. For a given latitude the winters get colder as we go from west to east. Air temperatures also vary locally with altitude. For instance temperatures at Eskdalemuir (altitude 250m) are about 1-2°C colder than those at nearby Dumfries (altitude 50m). The effect is more marked around the alps where winter temperatures in Turin (altitude 250m) are around 5°C lower than in Nice (at sea level) 150km away.

3. Prevailing Winds. The winter weather over most of North-West Europe is best described as circular. Large circulating cyclones and anti-cyclones drift across in a westerly direction. This means that although the prevailing wind is nominally south-westerly, it only blows slightly more often than a wind of any other direction.

For most of Europe north of the Alps the winds have distinctive properties. A westerly wind, the nominal prevailing wind, is liable to be relatively warm and bring rain. A south wind is liable to be warm and dry. A north-easterly wind may be bitterly cold and dry, bringing down cold air from the Arctic. Around the Alps and the Pyrenees there are other factors. Cold air from the mountains is likely to sink into the warmer low-lands as katabatic winds. Thus a south wind will bring cold air in such places as Southern Germany and similarly a north wind in northern Italy.

Sheltering buildings is so dependent on local microclimate that competitors should give a specification of their local weather conditions.

*Net Radiation Received by a Horizontal Surface at the Earth, Delft University Press, Netherlands '73.

DENSITIES AND SPECIFIC HEATS OF SAMPLE MATERIALS

MATERIAL	DENSITY kg/m³	SPECIFIC HEAT Wh/kg°C
Dense Concrete	2100	0.23
Brickwork	1700	0.20
Water	1000	1.16

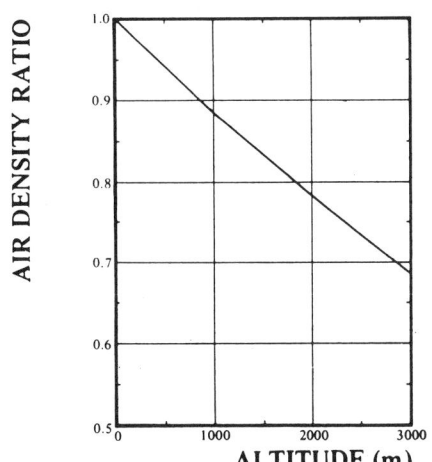

Fig. 7

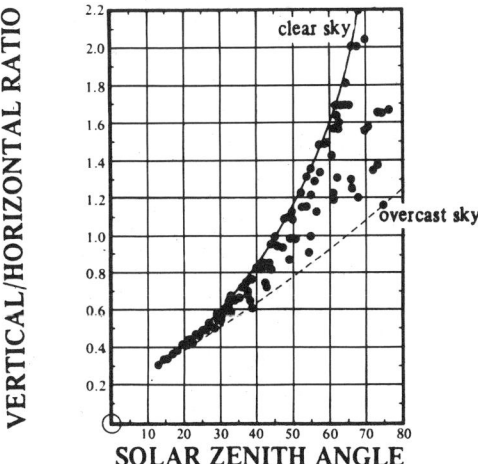

Fig. 8

4

COUNTRY DATA POINT DEGREE DAYS (Base 18.3°C)	LATITUDE LONGITUDE ALTITUDE	SOLAR RADIATION ON A VERTICAL SOUTH-FACING SURFACE (kWh/m² /month) MONTHLY AVERAGE AIR TEMPERATURES (°C) MEAN ANNUAL MINIMUM TEMPERATURE (°C)											
		JUL	AUG	SEP	OCT	NOV	DEC	JAN	FEB	MAR	APR	MAY	JUN
EIRE Valentia 2726	51° 56' N 10° 15' W Sea Level	87.7 15.0	94.2 15.4	81.9 14.0	64.2 11.6	41.4 9.1	27.6 7.8	34.4 7.0 −2.0	56.8 6.8	76.9 8.3	87.9 9.4	99.2 11.5	86.4 13.8
UNITED KINGDOM Aberporth 3137	52° 08' N 4° 34' W 150m	94.2 14.7	98.6 14.9	87.9 13.7	67.0 11.2	39.3 7.9	30.7 5.9	35.7 4.7 −3.7	51.0 4.6	82.5 6.3	93.0 8.2	99.5 10.7	98.1 13.3
Eskdalemuir 4055	55° 19' N 3° 12' W 250m	70.4 13.1	73.2 12.9	67.2 11.1	50.5 8.3	28.2 4.5	19.2 2.5	29.1 1.4 −9.7	39.5 1.5	59.2 3.7	75.9 6.1	85.3 8.9	79.8 11.9
Lerwick 4030	60° 09' N 1° 10' W Sea level	87.4 12.1	67.6 12.1	59.7 10.7	36.6 8.2	15.0 6.0	6.8 4.5	11.2 3.1 −5.2	27.2 2.9	52.7 3.9	81.0 5.5	89.0 7.8	90.0 10.0
London (Kew) 2798	51° 28' N 0° 19' W Sea Level	78.4 17.5	81.5 17.1	78.9 14.9	62.9 11.6	35.1 7.5	22.9 5.3	29.1 4.2 −4.2	38.1 4.5	67.3 6.6	72.9 9.5	84.3 12.6	80.7 15.9
NEDERLAND De Bilt 3145	52° 06' NB 5° 11' OL Om	78.7 17.4	87.7 17.2	75.9 14.7	59.8 10.4	34.5 6.1	24.2 3.0	28.8 1.8 −9.3	44.8 2.3	50.2 5.4	79.2 8.9	90.8 12.7	84.3 15.8
BELGIQUE/ BELGIE Bruxelles (Uccle) 2990	50° 48' NB 4° 22' OL 100m	80.9 17.4	88.4 17.2	82.8 15.5	65.1 11.4	39.6 6.0	23.3 2.9	30.7 1.5 −7.6	43.1 3.5	65.1 6.3	79.8 9.6	90.2 13.2	81.3 16.4
FRANCE Ajaccio 1639	41° 55' N 8° 48' E Niveau de la mer	103.2 22.0	114.2 22.2	128.4 20.3	121.4 16.3	95.9 11.8	93.1 8.7	91.5 7.7 −2.1	85.5 8.7	115.8 10.5	106.0 12.6	94.0 15.9	89.6 19.8
Limoges 2803	45° 49' N 1° 17' E 250m	89.9 18.4	96.1 17.8	97.8 15.3	95.2 10.7	63.0 6.7	50.2 3.8	70.1 3.1 −9.4	74.5 3.9	96.4 7.4	92.1 9.9	92.4 13.3	87.9 16.8
Nice 1520	43° 40' N 7° 12' E Niveau de la mer	96.8 22.7	118.1 22.5	122.1 20.3	128.7 16.0	113.1 11.5	112.5 8.2	106.5 7.5 0.7	100.2 8.5	131.1 10.8	116.4 17.3	100.1 16.7	86.5 20.1
Paris 2536	48° 49' N 2° 30' E 50m	83.4 20.0	88.0 19.2	86.7 16.5	73.2 11.8	42.9 7.3	32.9 4.3	43.5 3.5 −5.1	52.1 4.4	76.0 7.9	85.5 11.1	84.3 14.6	84.0 17.8
Tours 2609 (Rayonnement pour Baugé)	47° 25' N 0° 46' E 100m	92.4 19.1	99.2 18.7	99.6 16.2	89.3 11.7	59.4 7.2	47.7 4.3	62.4 3.5 −6.1	71.7 4.4	104.8 7.7	97.8 10.6	97.0 13.9	90.0 17.3

5

COUNTRY DATA POINT DEGREE DAYS (Base 18.3°C)	LATITUDE LONGITUDE ALTITUDE	SOLAR RADIATION ON A VERTICAL SOUTH-FACING SURFACE (kWh/m² /month) MONTHLY AVERAGE AIR TEMPERATURES (°C) MEAN ANNUAL MINIMUM TEMPERATURE (°C)											
		JUL	AUG	SEP	OCT	NOV	DEC	JAN	FEB	MAR	APR	MAY	JUN
ITALIA													
Bolzano 2430	46° 28' N 11° 20' E 250m	71.3 22.0	78.1 21.1	87.3 18.4	79.1 12.6	54.6 6.0	49.9 1.5	63.3 0.2 −8.3	61.3 7.3	81.5 8.8	76.2 13.1	74.4 16.9	70.2 20.1
Messina 844	38° 12' N 15° 33' E 50m	53.6 26.0	59.7 26.4	71.3 23.7	80.4 20.2	63.8 16.7	61.0 13.3	53.9 11.4 3.8	63.6 11.9	71.4 13.1	65.2 15.4	55.3 19.2	47.5 22.9
Roma 1401	41° 48' N 12° 35' E Livello del mare	90.3 25.0	100.8 24.6	109.7 21.6	111.2 17.2	89.1 12.7	80.7 9.5	97.7 7.8 −0.7	86.1 9.0	104.9 11.2	89.5 14.3	81.0 18.4	70.7 22.4
Torino 2382	45° 11' N 7° 39' E 250m	76.6 24.2	80.9 22.9	85.5 19.3	79.7 13.2	59.1 ·6.8	69.4 2.7	77.7 1.2 −7.4	70.8 3.6	93.9 8.7	83.7 13.4	77.2 18.0	68.7 21.6
DANMARK													
København 3558	55° 40' N 12° 18' Ø 0m	93.0 17.7	94.6 17.4	75.6 14.0	51.5 9.4	24.3 5.3	16.4 2.5	23.9 0.0 −6.5	42.0 −0.2	69.4 2.1	88.5 6.7	102.3 11.8	102.6 15.3
DEUTSCHLAND													
Hamburg 3416	53° 38' N 10° 00' O Meereshöhe	84.6 17.6	89.3 17.2	74.7 14.3	56.4 9.5	30.0 5.0	19.2 3.7	25.4 0.0 −11.8	44.5 0.3	65.7 3.2	83.4 8.0	93.9 12.3	90.3 15.6
Potsdam (Berlin) 3486	52° 23' N 13° 04' O 100m	93.9 18.4	97.7 17.7	90.3 14.2	67.3 8.9	33.3 4.2	24.5 0.7	32.2 −1.1 −12.5	44.0 −3.3	77.2 3.3	89.4 8.3	100.4 13.4	94.8 16.8
Wurzburg 3129	49° 48' N 9° 54' O 200m	91.8 19.2	92.4 18.6	90.3 15.3	76.3 9.9	41.7 5.0	36.6 1.3	44.6 −0.1 −12.8	60.8 1.2	81.5 5.3	90.9 10.0	96.1 14.3	91.5 17.4
ΕΛΛΑΔΑ													
'Αθήνα 1110	37° 58' Β 23° 43' Α 100m	80.0 27.9	97.0 27.8	109.0 23.9	114.0 18.7	104.0 15.0	89.0 11.4	87.0 9.4 1.0	86.0 10.3	91.0 11.7	83.0 15.8	78.0 20.6	72 .0 25.2
'Ηράκλειο 782	35° 20' Β 25° 08' Α Στάθμη θαλ.	76.0 26.4	92.0 26.4	108.0 23.6	107.0 20.3	103.0 17.2	87.0 13.9	79.0 12.3 3.0	81.0 12.5	86.0 13.8	81.0 16.8	75.0 20.4	69.0 24.4
Θεσσαλονίκη 1725	40° 38' Β 22° 57' Α Στάθμη Θαλ.	82.0 26.7	92.0 26.3	101.0 22.2	98.0 16.7	83.0 11.9	75.0 7.4	77.0 5.5 −5.0	78.0 7.0	83.0 9.9	81.0 14.6	78.0 19.7	72.0 24.1

6

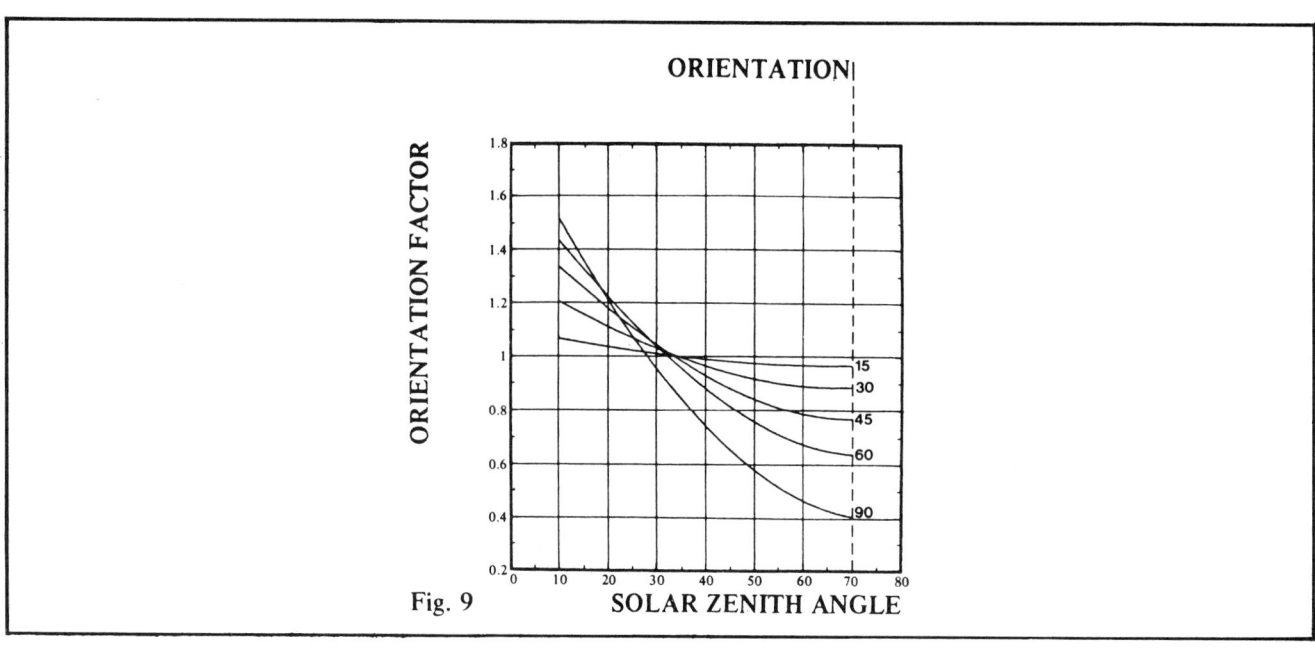

Fig. 9

SOLAR ZENITH ANGLE

TILT FACTORS

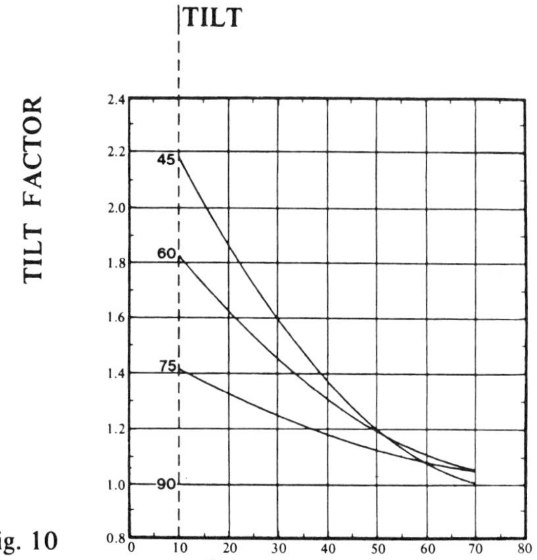

Fig. 10
ORIENTATION = 0° SOLAR ZENITH ANGLE

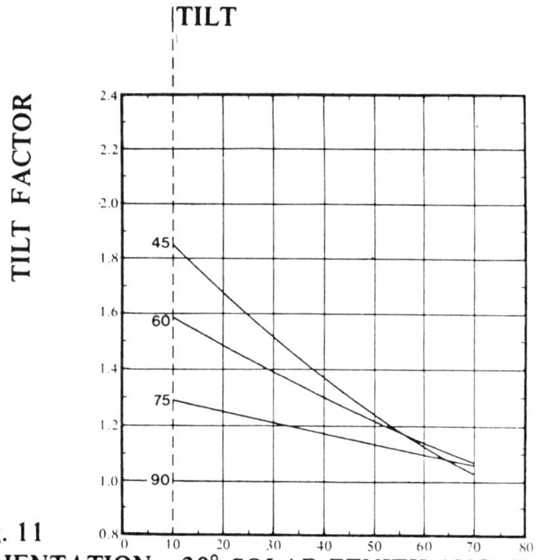

Fig. 11
ORIENTATION = 30° SOLAR ZENITH ANGLE

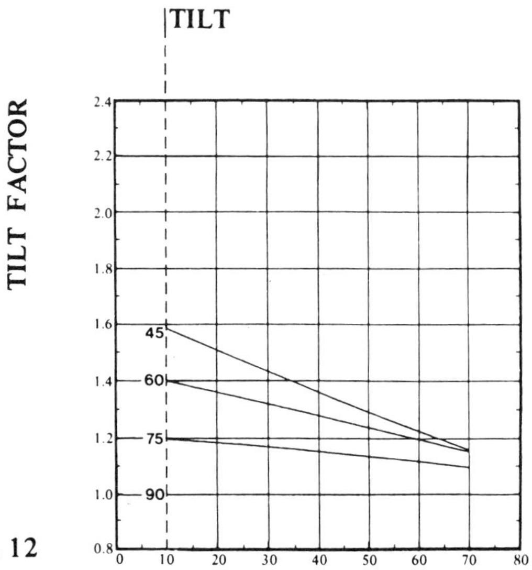

Fig. 12
ORIENTATION = 60° SOLAR ZENITH ANGLE

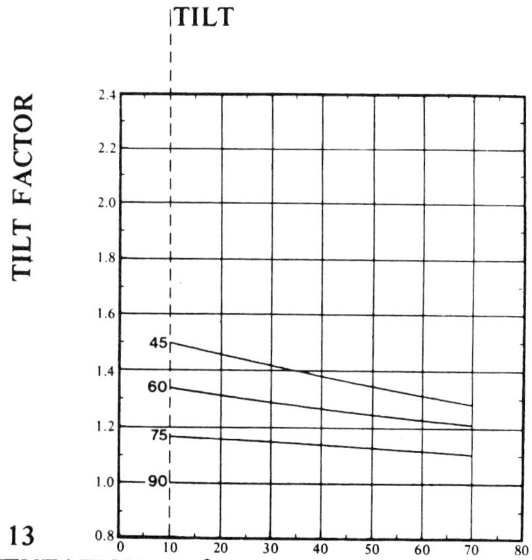

Fig. 13
ORIENTATION = 90° SOLAR ZENITH ANGLE

7

26

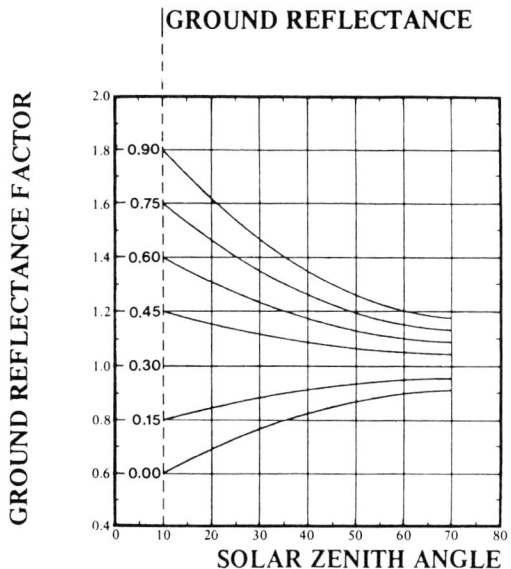

GROUND REFLECTANCE

Fig. 14

GROUND REFLECTANCES

Snow	Fresh		0.8-0.9
	Old		0.45-0.7
Water – Solar Zenith Angle:		50°	0.1
		60°	0.16
		70°	0.26
		80°	0.47
	Ice-covered		0.68
Grass			0.25
Agricultural Crops			0.18-0.25
Deciduous Forest			0.15-0.2
Coniferous Forest			0.05-0.2
Concrete	Clean		0.55
	Average		0.3
	Weathered		0.2
Brick			0.2-0.4
Asphalt			0.15

For example: Urban Average   0.10-0.27
              Snow-covered field,
                 wooded background   0.66-0.73

8

TYPICAL REFLECTOR GEOMETRIES

Aspect Ratio = $\dfrac{w}{h}$

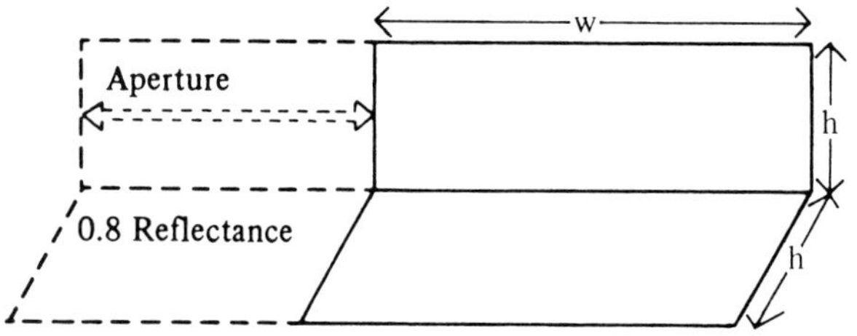

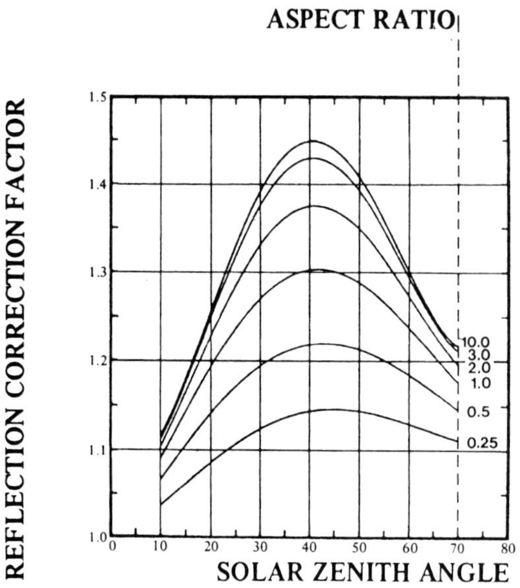

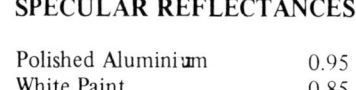

Aperture

0.8 Reflectance

ASPECT RATIO

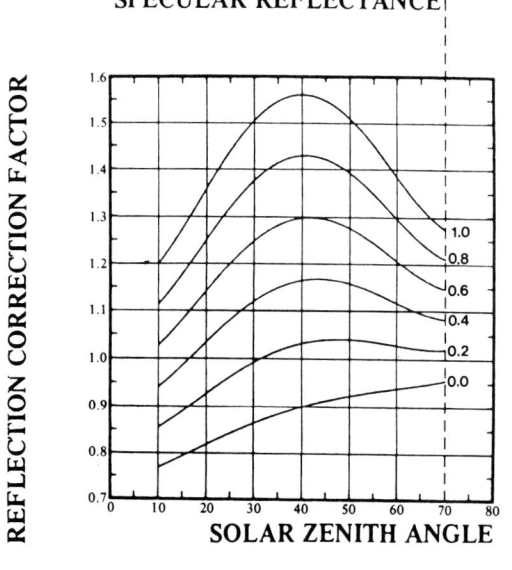

Fig. 15

Reflector Length = $\dfrac{l}{h}$

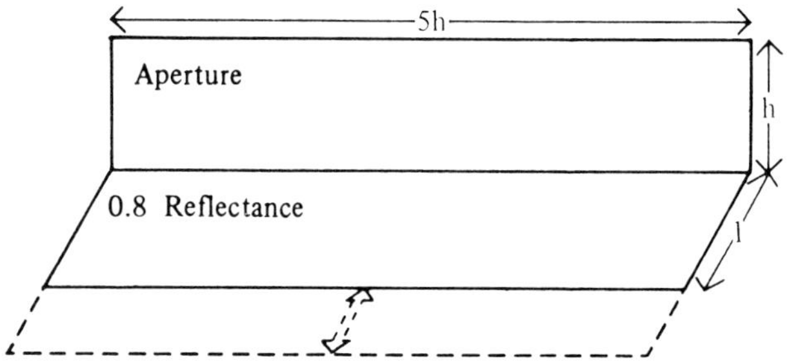

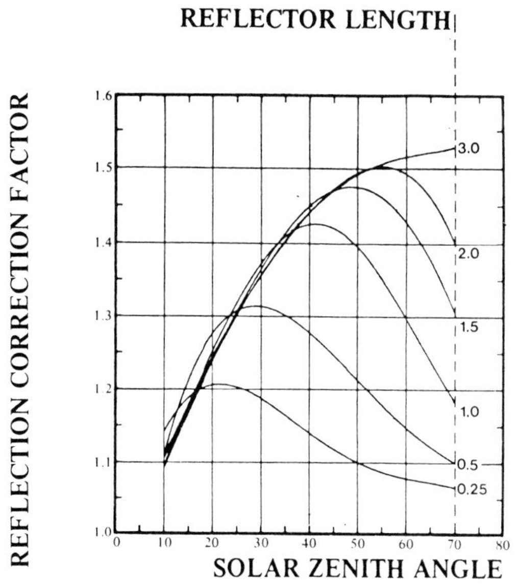

Aperture

0.8 Reflectance

REFLECTOR LENGTH

Fig. 16

SPECULAR REFLECTANCES

Polished Aluminium	0.95
White Paint	0.85
Aluminium Paint	0.70
Canary Yellow Paint	0.70

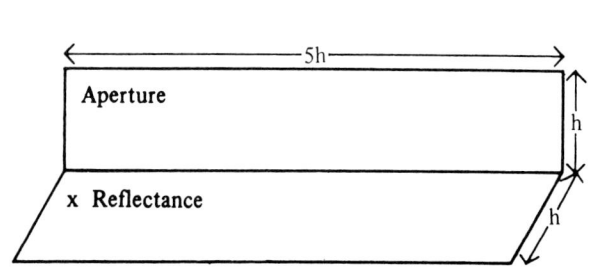

Aperture

x Reflectance

SPECULAR REFLECTANCE

Fig. 17

TRANSMITTANCE FACTORS

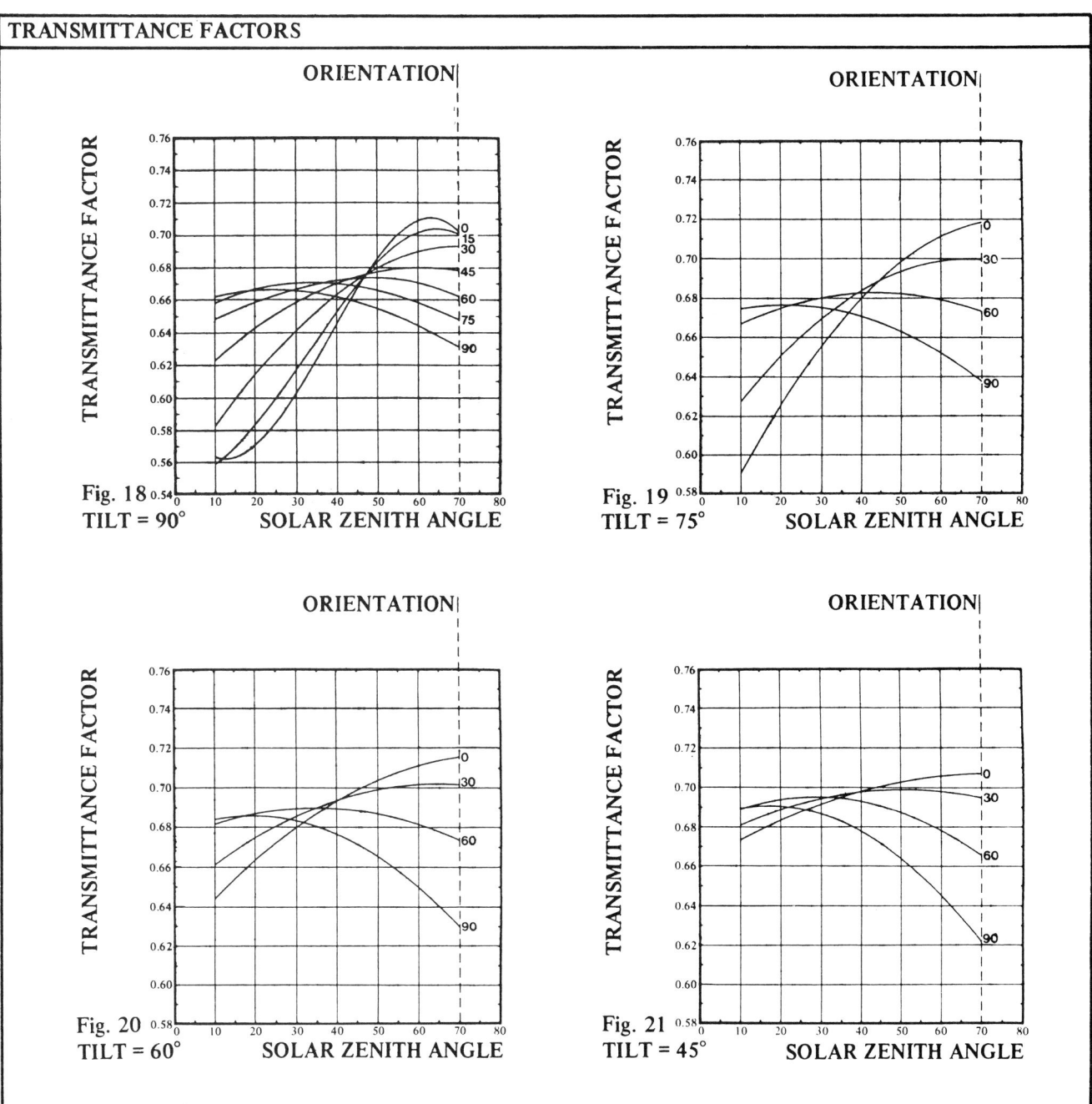

Fig. 18
TILT = 90°

Fig. 19
TILT = 75°

Fig. 20
TILT = 60°

Fig. 21
TILT = 45°

TYPICAL ABSORPTANCES

TYPICAL ABSORPTANCES

Matt Black Paint	0.95
Dark Brown Paint	0.88
Red Brick	0.70
Concrete	0.65
Light Buff Brick	0.60
White Gloss Paint	0.25
Polished aluminium sheet	0.12

10

OVERHANG FACTORS

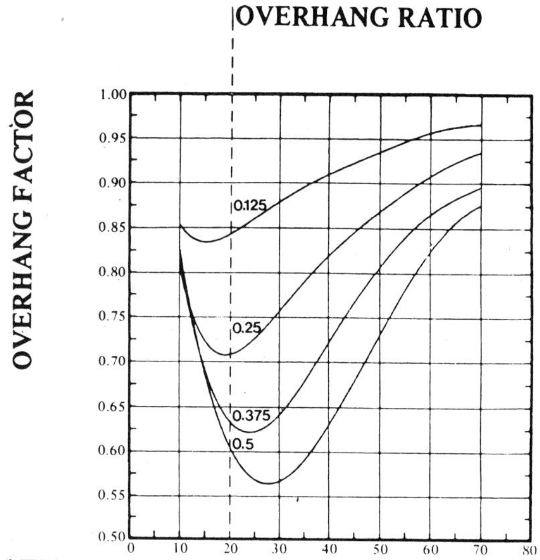

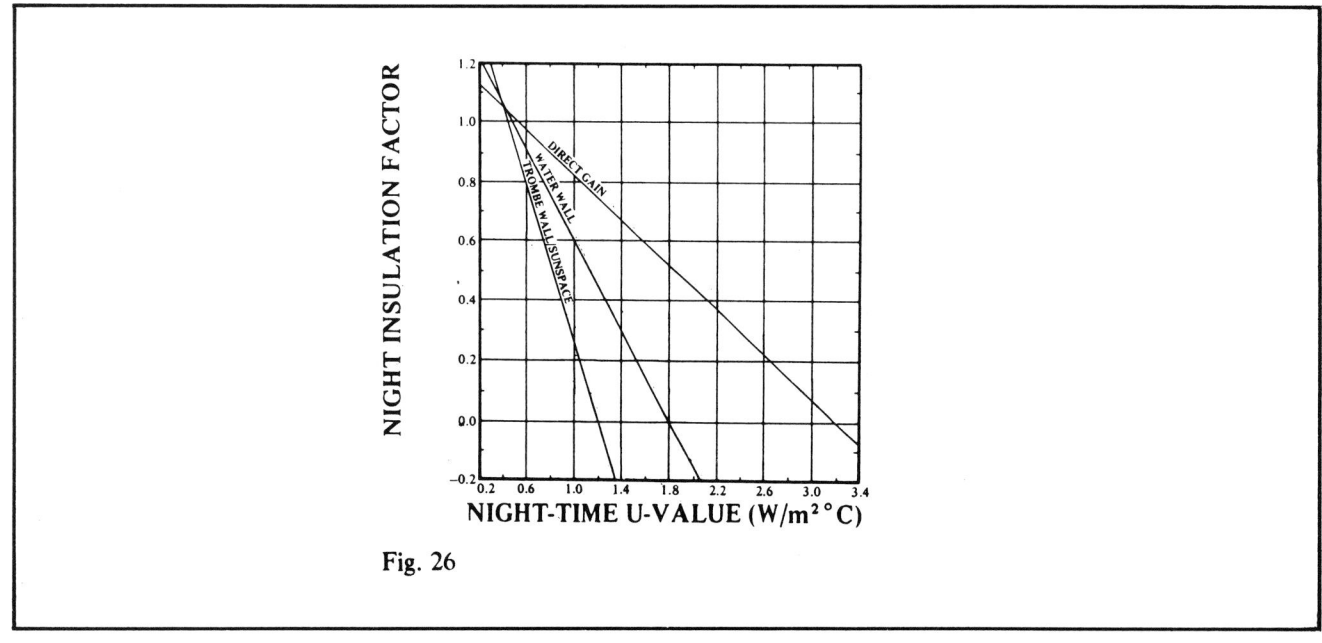

Fig. 22
SEPARATION RATIO = 0 SOLAR ZENITH ANGLE

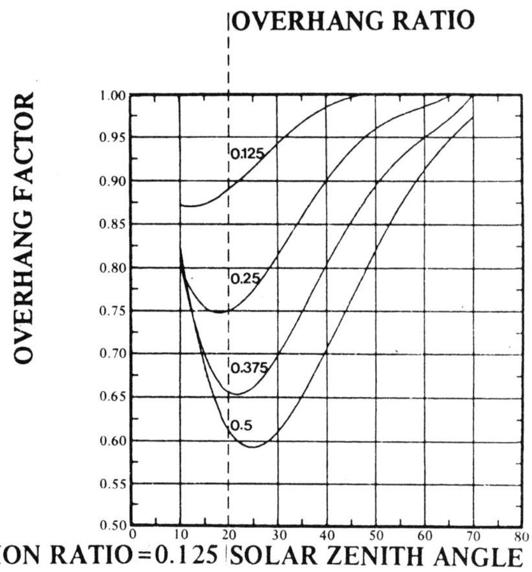

Fig. 23
SEPARATION RATIO = 0.125 SOLAR ZENITH ANGLE

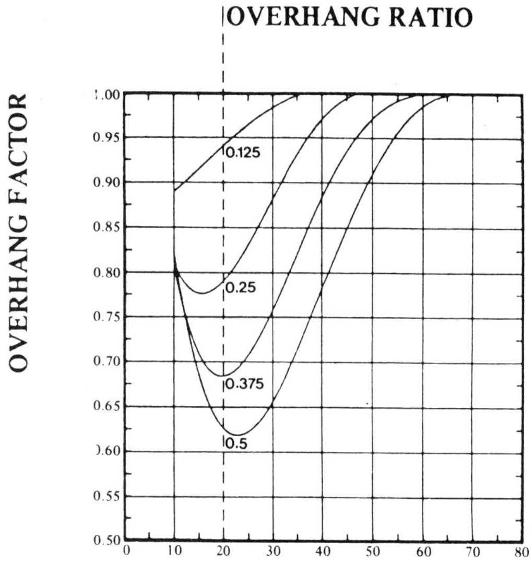

Fig. 24
SEPARATION RATIO = 0.25 SOLAR ZENITH ANGLE

Fig. 25
SEPARATION RATIO = 0.5 SOLAR ZENITH ANGLE

Fig. 26

11

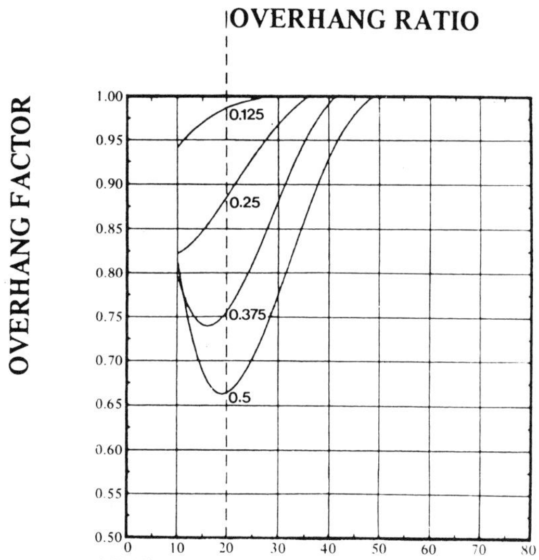

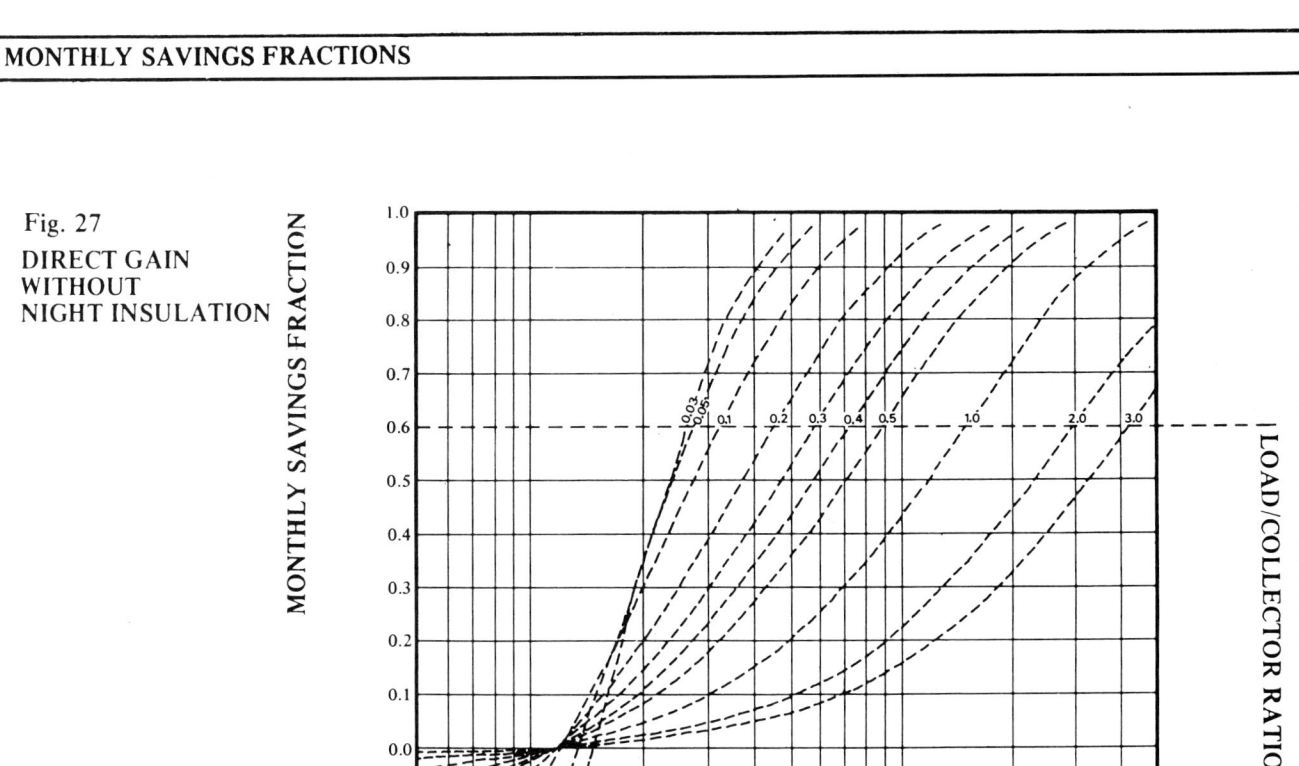

Fig. 27
DIRECT GAIN
WITHOUT
NIGHT INSULATION

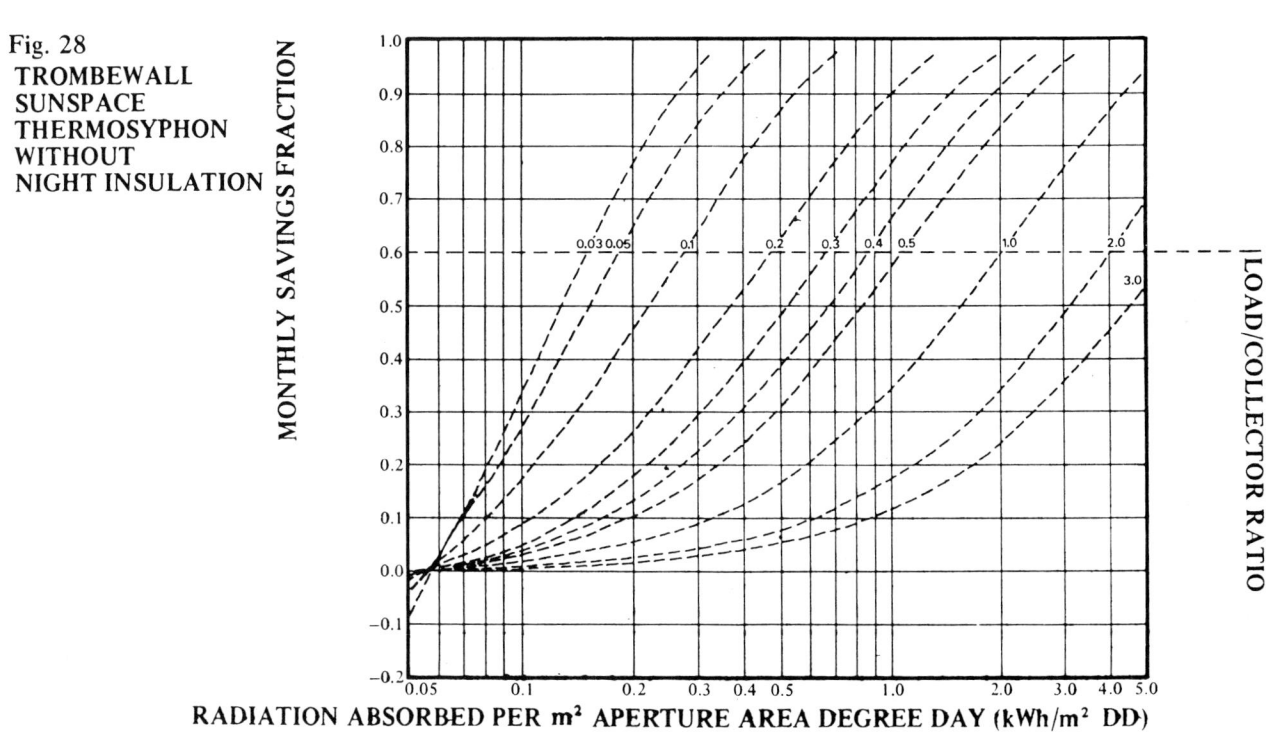

Fig. 28
TROMBEWALL
SUNSPACE
THERMOSYPHON
WITHOUT
NIGHT INSULATION

12

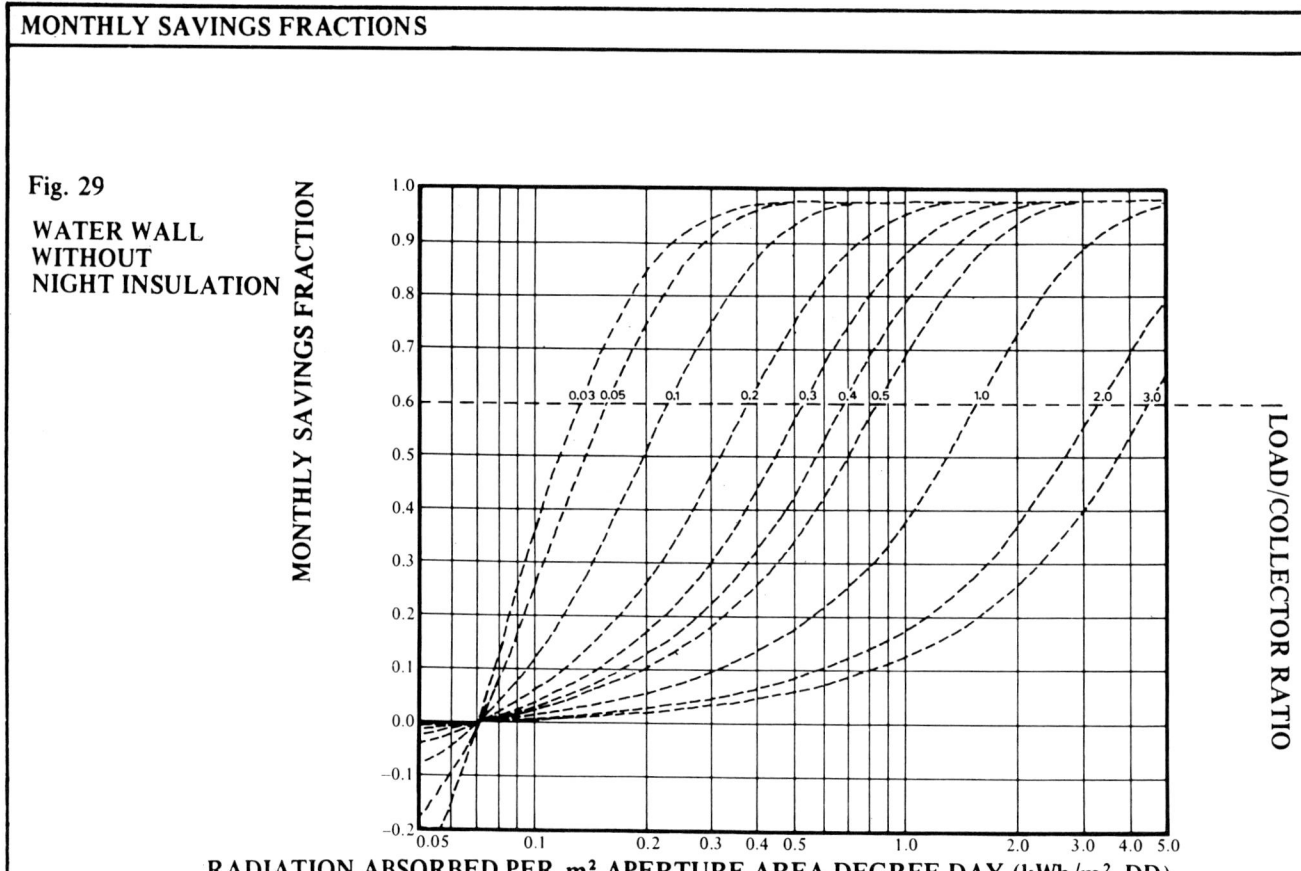

Fig. 29

WATER WALL
WITHOUT
NIGHT INSULATION

MONTHLY SAVINGS FRACTION

LOAD/COLLECTOR RATIO

RADIATION ABSORBED PER m² APERTURE AREA DEGREE DAY (kWh/m² DD)

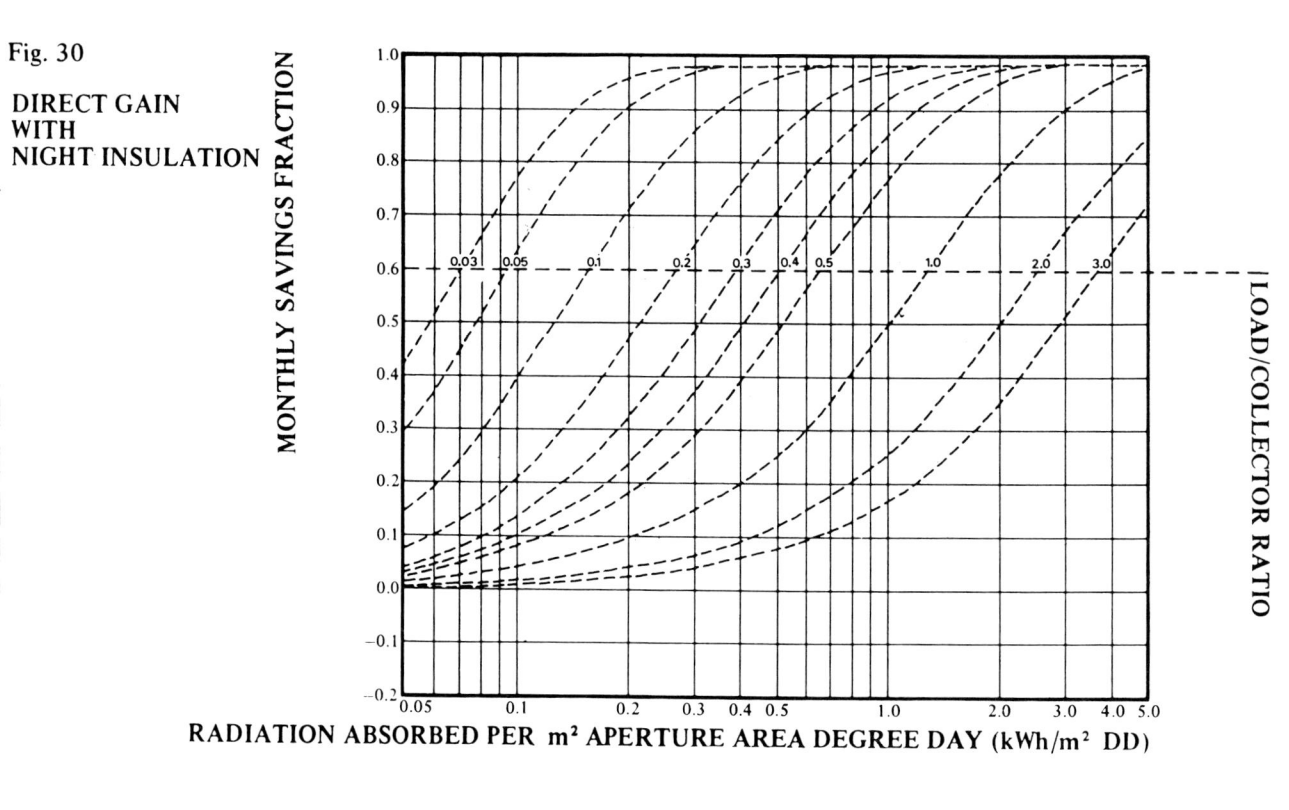

Fig. 30

DIRECT GAIN
WITH
NIGHT INSULATION

MONTHLY SAVINGS FRACTION

LOAD/COLLECTOR RATIO

RADIATION ABSORBED PER m² APERTURE AREA DEGREE DAY (kWh/m² DD)

13

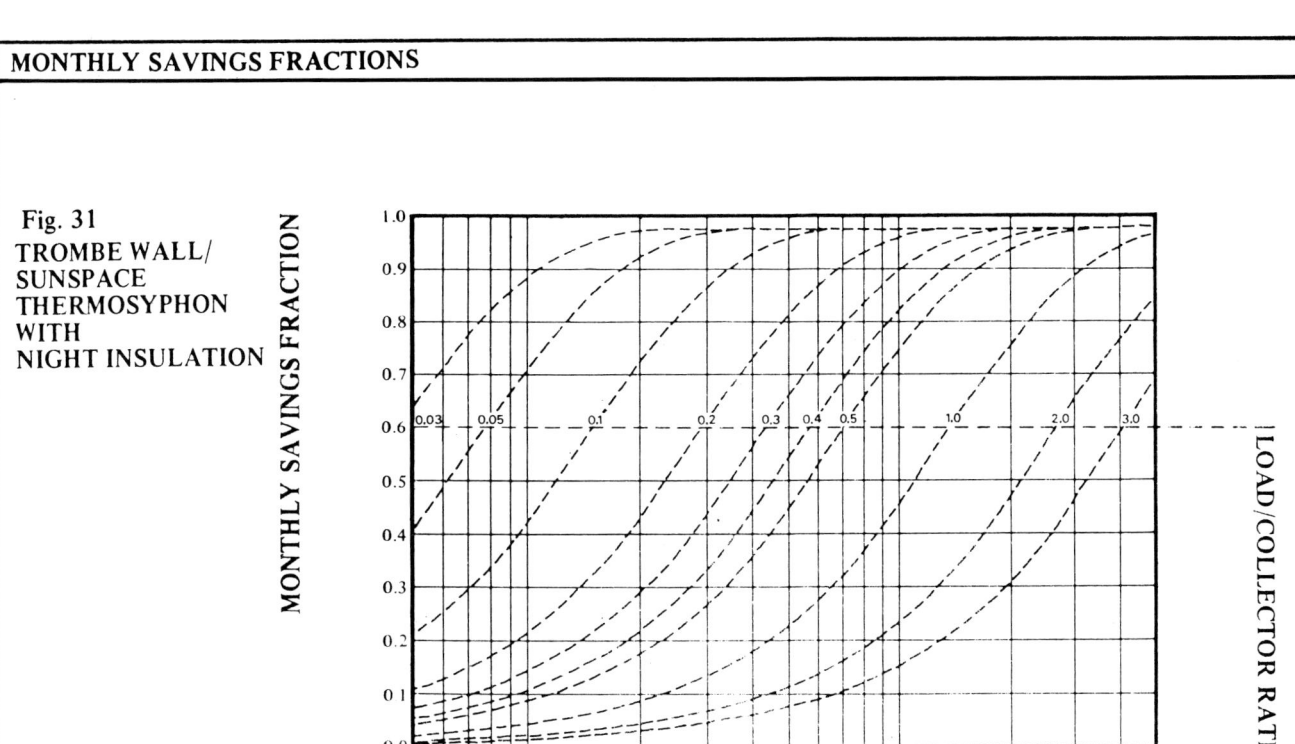

Fig. 31
TROMBE WALL/
SUNSPACE
THERMOSYPHON
WITH
NIGHT INSULATION

Fig. 32

WATER WALL
WITH
NIGHT INSULATION

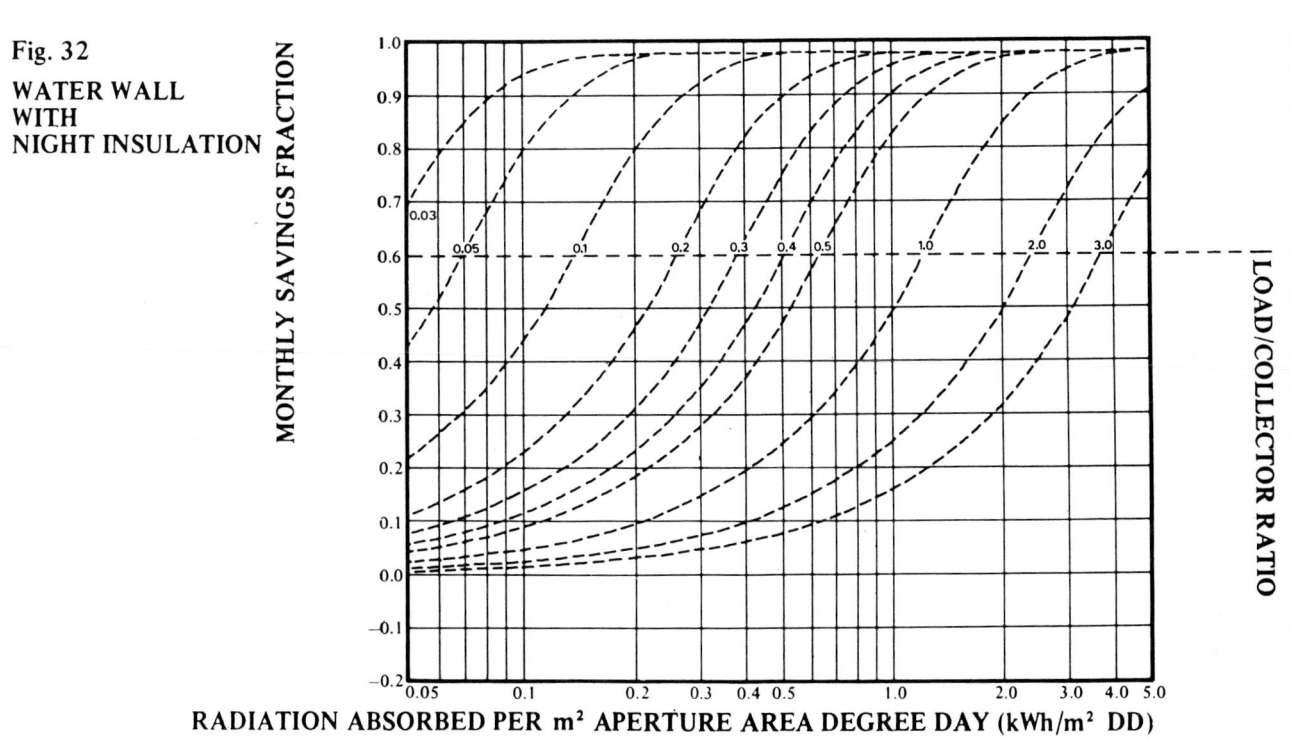

14

CATEGORY A
HIGH DENSITY, LOW-RISE
HOUSING

PRIZE WINNERS

FIRST PRIZE
CATEGORY A

35,000 French Francs

The housing scheme is situated on an approved building site in part of the city of Meylan. The site is near to the centre of the town and is scheduled for development in the near future. It will accommodate 2,500 new residents in an area of 40ha. In addition to the residential units (half of which will be for rent) other amenities will be provided and 8ha of green space will be preserved.

The area for residential development is 80 metres square. This requirement has been laid down by the Site Architect with whom we have had discussions. We have conformed to the required dwelling classification and those other regulations relevant to the development of an approved building site.

The site has a 5% fall towards the south with no obstruction to affect the availability of sunlight. As may be expected, we have decided upon an east/west orientation so that the buildings may gain the best possible advantage from the sunlight. As the existing site has dense vegetation, we have decided to incorporate climbing plants on the structures, planting boxes on the balconies and trees

within our design. This vegetation will also protect both the residential levels and communal spaces from the summer sun.

The form of the buildings creates a central communal area which is in a hollow, well protected from the wind. It is closed at an angle by banking which forms natural steps and also covers the garages.

The compact residential units have cavity walls. They are closed towards the north and open towards the south. They are served by an internal circulation area which has a glazed roof and which collects the solar gain. This space also acts as a buffer against heat loss from the dwellings and provides a warm communal area in the winter months.

The dwellings are also largely open towards the south and all adjoin a conservatory connected to a heat exchanger. The upper dwellings have access to a central conservatory which is situated above the inner passage. Openings on the northern side are made as small as possible and those rooms exposed to the north are protected by buffer zones such as garages, cellars or storage spaces.

DESIGN TEAM

Christian Blachot
Bernard Cogne

20 rue Gabriel Didier
38130 Echirolles
France

LOCATION
Meylan
France

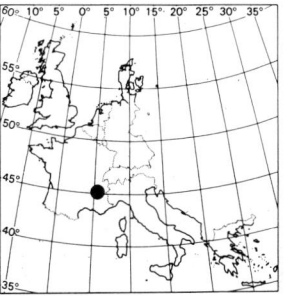

A. FRANCE SOUTH-EAST LATITUDE 45° 12´

LOCATION

MONT ST-EYNARD
(1350/1550m)
north wind protection
microclimate

ZAC of BEALIERES

MEYLAN

ZAC

l'isère

GRENOBLE

N

0 1 2km

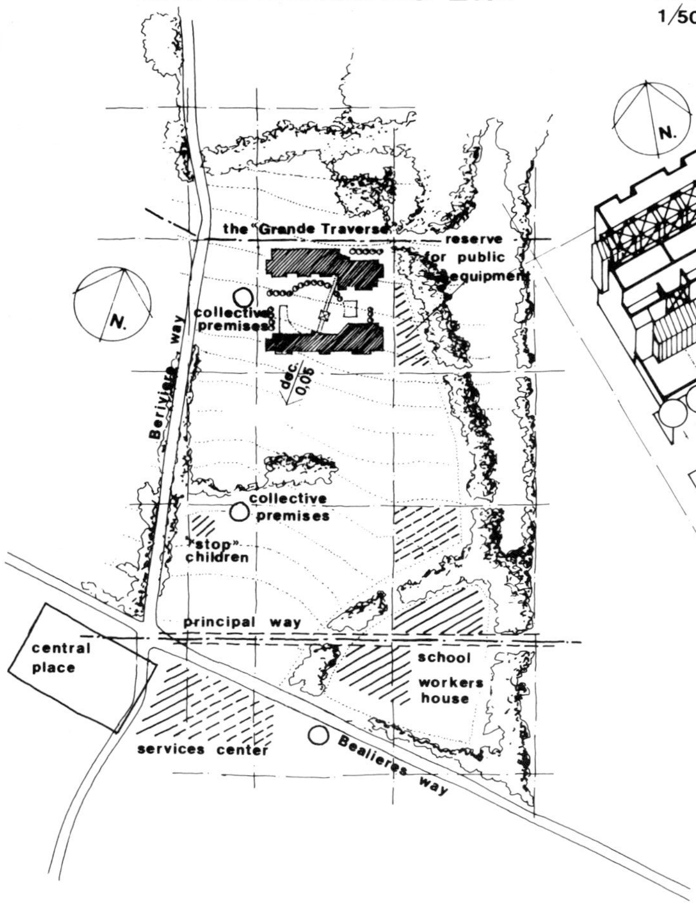

SITE PLAN
AXONOMETRY
1/500

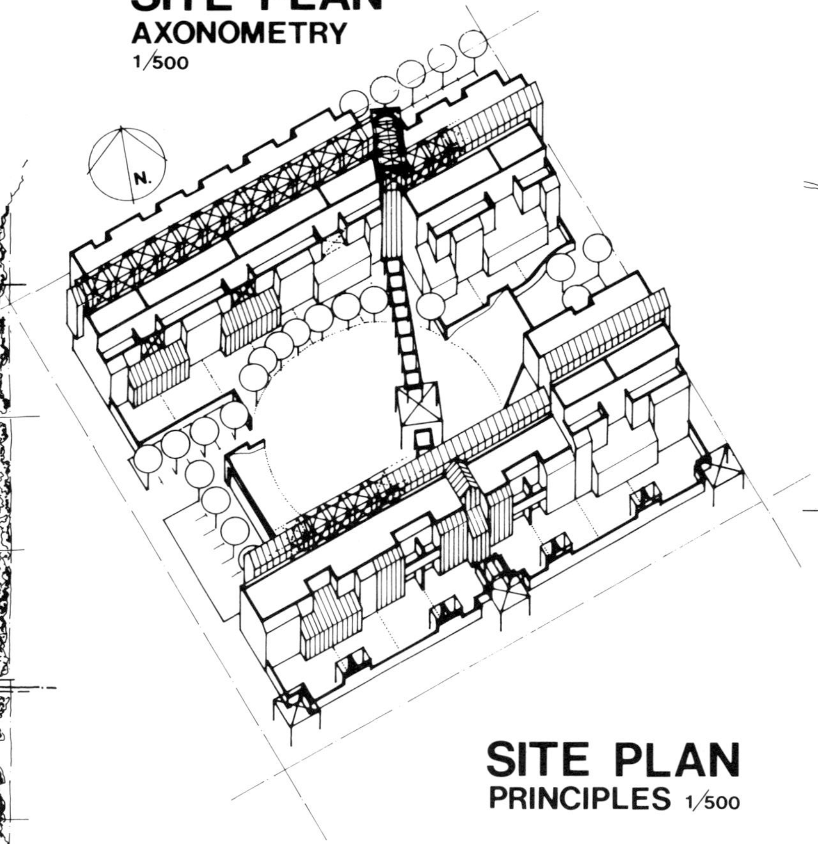

N.

TYPICAL DWELLING

7 4 1 6 1 2 7

1 3 5 5 1 7

6 4 4 4

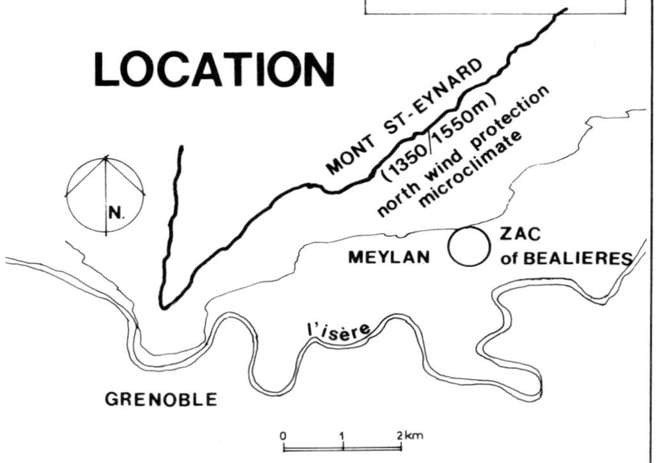

SITE PLAN
PRINCIPLES 1/500

1 apartments:
6 T2, 7 T3, 11 T4, 6 T5, 2 T6
2 glassed passage
3 collective area
4 car park
5 private gardens
6 interred garages
7 public space

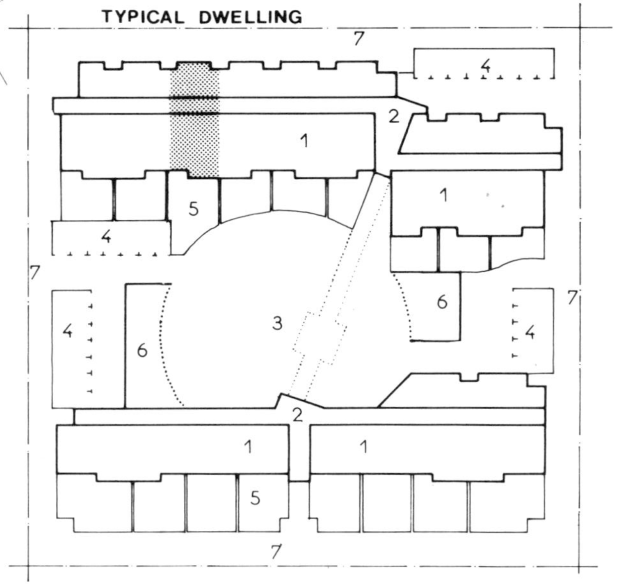

SITUATION
ZAC of BEALIERES Z H2
1/2000

N.

the "Grande Traverse"

reserve for public equipment

collective premises

collective premises

"stop" children

principal way

school

workers house

Bealieres way

services center

central place

Berlyier way

dec 0.05

JUDGES' COMMENTS

We thought that the scheme which most skilfully handled the creation of urban spaces with south-oriented houses was the one near Grenoble in south-east France, by Christian Blachot and Bernard Cogne, and we gave this the First prize of 35,000 French Francs.

The north and south sides of a semi-open ended courtyard are composed of three and a half floors of dwellings which stand on either side of a central glazed arcade and interlock across it at the higher levels. This enables the dwellings on both sides of the arcade to have their main living rooms on the south side, and at the same time allows the bedrooms of the northside dwellings to receive solar gain via the glazed roof of the arcade itself.

The garages on the north side are used as a source of summertime through ventilation in conjunction with the arcade roof. The central arcade or sunspace is used as a means to heat fresh air: an efficient and a very French device.

Skilful steps are then taken, through the manipulation and projection of the ends of these two terraces, to establish a north-south counterpoint and a static centre that largely neutralises the east-west directionality of the two terraces of dwellings. This is achieved by establishing a central shared space and using a linking covered path that connects the two terraces across that shared space. We especially liked the tumulus garages that (whilst facing conveniently outwards to east and west, like open mouths ready to receive the cars from the surrounding roads) helped in the creation of the saucer of central space by means of their sloping grassed roofs.

Like the plan and the section, the elevations showed a controlled and un-kooky balance of composition between the needs of domesticity and solar gain and, although shown on an isolated site, we were sure that such a scheme could make a useful contribution to the urban landscape. Despite a few instances of rather jerky planning in the dwellings and graphics that were not always of the highest standard, we were agreed that this was a truly worthy winner.

TECHNICAL ASSESSORS' COMMENTS

These two storey duplex apartments incorporate a sunspace which acts as a common circulation area. Good spacial organisation is achieved in relation to solar penetration and circulation. The scheme is mechanically ventilated, the incoming air being preheated in individual greenhouses or in the common sunspace. A heat exchanger is used to minimize heat loss through exhausted air.

Minor errors were discovered in the calculations.

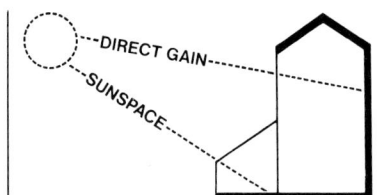

TECHNICAL DATA
This data has been recalculated.
For explanation of data see page 16.

Latitude: 45° 12'N
Altitude: 220 m
Data Point: Turin

DWELLING DESCRIPTION (Typical Unit)
Heated Volume: 427 m³

APERTURE	A	B	C	D
System Type	SS	SS	SS	DG
Net Area m²	16.0	11.5	4.0	10.0
Glazing Layers	1	2	2	2
Night Insulation	No	Yes	Yes	Yes
τ	0.60	0.55	0.55	0.55
Comment				

Aperture/Heated Volume: 0.097 m²/m³
Primary Mass/
   Related Aperture: 150.0 Wh/m²°C
Remote Mass/
   Related Aperture: —Wh/m²°C
Air Change Rate: 0.60 ac/h
Building Loss Coeff.: 6.86 kWh/DD
          : 286.00 W/°C

DWELLING PERFORMANCE (Typical Unit)
% Internal Gains: 21.0
% Auxiliary Heating: 37.0
% Useful Solar Gains: 42.0
Annual Solar Gains Fraction: 0.53
Figure of Merit: 0.011 kWh/DDm²
Useful Solar Gains/
   m² of Aperture: 161.3 kWh/m²yr
Min. Temp. without Heating: —1.7°C
Min. Outdoor Temperature: —7.4°C

ENERGY CHARACTERISTICS

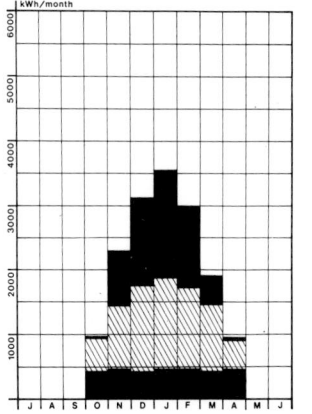

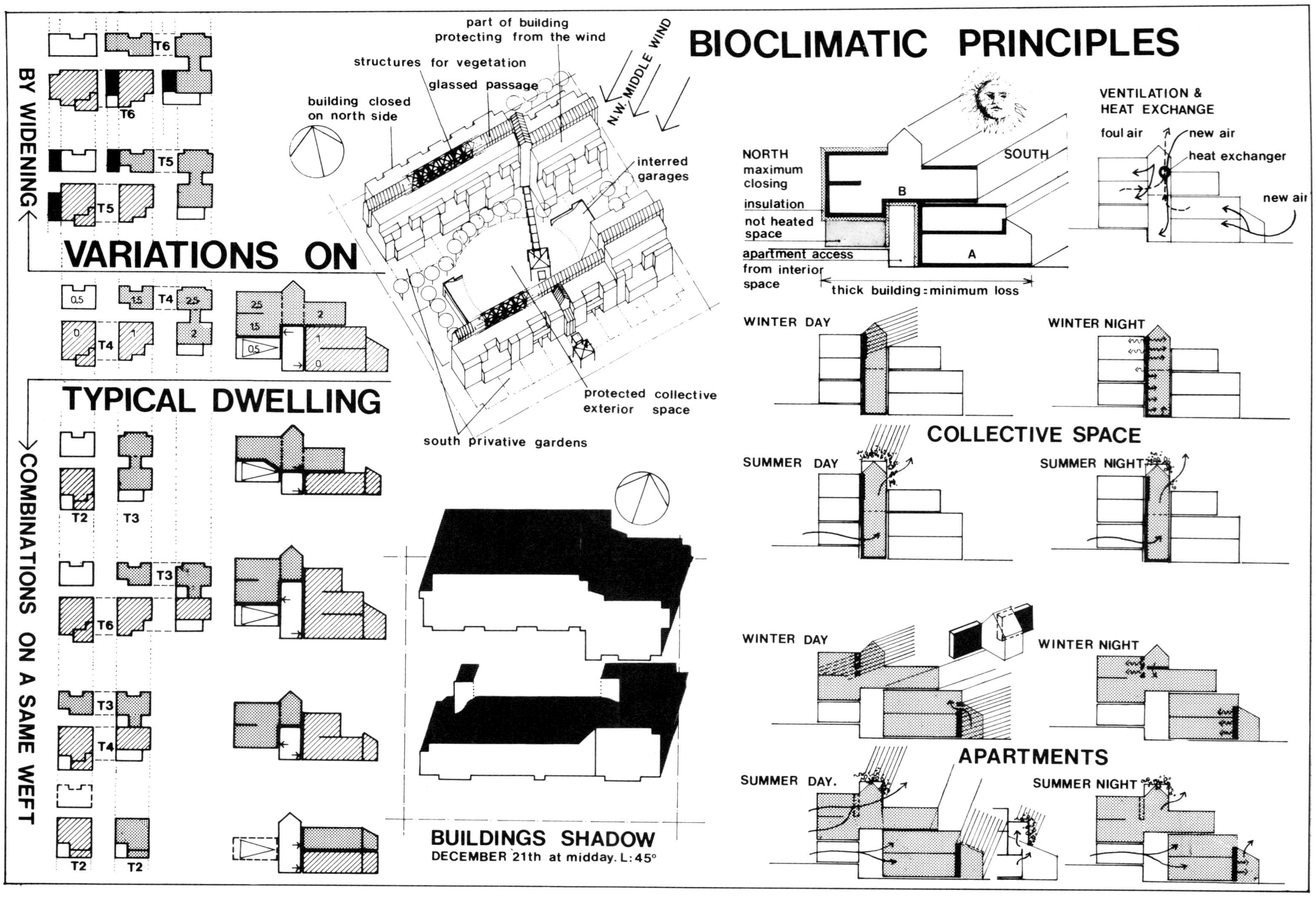

BIOCLIMATIC PRINCIPLES

VENTILATION & HEAT EXCHANGE

new air
heat exchanger
foul air
new air

SOUTH

NORTH
maximum closing
insulation
not heated space
apartment access from interior space
thick building = minimum loss

A
B

COLLECTIVE SPACE

WINTER NIGHT
WINTER DAY

SUMMER NIGHT
SUMMER DAY

APARTMENTS

WINTER NIGHT
WINTER DAY

SUMMER NIGHT
SUMMER DAY.

N.W. MIDDLE WIND

part of building protecting from the wind
interred garages
structures for vegetation
glassed passage
building closed on north side
protected collective exterior space
south privative gardens

BUILDINGS SHADOW
DECEMBER 21th at midday. L: 45°

VARIATIONS ON

BY WIDENING

T6
T6
T5
T5
T4
T4
T3
T3
T2
T2

0.5
1.5
2.5

TYPICAL DWELLING

→ COMBINATIONS ON A SAME WEFT

SCALE 1/100

FLAT B
FLAT A
FLAT A
FLAT B
A
A
B
B
garage

① SECTION ②

SCALE 1/100

SOUTH ELEVATION

GLASSED PASSAGE

FLAT B
SOLAR PANEL
SECOND FLOOR
1
3
9
10
4
5

FLAT A
FIRST FLOOR
4
4
9
4
5
6
GLASSED PASSAGE
4
7
FLAT B

FLAT A
GROUND FLOOR
SCALE 1/100
9
1
3
2
6
7
8
8

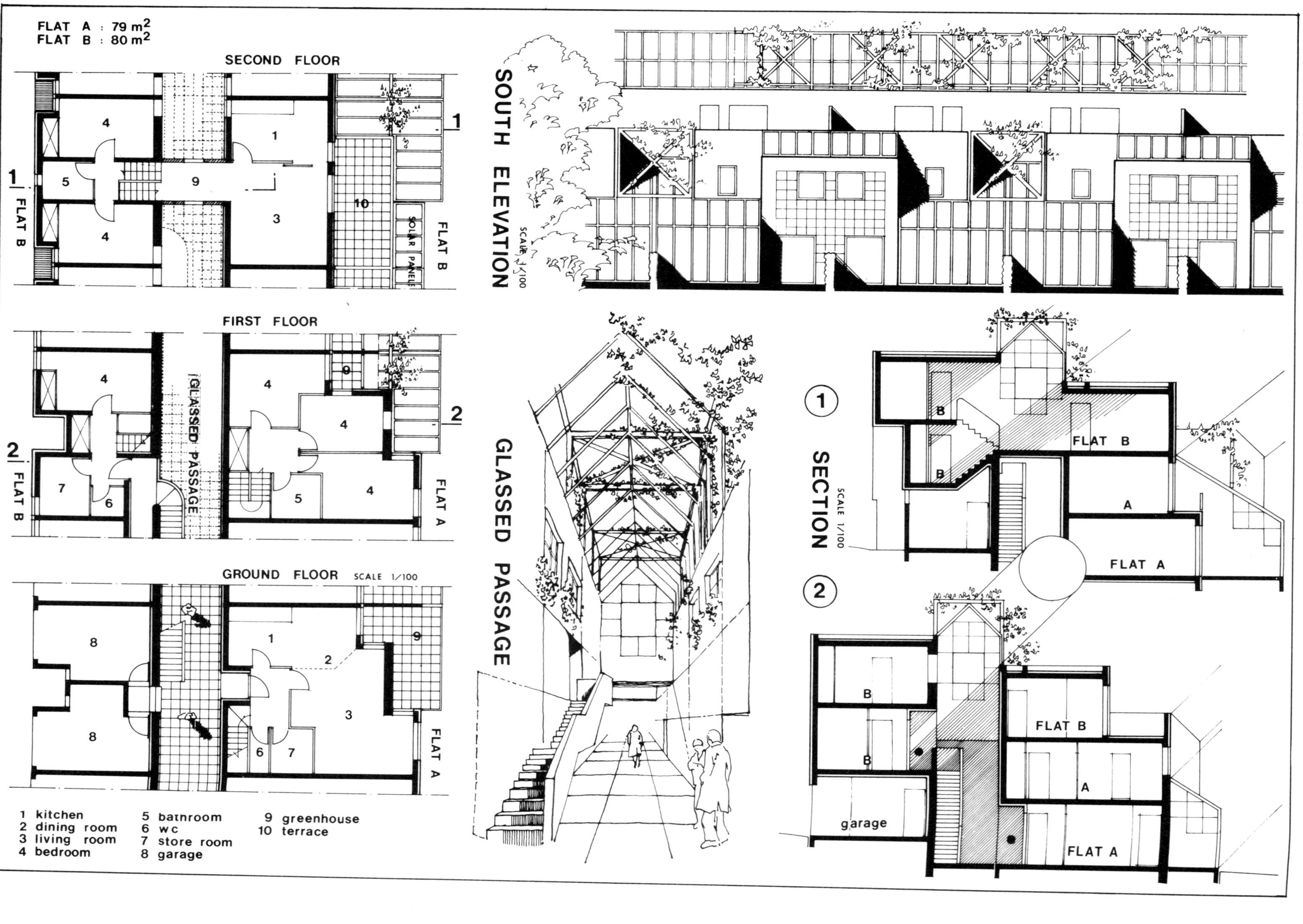

FLAT A : 79 m²
FLAT B : 80 m²

1 kitchen
2 dining room
3 living room
4 bedroom
5 bathroom
6 wc
7 store room
8 garage
9 greenhouse
10 terrace

SECOND PRIZE
CATEGORY A

4,000,000 Italian Lire

We decided to put forward proposals for a large scale 'model' development rather than to concentrate upon a single building for the following reasons:—

a. A large scale development creates a complex system of parts and functions which helps to give a true-to-life feel to the project.

b. The flexibility of such a development allows the creation of typically Italian urban features — such as colonnaded streets or squares with porticos and shops.

c. The proposals are not designed for any particular site but may be adapted to suit different configurations of land form and existing buildings.

Greater internal flexibility is achieved since the scheme is made up of units of differing volumes which are nevertheless homogeneous in their architectural composition and energy performance.

The residential units are particularly energy efficient. The rooms look inwards only

Site model.

DESIGN TEAM

Vincenzo Bacigalupi
Cristina Benedetti
Giancarlo Cavallera
Vitangelo Pugliese

via Rodolfo Benini 20
00191 Roma
Italy

towards a central, two storey high, atrium.

The atrium is enclosed by a glass skylight, the windows of which may be opened.

Our proposed development may be reproduced in a variety of materials by either traditional or industrialised construction methods — in either case it will be possible to incorporate factory-produced components.

For the competition a site at Serpentara, to the north of Rome was selected for the scheme.

The architect's objective here was to create a group of buildings which would link the various parts of the existing town to a village, Fidene, which has developed spontaneously and is therefore characterised by a lack of amenities and general untidiness.

We have achieved this by using our development model — by incorporating the colonnaded streets and squares and by the use of various unifying techniques. An open air theatre which takes advantage of the natural 'basin' form of the land is also incorporated into the design. This area also serves as a junction for the arteries which link the town to the village.

LOCATION
Serpentara
Italy

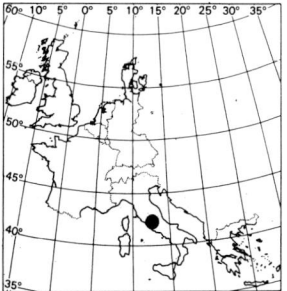

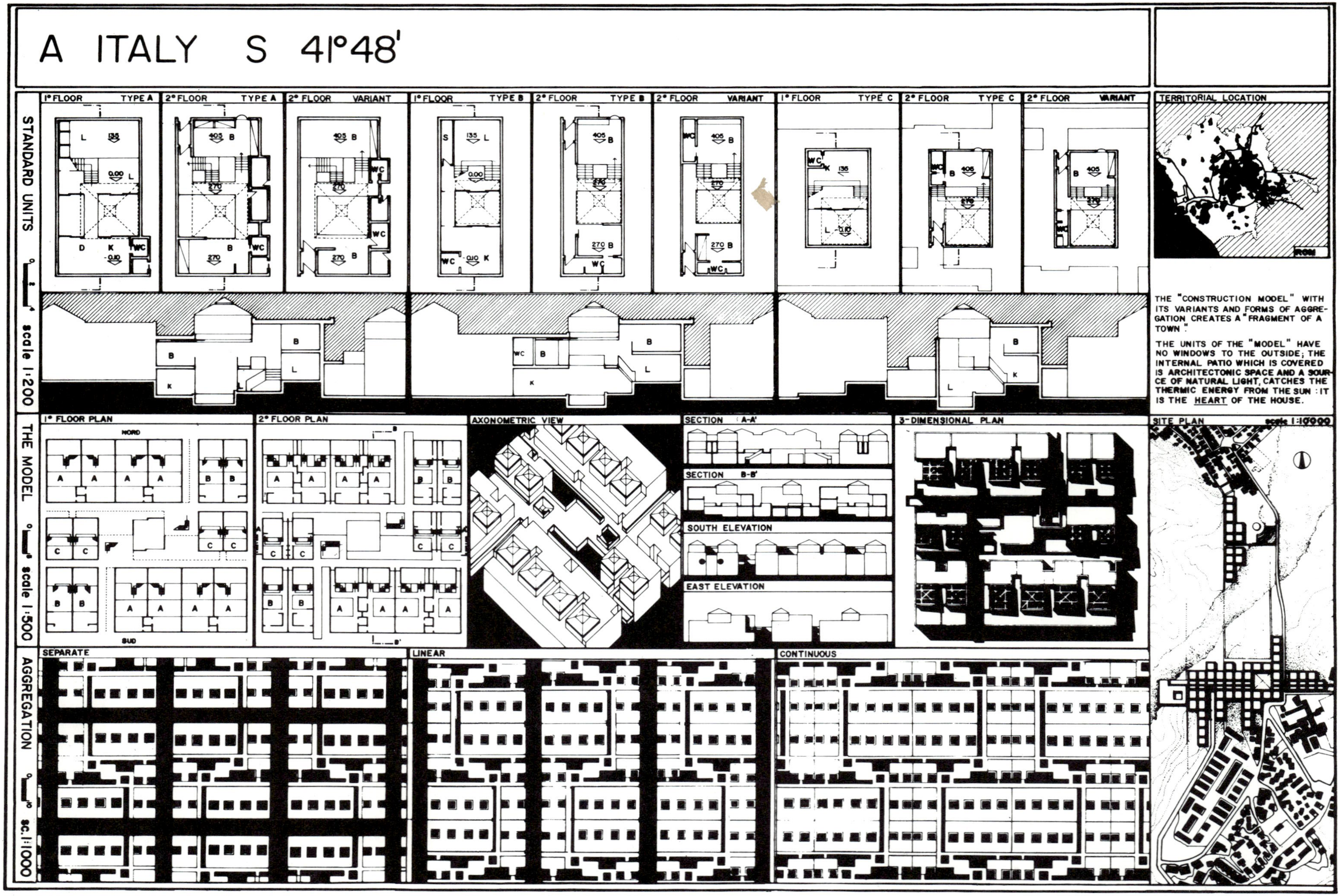

A ITALY S 41°48'
STANDARD UNITS scale 1:200
1° FLOOR TYPE A
2° FLOOR TYPE A
2° FLOOR VARIANT
1° FLOOR TYPE B
2° FLOOR TYPE B
2° FLOOR VARIANT
1° FLOOR TYPE C
2° FLOOR TYPE C
2° FLOOR VARIANT
TERRITORIAL LOCATION
THE "CONSTRUCTION MODEL" WITH ITS VARIANTS AND FORMS OF AGGREGATION CREATES A "FRAGMENT OF A TOWN".
THE UNITS OF THE "MODEL" HAVE NO WINDOWS TO THE OUTSIDE; THE INTERNAL PATIO WHICH IS COVERED IS ARCHITECTONIC SPACE AND A SOURCE OF NATURAL LIGHT, CATCHES THE THERMIC ENERGY FROM THE SUN: IT IS THE HEART OF THE HOUSE.
THE MODEL scale 1:500
1° FLOOR PLAN
NORD
SUD
2° FLOOR PLAN
AXONOMETRIC VIEW
SECTION A-A'
SECTION B-B'
SOUTH ELEVATION
EAST ELEVATION
3-DIMENSIONAL PLAN
SITE PLAN scale 1:10000
AGGREGATION sc. 1:1000
SEPARATE
LINEAR
CONTINUOUS

JUDGES' COMMENTS

In Category A, the Second prize of 4,000,000 Italian Lire goes to Vincenzo Bacigalupi for a scheme of houses to be built to the north of Rome.

A central atrium in each split-level house acts as a general and unifying space for the rooms which link and connect across and beside it; these rooms therefore form a progression of spaces related to the atrium whilst achieving different degrees of publicness and privateness within themselves.

Above the atrium is a highly adjustable lantern, biased to the south by means of a stepped section; the lantern collects heat through its sun-side faces whilst insulating to the north. It can open all its faces for ventilation and can be completely closed off by internal shutters during the winter nights.

By achieving solar gain and climate control through the stepped roof of the atrium, the house largely avoids the 'one pretty face' problem of many solar houses and the designer is able to show that he can thereby make a very varied urban pattern using these houses. A slight east-west grain is

counteracted by the introduction of vigorous paths or alleys that run, disjointedly, north-south. Together these east-west, north-south passages are used to create the varied and multi-directional open spaces that a city requires: passages, roads, streets, boulevards, terraces, gardens, parks, piazzas, courtyards and so on. So for a combination of microcosm and macrocosm in a solar context and an urban context we thought this to be an excellent prize winner.

TECHNICAL ASSESSORS' COMMENTS

Two storey urban dwellings in Rome with a central atrium. Direct gains to the atrium are used as a heat pump source. When the temperature in the atrium is cooled close to the outside air temperature, the heat pump then switches source to utilise the ambient air as a source. The atrium is also used for summer cooling. This is an interesting design but the control systems need to be further developed.   The calculations are correct.

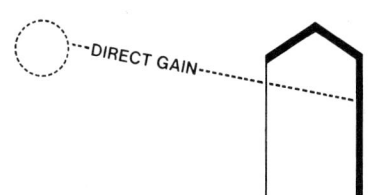

TECHNICAL DATA

For explanation of data see page 16.

Latitude: 41° 48'N
Altitude: 60 m
Data Point: Rome

DWELLING DESCRIPTION (Typical Unit)
Heated Volume: 410 m³

APERTURE	A	B	C	D
System Type	DG	DG	DG	
Net Area m²	5.2	5.2	5.2	
Glazing Layers	2	2	2	
Night Insulation	No	No	No	
τ		1.00	0.65	0.65
Comment		T	T	T
			+	+
			W	W

Aperture/Heated Volume: 0.06 m²/m³
Primary Mass/
    Related Aperture: 150.0 Wh/m²°C
Remote Mass/
    Related Aperture: —Wh/m²°C
Air Change Rate: 0.58 ac/h
Building Loss Coeff.: 5.55 kWh/DD
                          : 231.40 W/°C

DWELLING PERFORMANCE (Typical Unit)
% Internal Gains: 41.0
% Auxiliary Heating: 29.0
% Useful Solar Gains: 30.0
Annual Solar Gains Fraction: 0.52
Figure of Merit: 0.003 kWh/DDm²
Useful Solar Gains/
    m² of Aperture: 108.0 kWh/m²yr
Min. Temp. without Heating: 6.0°C
Min. Outdoor Temperature: —0.7°C

ENERGY CHARACTERISTICS

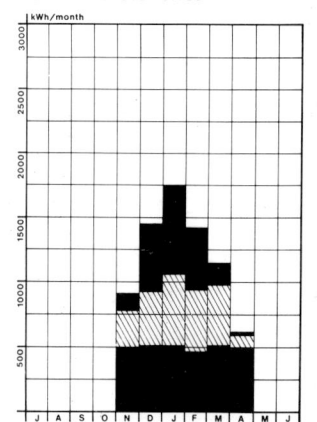

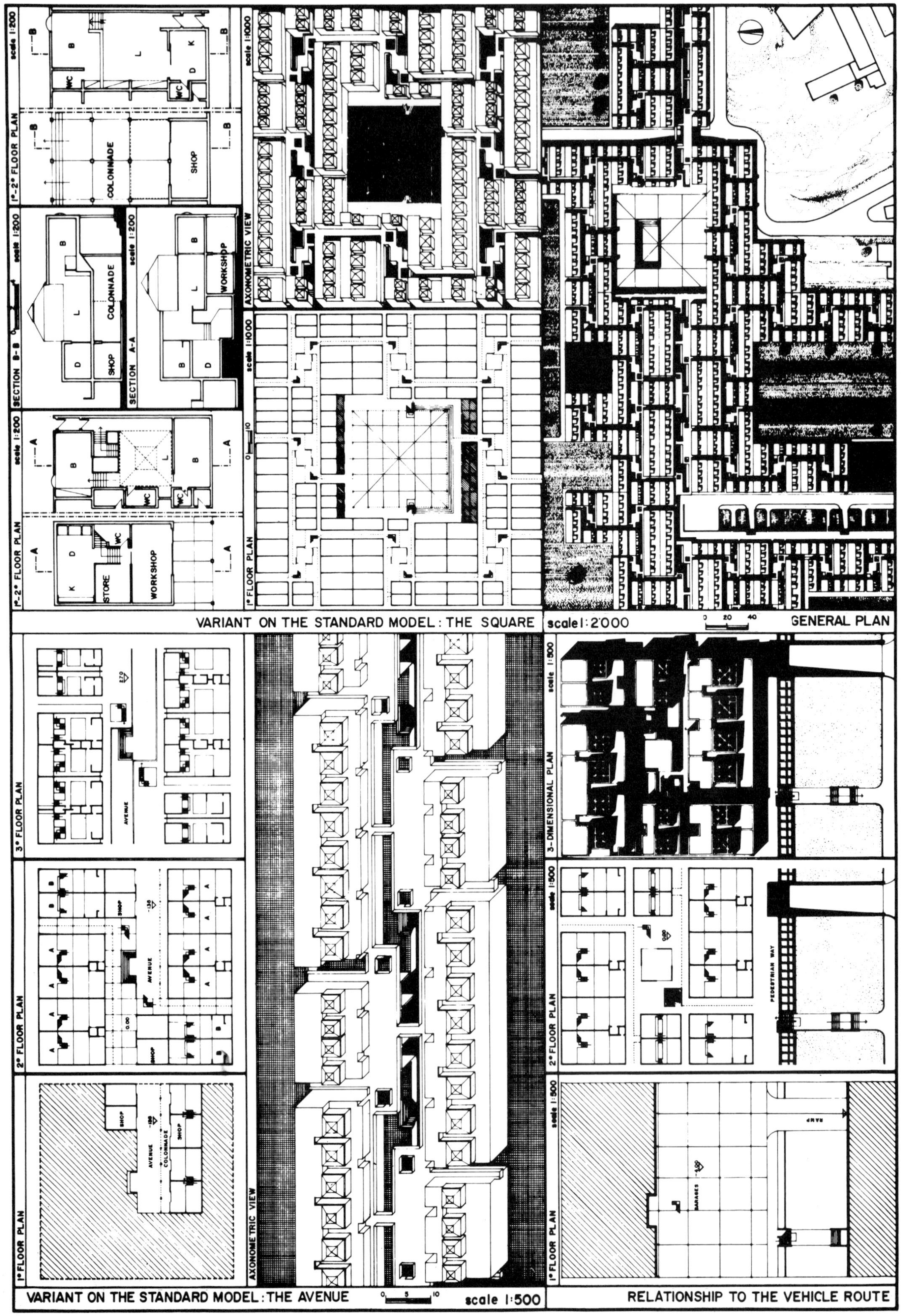

scale 1:200

SECTION B-B

scale 1:200

SECTION A-A

scale 1:200

1°-2° FLOOR PLAN

COLONNADE

SHOP

COLONNADE

SHOP

WORKSHOP

SHOP

STORE

WORKSHOP

1°-2° FLOOR PLAN

scale 1:1000

AXONOMETRIC VIEW

scale 1:1000

FLOOR PLAN

VARIANT ON THE STANDARD MODEL: THE SQUARE

scale 1:2000   GENERAL PLAN

3° FLOOR PLAN

2° FLOOR PLAN

1° FLOOR PLAN

AVENUE

SHOP

AVENUE

COLONNADE

SHOP

VARIANT ON THE STANDARD MODEL: THE AVENUE   scale 1:500

scale 1:500

AXONOMETRIC VIEW

scale 1:500

3-DIMENSIONAL PLAN

scale 1:500

2° FLOOR PLAN

scale 1:500

1° FLOOR PLAN

PEDESTRIAN WAY

RELATIONSHIP TO THE VEHICLE ROUTE

FLOORING cm 3
CONCRETE cm 3
WATERPROOFING
INSULATION cm 10
VAPOUR BARRIER

ALUMINIUM SEAL
SOLID BRICKS cm 12
INSULATION cm 10
PLASTER cm 2.5

CONCRETE FOR SLOPE min. cm 3
STRUCTURAL CONCRETE cm 18
PLASTER cm 2.5
PERFORATED BRICKS cm 8
SOLID BRICKS cm 12
INSULATION cm 10
PLASTER cm 2.5

WIND-UP CURTAINS AS PROTECTION AGAINS SOLAR RADIATION IN WIRE-GLASS COVERED WITH PVC
L-SHAPED IRON STRUCTURE
ALUMINIUM FIXTURES WITH "THERMIC CUT"
DOUBLE GLAZING

TOP SEALING
FIXED GLASS WITH SILICONE
ALUMINIUM SEAL
INSULATION PANEL WITH INTERNAL REFLECTING SURFACE

ALL FIXTURES WITH "HORIZONTAL CENTRE HUNG" OPENING CONTROLLED WITH A HANDLE AT LANDING LEVEL.

FIXED WINDOWS IN THE ANGLES

SLIDING INSULATION PANELS cm 10
INTERNAL ROOFING IN WOOD

GUIDE-RAIL FOR THE ACCOMODATION OF THE MOBILE WINDOWS

L-SHAPED TRACK FOR THE INSULATION PANELS TO SLIDE ALONG

C-SHAPED BEAM TO SUPPORT FIXTURE AND L-SHAPED TRACK

scale 1:20   PATIO ROOF SECTION (DETAIL)

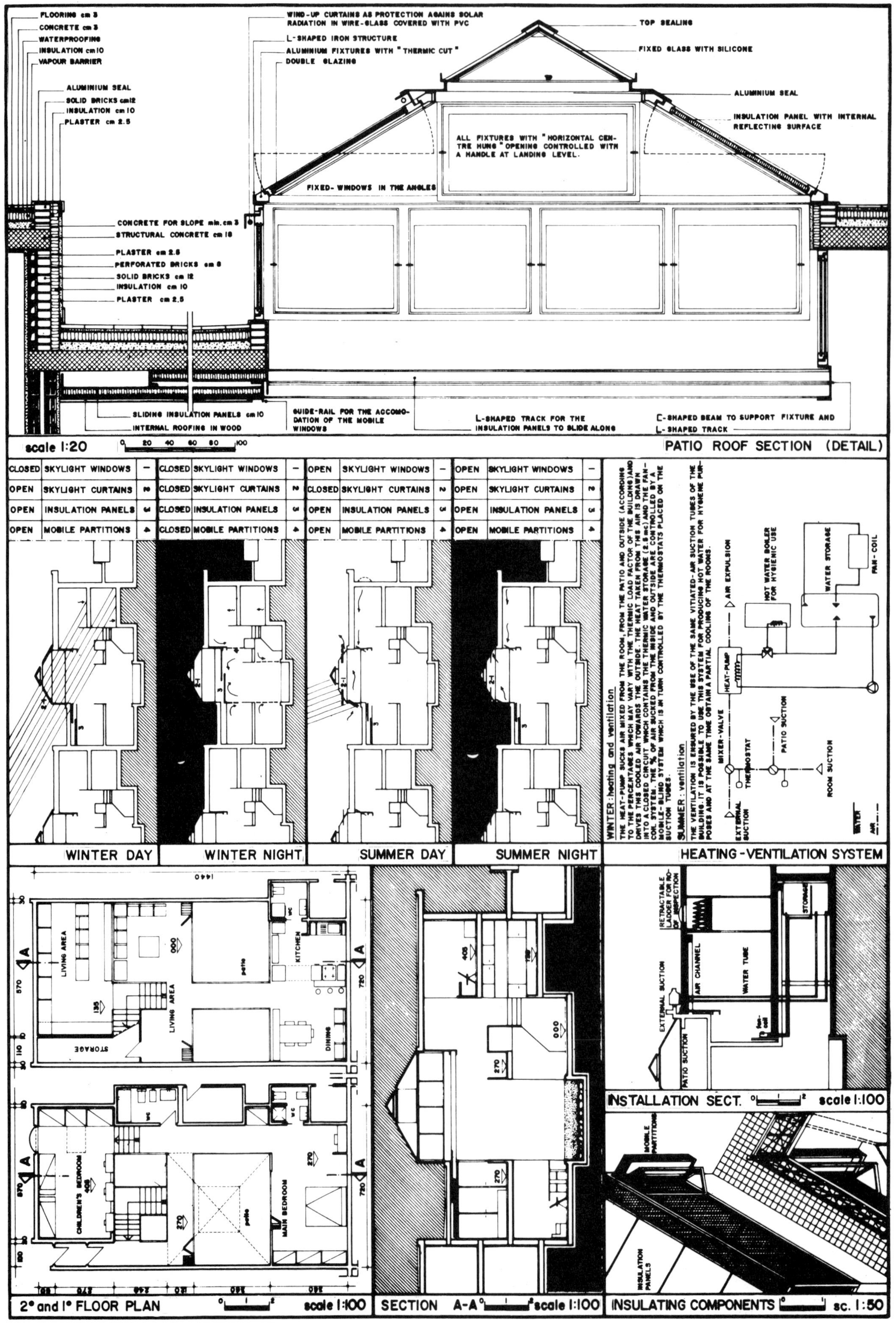

CLOSED	SKYLIGHT WINDOWS	CLOSED	SKYLIGHT WINDOWS	OPEN	SKYLIGHT WINDOWS	OPEN	SKYLIGHT WINDOWS
OPEN	SKYLIGHT CURTAINS	CLOSED	SKYLIGHT CURTAINS	CLOSED	SKYLIGHT CURTAINS	OPEN	SKYLIGHT CURTAINS
OPEN	INSULATION PANELS	CLOSED	INSULATION PANELS	OPEN	INSULATION PANELS	OPEN	INSULATION PANELS
OPEN	MOBILE PARTITIONS	CLOSED	MOBILE PARTITIONS	OPEN	MOBILE PARTITIONS	OPEN	MOBILE PARTITIONS

WINTER DAY   WINTER NIGHT   SUMMER DAY   SUMMER NIGHT   HEATING-VENTILATION SYSTEM

WINTER: heating and ventilation

SUMMER: ventilation

WATER STORAGE
HOT WATER BOILER FOR HYGIENIC USE
FAN-COIL
HEAT-PUMP
AIR EXPULSION
PATIO SUCTION
ROOM SUCTION
MIXER-VALVE
THERMOSTAT
EXTERNAL SUCTION
METER
WATER

LIVING AREA
LIVING AREA
KITCHEN
PATIO
DINING
STORAGE
CHILDREN'S BEDROOM
MAIN BEDROOM
WC
patio

2° and 1° FLOOR PLAN   scale 1:100

SECTION A-A   scale 1:100

INSTALLATION SECT.   scale 1:100

RETRACTABLE AIR CHANNEL FOR CLOSER POSITION
EXTERNAL SUCTION
PATIO SUCTION
AIR CHANNEL
WATER TUBE
STORAGE

MOBILE PARTITIONS
INSULATION PANELS

INSULATING COMPONENTS   sc. 1:50

THIRD PRIZE
CATEGORY A

£1,000

My aims were:-

1. To achieve successful passive solar housing on a thoroughly 'ordinary' site — a gap in the suburban fabric around Bath, England sloping northwards and bounded by busy commuter routes.

2. To establish an enclave of positive, recognisable solar architecture on the site and to explore the possibilities of perimeter housing in order to escape the parallel ranks of east-west terraces.

3. To exploit the few natural advantages of the site (the hospital chapel in the north-west corner, the pedestrian footpath system and the playing fields to the south) and create a focus for the surrounding community.

DESIGNER

Steve Tompkins

3 Oxford Place
Combe Down
Bath
United Kingdom

LOCATION
Bath
England

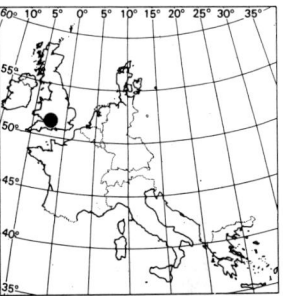

4. To explore the idea of the solar house in subjective terms as well as technical:-

 a. Can the internal space of the home be made to perform as a sundial, whereby the occupants can experience the different times of day and year from inside?
 b. Can the house be seen as a flower, which, whatever its position on the ground, orientates itself towards the sun — i.e. can a house address itself both to the sunshine and to the street on which it is built?
 c. Can the sectional and plan form be arranged both to enhance the enjoyment of different weather conditions by the occupants and to optimise the technical response of the building in terms of air movement, solar stack effects, etc.?

5. To reduce the annual heating load to an absolute minimum by the use of 'free' auxiliary as well as principal heating systems — in this case waste heat from domestic hot water.

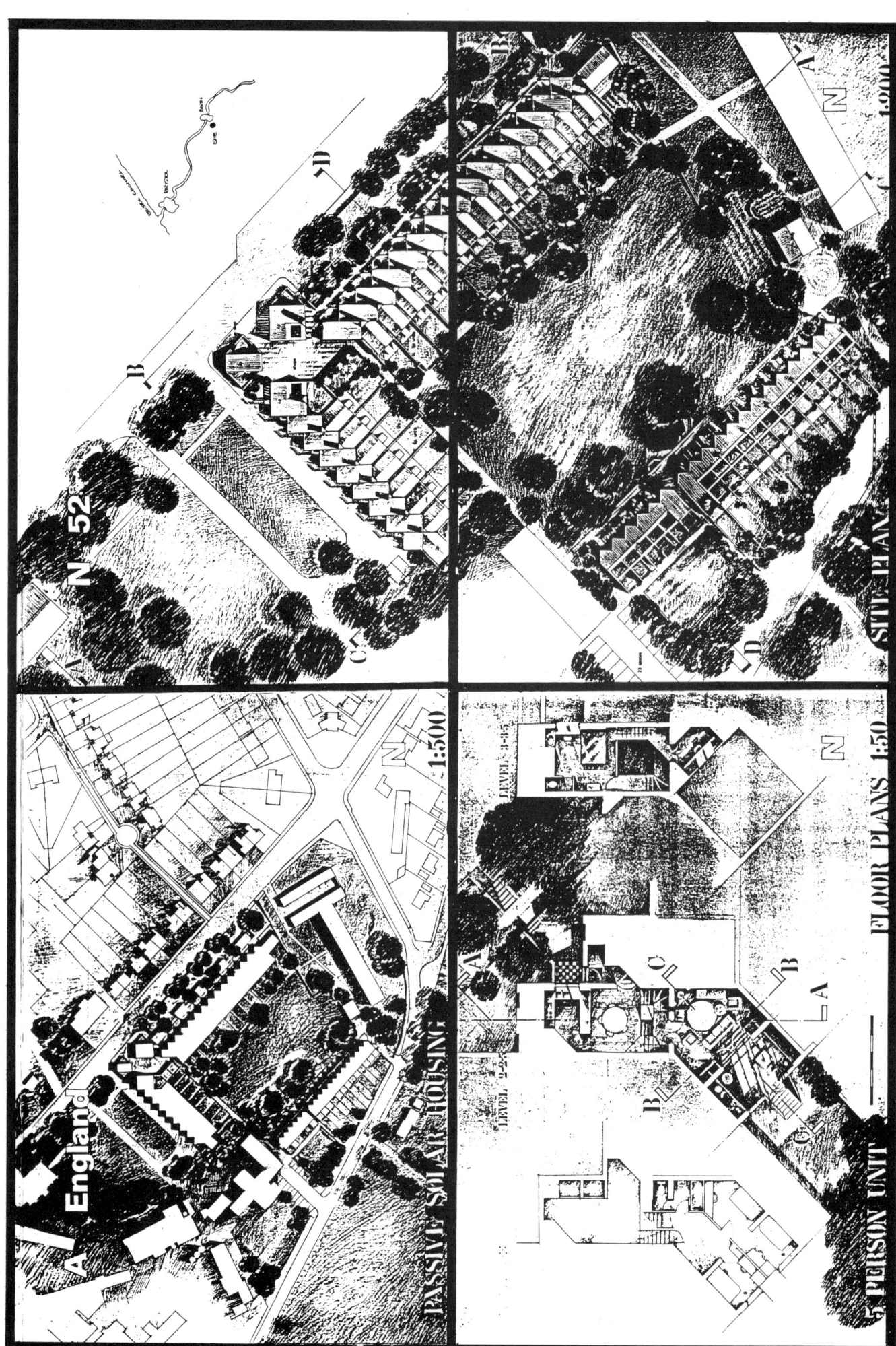

PASSIVE SOLAR HOUSING

SITE PLAN

FLOOR PLANS 1:50

5 PERSON UNIT

England

N 52

1:500

LEVEL 3-85

LEVEL 2-2-

JUDGES' COMMENTS

Our Third prize of £1,000 goes to Steve Tompkins for his scheme of houses on the outskirts of Bath in England. A problem with the individual row house, as with suburbia, is to create a place which as a whole adds up to more than just the sum of the separate parts; to do this with passive solar buildings is a significant achievement in ingenuity of composition.

We especially enjoyed the way that the houses faced mainly south to collect the sun, but turned their heads, like sunflowers, making their living rooms and main bedrooms wider and larger, creating an elevation fit to bound the open space which they all share. Existing buildings are incorporated into the boundaries of the main open space, which has a happy and flexible balance with the private gardens that bound it. We liked the way the two turned terraces achieved a final turn, at their northern confluence, to create a minor but linked open space for the shops.

Not least for the lovely drawings, this was a fine third prize.

TECHNICAL ASSESSORS' COMMENTS

A cranked terrace arrangement of deep plan dwellings with upper floor living spaces. Solar gains to a fan assisted sun space and a vertically glazed roof space are used together with direct gains through clerestory windows. The study of form in relation to solar penetration is commendable. The scheme is lacking some technical details and it is difficult to relate the larger scale drawings to the site plan. The back-up heating system has been oversized.

The calculations are correct.

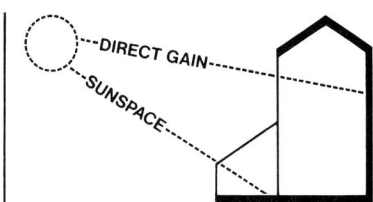

TECHNICAL DATA

For explanation of data see page 16.

Latitude: 51° 22'N
Altitude: 160 m
Data Point: London/Aberporth

DWELLING DESCRIPTION (Typical Unit)
Heated Volume: 261 m³

APERTURE	A	B	C	D
System Type	DG	SS	DG	
Net Area m²	9.5	20.5	4.0	
Glazing Layers	2	2	2	
Night Insulation	Yes	Yes	Yes	
τ	0.60	0.45	0.20	
Comment	O/H	O/H	O	
	+	+	+	
	O	SE	E	

Aperture/Heated Volume: 0.130 m²/m³
Primary Mass/
    Related Aperture: 129.0 Wh/m²°C
Remote Mass/
    Related Aperture: 2109.0 Wh/m²°C
Air Change Rate: 0.75 ac/h
Building Loss Coeff.: 3.13 kWh/DD
       : 130.60 W/°C

DWELLING PERFORMANCE (Typical Unit)
% Internal Gains: 50.8
% Auxiliary Heating: 14.2
% Useful Solar Gains: 35.0
Annual Solar Gains Fraction: 0.32
Figure of Merit: 0.0018 kWh/DDm²
Useful Solar Gains/
m² of Aperture: 80.9 kWh/m²yr
Min. Temp. without Heating: 9.0°C
Min. Outdoor Temperature: −4.0°C

ENERGY CHARACTERISTICS

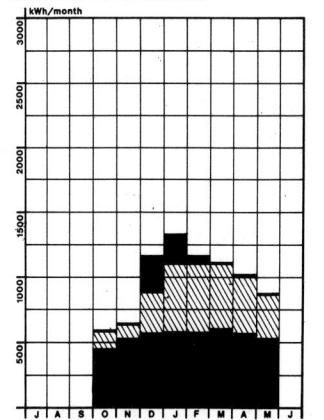

AA

CC

DD

1:200

AA

CC

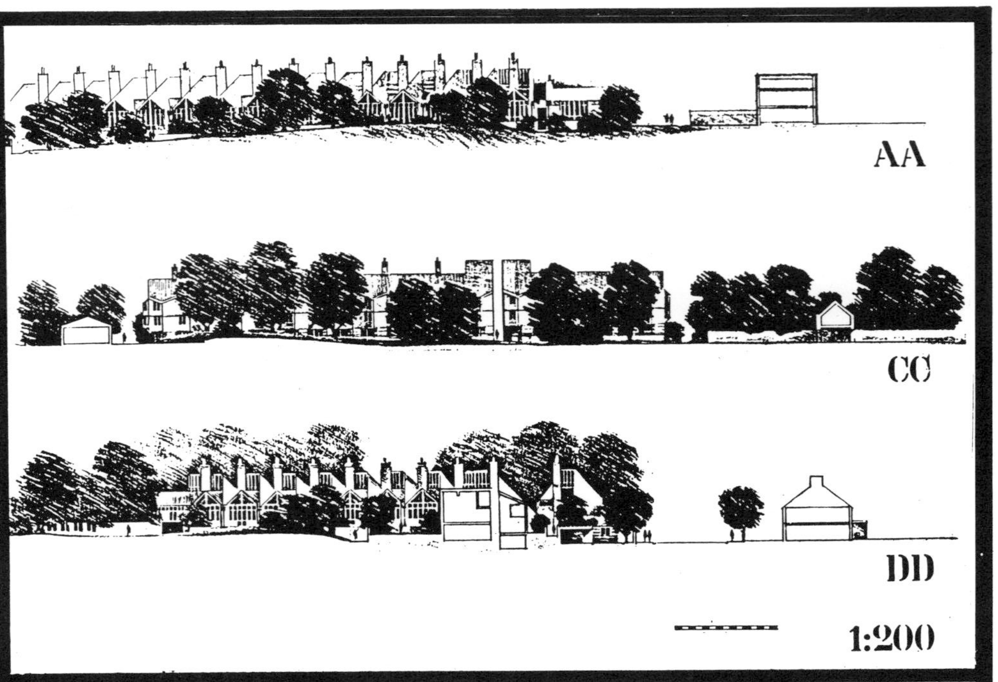

SECTIONS 1:50

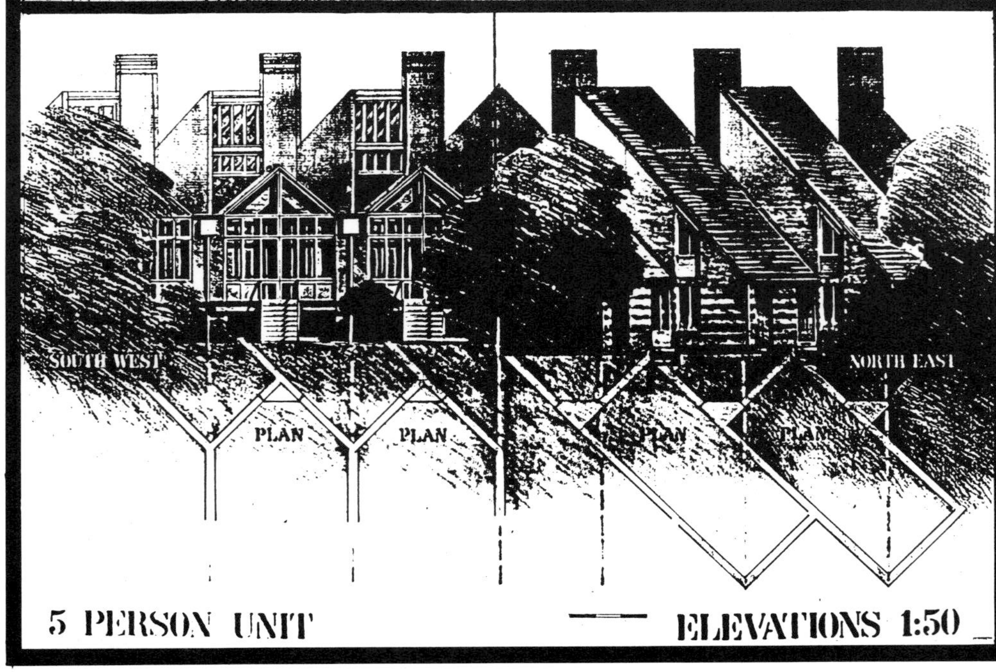

5 PERSON UNIT

BB

5 PERSON UNIT

SITE SECTIONS

ELEVATIONS 1:50

NORTH EAST

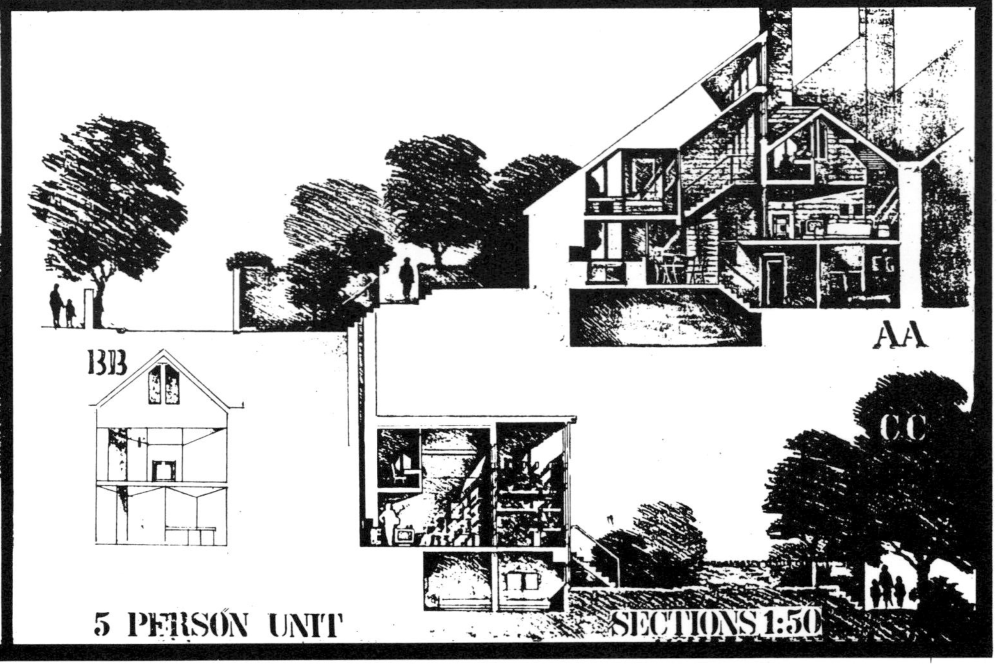

SOUTH WEST

PLAN

PLAN

PLAN

5 PERSON UNIT

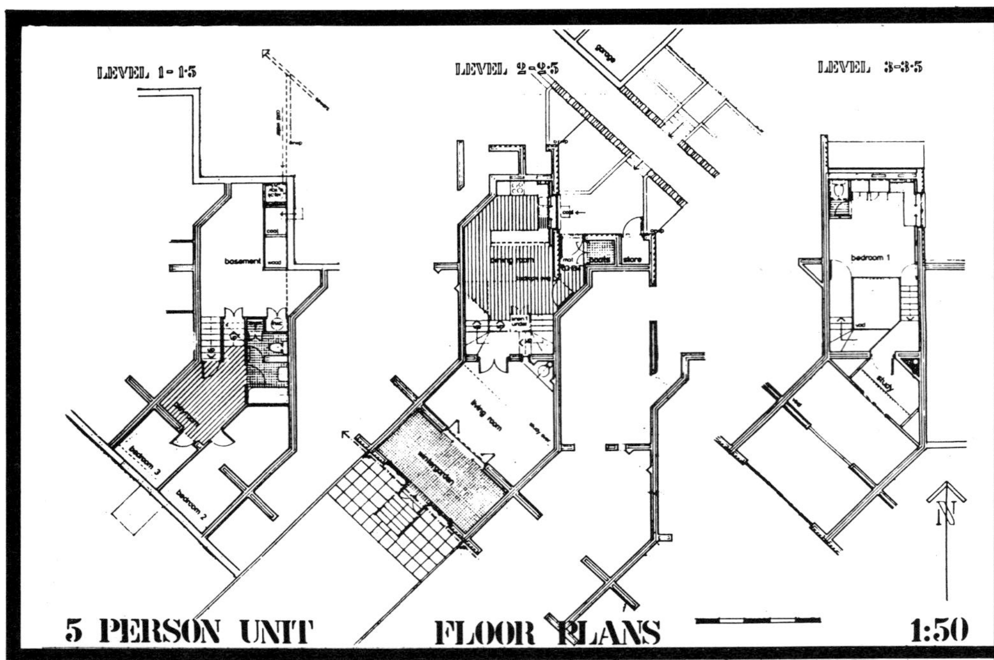

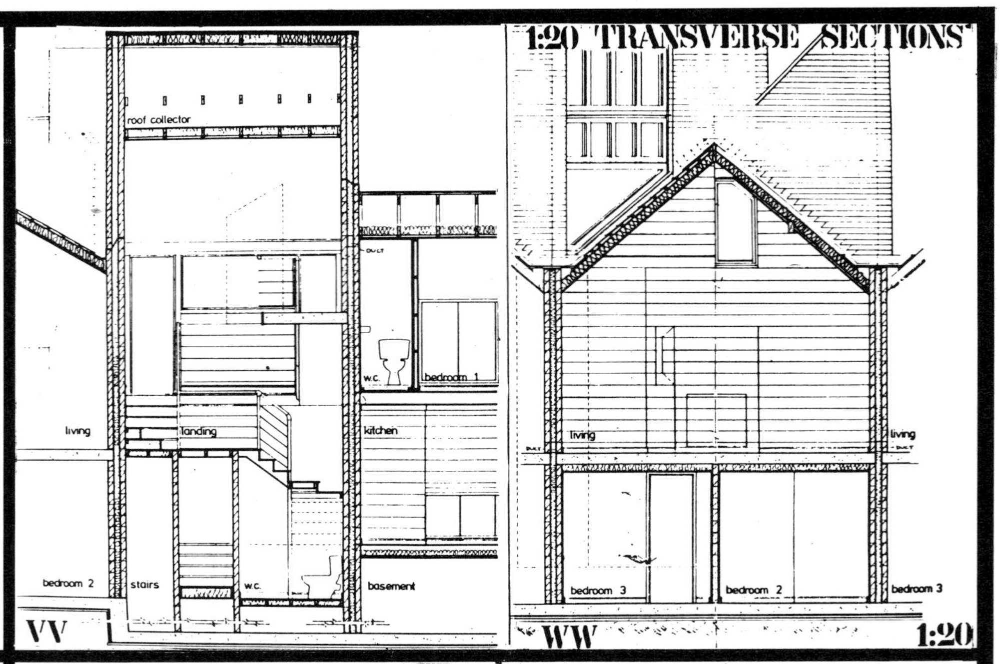

1:20 TRANSVERSE SECTIONS

1:20

WW

VV

living

bedroom 3

bedroom 2

w.c.

kitchen

basement

stairs

playroom

living

WORK ROOM

bedroom 2

living

1:20

bedroom

kitchen

code

basement

SECTION UU

SEE SECTION XX

roof collector

dining

living

playroom

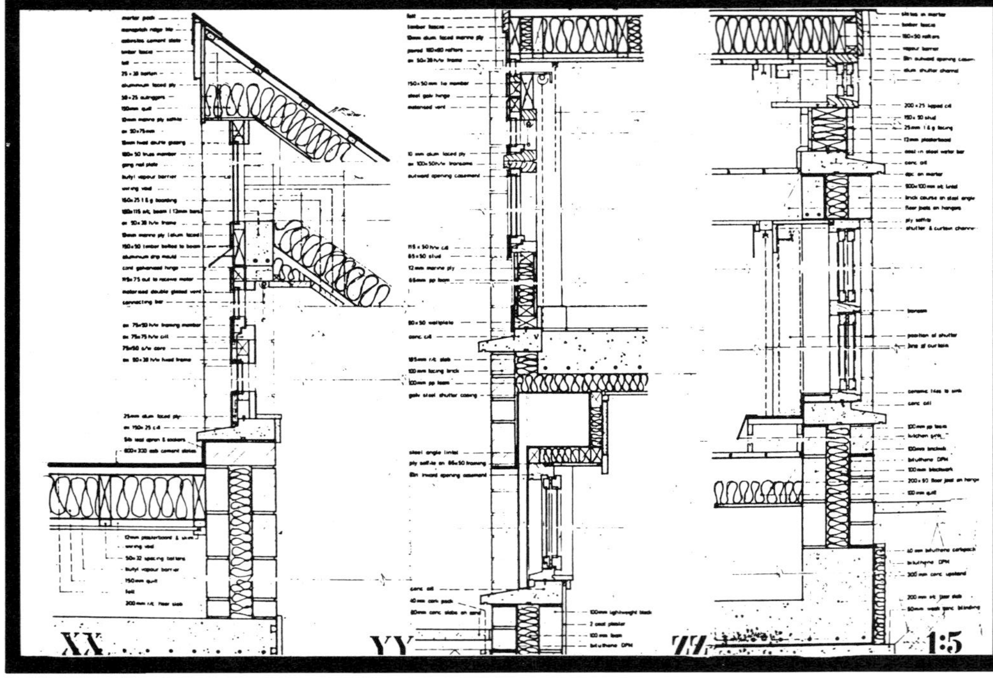

SEE SECTION YY

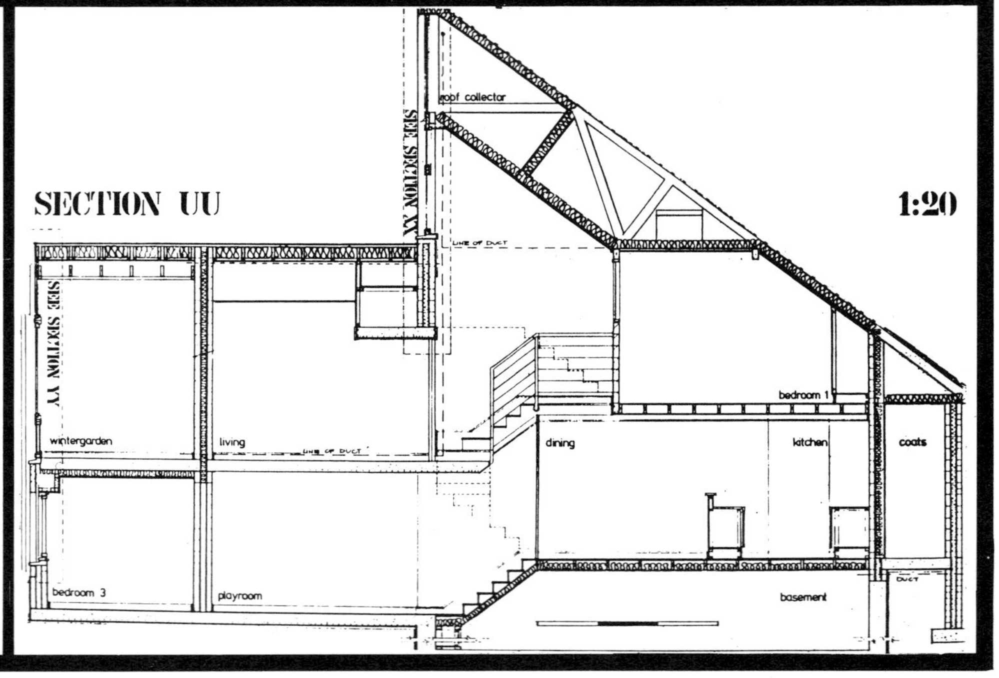

bedroom 3

wintergarden

1:50

LEVEL 3-4-5

bedroom 1

LEVEL 2-3-5

garage

LEVEL 1-2-5

basement

bedroom 2

FLOOR PLANS

1:5

5 PERSON UNIT

XX

YY

ZZ

Submitted Drawings: Third Prize Category A

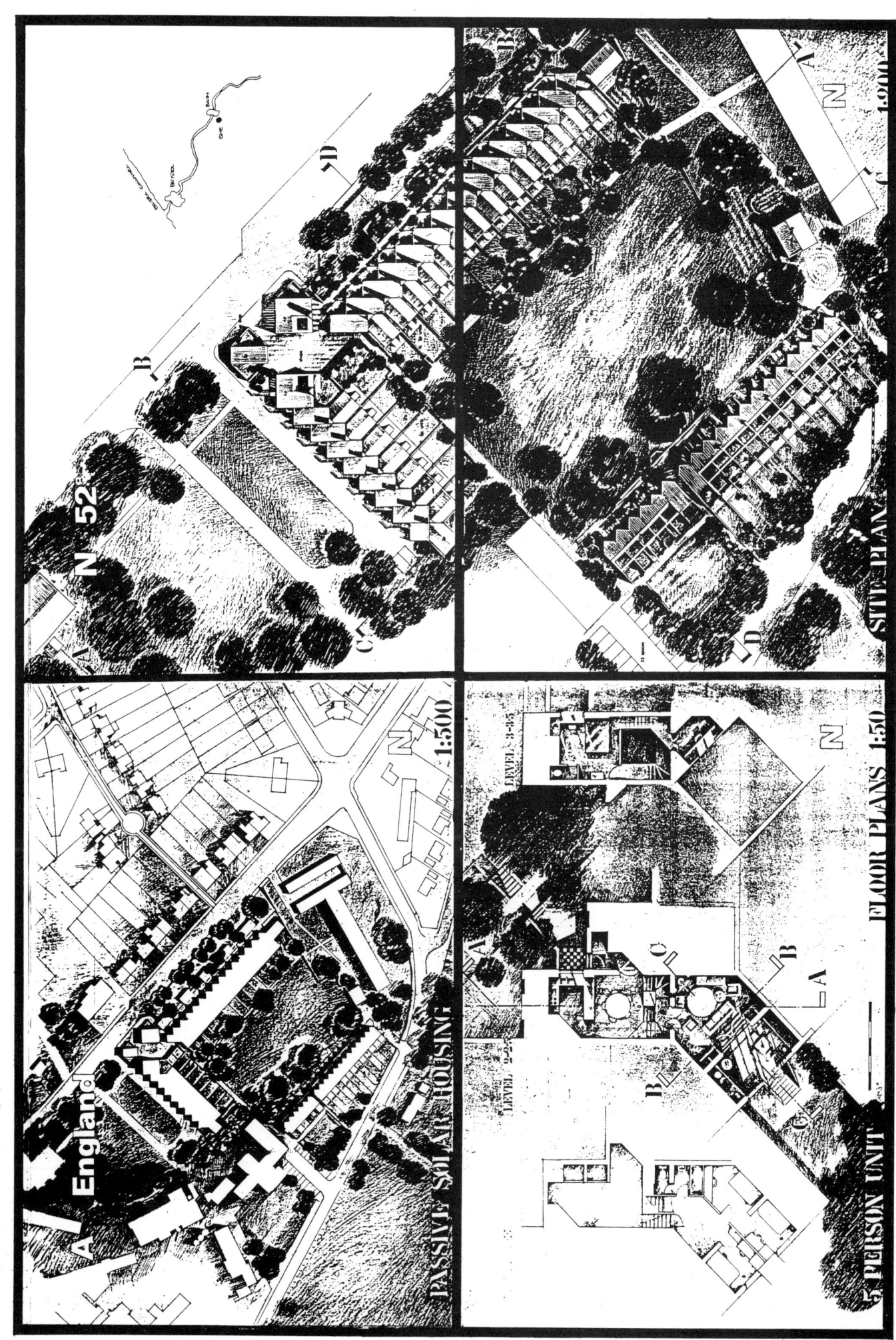

THIRD PRIZE
CATEGORY A

£1,000

My aims were:-

1. To achieve successful passive solar housing on a thoroughly 'ordinary' site — a gap in the suburban fabric around Bath, England sloping northwards and bounded by busy commuter routes.

2. To establish an enclave of positive, recognisable solar architecture on the site and to explore the possibilities of perimeter housing in order to escape the parallel ranks of east-west terraces.

3. To exploit the few natural advantages of the site (the hospital chapel in the north-west corner, the pedestrian footpath system and the playing fields to the south) and create a focus for the surrounding community.

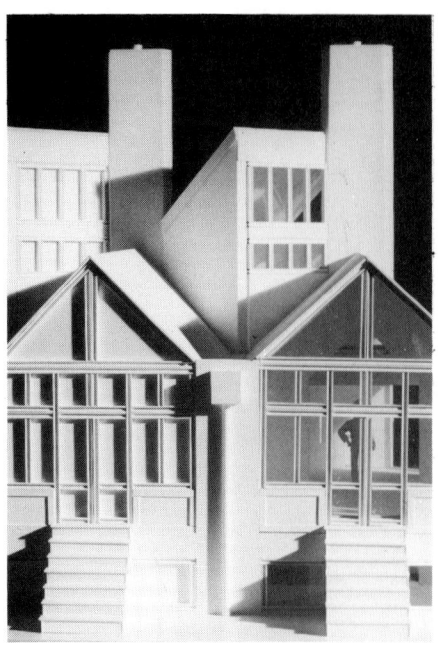

DESIGNER

Steve Tompkins

3 Oxford Place
Combe Down
Bath
United Kingdom

4. To explore the idea of the solar house in subjective terms as well as technical:-

   a. Can the internal space of the home be made to perform as a sundial, whereby the occupants can experience the different times of day and year from inside?
   b. Can the house be seen as a flower, which, whatever its position on the ground, orientates itself towards the sun — i.e. can a house address itself both to the sunshine and to the street on which it is built?
   c. Can the sectional and plan form be arranged both to enhance the enjoyment of different weather conditions by the occupants and to optimise the technical response of the building in terms of air movement, solar stack effects, etc.?

5. To reduce the annual heating load to an absolute minimum by the use of 'free' auxiliary as well as principal heating systems — in this case waste heat from domestic hot water.

LOCATION
Bath
England

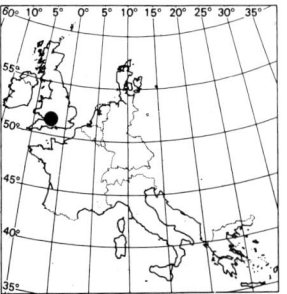

FOURTH PRIZE
CATEGORY A

2,000 Deutsch Marks

On the outskirts of the towns in West Germany — and, as far as we know, around towns elsewhere — there are allotment gardens where many people spend their leisure time. Here they have made for themselves creative oases which stand in contrast to their normal, impersonal life styles in rented apartment buildings. In these times of economic stagnation these allotments are the alternative, particularly for young couples with children and for the less well off in general, to a house with a garden.

Our proposals therefore consist of a self-build estate of small terraced houses. The basic structure of the houses would be erected with the assistance of local craftsmen (possibly working as a cooperative) but they would then be individually completed with additions chosen by the tenants, so that the final form of the buildings will depend upon the wishes and finances of the owners.

The project is in a transition zone between the high density medieval buildings of the small town of Markgroningen and an estate of detached family houses with gardens built in the '60s.

It therefore seemed that medium density housing would be most appropriate for this site. Building at this density also means that open landscaped communal areas and

DESIGN TEAM

Johannes T Brucker
Angelica Fellhaver
Reinhard A Langner
Manfred Vietz

Strohberg 4
D 7000 Stuttgart 1
F R Germany

LOCATION
Markgroningen
F R Germany

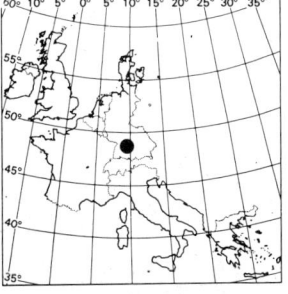

medium sized private gardens could also be incorporated.

At the centre of the scheme a workshop for use during the construction of the buildings will be provided — later it will be used as a community centre. The houses will be constructed using local traditional methods and will be laid out in short terraces. They will utilize passive solar principles.

The houses make use of a highly insulating cladding system and reflectors to increase the amount of usable solar radiation available.

The houses may also be extended with a choice of additions. A verandah, vine-terrace, greenhouse or shed may be constructed, the choice depending upon the local traditional form of building.

Integration into the ecological cycle will be possible because:-

1. Energy requirements of the materials and construction of buildings will be low.

2. Conservation of air, water, earth, flora and fauna is ensured.

3. It will be possible to create cycles of provision and disposal, e.g. -

   — composting toilet
   — manure
   — food provision.

A /High-density low-rise housing /South Germany /49 °

LOW-COST + LOW-ENERGY HOUSING PROJECT

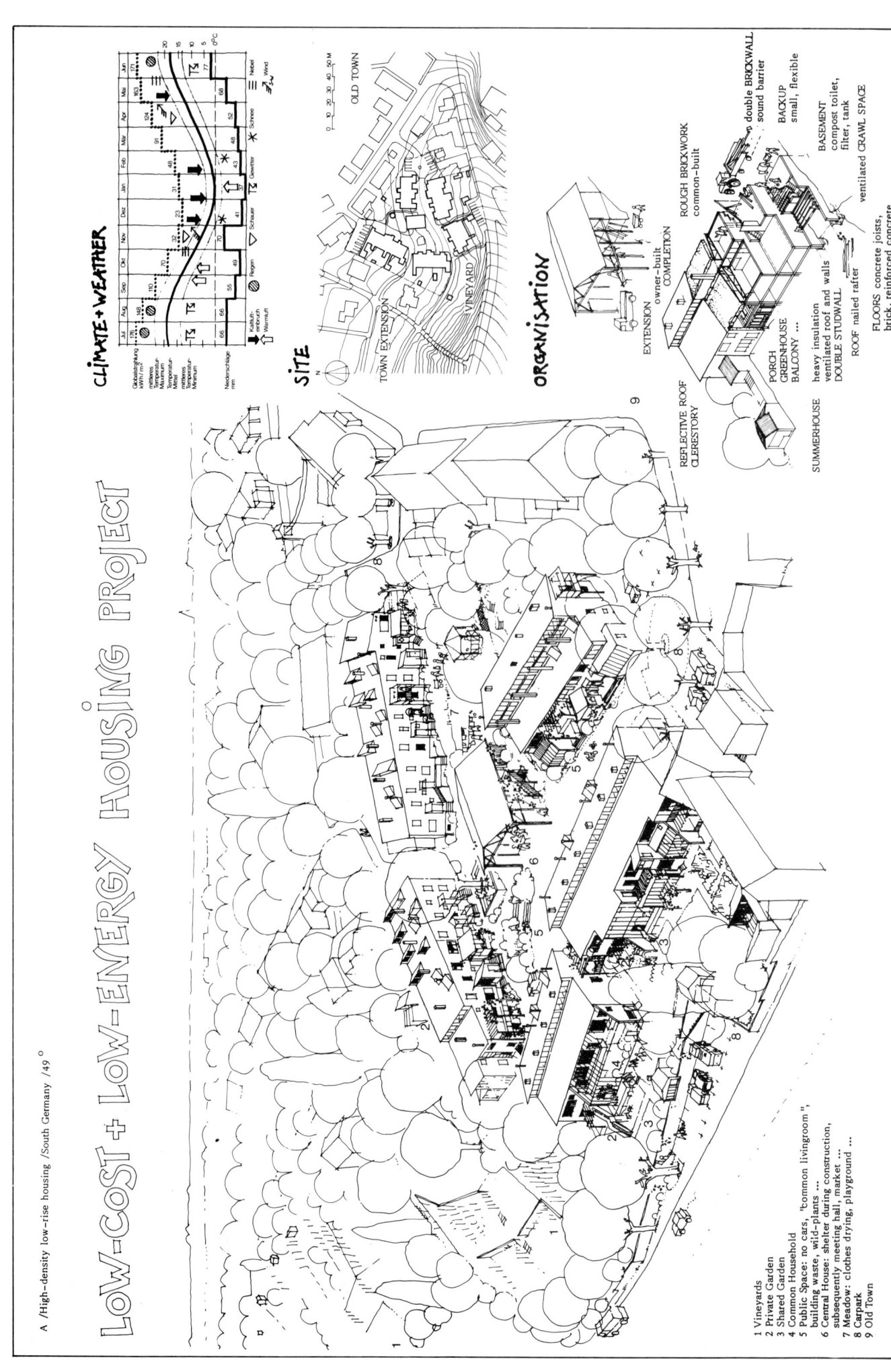

CLIMATE + WEATHER

SITE

OLD TOWN

VINEYARD

TOWN EXTENSION

0 10 20 30 40 50 M

ORGANISATION

EXTENSION
owner-built
COMPLETION

ROUGH BRICKWORK
common-built

double BRICKWALL
sound barrier

BACKUP
small, flexible

BASEMENT
compost toilet,
filter, tank
ventilated CRAWL SPACE

PORCH
GREENHOUSE
BALCONY ...

heavy insulation
ventilated roof and walls
DOUBLE STUDWALL

ROOF nailed rafter

FLOORS concrete joists,
brick, reinforced concrete

REFLECTIVE ROOF
CLERESTORY

SUMMERHOUSE

1 Vineyards
2 Private Garden
3 Shared Garden
4 Common Household
5 Public Space: no cars, "common livingroom",
  building waste, wild-plants ...
6 Central House: shelter during construction,
  subsequently meeting hall, market ...
7 Meadow: clothes drying, playground ...
8 Carpark
9 Old Town

56

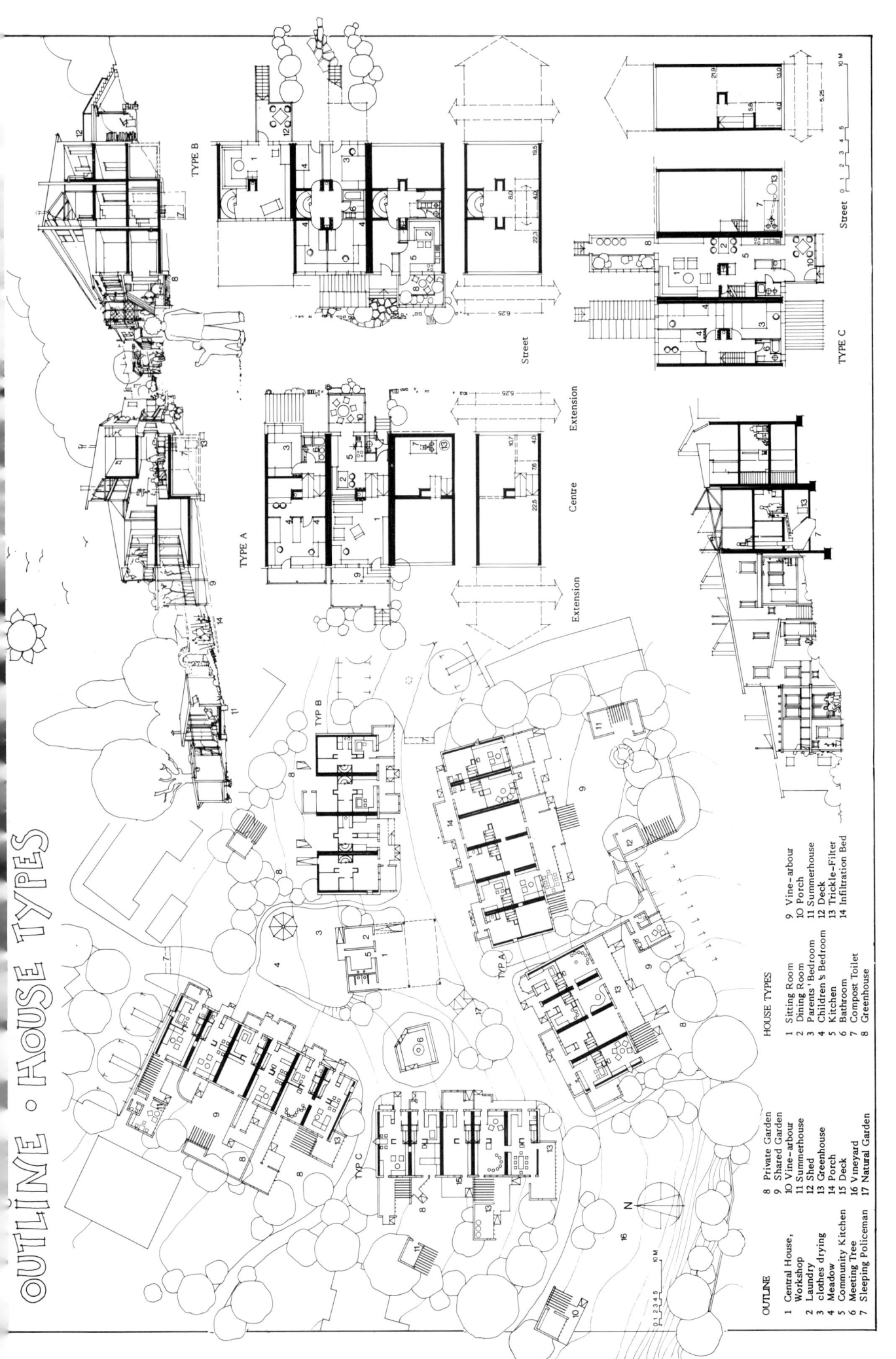

OUTLINE · HOUSE TYPES

TYPE B

TYPE A

Street

Extension   Centre   Extension

TYPE C

Street

0 1 2 3 4 5   10 M

TYP B

TYP A

TYP C

N

0 1 2 3 4 5   10 M

OUTLINE

1 Central House,
  Workshop
2 Laundry
3 clothes drying
4 Meadow
5 Community Kitchen
6 Meeting Tree
7 Sleeping Policeman

8 Private Garden
9 Shared Garden
10 Vine-arbour
11 Summerhouse
12 Shed
13 Greenhouse
14 Porch
15 Deck
16 Vineyard
17 Natural Garden

HOUSE TYPES

1 Sitting Room
2 Dining Room
3 Parents' Bedroom
4 Children's Bedroom
5 Kitchen
6 Bathroom
7 Compost Toilet
8 Greenhouse

9 Vine-arbour
10 Porch
11 Summerhouse
12 Deck
13 Trickle-Filter
14 Infiltration Bed

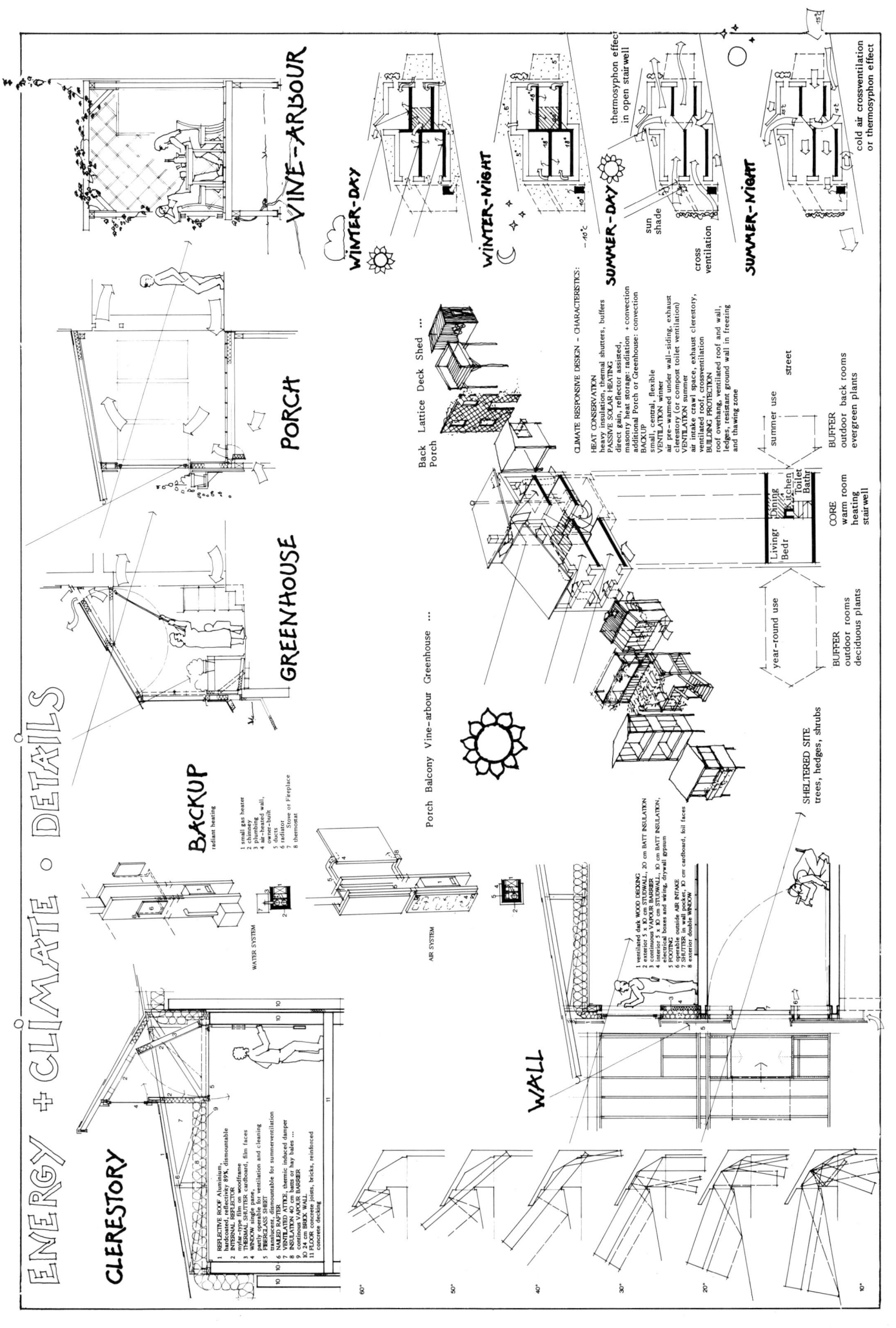

JUDGES' COMMENTS

Our fourth prize of 2,000 Deutsch Marks goes to Johannes T Brucker for his thoroughly instructive scheme of self build houses on a south sloping hillside in Stuttgart.

The very clear, skilful and joyful drawings show a scheme that is clearly capable of being built by its inhabitants. It uses direct gain combined with a simple set of controls and ample insulation to achieve a high level of solar gain and efficient ventilation.

Some of the judges were slightly doubtful about the sameness of north-south and east-west houses. We all found the lightly organised campus type planning on the site to be quite satisfactory.

We were glad to be able to include such a scheme among the winners since it represents a self-build tradition which interests us and many of the competitors. To have that tradition represented by someone with such a clear feel for the simplicities of building construction and such a capacity for graphic illustration is delightful.

TECHNICAL ASSESSORS' COMMENTS

This split level clustered housing on a south facing hill utilizes direct and some sunspace gains and incorporates buffer zones. The basic pre-cast concrete and passive elements are designed for self build and are selected according to the choice of the occupant. Well detailed and easily controlled insulating panels and reflective surfaces are incorporated in the scheme — but fans would be required to improve air circulation.

Errors were discovered in the calculations.

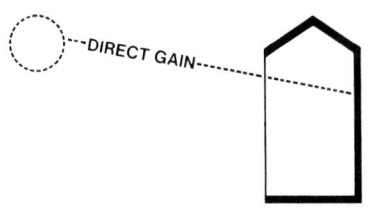

TECHNICAL DATA

This data has been recalculated.
For explanation of data see page 16.

Latitude: 48° 53'N
Altitude: 260 m
Data Point: Ludwigsburg

DWELLING DESCRIPTION (Typical Unit)
Heated Volume: 219 m³

APERTURE	A	B	C	D
System Type	DG	DG	DG	
Net Area m²	6.3	5.4	4.3	
Glazing Layers	2	2	2	
Night Insulation	Yes	Yes	Yes	
τ	0.70	0.70	1.05	
Comment	R			

Aperture/Heated Volume: 0.073 m²/m³
Primary Mass/
　　Related Aperture: 379.8 Wh/m²°C
Remote Mass/
　　Related Aperture: —Wh/m²°C
Air Change Rate: 0.75 ac/h
Building Loss Coeff.: 3.11 kWh/DD
　　　　　　　　　: 129.60 W/°C

DWELLING PERFORMANCE (Typical Unit)
% Internal Gains: 39.0
% Auxiliary Heating: 18.2
% Useful Solar Gains: 42.8
Annual Solar Gains Fraction: 0.75
Figure of Merit: 0.002 kWh/DDm²
Useful Solar Gains/
　　m² of Aperture: 238.8 kWh/m²yr
Min. Temp. without Heating: 4.8°C
Min. Outdoor Temperature: −12.0°C

ENERGY CHARACTERISTICS

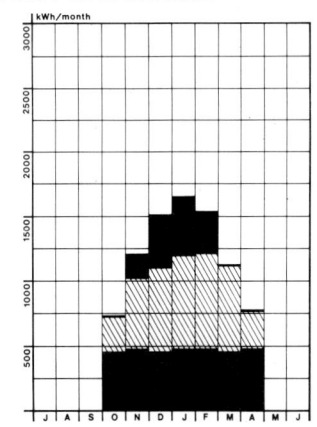

CATEGORY A
HIGH DENSITY, LOW-RISE HOUSING

COMMENDATIONS

OTHER DETAILS OF INTEREST

We have tried with this scheme to recover the spacial and morphological value from the surrounding urban tissue. By placing the project in an area that is already partially developed we have had to take into account the history of this part of the city, its continuing evolution and its present needs. The district, located in the first peripheral band around Florence, has, since the seventeenth century, continued to grow with the gradual congestion of three main roads. This congestion has affected even the interior areas where there are alleys and passages which connect the residential areas to work places. These form a system of articulated spaces that are also very interesting bioclimatically. In general the existing houses are two or three storeys high and contain more than one family. The houses have rooms which open on to internal courtyards. These rooms can be closed off during certain seasons by windows, curtains or awnings. This form of building tends to strengthen the relationship between neighbouring families. This is the case here where the inhabitants are of working-class origin. With the creation of two new roads, the project intends to further the development of this area. Reference was made to previous unrealised projects which attempted to distribute the building density to the already developed bordering districts. Within the new building complex an east/west road axis was favoured to give the best possible conditions for passive solar design.

We have designed a system of topological and spatial relationships with which to create an 'urban form'. From an analysis of the existing topography, both in and around the site, it became possible to identify some simple spatial relationships. The use of these relationships in both the vertical and horizontal planes led to the development of an area/volume ratio for groups of dwellings at different densities.

By designing according to these rules (which are to be found in the planning — not in the structure) the relationship between the spacing of the buildings with respect to their

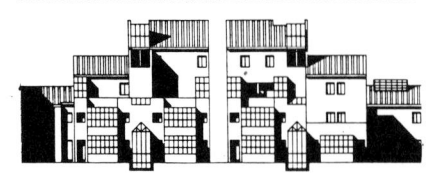

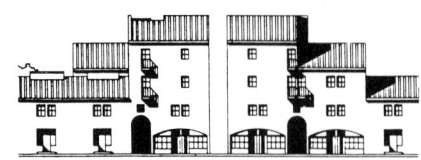

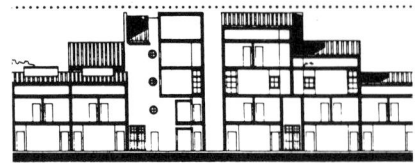

DESIGN TEAM

Marco Sala
Alessandro Gioli
Andrea Corsi
Branka Jankovich
Adriana Toti

via Circondaria 56/1
50127 Firenze
Italy

requirements can be preserved. In this way it became possible not only to standardize the dimension of the building elements (thus making it possible to use industrialized construction methods) but also to identify and standardize the optimum criteria for the passive solar elements of the design.

By using different configurations of the basic elements it became possible to identify ways of grouping the houses together along a roadside so that they responded to the orientation of the road. The variety of solutions possible within this system are illustrated. By using the same procedure it was also possible to design factories and retail shops which are also in keeping with the character of the area.

JUDGES' COMMENTS

Existing cities and towns are full of gaps in terraces, partly empty blocks and other hiccoughs of many varieties; the ordering or graceful completion of the urban fabric within itself is therefore of great interest. We therefore commend Alessandro Gioli and Marco Sala for a well ordered and integrated row of houses and apartments inserted into the existing street pattern of Florence. The scheme achieves a suitable urban scale through the composed interplay of solid external wall and light weight skin and, within the apartments, the spaces were comfortable, and well organised around the shared stairs.

TECHNICAL ASSESSORS' COMMENTS

Small urban housing units of 2,3 and 4 storeys with a high ratio of surface to heated volume utilizing direct and sun space gains. Some devices are not explained — such as the rock bed without air circulation. Mechanical ventilation is used to transfer heat from southern to northern units. Using ventilation from the common staircase for summer cooling purposes may create a fire hazard.

Errors were discovered in the calculations.

LOCATION
Florence
Italy

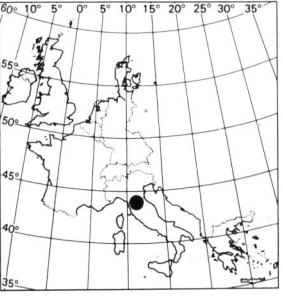

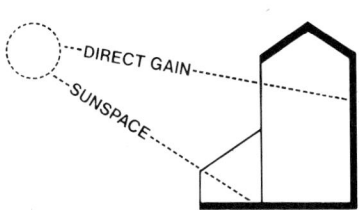

TECHNICAL DATA

This data has been recalculated.
For explanation of data see page 16.

Latitude: 43° 48'N
Altitude: 73 m
Data Point: Rome

DWELLING DESCRIPTION (Typical Unit)
Heated Volume: 251 m³

APERTURE	A	B	C	D
System Type	SS	DG		
Net Area m²	8.1	4.3		
Glazing Layers	2	2		
Night Insulation	Yes	Yes		
τ	0.70	0.70		
Comment				

Aperture/Heated Volume: 0.049 m²/m³
Primary Mass/
    Related Aperture: 114.9 Wh/m²°C
Remote Mass/
    Related Aperture: —Wh/m²°C
Air Change Rate: 1.00 ac/h
Building Loss Coeff.: 3.15 kWh/DD
    : 131.05 W/°C

DWELLING PERFORMANCE (Typical Unit)
% Internal Gains: 62.3
% Auxiliary Heating: 5.0
% Useful Solar Gains: 32.7
Annual Solar Gains Fraction: 0.87
Figure of Merit: 0.0004 kWh/DDm²
Useful Solar Gains/
    m² of Aperture: 99.3 kWh/m²yr
Min. Temp. without Heating: 10.7°C
Min. Outdoor Temperature: —0.7°C

ENERGY CHARACTERISTICS

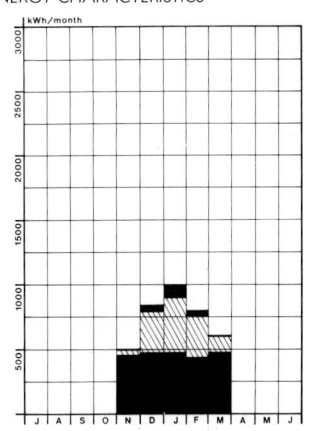

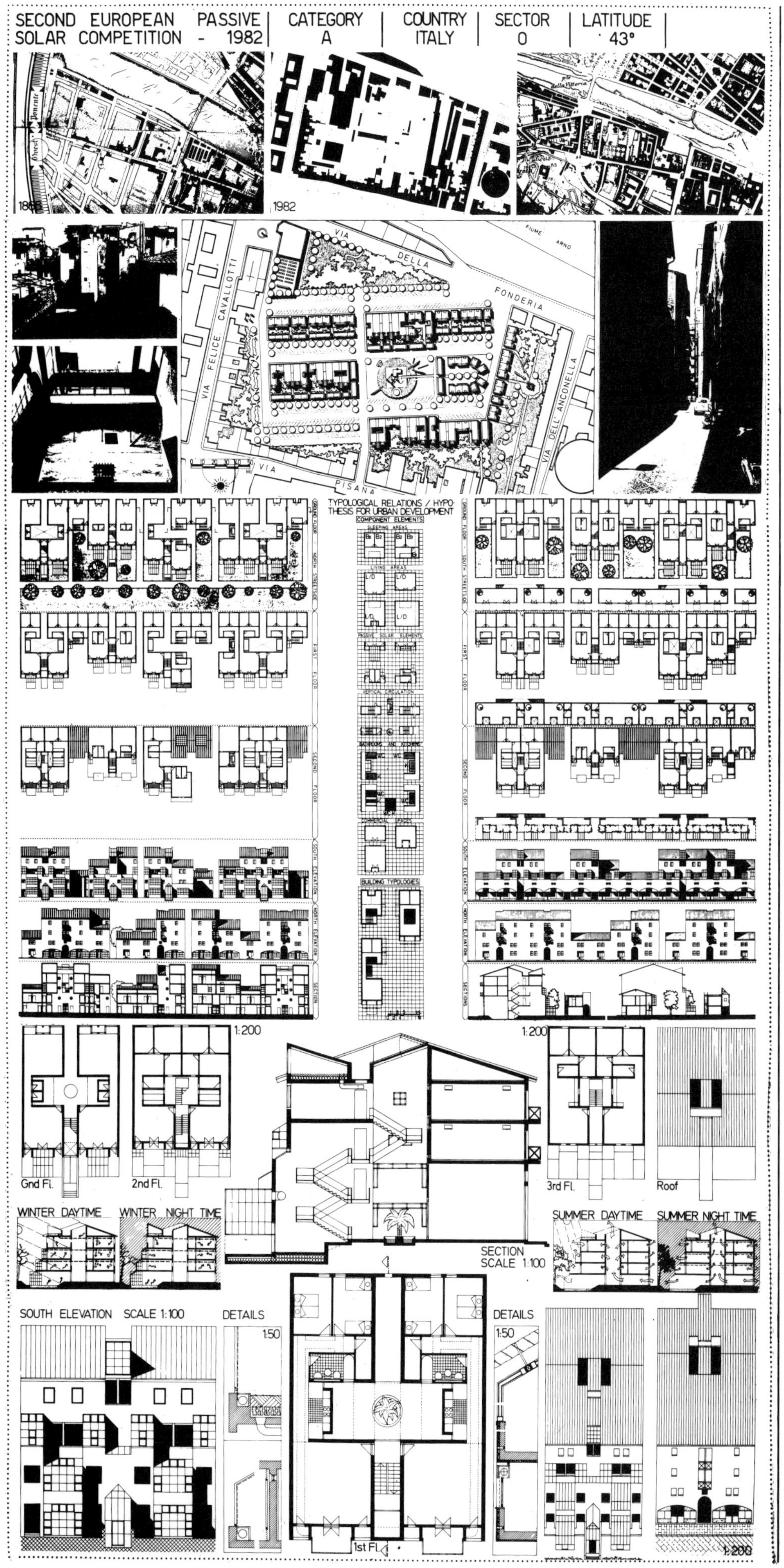

DIRECT GAIN
SUNSPACE

TYPOLOGICAL RELATIONS / HYPOTHESIS FOR URBAN DEVELOPMENT
[COMPONENT ELEMENTS]

Gnd Fl.   2nd Fl.   3rd Fl.   Roof

1:200   1:200

WINTER DAYTIME   WINTER NIGHT TIME   SUMMER DAYTIME   SUMMER NIGHT TIME

SECTION SCALE 1:100

SOUTH ELEVATION SCALE 1:100   DETAILS 1:50   DETAILS 1:50

1st Fl.   1:200

COMMENDATION
CATEGORY A

Our scheme provides 56 dwellings for at least 254 inhabitants in an area of 11,537m² (a density of 220p.p.ha.).

The site is to be found in the neighbourhood of Arras. The area plays a subservient role compared with the nearby town centre where most activities take place. The area consists mainly of small semi-detached houses which date from the 1920s and '30s. These housing developments were built around industries that are now in decline leaving huge industrial estates that are almost closed down — future development is hard to visualize.

The plots of land are long and narrow — 20m x 6m approx. The existing houses are generally three storeys high and occupied by one family. This generates rather high densities since the plot ratio is, on average, 0.9.

We propose the 'opening up' of a block of buildings that has the same characteristics as those outlined above. A new street has been created to break up the block, create more interest and make it possible to achieve higher densities. We also propose to promote cultural, craft and commercial centres in order to encourage people to stay in the area.

The Arras region has a moderate ocean climate. Generally the characteristics are as follows (data for Lille and Cambrai):-

— high humidity (84%),
— low temperatures (9 to 10°C),
— severe depressions (640mm),
— 79 days of fog per year
— an average number of sunshine hours (1574 hours).

Typical characteristics of the various seasons are as follows:-

winter
— weak sunshine
— frequent westerly winds bringing rain
— morning fog
— relatively mild temperatures (2.5°C to 3.5°C)

THE GLASSHOUSE IS A HABITABLE ROOM

THE GLASSHOUSE IS DYNAMIC

DESIGNER

Bernard F M Andral

*5 rue de Vouille
75015 Paris
France*

spring and autumn
— long hours of sunshine
— wind from north-east bringing clear skies
— morning fog
— average temperatures (6.2°C to 12.4°C)

summer
— weak sunshine
— frequent westerly winds bringing rain
— frequent heavy rain
— not very high temperatures (15°C to 17.4°C)

Passive solar solutions are particularly appropriate in Arras since more sunlight is available during the intermediate seasons than in the summer. We propose that solar energy be collected by means of the windows and conservatories of the development. A rapid response storage system and high levels of exterior insulation would also be incorporated in the scheme.

JUDGES' COMMENTS

We commend Bernard F M Andral whose scheme in Arras seeks to complete a duller and more disorderly block than the one in the previous scheme in Florence. He does so with considerable variation and flair, using many different plan-types and house-sizes in a variety of one, two and four storey buildings according to location and the needs of solar gain and ventilation. We had some doubts about the style of the elevations but no doubt that the scheme merited commendation.

TECHNICAL ASSESSORS' COMMENTS

These 1,2 and 4 storey buildings are constructed from prefabricated elements. The main solar component is a green house separated from the rest of the accommodation by a mass storage wall. Ventilation air is preheated before being admitted to the building, first by a heat exchanger and then by passing through the greenhouse. Good studies of solar penetration into the different units were submitted but the description of the operation of shutters and blinds was poor.

The calculations are correct.

LOCATION
Arras
France

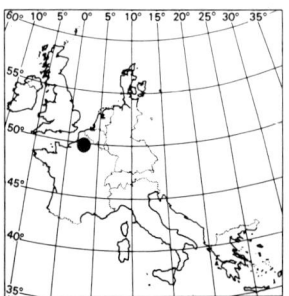

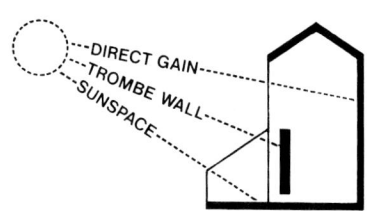

—DIRECT GAIN
—TROMBE WALL
—SUNSPACE

TECHNICAL DATA

For explanation of data see page 16.

Latitude: 49° 5'N
Altitude: 50 m
Data Point: Lille

DWELLING DESCRIPTION (Typical Unit)
Heated Volume: 189 m³

APERTURE	A	B	C	D
System Type	DG	SS	TW	
Net Area m²	6.0	14.9	4.0	
Glazing Layers	1	1	2	
Night Insulation	No	Yes	Yes	
τ	0.50	0.50	0.50	
Comment	SE	SE	SE	
	or	or	or	
	SW	SW	SW	

Aperture/Heated Volume: 0.131 m²/m³
Primary Mass/
  Related Aperture: 107.5 Wh/m²°C
Remote Mass/
  Related Aperture: —Wh/m²°C
Air Change Rate: 0.70 ac/h
Building Loss Coeff.: 3.47 kWh/DD
  : 144.70 W/°C

DWELLING PERFORMANCE (Typical Unit)
% Internal Gains: 38.0
% Auxiliary Heating: 41.0
% Useful Solar Gains: 21.0
Annual Solar Gains Fraction: 0.33
Figure of Merit: 0.007 kWh/DDm²
Useful Solar Gains/
  m² of Aperture: 98.0 kWh/m²yr
Min. Temp. without Heating: 5.7°C
Min. Outdoor Temperature: −5.0°C

ENERGY CHARACTERISTICS

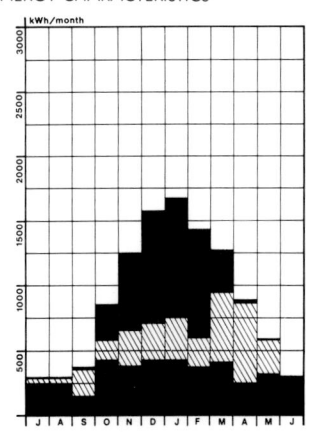

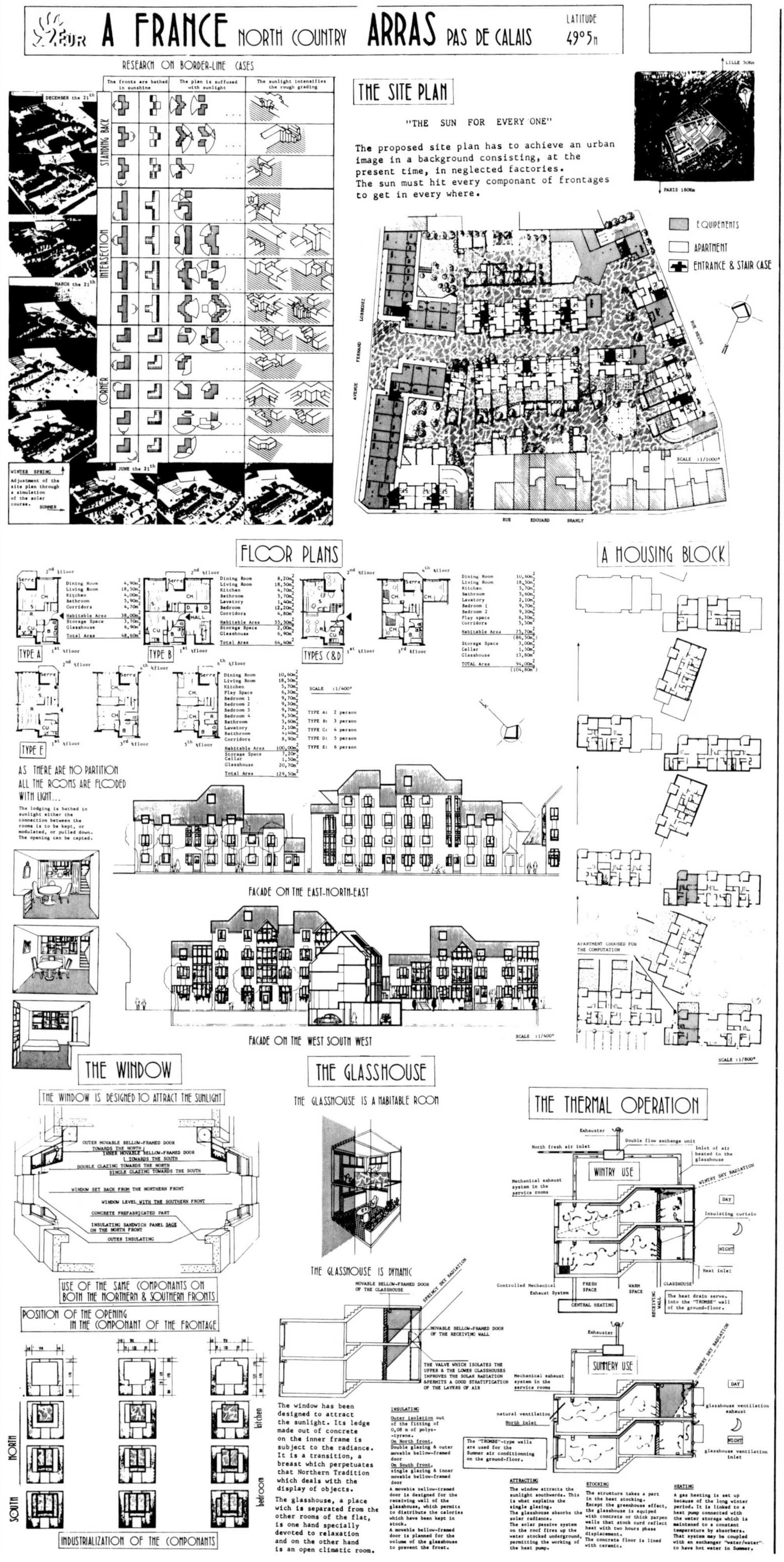

kWh/month

J A S O N D J F M A M J

A FRANCE NORTH COUNTRY ARRAS PAS DE CALAIS
LATITUDE 49°5'N

RESEARCH ON BORDER-LINE CASES

The fronts are bathed in sunshine	The plan is suffused with sunlight	The sunlight intensifies the rough grading

STANDING BACK
INTERSECTION
CORNER

DECEMBER the 21th
MARCH the 21th
JUNE the 21th

WINTER SPRING
Adjustment of the site plan through a simulation of the solar course.
SUMMER

THE SITE PLAN

"THE SUN FOR EVERY ONE"

The proposed site plan has to achieve an urban image in a background consisting, at the present time, in neglected factories.
The sun must hit every componant of frontages to get in every where.

LILLE 50Km
PARIS 180Km

EQUIPEMENTS
APARTMENT
ENTRANCE & STAIR CASE

SCALE 1/1000°

RUE EDOUARD BRANLY

FLOOR PLANS

TYPE A
Dining Room	4,90m
Living Room	18,50m
Kitchen	5,70m
Bathroom	4,40m
Bedroom	4,70m
Habitable Area	38,00m
Storage Space	3,70m
Glasshouse	6,90m
Total Area	48,60m

TYPE B
Dining Room	8,20m
Living Room	18,50m
Kitchen	5,70m
Bathroom	6,90m
Lavatory	12,20m
Bedroom	6,90m
Corridors	4,80m
Habitable Area	53,50m
Storage Space	3,70m
Glasshouse	6,90m
Total Area	64,40m

TYPES C & D
Dining Room	10,50m
Living Room	18,50m
Kitchen	5,70m
Bathroom	5,60m
Lavatory	2,10m
Bedroom 1	9,30m
Bedroom 2	9,30m
Play space	5,50m
Corridors	5,50m
Habitable Area	75,70m
	(86,50m)
Storage Space	3,70m
Cellar	1,50m
Glasshouse	13,80m
TOTAL AREA	94,00m
	(105,80m)

TYPE E
Dining Room	10,50m
Living Room	18,50m
Kitchen	5,70m
Play Space	9,70m
Bedroom 1	9,30m
Bedroom 2	9,30m
Bedroom 3	9,30m
Bedroom 4	4,60m
Bathroom	5,60m
Lavatory	2,10m
Bathroom	4,60m
Corridors	8,90m
Habitable Area	100,00m
Storage Space	3,70m
Cellar	1,50m
Glasshouse	20,70m
Total Area	129,50m

TYPE A: 2 person
TYPE B: 3 person
TYPE C: 4 person
TYPE D: 5 person
TYPE E: 6 person

AS THERE ARE NO PARTITION ALL THE ROOMS ARE FLOODED WITH LIGHT...

The lodging is bathed in sunlight either the connection between the rooms is to be kept, or modulated, or pulled down. The opening can be capted.

SCALE 1/400°

FACADE ON THE EAST-NORTH-EAST

FACADE ON THE WEST SOUTH WEST

SCALE 1/400°

A HOUSING BLOCK

APARTMENT LOADGED FOR THE COMPUTATION

SCALE 1/800°

THE WINDOW

THE WINDOW IS DESIGNED TO ATTRACT THE SUNLIGHT

OUTER MOVABLE BELLOW-FRAMED DOOR TOWARDS THE NORTH
INNER MOVABLE BELLOW-FRAMED DOOR TOWARDS THE SOUTH
DOUBLE GLAZING TOWARDS THE NORTH
SINGLE GLAZING TOWARDS THE SOUTH
WINDOW SET BACK FROM THE SOUTHERN FRONT
WINDOW LEVEL WITH THE SOUTHERN FRONT
CONCRETE PREFABRICATED PART
INSULATING SANDWICH PANEL SAGE ON THE NORTH FRONT
OUTER INSULATING

USE OF THE SAME COMPONANTS ON BOTH THE NORTHERN & SOUTHERN FRONTS

POSITION OF THE OPENING IN THE COMPONANT OF THE FRONTAGE

NORTH
SOUTH
kitchen
bedroom
INDUSTRIALIZATION OF THE COMPONANTS

The window has been designed to attract the sunlight. Its ledge made out of concrete on the inner frame is subject to the radiance. It is a transition, a breast which perpetuates that Northern Tradition which deals with the display of objects.

The glasshouse, a place wich is separated from the other rooms of the flat, is one hand specially devoted to relaxation and on the other hand is an open climatic room.

THE GLASSHOUSE

THE GLASSHOUSE IS A HABITABLE ROOM

THE GLASSHOUSE IS DYNAMIC

MOVABLE BELLOW-FRAMED DOOR OF THE GLASSHOUSE

MOVABLE BELLOW-FRAMED DOOR OF THE RECEIVING WALL

THE VALVE WHICH ISOLATES THE UPPER & THE LOWER GLASSHOUSES IMPROVES THE SOLAR RADIATION & PERMITS A GOOD STRATIFICATION OF THE LAYERS OF AIR

INSULATING
Outer isolation out of the fitting of 0,08 m of poly-styrene.
On North front,
Double glazing & outer movable bellow-framed door
On South front,
single glazing & inner movable bellow-framed door
A movable bellow-framed door is designed for the receiving wall of the glasshouse, which permits to distribute the calories which have been kept in stock.
A movable bellow-framed door is planed for the volume of the glasshouse to prevent the frost.

THE THERMAL OPERATION

Exhauster
North fresh air inlet
Double flow exchange unit
Inlet of air heated in the service rooms
WINTRY USE
Mechanical exhaust system in the service rooms
DAY
Insulating curtain
NIGHT
Heat inlet

Controlled Mechanical Exhaust System
FRESH SPACE
WARM SPACE
GLASSHOUSE
CENTRAL HEATING

The heat drain serves into the "TROMBE" wall of the ground-floor.

Exhauster
SUMMERY USE
Mechanical exhaust system in the service rooms
DAY
natural ventilation
North inlet
glasshouse ventilation exhaust
NIGHT
glasshouse ventilation inlet

The "TROMBE"-type walls are used for the Summer air conditioning on the ground-floor.

ATTRACTING
The window attracts the sunlight southwards. This is what explains the single glazing. The glasshouse absorbs the solar radiance. The solar passive system on the roof fires up the water stocked underground, permitting the working of the heat pump.

STOCKING
The structure takes a part in the heat stocking. Except the greenhouse effect, the glasshouse is equiped with concrete or thick carpen walls that stock curf reflect heat with two hours phase displacement. The concrete floor is lined with ceramic.

HEATING
A gas heating is set up because of the long winter period. It is linked to a heat pump connected with the water storage which is maintioned to a constant temperature by absorbers. That system may be coupled with an exchanger "water/water" to have hot water in Summer.

COMMENDATION
CATEGORY A

The heroic aspect of passive solar heating — learning from the past, and offering a brighter future — evokes an architectural response. We are proposing a project which will encircle the historic core of Dublin along the line of its eighteenth century canals with a 12km long wall of passive solar housing. This is a roof-top promenade, a tourist attraction, a desirable place for 8,000 people to live and in the process it will restore many damaged areas of the city.

The canals run mainly east-west; the housing has living areas facing south over the canals with servant spaces to the north. The lowered ground floor holds shops, workshops, crêches and similar accommodation. The wall steps down to permit through views and access, and it also spans across streets. The roof-top park which is closed to the public at night offers views across the city to the mountains and a safe place in which to practise running.

The largest flats are at ground level whilst the smallest, student, flats are on the top floor. The 'Crystal Glasshouse' image evokes Richard Turner's pioneering nineteenth century greenhouses at Dublin's Botanic Gardens, and the building height is similar to that of the eighteenth century streets which the wall encloses.

Technical assumptions in the calculations. The flat at the lowest level is chosen because it is the largest, and also partly exposed. The shop is heated by day but not by night. The existing deciduous trees on the opposite bank are retained for shading.

DESIGN TEAM

David McHugh
Eoin O'Cofaigh
Flemming Rasmussen

13 Lower Baggot Street
Dublin 2
Ireland

JUDGES' COMMENTS

We commend David McHugh, Eoin O'Cofaigh and Flemming Rasmussen for their powerful scheme of apartments that stretch along the side of the canal in Dublin. The judges were not at all sure that the scheme should be realised to its full and final extent because they thought it might have the effect of bisecting the city. They were sure however, that the piece presented was a fine example of the combination of good and enjoyable plans with terraces, conservatories and balconies to make a scheme for solar apartments that also achieved a noble and balanced urban scale and, as far as it went, fitted well but definitely into the existing grain of the city.

TECHNICAL ASSESSORS' COMMENTS

This terraced wall of apartment houses follows the line of Dublin's two canals and incorporates sunspaces on the south facade. The operation of the solar system is not well developed, for instance there is heavy reliance on manual controls and inadequate development of storage walls.

The calculations are correct.

LOCATION
Dublin
Ireland

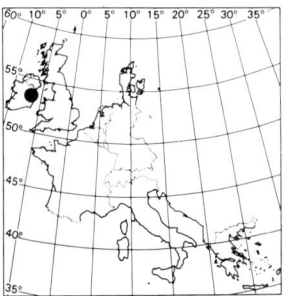

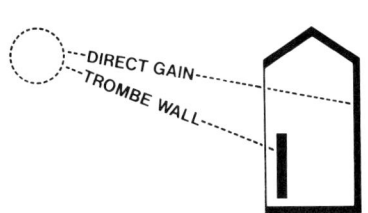

TECHNICAL DATA

For explanation of data see page 16.

Latitude: 53° 20'N
Altitude: 10 m
Data Point: Valentia

DWELLING DESCRIPTION (Typical Unit)
Heated Volume: 208 m³

APERTURE	A	B	C	D
System Type	DG	TW		
Net Area m²	1.7	30.0		
Glazing Layers	2	2+		
Night Insulation	Yes	Yes		
τ	0.50	0.60		
Comment	O			

Aperture/Heated Volume: 0.152 m²/m³
Primary Mass/
    Related Aperture: 157.0 Wh/m²°C
Remote Mass/
    Related Aperture: —Wh/m²°C
Air Change Rate: 1.25 ac/h
Building Loss Coeff.: 4.12 kWh/DD
    : 171.40 W/°C

DWELLING PERFORMANCE (Typical Unit)
% Internal Gains: 49.0
% Auxiliary Heating: 19.0
% Useful Solar Gains: 32.0
Annual Solar Gains Fraction: 0.64
Figure of Merit: 0.0035 kWh/DDm²
Useful Solar Gains/
    m² of Aperture: 111.0 kWh/m²yr
Min. Temp. without Heating: 7.0°C
Min. Outdoor Temperature: —2.0°C

ENERGY CHARACTERISTICS

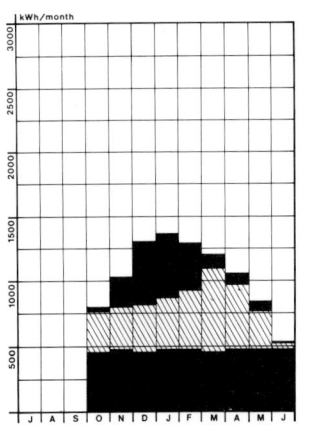

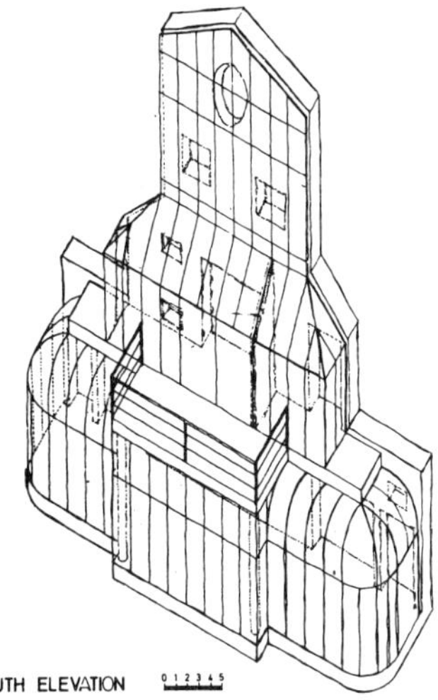

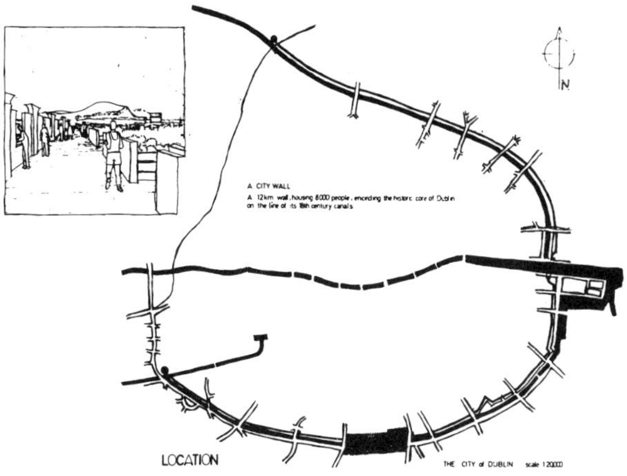

SOUTH ELEVATION

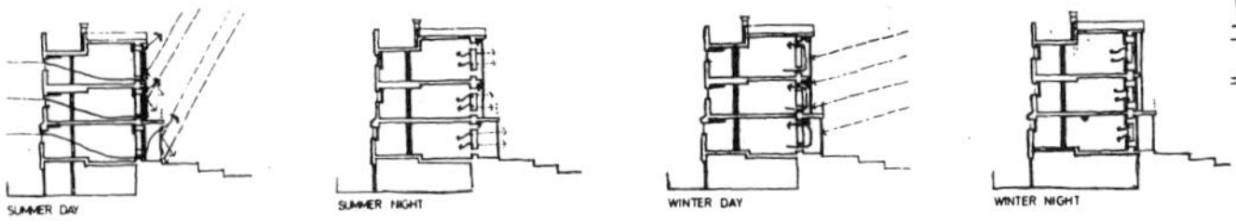

LOCATION

THE CITY of DUBLIN   scale 1:20000

SUMMER DAY   SUMMER NIGHT   WINTER DAY   WINTER NIGHT

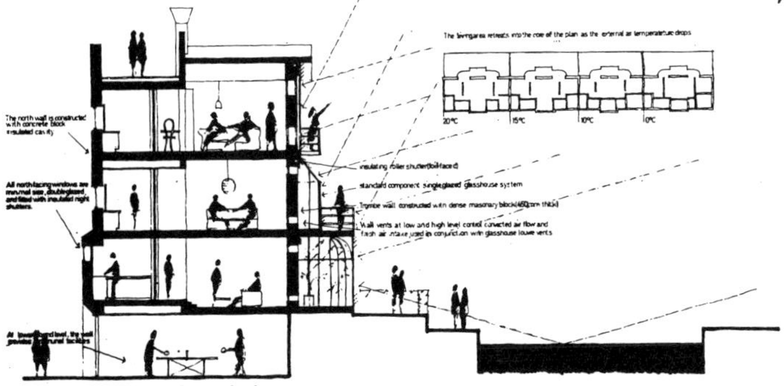

SITE PLAN

TYPICAL SECTION

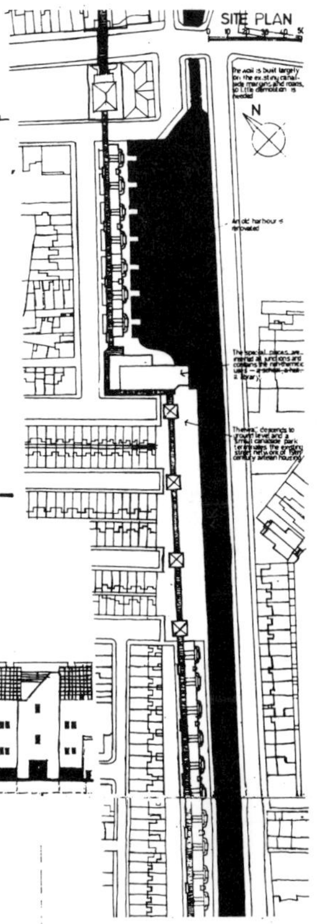

NORTH ELEVATION

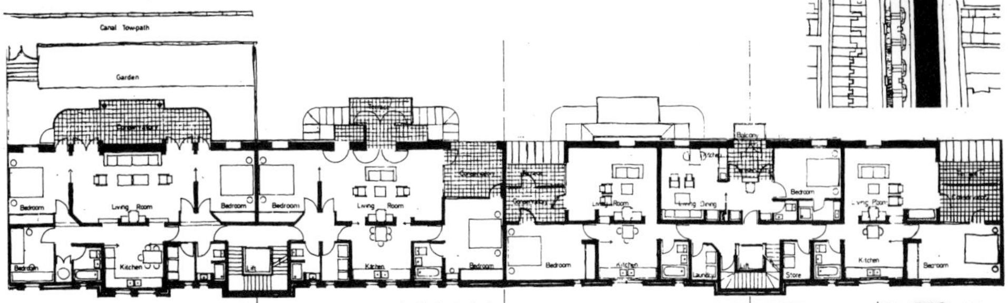

GROUND FLOOR   FIRST FLOOR   SECOND FLOOR

ROOF PLAN

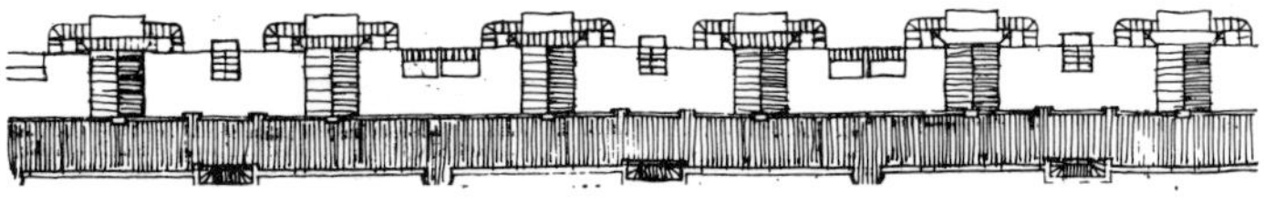

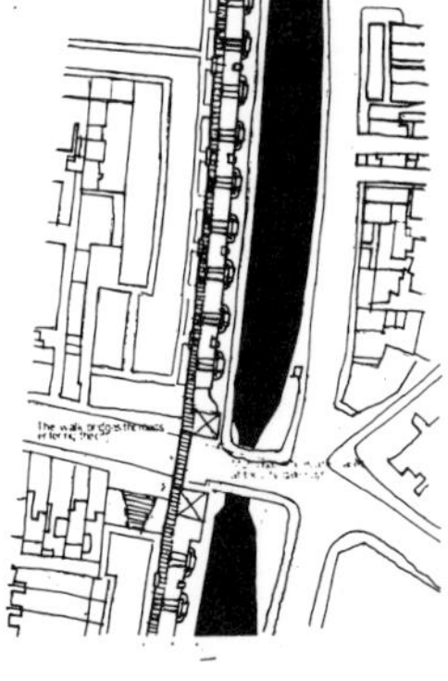

COMMENDATION
CATEGORY A

The project is situated in an urban zone which is under construction on the outskirts of the new town, St Quentin en Yvelines.

The expected density of the site is very high: approximately 50 dwellings on a site covering about half a hectare.

Compliance with the height and alignment restraints on the streets is essential. In practice, these constraints tend to concentrate the general massing of the buildings. Because of this the buildings tend to act as screens.

The project is situated on a site that is almost level and which has little vegetation to reduce the amount of solar energy available.

Local climatic characteristics are extremely well recorded by data received from the nearby meteorological station at Trappes.

Both urban and high density restraints reduced the amount of planning that could be carried out to ensure sufficient insolation to the main facades. The buildings on the site are in four groups, each of which comprises a corner unit with two linear units which look out on to the street. Vertical circulation is provided within the corner unit and the linear circulation zones are located next to this unit. This has been done in order to minimize the area of the communal circulation areas. Because the north-south line lies diagonally across the site, each building has a sunny aspect and looks either on to the other sides of the block or on to the streets to the south of the block. Access to each building can be gained at each of the corners of the block.

The street level dwellings have direct access either on to the street or on to the courtyard.

Car parking is provided in the basement underneath the northern part of the block. Vehicles may gain access by means of a ramp which is situated at the eastern angle of the block. Pedestrians gain access by means of a stairway outside the building which faces on to the inner courtyard.

Taking into account the urban restraints and previous experience with economical building techniques, our main proposals for the internal spaces were as follows:-

— Adjoining each dwelling there is to be a conservatory space which is both spatially and thermally habitable. This has been provided more for functional and 'quality of life' reasons than for thermal reasons.

SOUTH WEST

SOUTH EAST

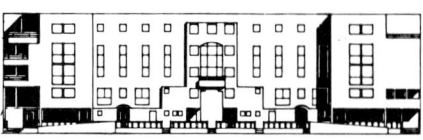

NORTH WEST

DESIGN TEAM

Jean Pierre Franca
Brigitte Ferrand

14 Villa des Fleurs
92120 Montrouge
France

LOCATION
St Quentin en Yvelines
France

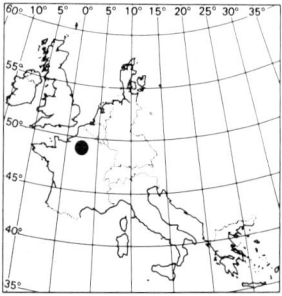

— Each dwelling is arranged to enable communication both with the semi-public space at the interior of the site and with the exterior of the site.

— The living areas of each dwelling are orientated towards the south-east and each street level dwelling also has the benefit of an exterior sunlit space.

Taking into account the organisation of the site as well as the layout of the buildings, our thermal planning criteria were as follows:-

— to reduce as far as possible any heat losses by incorporating high levels of insulation and by the recirculation of extract air.

— to achieve the maximum passive solar contribution for each dwelling — by means of the conservatory and by means of well orientated windows.

— to use the solar contribution in the communal circulation areas in such a way that parts of the dwellings which do not have access to a direct solar contribution may also benefit.

JUDGES' COMMENTS

We commend Jean-Pièrre Franca and Brigitte Ferrand for their courtyard scheme in the new town at Saint Quentin. The judges wondered why the scheme did not have its entrance at the southern corner or rise to its greatest height to the north. Nevertheless we thought that it was a good example of how a solar heated scheme which utilises sun spaces to preheat the ventilation air could adopt the simple block format of the rest of the city and offer clearly organised and well scaled elevations to that city.

TECHNICAL ASSESSORS' COMMENTS

This five storey apartment complex encloses a courtyard. The solar system consists of both common and private sunspaces — those gains to the common sunspaces being used to preheat ventilation air. Technically this scheme is impressive. Auxiliary heat pumps are connected to the ventilation system.

The calculations are correct.

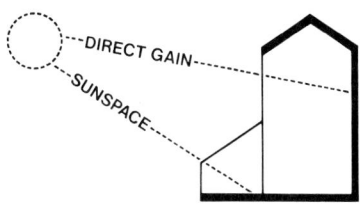

DIRECT GAIN
SUNSPACE

TECHNICAL DATA

For explanation of data see page 16.

Latitude: 48° 48'N
Altitude: 50 m
Data Point: Trappes

DWELLING DESCRIPTION (Typical Unit)
Heated Volume: 211 m³

APERTURE	A	B	C	D
System Type	DG	SS		
Net Area m²	4.0	6.4		
Glazing Layers	2	2		
Night Insulation	Yes	No		
τ	0.45	0.45		
Comment	SE+O	SE+O		

Aperture/Heated Volume: 0.049 m²/m³
Primary Mass/
    Related Aperture: 276.0 Wh/m²°C
Remote Mass/
    Related Aperture: —Wh/m²°C
Air Change Rate: 0.71 ac/h
Building Loss Coeff.: 2.26 kWh/DD
          : 94.20 W/°C

DWELLING PERFORMANCE (Typical Unit)
% Internal Gains: 39.0
% Auxiliary Heating: 33.0
% Useful Solar Gains: 28.0
Annual Solar Gains Fraction: 0.46
Figure of Merit: 0.0041 kWh/DDm²
Useful Solar Gains/
    m² of Aperture: 180.0 kWh/m²yr
Min. Temp. without Heating: 4.8°C
Min. Outdoor Temperature: 0.2°C

ENERGY CHARACTERISTICS

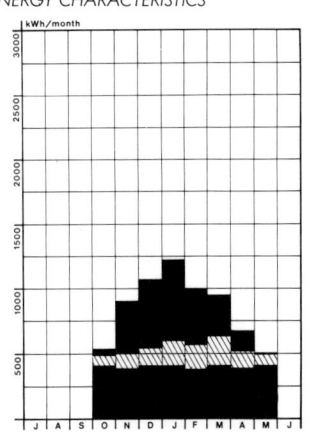

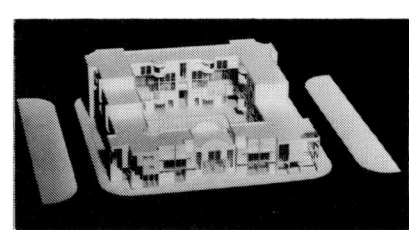
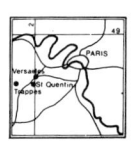

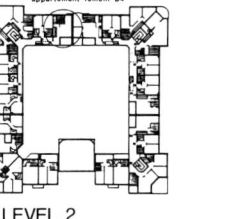
appartement témoin D4
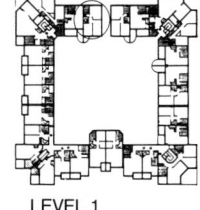
appartement témoin D4

LEVEL 3   LEVEL 2   LEVEL 1   LOCATION

ech 1/500   ech 1/2000

LEVEL 4

GROUND FLOOR PLAN

ech 1/500

SOUTH WEST ELEVATION

SOUTH EAST ELEVATION

NORTH WEST ELEVATION   SECTION A

ech 1/250

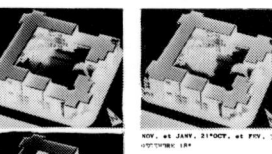

NOV. et JANV. 21°OCT. et FEV. 30° SEP. et MARS 41° AOUT et AVR. 53° JUIL. et MAI 61° JUIN 64°
DECEMBRE 18°

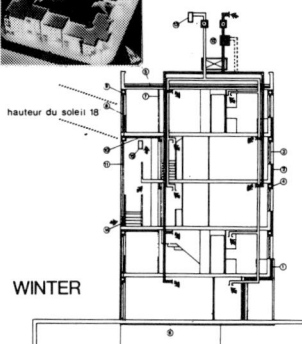

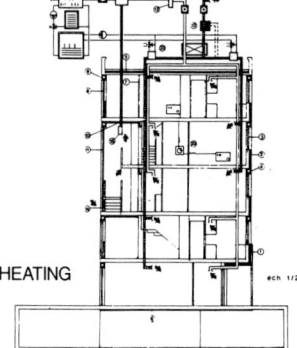

hauteur du soleil 18   hauteur du soleil 63°

WINTER   SUMMER   HEATING

ech 1/200

1. EXTERIOR CONSTRUCTION OF 100mm INSULATION + AIR SPACE + FACING BRICKS.
2. EXTERIOR CONSTRUCTION OF 100mm INSULATION WITH PLASTIC COATED EXTERNAL SKIN.
3. DOUBLE GLAZING IN TIMBER FRAME.
4. EXTERIOR PVC ROLLER SHUTTERS.
5. 6mm OR 60mm POLYSTYRENE INSULATION.
6. 80mm INSULATION APPLIED TO UNDERSIDE OF FLOOR.
7. 60mm OF POLYSTYRENE INSULATION TO OPAQUE ELEMENT OF PARTITION – TRANSPARENT PARTS ARE OF SINGLE GLAZING IN TIMBER FRAMES.
8. EXTERIOR INSULATION TO OPAQUE PARTS OF PARTITION TO SAME STANDARD AS THE REST OF THE DWELLING – TRANSPARENT ELEMENTS ARE OF DOUBLE GLAZING IN METAL WINDOW FRAMES.
9. EXTERIOR PVC SHUTTERS.
10. 80mm POLYSTYRENE INSULATION
11. SINGLE GLAZING IN METAL FRAMES
12. EXTRACT AIR INPUT WITH HEAT EXCHANGER
13. EXTRACTED AIR IS DUCTED TO THE HEAT PUMP
14. FRESH AIR INPUT TO CONSERVATORY – AIR IS EXTRACTED FROM THE CONSERVATORY AT A RATE OF 390m³ PER HOUR
15. AIR EXTRACTED FROM THE CONSERVATORY AREAS IS DUCTED TO THE CIRCULATION SPACES
16. FROM HUT ONWARDS THE HEAT EXCHANGER IS BYPASSED
17. PARTIAL SHADING OF THE SE WINDOW IS ACHIEVED BY THE USE OF ROLLER SHUTTERS
18. PARTIAL SHADING OF THE SE WINDOW IS ACHIEVED BY THE USE OF ROLLER SHUTTERS
19. SUPPLEMENTARY NATURAL VENTILATION VIA 'MACON' TYPE VENTILATORS.
20. SUPPLEMENTARY NATURAL VENTILATION BY THE OPENING OF WINDOWS.
21. THE CONSERVATORY IS LARGELY OPEN BOTH TO THE DWELLING AND TO THE OUTSIDE
22. BACK UP ELECTRIC CONVECTION HEATERS
23. CONSTANT ENVIRONMENTAL CONDITIONS ARE MAINTAINED BY THE AIR AND WATER COILS OF THE FRESH AIR SYSTEM. THESE ARE REGULATED ACCORDING TO THE OUTSIDE TEMPERATURE, THE DEGREE OF INSULATION ON THE FACADE OF THE BUILDING, AND BY THE TEMPERATURE OF THE EXTRACTED AIR.
24. HEAT PUMP UTILISES THREE SOURCES: EXTRACTED AIR (AFTER IT HAS PASSED THROUGH THE HEAT EXCHANGER) AIR WHICH HAS BEEN PREHEATED IN THE CONSERVATORY AREAS AND THE AMBIENT AIR. THE TEMPERATURE OF THE WATER IN THE HOT WATER TANKS IS MAINTAINED BY THE REGULATION OF THE HEAT PUMP. THESE SOURCES OF HEAT ARE USED MAINLY FOR SPACE HEATING IN THE WINTER AND SOLELY FOR DOMESTIC HOT WATER IN THE SUMMER.

COMMENDATION
CATEGORY A

Our project is situated in the site scheduled by the Tricesimo Community Village as an area for District Council Housing and Cooperatives. Our scheme attempts to provide the people of the region with the low cost independent houses that they have often requested. Our project attempts to give architectural dignity to the everyday terraced house.

The site is basically level with the winter winds from the north and north-east. Therefore an artificial or a natural wind break is required to the north of the site. Evergreen trees or hedges are to be used for this purpose in our scheme. Where there is an entrance on the north side it has been protected both by a porch and a double door.

Our buildings could be entirely of industrialised or prefabricated construction. There are three main slab lengths: 2.5m, 3m and 5m, while the width has a 1,200mm module. The following elements have standard dimensions: bathrooms, laundry-rooms, kitchens, bedrooms, wardrobes and staircases. The sizes of the flats are in keeping with the limits imposed on low-rent housing by National and Regional regulations, thus: two person dwellings have an area of 50m², three/four persons have 65m², four persons have 80m² and five persons have 95m². A 'studio' for one/two persons (28m²) may be joined to four/five person dwellings.

The dwellings are "U" shaped: almost fully enclosed on three sides by insulating walls and completely open towards the south.

The entrance is on the north side: a wide porch and a double door give protection from the stormy winter weather. An extra entrance is provided on the south side in a sheltered area protected by overhanging eaves. The windows facing north are designed as thin 'slits'. A continuous space gives form to the house: this is the dining-living-mezzanine space into which all the surrounding rooms (the bedrooms, kitchens and bathrooms) lead.

DESIGN TEAM

Vittorio Zanfagnini
Pierluigi de Col Impiantista
Roberto Verzegnassi
Magda Ferreghini

Viale Venezia 96
33100 Udine
Italy

This space is given life by two architectural means:-

1. A huge window two storeys high is open to the south and provides a pleasant garden view. Through this opening one is in touch with nature and the sun which provides both daylighting and the main source of thermal energy.

2. A large fire-place is situated under the mezzanine level opposite the window and around this the whole space flows; it provides auxiliary heating and becomes the living heart of the house.

JUDGES' COMMENTS

For a scheme with a satisfactorily urban quality, we commend Vittorio Zanfagnini for his studio style houses in Udine. Though there was not a really satisfactory site plan we enjoyed these houses for their large scale and for the stylish way of life that they represent. The studio or gallery section has long been a pre-occupation of modern architects, and rightly so, since it can represent an advance on the rigid compartmentation of many houses. This scheme (and some others) starts to show that the need for solar gain and efficient ventilation can be a stimulus to the invention of more fluid interior spaces.

TECHNICAL ASSESSORS' COMMENTS

These are single storey terraced dwellings with a mezzanine level. Direct gains are utilized together with active domestic hot water collectors mounted on the roof. The building is well insulated and has a high thermal capacity but it is thought that the large areas of moveable glazing are impractical.

The U-values used in the calculations were rather optimistic.

LOCATION
Tricesimo
Italy

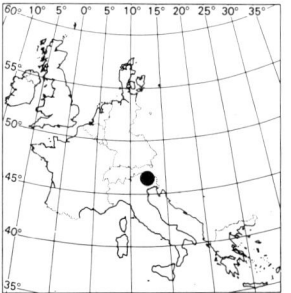

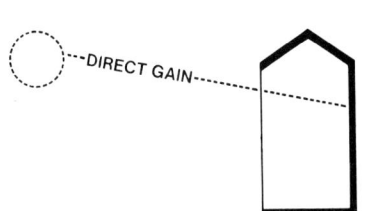
—DIRECT GAIN—

TECHNICAL DATA

For explanation of data see page 16.

Latitude 46°09'N
Altitude: 180 m
Data Point: Udine

DWELLING DESCRIPTION (Typical Unit)
Heated Volume: 322 m³

APERTURE	A	B	C	D
System Type	DG			
Net Area m²	30.1			
Glazing Layers	2			
Night Insulation	Yes			
τ	0.70			
Comment				

Aperture/Heated Volume: 0.09 m²/m³
Primary Mass/
    Related Aperture: 338.7 Wh/m²°C
Remote Mass/
    Related Aperture: 603.7 Wh/m²°C
Air Change Rate: 0.75 ac/h
Building Loss Coeff.: 3.50 kWh/DD
            : 147.00 W/°C

DWELLING PERFORMANCE (Typical Unit)
% Internal Gains: 32.4
% Auxiliary Heating: 13.8
% Useful Solar Gains: 53.8
Annual Solar Gains Fraction: 0.80
Figure of Merit: 0.002 kWh/DDm²
Useful Solar Gains/
    m² of Aperture: 157.4 kWh/m²yr
Min. Temp. without Heating: 7.6°C
Min. Outdoor Temperature: −4.0°C

ENERGY CHARACTERISTICS

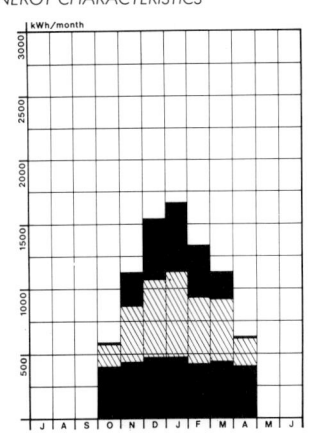

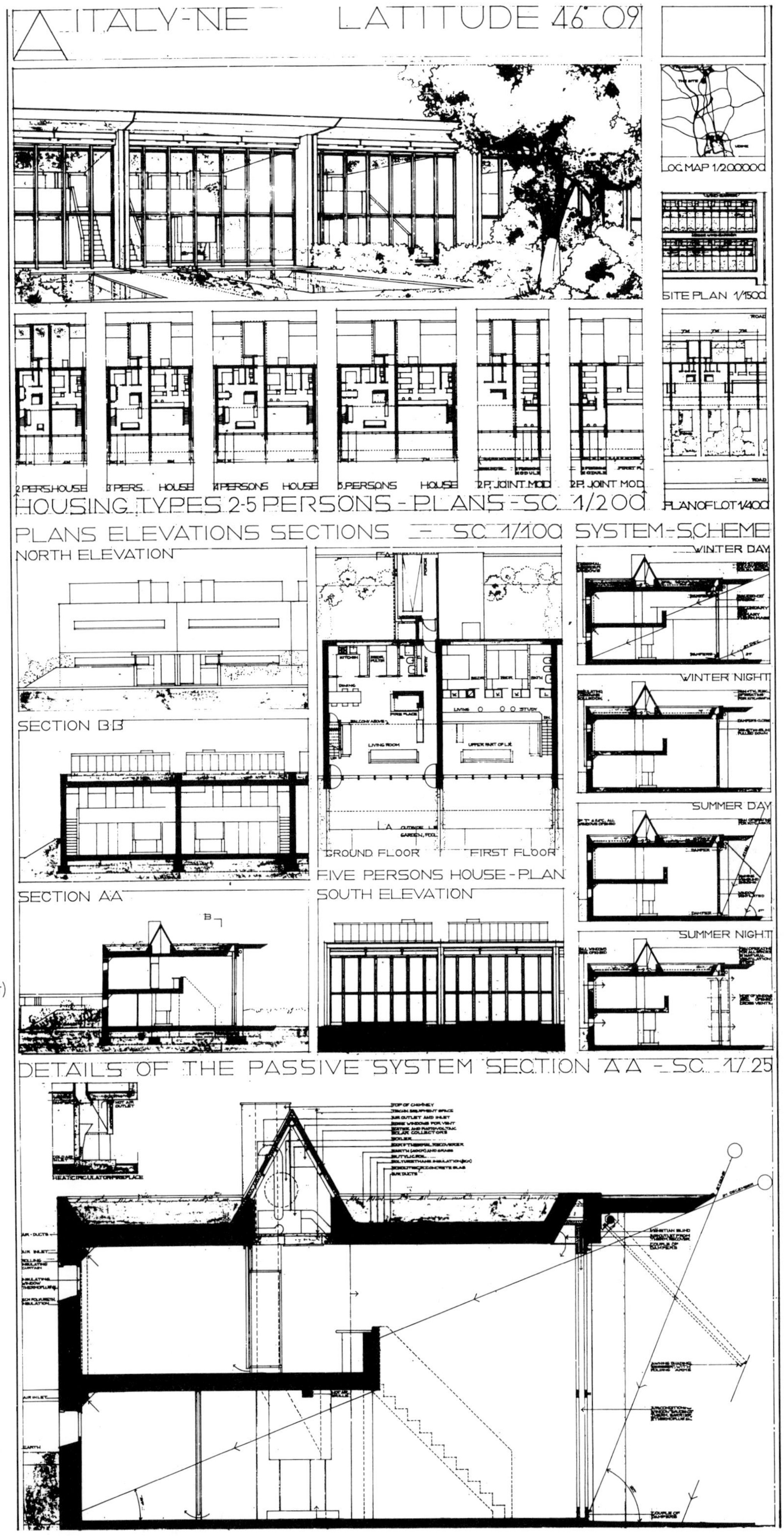

ITALY-NE   LATITUDE 46°09'

LOC. MAP 1/200000
SITE PLAN 1/1500

2 PERS. HOUSE   3 PERS. HOUSE   4 PERSONS HOUSE   5 PERSONS HOUSE   2 P. JOINT MOD   2 P. JOINT MOD

HOUSING TYPES 2-5 PERSONS - PLANS - SC. 1/200   PLAN OF LOT 1/400

PLANS ELEVATIONS SECTIONS = SC. 1/100   SYSTEM - SCHEME

NORTH ELEVATION

SECTION BB

SECTION AA

SOUTH ELEVATION

GROUND FLOOR   FIRST FLOOR

FIVE PERSONS HOUSE - PLAN

WINTER DAY
WINTER NIGHT
SUMMER DAY
SUMMER NIGHT

DETAILS OF THE PASSIVE SYSTEM SECTION AA - SC. 1/25

HEAT CIRCULATOR FIREPLACE

COMMENDATION
CATEGORY A

The site is situated on the south-westerly border of Berlin and it is surrounded by detached houses and allotment gardens.

The planning of our scheme is based upon symmetrically organised south-orientated short terraces of housing, rhythmically spaced and separated by greenhouses. The various sections are linked by glass connections to reduce the exposed areas.

Access to the dwellings is from the north via residential streets forming a pincer-shaped road system.

At the centre of the access system is a square which functions as a communications area. The north-westerly block of the scheme, with its three different types of housing, is typical of the planning of the development.

Type A — A two-storey terraced house for four people

Type B — A two and half-storey terraced dwelling for six people

Type C — A single storey atrium house for four people

A fourth *'Type D'* house is on the southern border of the development — this is a one and a half-storey terraced house for three people.

The following measures were taken to exploit the available solar energy:-

1. The external surface area is reduced by the terracing and stacking of buildings and by the covering of exposed walls with vegetation.

2. All living areas are arranged to face south.

3. Floor plans are zoned and all the north facing aspects are buffered by conservatories and built-in cupboards.

4. Central areas receive sunlight via adjustable reflectors.

5. All level roof areas are to be planted with vegetation to improve heat conservation and provide ecological conditions.

DESIGN TEAM

Michael Stosslein
Karin Warthmann
Bernd Sinning

Neumanstr 38
85150 Fürth
F R Germany

Those areas of wall and ceiling on to which direct sunlight falls will act as both primary and secondary storage. The rock stores will be charged via a hybrid system. Conservatories, atriums, sun-traps and pools of water will increase collection of the solar radiation and these form the passive solar elements of the design. Overhanging roofs, trellis frames and venetian or roller blinds will provide shade.

The basic heating and hot-water provision is supplied by individual gas heating systems and at peak times supply will come from tiled Dutch stoves or fire-places in the terraced houses. Dense plant growth on the northern and eastern side of the development protects the buildings against cold winds.

JUDGES' COMMENTS

For a scheme that has a more carpet-like, almost suburban, character in Berlin, we commend Michael Stosslein, Karin Warthmann and Bernd Sinning. Their scheme is in the context of an existing pattern of roads and medium density urban landscape. They respond to this with a very clever interlocking section that performs well climatically and shows it can make private and public outdoor spaces which both have a tangible quality and form an enjoyable sequence.

TECHNICAL ASSESSORS' COMMENTS

These 3 storey terraced houses use solar gains from a sunspace, atrium and a light well. A rock store is situated in the light well but it is doubtful whether this component will become properly charged. The greenhouse is equipped with movable reflecting blinds and the glazing between the greenhouse and the dwelling is insulated at night.

A straight forward design backed up with good calculations.

LOCATION
Berlin
F R Germany

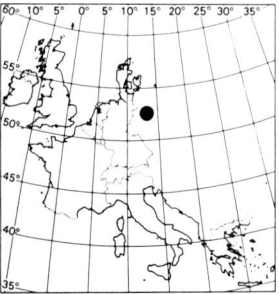

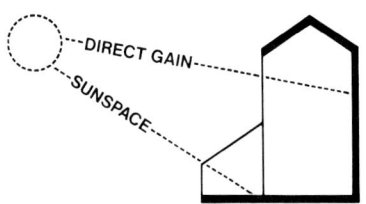

DIRECT GAIN
SUNSPACE

TECHNICAL DATA

For explanation of data see page 16.

Latitude: 52° 23'N
Altitude: 100 m
Data Point: Berlin

DWELLING DESCRIPTION (Typical Unit)
Heated Volume: 430 m³

APERTURE	A	B	C	D
System Type	SS	SS	SS	DG
Net Area m²	12.0	8.5	5.1	3.2
Glazing Layers	3	3	3	3
Night Insulation	Yes	Yes	Yes	Yes
τ	0.30	0.40	0.60	0.65
Comment	O/H	O/H	O/H	O/H
	+	+	+	+
	off S	off S	off S	off S

Aperture/Heated Volume: 0.07 m²/m³
Primary Mass/
    Related Aperture: 435.4 Wh/m²°C
Remote Mass/
    Related Aperture: 1779.6 Wh/m²°C
Air Change Rate: 0.75 ac/h
Building Loss Coeff.: 6.70 kWh/DD
           : 278.97 W/°C

DWELLING PERFORMANCE (Typical Unit)
% Internal Gains: 18.5
% Auxiliary Heating: 68.0
% Useful Solar Gains: 13.5
Annual Solar Gains Fraction: 0.17
Figure of Merit: 0.011 kWh/DDm²
Useful Solar Gains/
    m² of Aperture: 108.8 kWh/m²yr
Min. Temp. without Heating: −7.0°C
Min. Outdoor Temperature: −12.5°C

ENERGY CHARACTERISTICS

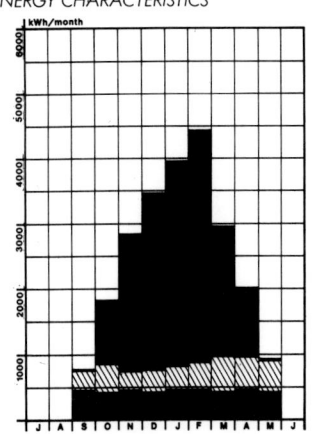

kWh/month

J A S O N D J F M A M J

A   DEUTSCHLAND   BERLIN (WEST)   52° 23'N

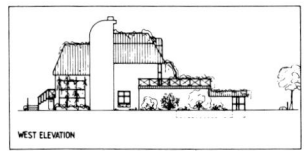

WEST ELEVATION

DISTRICT NEUKOLLN/BUCKOW

NORTH ELEVATION

SOUTH ELEVATION

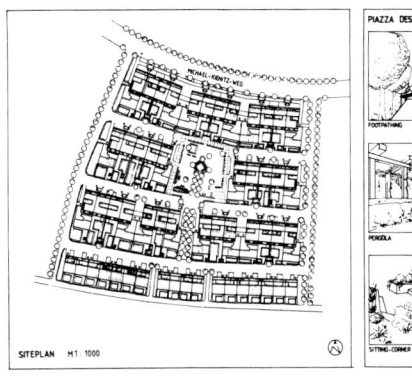

SITEPLAN M1: 1000

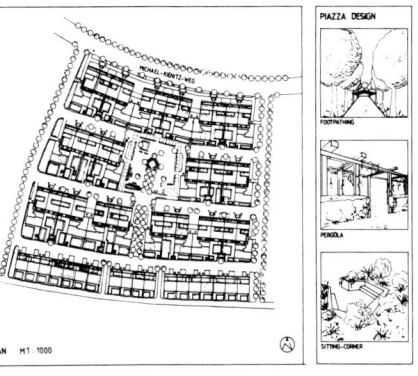

PIAZZA DESIGN

FOOTPATHING

PERGOLA

SITTING-CORNER

Town-planning conception

The property is situated at the southwestern city boundary of Berlin; it is surrounded with a site covered with single-family homes and allotments.

The zoning proposal is based upon a ribbon building which is symmetrically directed southwards. It is rhythmically interrupted and divided by putting under atrium houses. The several groups are joined together by glass hinges in order to reduce the outer surfaces.

On the north side the house-types are developed by residential streets with the help of a system of streets which is laid out in the form of tongs. The heart of the development system is a square which has the function of a communication area.

For a thorough study in a plan there has been consulted the northwestern part of the zoning conception, which includes three different types of houses:

Type A: serial house, 2 floors, 4 persons;
Type B: serial house, 2 1/2 floors, 6 persons;
Type C: atrium house, 1 floor, 4 persons.

The southern line of the property consists of a fourth house-type:
Type D: serial house, 1 1/2 floors, 3 persons.

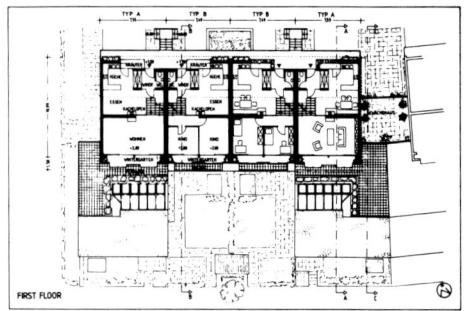

FIRST FLOOR

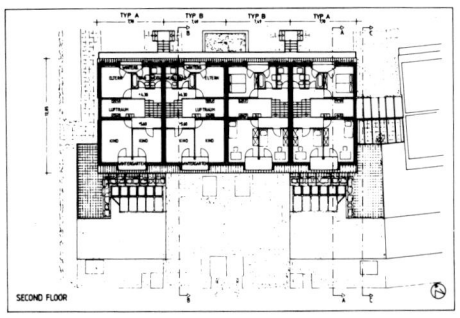

SECOND FLOOR

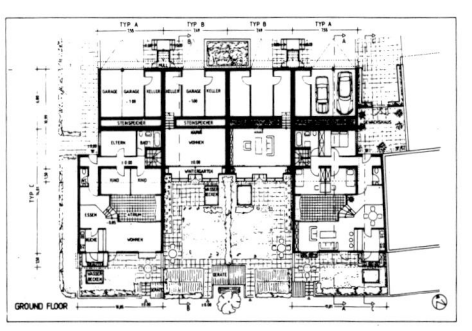

GROUND FLOOR

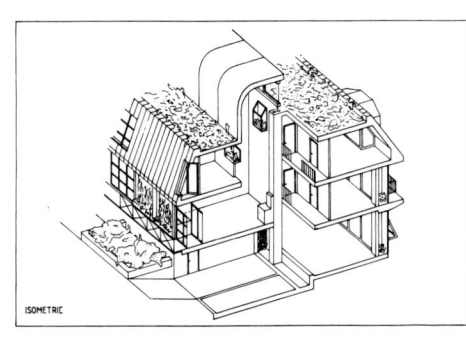

ISOMETRIC

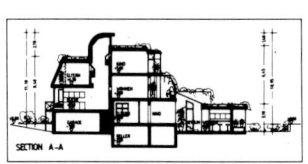

SECTION A-A

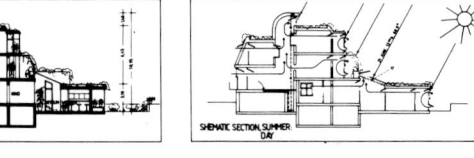

SHEMATIC SECTION: SUMMER DAY

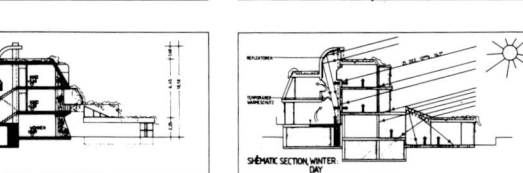

SECTION B-B

SHEMATIC SECTION: WINTER DAY

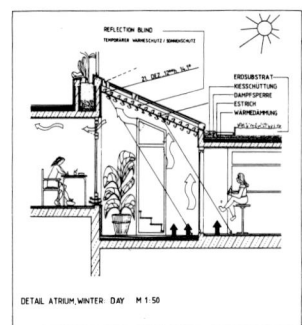

DETAIL ATRIUM: WINTER DAY M 1:50

SECTION C-C

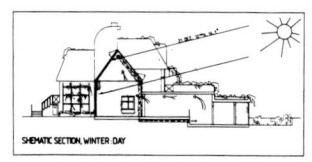

SHEMATIC SECTION: WINTER DAY

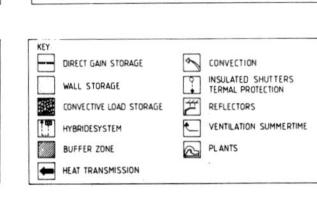

KEY

DIRECT GAIN STORAGE — CONVECTION
WALL STORAGE — INSULATED SHUTTERS / TERMAL PROTECTION
CONVECTIVE LOAD STORAGE — REFLECTORS
HYBRIDESYSTEM — VENTILATION SUMMERTIME
BUFFER ZONE — PLANTS
HEAT TRANSMISSION

Energy conception

As a basis for the passive utilizing of solar energy the following measures will be taken:

1. Diminution of the outer surfaces by building houses in rows and stockpile them. Turfing of the bare walls.
2. Orientation of the rest rooms towards south.
3. Zonation of the ground plans and buffering of the north side by means of winter gardens and unit cupboards.

4. Insolation of the main zones by adjustable reflectors.
5. Plantin of all flat roofs in order to improve the thermal protection and the ecological conditions.

Walls and ceilings upon which the sun shines directly serve as primary and secondary storage. Utilizing the hothouse effect, the stone storages are charged by means of a hybrid system. Winter gardens, atria, sun traps and basins which intensify the insolation on the winter gardens are planned as passive solar elements.

Projecting roofs, scaffolds for climbing plants and Venetian blinds of shutters are assigned to give shade.

A separate gas heating provides for the sheer failure load and the hot-water supply; a tile stove or a fire place have the peak load in the ribbon buildings.

A thick turfing at the north side and west side of the property has the function to protect the buildings from cold winds.

73

COMMENDATION
CATEGORY A

The project consists of a group of small blocks of flats that forms part of a scheme of more than 160 dwellings — including adjacent private houses. These dwellings are to be used as permanent homes for the employees of the tourist industry in Barcares. The site is situated in an urban zone more than 5km wide between the Mediterranean Sea and the Etang de Salses.

The blocks with which this scheme is concerned are built around a communal area on top of ground floor commercial premises.

Our architectural response was determined by the prevalent north-westerly winds (the Tramontante), the large quantity of sunshine available here and the need for heating in winter. The general plan has been arranged to reduce the effect of the Tramontante without losing the fresh breezes which come in off the sea in summer.

Each block receives a minimum of 5 hours sunshine each day during the month of December. The direct or indirect catchment areas are equipped with night insulation systems and solar protection devices in order to control the energy flow during the day and the night both in winter and in summer.

Access to the dwellings is via a large flight of stairs on the north side. These are over a plenum which is the source of ventilation from which each dwelling receives the fresh air that has been extracted from the southern facade by suction from the solar chimney. The flow of air through an underground duct stabilizes the temperature of the fresh air all year round.

The structure (floors and cross walls) is heavy and the southern and northern facades are of light timber; this type of construction

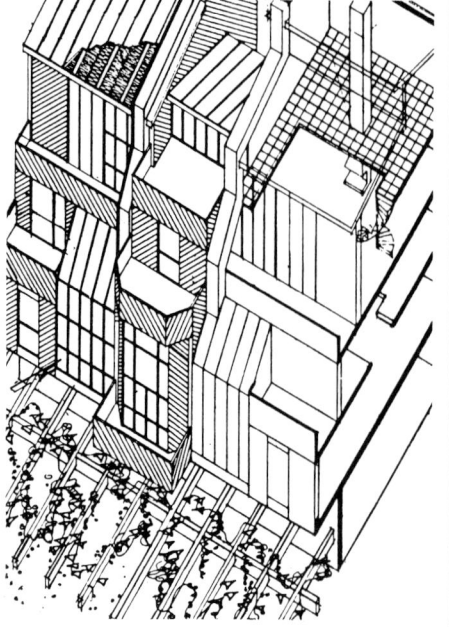

DESIGN TEAM

Anne-Marie Adenis
Gerard Baldet
Mimi Tjoyas
Ch. Marzo
Bernard Cabanne
Clean Energy
Isomobile

3 rue Joseph Pal
66000 Perpignan
France

is new to this area.

The existing vegetation on the site serves as a wind break and is planted in south-westerly and north-easterly directions. The preservation of these trees and vegetation will give protection against the wind in winter and create cool areas in summer.

JUDGES' COMMENTS

For a scheme on an open site, by the Mediterranean near Perpignan, we commend Anne-Marie Adenis, Gerard Baldet and Mimi Tjoyas. Their design showed how an existing layout of low density houses might be terminated and completed by forming a coherent space between two rows of quite high (5 storey) apartment buildings. This scheme was both elegantly designed to contribute to that outside space and extremely efficient from the climatic point of view.

TECHNICAL ASSESSORS' COMMENTS

A terraced 5 storey building with duplex apartments over commercial units utilizing direct gains, sun spaces and a water wall — although not all these aspects are used in one apartment. A solar chimney is incorporated with a fresh air intake via underground tubes — it appears to be an oversight not to use the chimney effect of the sunspace as an alternative. Thermosyphon domestic hot water collectors are also incorporated in this clearly presented scheme.

The calculations are correct.

LOCATION
Barcares
France

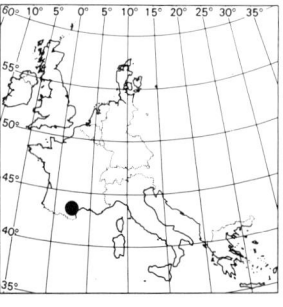

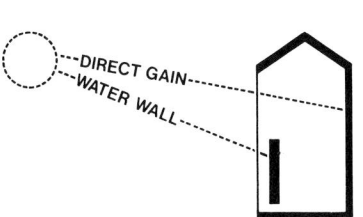

- - - DIRECT GAIN - - -
- - - WATER WALL - - -

TECHNICAL DATA

For explanation of data see page 16.

Latitude: 42° 42'N
Altitude: 2 m
Data Point: Nice

DWELLING DESCRIPTION (Typical Unit)
Heated Volume: 230 m³

APERTURE	A	B	C	D
System Type	WW	DG	DG	DG
Net Area m²	6.8	5.3	1.7	1.3
Glazing Layers	1	1	1	1
Night Insulation	Yes	Yes	Yes	Yes
τ	0.53	0.46	0.68	0.68
Comment	O/H	O/H		

Aperture/Heated Volume: 0.066 m²/m³
Primary Mass/
    Related Aperture: 209.0 Wh/m²°C
Remote Mass/
    Related Aperture: —Wh/m²°C
Air Change Rate: 0.60 ac/h
Building Loss Coeff.: 3.73 kWh/DD
    : 155.60 W/°C

DWELLING PERFORMANCE (Typical Unit)
% Internal Gains: 36.0
% Auxiliary Heating: 14.0
% Useful Solar Gains: 50.0
Annual Solar Gains Fraction: 0.78
Figure of Merit: 0.002 kWh/DDm²
Useful Solar Gains/
    m² of Aperture: 163.0 kWh/m²yr
Min. Temp. without Heating: 3.9°C
Min. Outdoor Temperature: 0.7°C

ENERGY CHARACTERISTICS

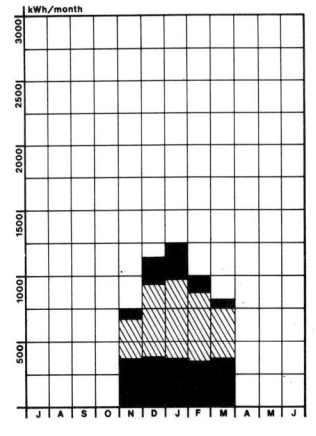

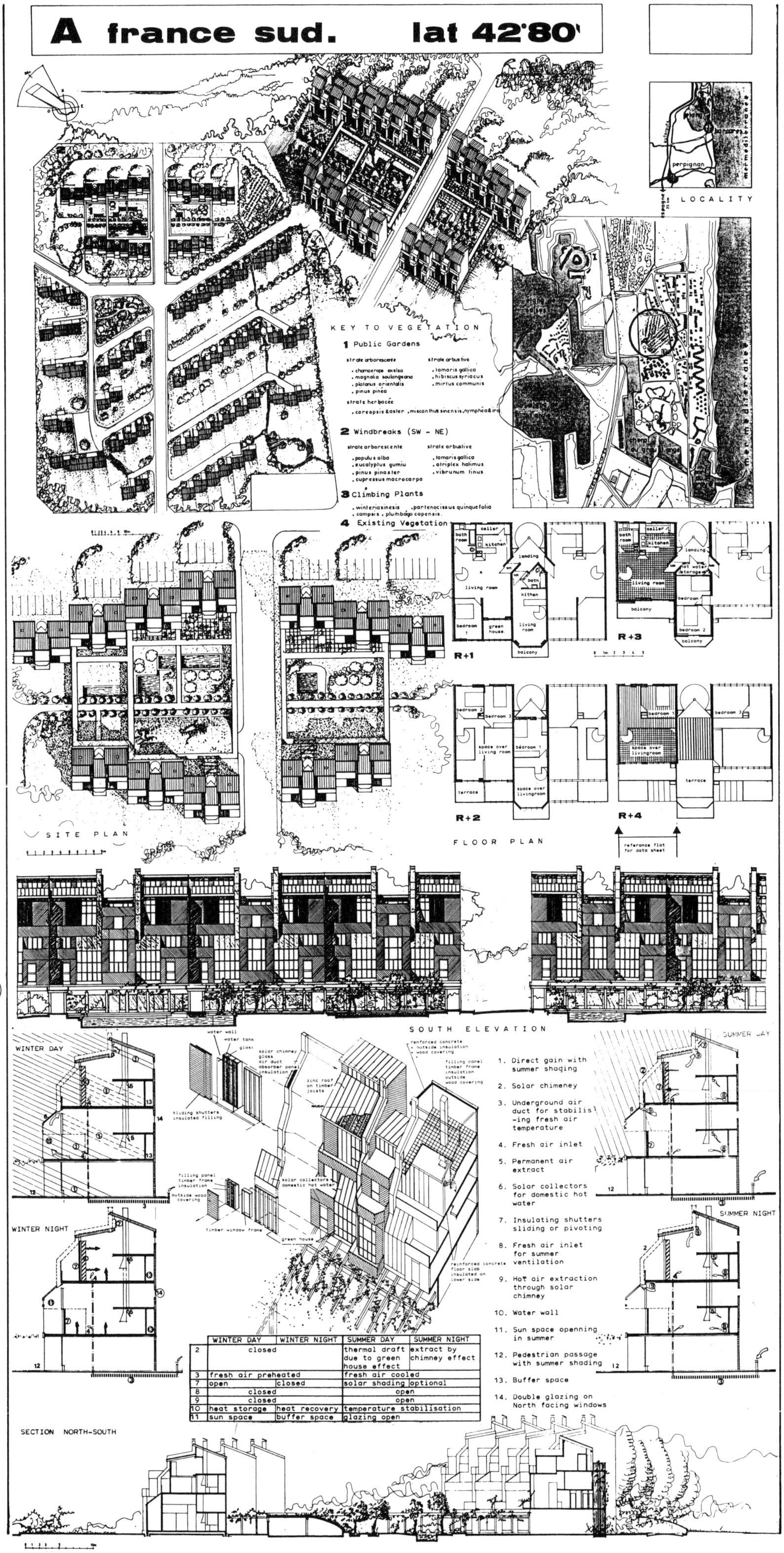

A france sud. lat 42°80'

LOCALITY

KEY TO VEGETATION

1 Public Gardens

strate arborescente
- chamaerops excelsa
- magnolia soulangeana
- platanus orientalis
- pinus pinea

strate arbutive
- tamaris gallica
- hibiscus syriacus
- mirtus communis

strate herbacee
- coreopsis Easter · miscanthus sinensis, nymphéa & iris

2 Windbreaks (SW - NE)

strate arborescente
- populus alba
- eucalyptus gumiu
- pinus pinaster
- cupressus macrocarpa

strate arbutive
- tamaris gallica
- atriplex halimus
- viburnum tinus

3 Climbing Plants
- winter jasmine · partenocissus quinquefolia · campsis · plumbago capensis

4 Existing Vegetation

SITE PLAN

R+1   R+3

R+2   R+4

FLOOR PLAN

reference flat for data sheet

SOUTH ELEVATION

WINTER DAY

WINTER NIGHT

SUMMER DAY

SUMMER NIGHT

1. Direct gain with summer shading
2. Solar chimney
3. Underground air duct for stabilising fresh air temperature
4. Fresh air inlet
5. Permanent air extract
6. Solar collectors for domestic hot water
7. Insulating shutters sliding or pivoting
8. Fresh air inlet for summer ventilation
9. Hot air extraction through solar chimney
10. Water wall
11. Sun space opening in summer
12. Pedestrian passage with summer shading
13. Buffer space
14. Double glazing on North facing windows

	WINTER DAY	WINTER NIGHT	SUMMER DAY	SUMMER NIGHT
2		closed	thermal draft due to green house effect	extract by chimney effect
3	fresh air preheated		fresh air cooled	
7	open	closed	solar shading	optional
	closed			open
9		closed		open
10	heat storage	heat recovery	temperature stabilisation	
11	sun space	buffer space	glazing open	

SECTION NORTH-SOUTH

COMMENDATION
CATEGORY A

O ur scheme has the characteristics of a direct solar system in combination with an indirect air-based heating system connected to a solar roof.

The houses are equipped with a solar-roof which is directly connected both to crawlspaces below the ground floor and the tie-free cavity walls separating neighbouring houses. The collected heat is thus transported to parts of the internal building envelope, where it is stored and gradually released into the living zones by means of radiation and convection. The envelope thus acts as an indirect heating system which is actively charged by solar heated air flowing within an air-tight circuit. The circuit consists of the solar collector outlet duct, crawlspace, cavity wall and inlet duct.

All the computations necessary to determine the thermal behaviour of the house were carried out with the help of the finite element-based computer program 'BFEP'. The program enabled an accurate analysis of all the major heat transport processes to be made. The operations of all the controls regulating the collector, the back-up heat supply and the solar blinds and shutters were taken into full consideration. The computer showed that although obstacles in the cavity considerably increased the heat exchange factor, they did not result in a substantial increase in the supply of solar energy in winter. The computer also:-

— showed that the draughtproofing of the building construction is as critical as the thermal insulation in low energy houses.

— enabled movable insulating shutters to be designed.

— showed that the use of plastic, rather than iron, ties in the external cavity walls reduces the conduction of heat through these walls.

— showed the layer of insulation in all the foundations also reduced the heat losses.

As a consequence of the draught-proofing of the house, the natural ventilation is not sufficient to maintain comfortable conditions and so a mechanical ventilation system is

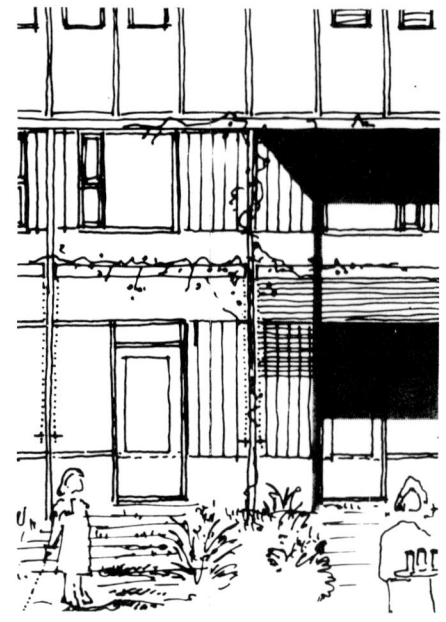

DESIGN TEAM

Jón Kristinsson
Godfried Augenbroe
Edward Tumbuan

Noordenbergsingel 10
7411 SE Deventer
The Netherlands

LOCATION
Enschede
The Netherlands

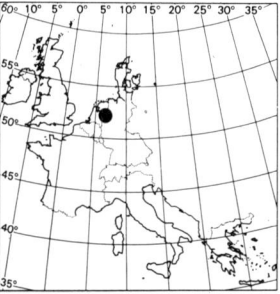

required. The system consists of a ventilation-unit for balanced ventilation, heat reclamation and space heating devices and all the necessary pipe-work. The heat exchanger used is an aluminium cross current plate exchanger with an efficiency of seventy per cent.

Warm, humid air is extracted and the heat from the exhaust air is transferred to the supply air. The fresh air passes through the heater element and is introduced as ventilation-spaceheating air. All the rooms are ventilated in this manner.

The flue gases from the gas water heater are expelled via the heat exchanger. In this way the heat remaining in the flue gases is regained and a high performance system is created. Outside the heating-season it is possible to open windows to increase ventilation.

JUDGES' COMMENTS

We commend J. Kristinsson, Godfried Augenbroe and Edward Tumbuan for this scheme of houses which are fitted into a medium density area of Enschede in Holland. Though the site layout is not very fully developed or shown in any great detail, the judges wished to commend the very simple, well-tried system of solar gain and ventilation combined with well worked out and liveable house plans. This scheme appeared to achieve an exceptionally high solar contribution although the calculations used were based on an alternative competition method whose characteristics are not revealed.

TECHNICAL ASSESSORS' COMMENTS

A terrace of two storey houses with an air collector system and ineffectively utilized direct gains. The collection and distribution system used is interesting in the context of the Netherlands and is already proving to be popular. This is a good example of a hybrid system.

The calculations used an alternative, competition based method, whose characteristics were not revealed.

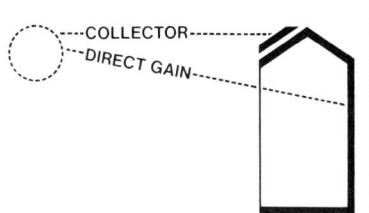

─ COLLECTOR ─
─ DIRECT GAIN ─

TECHNICAL DATA
This data has been recalculated.
For explanation of data see page 16.

Latitude 50° 13'N
Altitude: m
Data Point: De Bilt

DWELLING DESCRIPTION (Typical Unit)
Heated Volume: 309 m³

APERTURE	A	B	C	D
System Type	DG	DG	AC	
Net Area m²	5.9	1.7	27.0	
Glazing Layers	2	2	2	
Night Insulation	Yes	Yes	No	
τ	0.60	0.50	0.95	
Comment	O/H			

Aperture/Heated Volume: 0.112 m²/m³
Primary Mass/
    Related Aperture: 89.6 Wh/m²°C
Remote Mass/
    Related Aperture: 343.3 Wh/m²°C
Air Change Rate: 1.00 ac/h
Building Loss Coeff.: 3.17 kWh/DD
           : 129.00 W/°C

DWELLING PERFORMANCE (Typical Unit)
% Internal Gains: 40.0
% Auxiliary Heating: 29.0
% Useful Solar Gains: 31.0
Annual Solar Gains Fraction: 0.51
Figure of Merit: 0.003 kWh/DDm²
Useful Solar Gains/
    m² of Aperture: 83.2 kWh/m²yr
Min. Temp. without Heating: 2.5°C
Min. Outdoor Temperature: −9.3°C

ENERGY CHARACTERISTICS

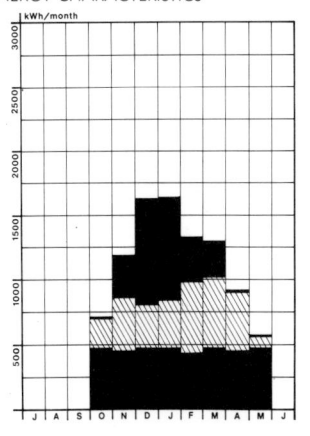

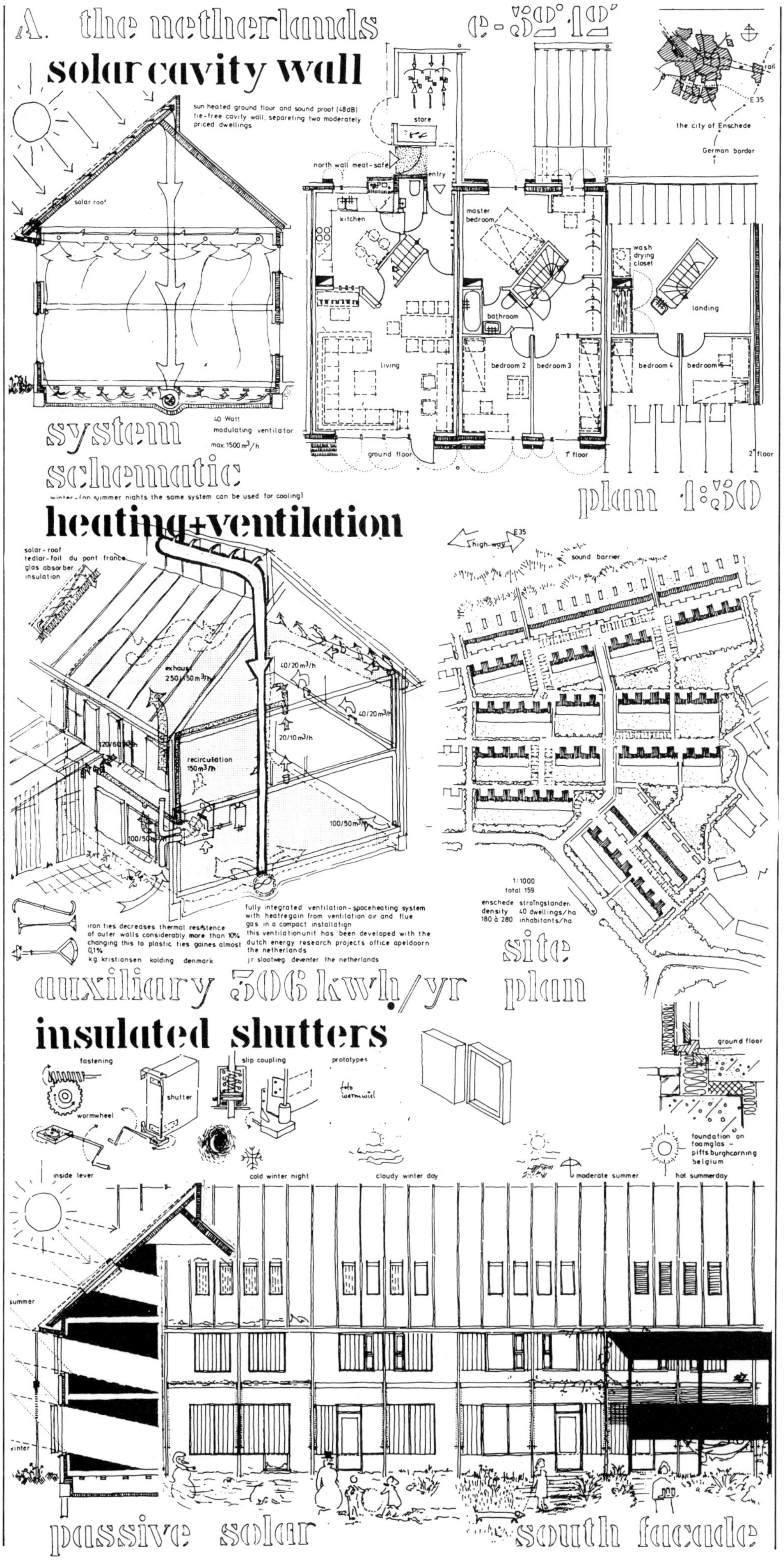

A. the netherlands
solar cavity wall

sun heated ground floor and sound proof (48dB)
tie-free cavity wall, separating two moderately
priced dwellings

solar roof

40 Watt modulating ventilator
max.1500 m³/h

north wall meat-safe

store

entry

kitchen

master bedroom

wash drying closet

landing

bathroom

living

bedroom 2 bedroom 3

bedroom 4 bedroom 5

ground floor   1ᵉ floor   2ᵉ floor

plan 1:250

system
schematic
winter (on summer nights the same system can be used for cooling)

heating+ventilation

solar - roof
tedlar - foil du pont france
glas absorber
insulation

exhaust
250/150 m³h

40/20 m³/h

40/20 m³/h

120/60 m³/h

20/10 m³/h

recirculation
150 m³/h

100/50 m³/h

100/50 m³/h

iron ties decreases thermal resistance
of outer walls considerably more than 10%
changing this to plastic ties gains almost
0.1%
kg kristiansen kolding denmark

fully integrated ventilation-spaceheating system
with heatregain from ventilation air and flue
gas in a compact installation
this ventilationunit has been developed with the
dutch energy research projects office apeldoorn
the netherlands
jr slootweg deventer the netherlands

high-way E35

sound barrier

1:1000
total 159
enschede stroingslanden
density 40 dwellings/ha
180 à 280 inhabitants/ha

site plan

auxiliary 306 kwh/yr

insulated shutters

fastening   slip coupling   prototypes

wormwheel

shutter

inside lever

cold winter night   cloudy winter day   moderate summer   hot summerday

ground floor

foundation on
foamglas –
pitts burghcorning
belgium

summer

winter

passive solar
south facade

COMMENDATION
CATEGORY A

I n 1981 the public were invited to submit ideas for the town planning of the Altfeldgebiet Zirndorf development. The competition site covered an area of over 40ha and plans for the development of this area are being considered by other architects.

We propose the saving of energy by:-

1. Utilising high density forms and simple solar systems.

2. Changing the attitude of the inhabitants of the dwellings so that they will become accustomed to lower temperatures and larger temperature swings. The tenants must also change their usage of the rooms in the dwellings according to the season — this is possible since the rooms are of similar dimensions.

3. Furnishing the various rooms without the loss of storage capacity.

Our proposals would also ensure the retention of:-

1. Urban qualities (streets, open areas, shops, mixture of dwelling-types).

2. Social and spacial relationships between the public spaces and the semi-public spaces in front of the dwelling and between these and the private roof terrace or winter garden and between these and the communal spaces — vegetable gardens, greenhouse stores, childrens' playgrounds etc.

3. The possibility of self identification for the residents — for instance the chance of self build.

The back-to-back concept of construction that we have chosen was evolved from the

DESIGN TEAM

Hans-Peter Hebensperger
Werner Sporrer

Pfeuferstr 30
8000 Munchen 70
F R Germany

design of the existing buildings on the competition site. It may be thought that a terraced house would be able to utilise solar energy more economically than the back-to-back layout that we propose whilst achieving almost as great a density. However, the back-to-back layout is very flexible and enables space to be made available for common usage (for example for childrens' playgrounds or workshops) and therefore this type of building not only saves energy but also can create an environment that will be of benefit to the residents.

JUDGES' COMMENTS

For the skilful use of a well-tried system, we commend Hans-Peter Hebensperger and Werner Sporrer for their carpet of houses near Nurnberg. We had some trouble choosing the best of many schemes designed along these lines, but eventually chose this scheme for the quality of space created between the houses, the good organisation of spaces within a climatically very efficient section, and the flexibility of arrangement possible within and without.

TECHNICAL ASSESSORS' COMMENTS

This tight layout of terraced housing situated on a south facing slope utilises direct and sunspace gains. The competition drawings mainly illustrate the planning layout — however, the system is both simple and classic and of a type which already exists in some parts of France. The construction and operation of the simple manual controls are unexplained.

The calculations are correct.

LOCATION
Zirndorf
F R Germany

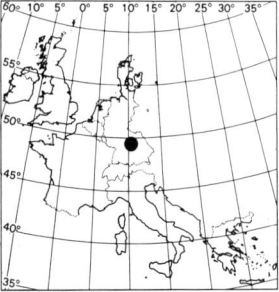

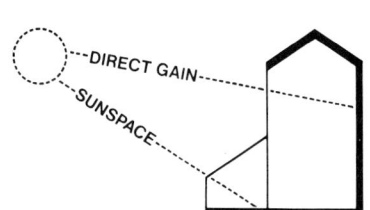

DIRECT GAIN
SUNSPACE

TECHNICAL DATA

For explanation of data see page 16.

Latitude: 49° 26'N
Altitude: m
Data Point: Munich

DWELLING DESCRIPTION (Typical Unit)
Heated Volume: 330 m³

APERTURE	A	B	C	D
System Type	DG	SS		
Net Area m²	10.0	10.0		
Glazing Layers	2	2		
Night Insulation	Yes	Yes		
τ	0.70	0.60		
Comment				

Aperture/Heated Volume: 0.061 m²/m³
Primary Mass/
   Related Aperture: 202.0 Wh/m²°C
Remote Mass/
   Related Aperture: — Wh/m²°C
Air Change Rate: 0.50 ac/h m.v.
Building Loss Coeff.: 5.40 kWh/DD
         : 225.00 W/°C

DWELLING PERFORMANCE (Typical Unit)
% Internal Gains: 20.0
% Auxiliary Heating: 49.9
% Useful Solar Gains: 31.0
Annual Solar Gains Fraction: 0.39
Figure of Merit: 0.008 kWh/DDm²
Useful Solar Gains/
   m² of Aperture: 311.0kWh/m²yr
Min. Temp. without Heating: —10.9°C
Min. Outdoor Temperature: —18.0°C

ENERGY CHARACTERISTICS

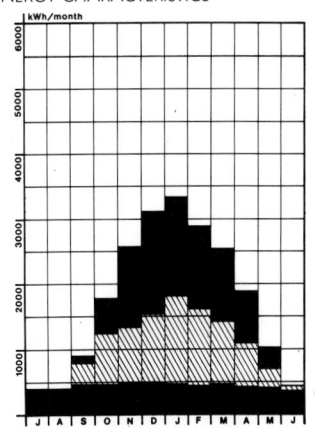

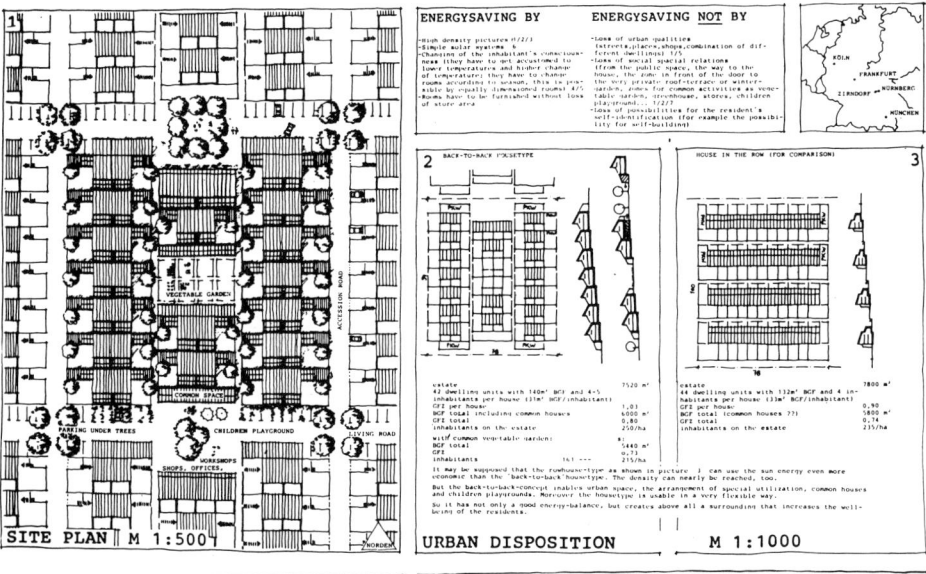

BUNDESREPUBLIK DEUTSCHLAND BAYERN

BUNDESREPUBLIK DEUTSCHLAND BAYERN
STADT ZIRNDORF ALTFELDGEBIET

GEOGRAPHISCHE BREITE 48°
GEOGRAPHISCHE LÄNGE 11°6'

SITE PLAN M 1:500

URBAN DISPOSITION M 1:1000

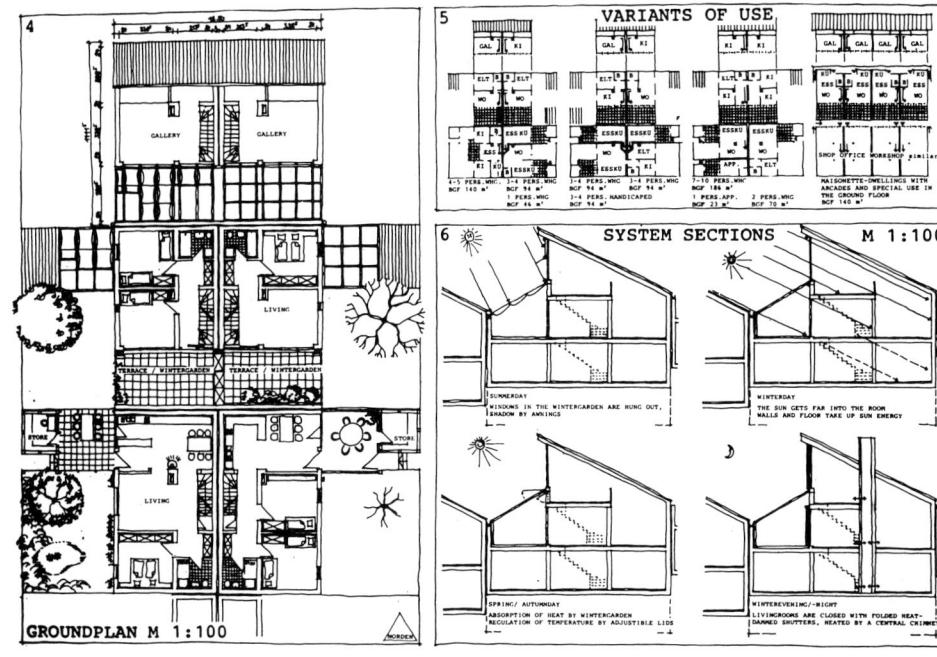

GROUNDPLAN M 1:100

VARIANTS OF USE

SYSTEM SECTIONS M 1:100

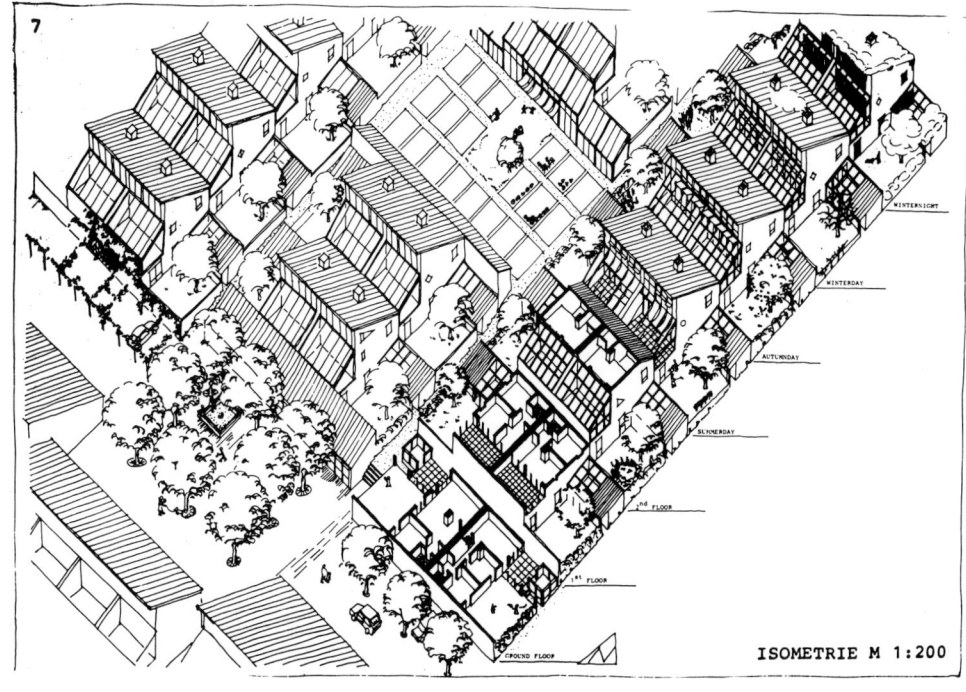

ISOMETRIE M 1:200

79

COMMENDATION
CATEGORY A

The buildings are to be situated in an undeveloped site in the village of Vekso, located on the top of a plateau approximately 20km to the west of Copenhagen. The development of Vekso has been generally towards the south on sloping areas separated by green belts. The sloping site on which the housing is to be built falls approximately 15m towards the south. The municipal regulations for this area call for densities higher than one would normally expect for a development of single family dwellings. Our proposals divide the site into small building plots which share approach roads, parking spaces, playgrounds and communal buildings. Each plot consists of one, two and three storey buildings in order to create interest. The larger changes of level within the site are accommodated within the two storey buildings.

The length of each block can be altered by varying the number of buildings within it but it is envisaged that, for the two and three storey buildings at least, the length of the blocks will be as proposed here. The upper floor of the three storied house consists of a small flat for one or two young persons. The house upon which the calculations have been performed is an end-of-terrace dwelling from a one storey block of five. The interior of the buildings is characterised by timber construction, massive concrete roof supports (or consoles) behind the windows and tiled floors. The roof and external walls are finished in yellow tiles. The southern facade of windows, solar collectors and greenhouses is of an elegant glass and aluminium construction.

The proposed buildings are direct gain passive solar houses with sloping windows on the south front, with internal insulating shutters and a large amount of primary mass in the form of the concrete consoles (perpendicular to the windows and immediately behind them) and also in the concrete floor between these walls — the walls absorb the solar radiation as it enters the house and are heated from both sides during the day. At midday, when the sun is at its highest position, the radiation is almost at right angles to the sloping glazing and is absorbed by the floor. Heat is distributed to the rest of the dwelling by natural convection. The 150mm concrete inner leaf of the external wall helps to stabilise the temperature at the

To keep the solar energy out the shutters are pulled down in a midway position for reflection. Further reflection is provided by a curtain. The windows are open for ventilation. The sectioned shutters allow for optimum comfort adjustment during spring and autumn.

DESIGN TEAM

Jørgen Andersen
Ove Jørgensen

Thermal Insulation Laboratory
Technical University of Denmark
DK 2800 Lyngby
Denmark

rear and at the east and west ends of the house. The southern facade of the dwelling module may have either solar collectors or an attached greenhouse in place of the glazing.

The proposed buildings do not differ substantially from most Danish house types either in layout or in site planning. However they do offer the potential of responding to the Danish climate in a much more appropriate way and the users may control their thermal environment simply and with a minimum of effort. The thickness of insulation in the external walls and roof is the maximum practicable with present day building techniques without creating unreasonable construction costs. The glazed area, at about 20% of the floor area, is chosen so that minor changes in the area do not change the thermal performance of the house considerably. The dwelling, which can be called a truly passive building, gives to users a high level of thermal comfort but with roughly one-third of the energy consumption of a traditionally built Danish house — hot water is supplied for roughly half the usual energy consumption.

Our design complies with the regional planning policy of the area in all respects.

JUDGES' COMMENTS

We commend Jørgen Andersen and Ove Jørgensen for a graceful section that steps up from one to two to three floors on a south facing hillside; for their great attention and detailed drawings of the system of solar gain, shading and ventilation, and their examination of prefabricated elements. The clearly drawn plans indicate that the scheme is capable of having apartments of different sizes and variable layouts. It would obviously be a relaxed and comfortable place to live.

TECHNICAL ASSESSORS' COMMENTS

This terraced housing on a south facing hillside uses both sun space and direct gains through sloping apertures. The emphasis is on industrialisation of the construction using a well insulated pre-cast concrete system. An interestingly detailed shutter design is illustrated.

The calculations are correct.

LOCATION
Vekso
Denmark

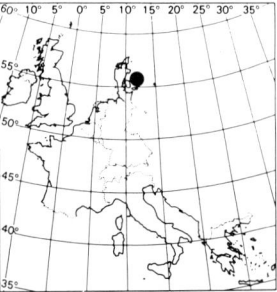

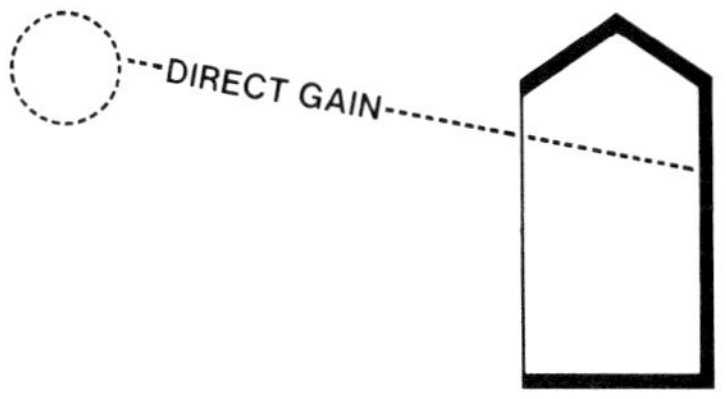

TECHNICAL DATA

For explanation of data see page 16.

Latitude: 55° 45'N
Altitude: 25 m
Data Point: Copenhagen

DWELLING DESCRIPTION (Typical Unit)
Heated Volume: 270 m^3

APERTURE	A	B	C	D
System Type	DG			
Net Area m^2	23.75			
Glazing Layers	2			
Night Insulation	Yes			
τ	0.85			
Comment	S			

Aperture/Heated Volume: 0.088 m^2/m^3
Primary Mass/
Related Aperture: 244.0 $Wh/m^2°C$
Remote Mass/
Related Aperture: 117.0 $Wh/m^2°C$
Air Change Rate: 0.75 ac/h
Building Loss Coeff.: 3.58 kWh/DD
: 149.10 W/°C

DWELLING PERFORMANCE (Typical Unit)
% Internal Gains: 34.0
% Auxiliary Heating: 28.4
% Useful Solar Gains: 37.6
Annual Solar Gains Fraction: 0.57
Figure of Merit: 0.0034 kWh/DDm^2
Useful Solar Gains/
m^2 of Aperture: 184.0 kWh/m^2yr
Min. Temp. without Heating: −0.9°C
Min. Outdoor Temperature: −6.5°C

ENERGY CHARACTERISTICS

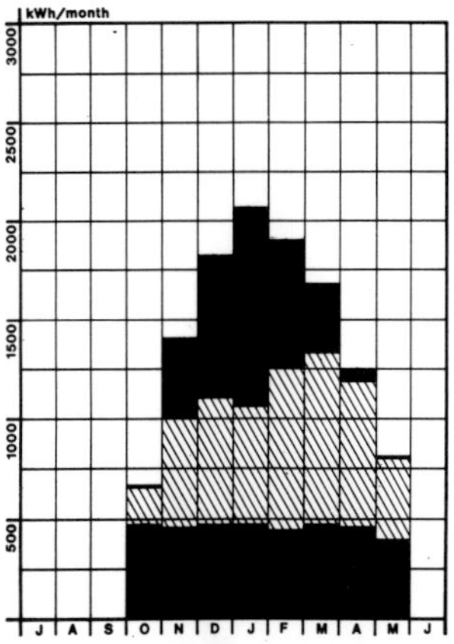

A — DENMARK - EAST - 56°

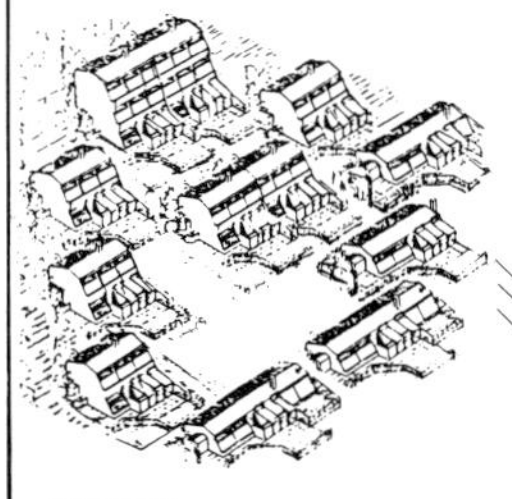

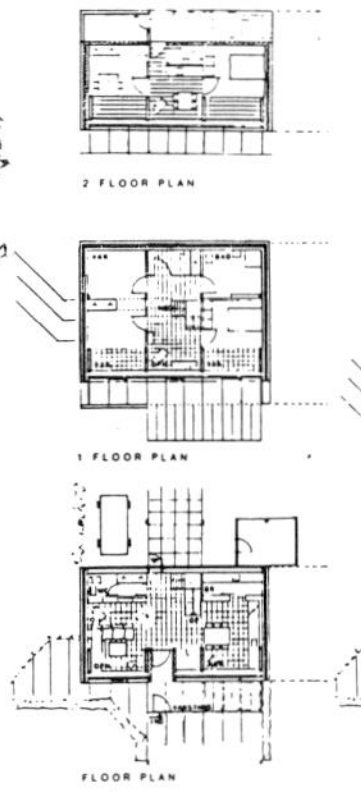

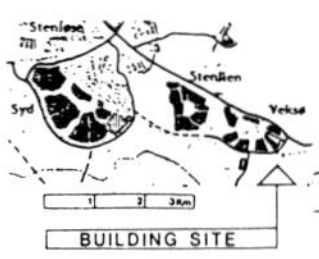

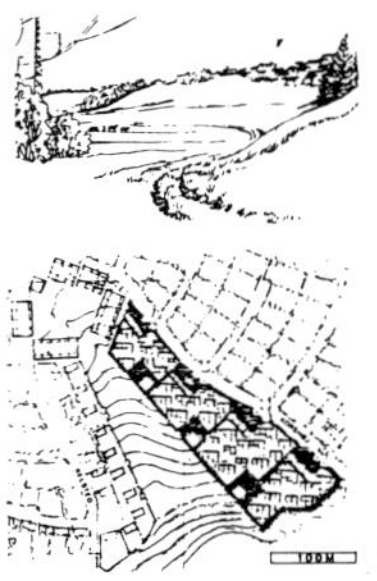

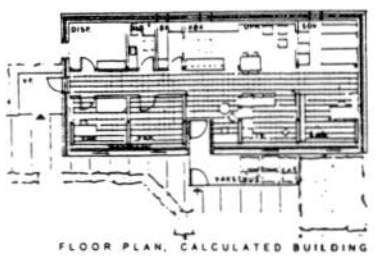

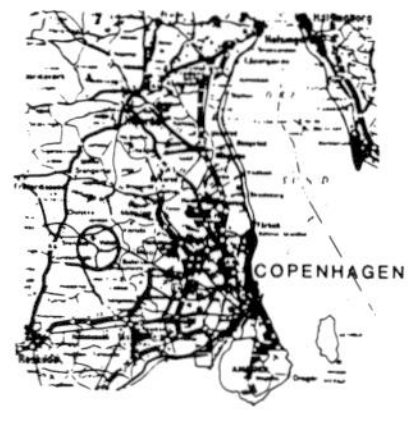

PASSIVE CONCEPTS

A direct gain system has the potential of collecting solar energy at the highest efficiency because it collects heat at the lowest operation temperature. A condition is, however, an adequate amount of primary mass. If this is not provided excess heat will be ventilated out.

A Trombe-Wall System has the potential of providing the best thermal comfort because of the time delay occuring between collecting the energy in the large amount of primary mass and from that releasing it to the house. However, to operate satisfactorily shutters placed outside the mass wall are a necessity in Denmark.

Inside shutters are more likely to be used regularly than outside shutters because of ease of operation. Furthermore they will be more reliable and take less maintenance.

Attached greenhouses ad an attractive additional living area to the house in the greater part of the year and collect a considerable amount of energy.

Sloping windows towards south maximizes solar gain during spring and autumn - the time of the year of highest energy output for a passive system in Denmark. The sloping windows allow for an integration of a solar collector array for a domestic hot water solar heating system, which is satisfying both from an architectural viewpoint and with regard to solar insolation.

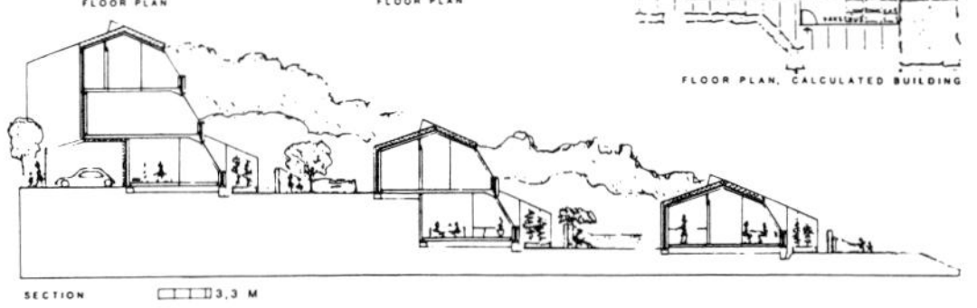

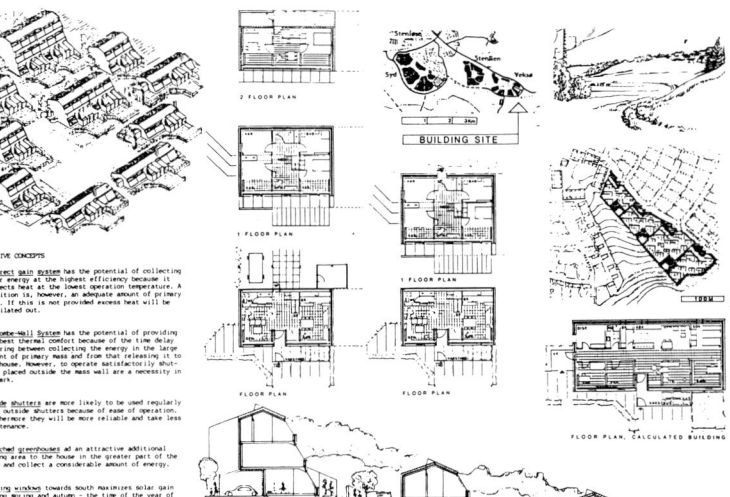

THE BUILDINGS

The buildings are placed on an unbuilt area approx. 20 km west of Copenhagen. The village Vekse has a characteristic situation on the top of a plateau in the landscape. The development of Vekse has been planned towards south on sligthly sloping areas carved up by green wedges. The south-sloping area for which the houses have been planned has a difference in ground levels of 15 m.

In the municipality regulations for this area is called for a higher density than for ordinary singlefamily dwellings. The area is divided into smaller building sites sharing the approach roads and the parking lot. Likewise a communal dwelling and playgrounds.

As is seen each group of houses has been combined of one-, two- and three-storied buildings to create character and variation. The two-storied houses take up greater recesses in the terrain.

The size of the buildings can be varied by the number of modules used, but the shown sizes of the two- and three-storied houses are the more likely to be chosen. The upper floor of the three-storied house is planned to be a small flat for one or two young people. The house which is used for the calculations in the calculation booklet is the one-storied house consisting of 5 modules shown on the rightmost floor-plan.

The interior of the buildings is characterized by the timber-construction, the massive consoles and the clinkers in the floor. The external facing of the walls and the roof covering are yellow tiles. The south facade appears as an elegant glass-aluminium construction - windows - solar collectors - greenhouse.

The proposed building is a direct gain passive house with sloping windows on the south front, with inside insulating shutters and a large amount of primary mass in the form of concrete consoles perpendicular to the window area, placed right behind it, and ind the concrete floor between the consoles. The consoles absorps the solar radiation as it enters the house and is heated from both sides during the day. At midday the sun is at its highest position, the radiation is almost perpendicular to the sloped glazing and the radiation is absorped by the floor under the windows. The heat is distributed to the rest of the house by natural convection. A 15 cm inner concrete part of the external wall stabilizes the temperatures at the rear and at the east and west ends of the house. The southern front of the module can in place of the glazing be equipped with either solar collectors or an attached greenhouse.

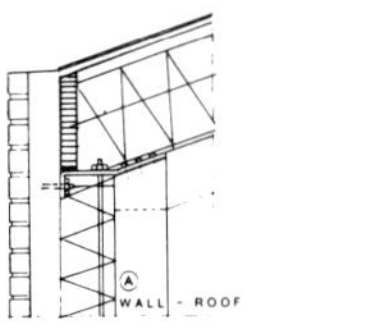

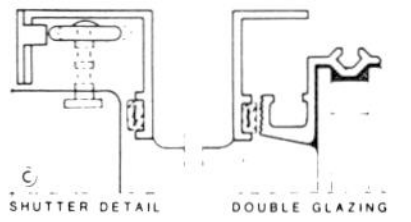

CONSTRUCTION DETAILS

The basic idea of the construction is the "industrialized module". The module has 45 cm external walls (5 cm quarter bats cast into 10 cm of light concrete, 15 cm of mineral wool and 15 cm of heavier concrete), roof coffers with 25 cm of insulation and a load-bearing construction of 15 heavy concrete consoles combined with timber. These are all industialized components to be assempled at the building site.

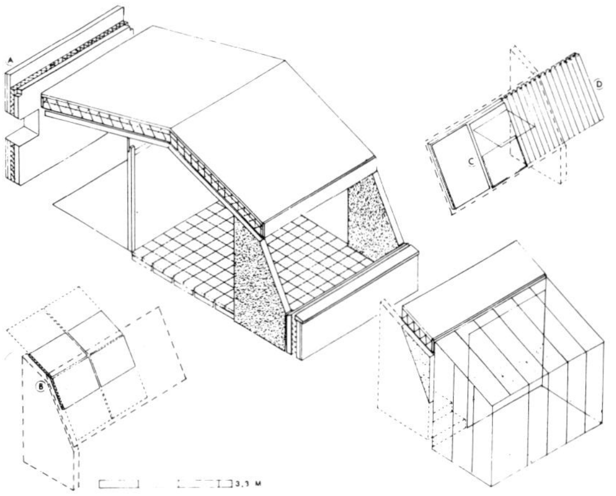

GLAZING

The details of the glass-construction is based on a newly designed aluminium-profile which is glued to the double-glazed thermopanes with a UV-resistant glue. In this profile hinges for different types of windows can be mounted, i.e. fixed windows, sliding windows and pivot windows. The profile eliminates the need for traditional framing of the window, thus minimizing the use of aluminium and maximizing the aperture/window area relationship of the entire facade.

The drawing shows a fixed window of 1.6 m by 1.1 m and a field sectioned in two, each .8 m by 1.1 m. Above a sliding pivot window, suitable for ventilation. Below a horizantally sliding window. This configuration can be used in the children's rooms. In the living room the sectioned window is replaced by one large sliding window allowing for optimum contact to the ambient and the firmament. This window can be pushed out and locked for nighttime-ventilation.

SHUTTERS

The sloping south front of the house allows for an easy operation of inside shutters. From the open position beneath the roof they can slide down and effectively close the glazed area without interfering with pot plants placed close by the windows. In a half-way position the shutters can be used for solar shading. For each module the shutters are sectioned following the glazing for more flexible operation. The shutters are made of an insulating foam, polyisocyanat, produced by a Danish factory. The foam is a non-inflamable, form-stable material with a high practical R-value. The 65 mm thickness of the shutters results in a R-value corresponding to 100 mm of mineral wool. The foam is covered by a 40 micron aluminiumfoil for moisture control and solar reflection. Each shutter is framed with a strip giving extra strength and allowing for the mounting of weather-stripping and spindles for the plastic wheels carrying the shutter. The wheels are running in an aluminiumprofile, which has been given small jogglings at the closed position in order that the shutters close tight.

Each shutter has a weight of 2.5 kg but is counterbalanced in such a way that when the handle is clutched it moves upwards by itself. When the handle is released the shutter can be locked in any position.

SOLAR COLLECTORS

The absorbers installed behind the glazing are of the make Sun-Strip produced by a Swedish factory. They consist of 14 cm wide strips of selective coated elements mounted in parallel on the headers. The strips are produced in any length up to 6 m and can be assempled at any number. For an even distribution of the passive direct gain two building modules are sharing a complete collector array of about 4 m^2 Behind the absorber elements 15 cm of mineralwool provide an effective backside insulation of the collector. In front of the absorber one pane glazing is used to avoid cracking because of heat-stresses.

ATTACHED GREENHOUSE

The module can also be equipped with an attached greenhouse which made of thermopanes in aluminiumframing fits into the architecture and at the same time provides additional exciting living space at the greater part of the year. Finally it increases the passive gain and adds flexibility to the use of the house. To prevent overheating the greenhouse is equipped with ventilation windows and a reflective curtain.

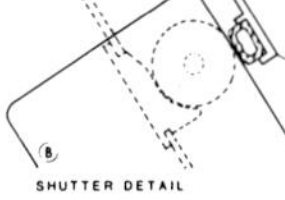

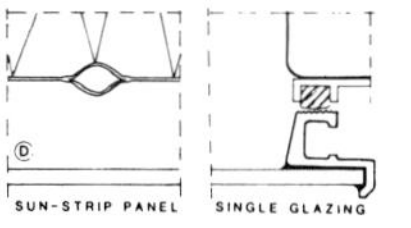

The proposed building does not differ substantially from typical Danish houses with regard to plan arrangements and site plan. It has, however, the potential of responding to the Danish climate in a much more appropriate way. The house appears as an offer to the users to control their thermal environment in an unsophisticated way at a minimum level of effort. The chosen thicknesses of insulation in the external walls and in the roof approaches what is within the reach of present building techniques without causing drastic increases in the constructon costs. The glass area of approx. 20 % of the floor area is chosen such that minor changes in the area does not change the thermal performance of the house considerably. The house, which can be designated as a truly passive house, provides the users with a high level of thermal comfort at about one third of the energy consumption of a traditionally built Danish house and supplies hot water at about half the energy consumption.

WINTER DAY

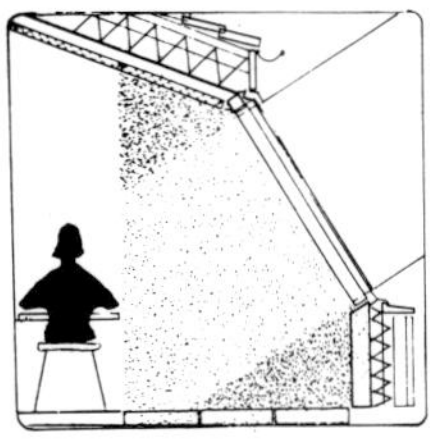

The shutters are opened allowing the solar radiation to directly heat the primary thermal mass. The sloping windows maximizes solar gains in spring and autumn.

WINTER NIGHT

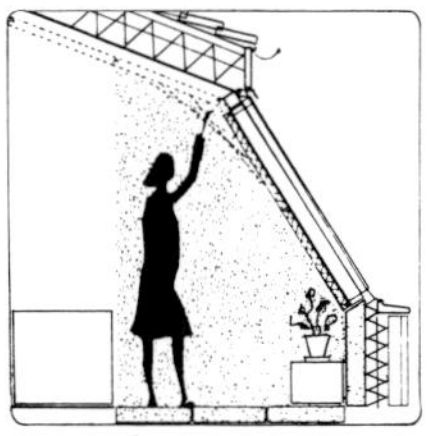

The insulating shutters have been closed down and the south front of the house is now completely insulated without thermal bridges to reduce heatlosses to a minimum.

SUMMER DAY

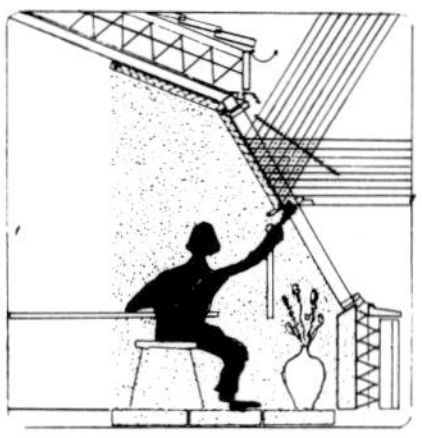

To keep the solar energy out the shutters are pulled down in a midway position for reflection. Further reflection is provided by a curtain. The windows are open for ventilation. The sectioned shutters allow for optimum comfort adjustment during spring and autumn.

SUMMER NIGHT

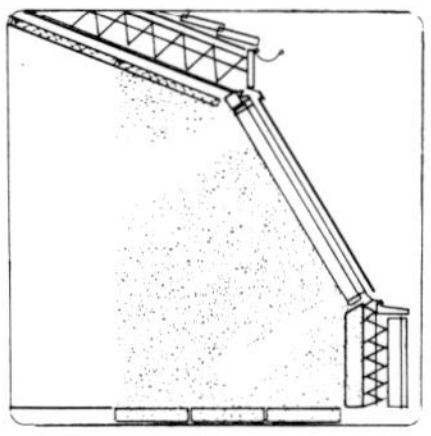

The shutters are hidden at the roof allowing for radiative cooling of the primary mass to the sky via the sloped glazing. The sliding windows have been pushed out and locked in that position for increased ventilation. If necessary windows at the east or west side of the house are open for cross flow ventilation.

DYNAMIC SIMULATIONS

To investigate how the house thermally responds to different climate conditions it has been modelled by a dynamic simulation model using hourly data from three periods of three consecutive days representing respectively a cold winter period, a warm summer period and a typical spring/autumn period. These data have been taken from the Danish Test Reference year which is based on climatic data from a 10 year period.

The model used is a thermal network model which implicitly solves the differential equations hour by hour using a matrix inversion technique (similar to the model PASOLE used for the development of the SLR-technique on which the calculations in the calculation booklet is based). The house has been modelled as 14 nodes. The southern rooms have been considered as one zone (node) and the northern rooms as another. The rest of the nodes have been placed in the consoles, the floor and the external walls. The natural convection heat flow that supplies the northern rooms with heat from the southern rooms has been modelled as proposed by Balcomb (1981).

The type of house modelled is the same as that used for the calculations in the calculation booklet, i.e. the one-storey house, consisting of 5 modules, equipped with sloping windows and shutters. The operation of the shutters in the winter period is optimal from a thermal point of wiev. The shutters only open when there is a positive net gain. In the summer situation three quarters of the shutters has been drawn down for reflection during daytime and opened for radiative cooling during nighttime. The windows are opened for cross flow ventilation. In the spring/autumn situation the shutters are open and the windows closed during the whole three day period.

Ref.: Balcomb, J.D. (1981). Heating remote rooms in passive solar houses, ISES Solar World Forum, Brighton, England, August 23-28.

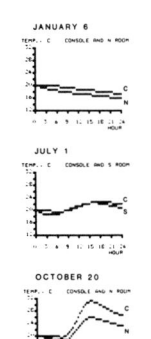

JANUARY 6

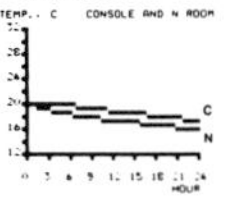

JANUARY 7

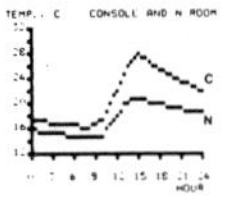

JANUARY 8

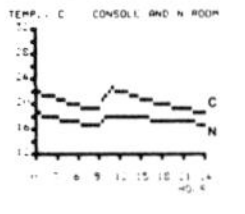

JULY 1

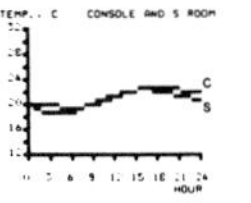

JULY 2

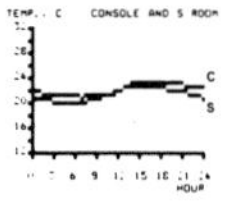

JULY 3

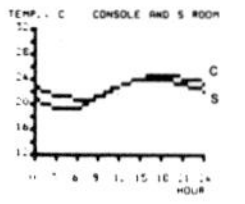

OCTOBER 20

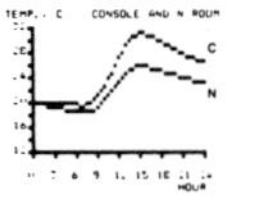

OCTOBER 21

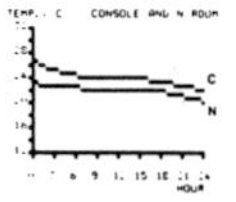

OCTOBER 22

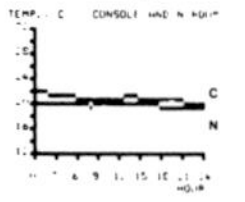

WINTER

The large time-constant of the house with closed shutters makes the temperatures drop very slowly on January 6. January 7 is a clear day, the consoles collect a lot of energy, reach high temperatures and release it slowly as the rooms cool down. In this way the consoles act very much like a Trombe-wall. They collect heat without causing thermal discomfort by overheating of the room air and delay the release of the energy until it is needed. The proposed system could be designated a Trombe-wall system of second order. On January 8 it is seen that even a very small amount of sunshine is enough to keep the temperature level for 18 hours.

SUMMER

The three very warm and sunny summer days try out the capability of the house to prevent overheating during daytime and to cool down during nighttime. Note that the room temperature shown in this case is the temperature in the southern rooms which are directly exposed to the sun. From the curves it is seen that the use of the shutters for reflection and the windows for cross-flow ventilation prove effective for preventing overheating during the day. Likewise the radiative cooling and ventilation at night seem to work properly.

AUTUMN/SPRING

The temperature plot of October 20 looks very similar to that of January 7. The consoles are heated to close to 30 C while the room temperature stay at comfort levels. What is interesting is that the higher ambient temperatures means that the shutters do not have to be used. The energy collected the first day last for the following two overcast days. This means that for a greater part of the year the house will provide thermal comfort at no use of auxiliary energy with a minimum operation effort.

3,3 M

This project aims to estimate the influence of using passive solar heating systems on the structure of buildings and on the urban form.

In choosing which of the systems to adopt, the peculiar climatic situation of Palermo was taken into account. Here the thermal aspects are of equal importance both in winter and summer. This consideration led to the exclusion of systems such as 'Trombe' walls since these are known to produce insoluble overheating problems even in winter months.

The use of lean-to conservatories and solar windows which can be screened when needed — will, in our opinion, provide an adequate solution to the problem here. The system is also thought to be suitable because of the low levels of maintenance and operation it requires. Particular attention was paid to providing the building with considerable thermal capacity — examination of the existing architecture of the area pointed us in this direction.

Finally, we consider that the system proposed for the storage of heat in the floors and ceilings of the building will also help to obtain the most comfortable thermal conditions possible, in order to gain the maximum profit from the heat circulating in the rooms.

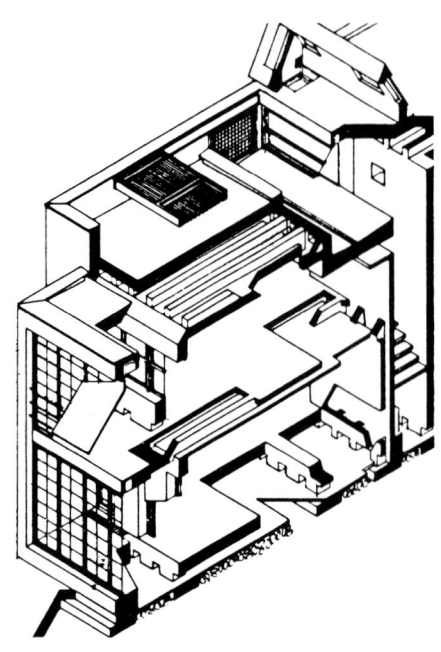

DESIGN TEAM

Aldo Lauritano
Anna Maria Cuccia
Antonino Caleca

Via Demetra 5 (Mondello)
90149 Palermo
Italy

LOCATION
Acquasanta
Italy

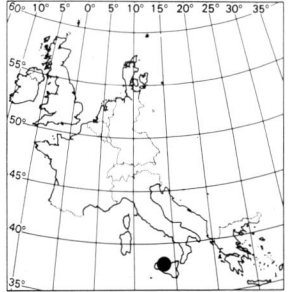

JUDGES' COMMENTS

For a scheme in the centre of Palermo, we commend a unique design by Aldo Lauritano which not only builds fairly logically into the existing city fabric but seriously tackles the problem of cooling, as well as the rather lesser problem of heating in southern climates. It does so with a system of double walls and roof with central chimney which fit very well with the southern character of the houses themselves.

TECHNICAL ASSESSORS' COMMENTS

These low-rise high density terraced houses utilize an original and technically sound passive cooling system. The winter heating mode needs some modification since the northern rooms are underheated and the natural convection is unlikely to operate as designed. This would be an expensive solution.

Errors were discovered in the calculations.

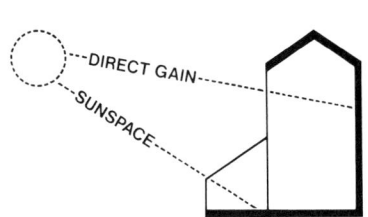

DIRECT GAIN

SUNSPACE

TECHNICAL DATA

This data has been recalculated.
For explanation of data see page 16.

Latitude: 38° 8'N
Altitude: 10 m
Data Point: Messina

DWELLING DESCRIPTION (Typical Unit)
Heated Volume: 330 m³

APERTURE	A	B	C	D
System Type	SS	SS	DG	
Net Area m²	6.9	6.9	5.2	
Glazing Layers	1	1	1	
Night Insulation	Yes	Yes	Yes	
τ	0.5	0.5	0.5	
Comment	O	O	O	

Aperture/Heated Volume: 0.06 m²/m³
Primary Mass/
   Related Aperture: 130.0 Wh/m²°C
Remote Mass/
   Related Aperture: —Wh/m²°C
Air Change Rate: 0.50 ac/h m.v.
Building Loss Coeff.: 8.55 kWh/DD
   : 356.29 W/°C

DWELLING PERFORMANCE (Typical Unit)
% Internal Gains: 37.0
% Auxiliary Heating: 32.0
% Useful Solar Gains: 31.0
Annual Solar Gains Fraction: 0.49
Figure of Merit: 0.008 kWh/DDm²
Useful Solar Gains/
   m² of Aperture: 107.0 kWh/m²yr
Min. Temp. without Heating: 9.9°C
Min. Outdoor Temperature: 3.8°C

ENERGY CHARACTERISTICS

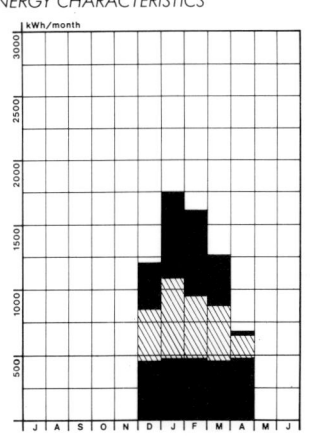

PALERMO

WEST ELEVATION

NORTH ELEVATION

SOUTH ELEVATION

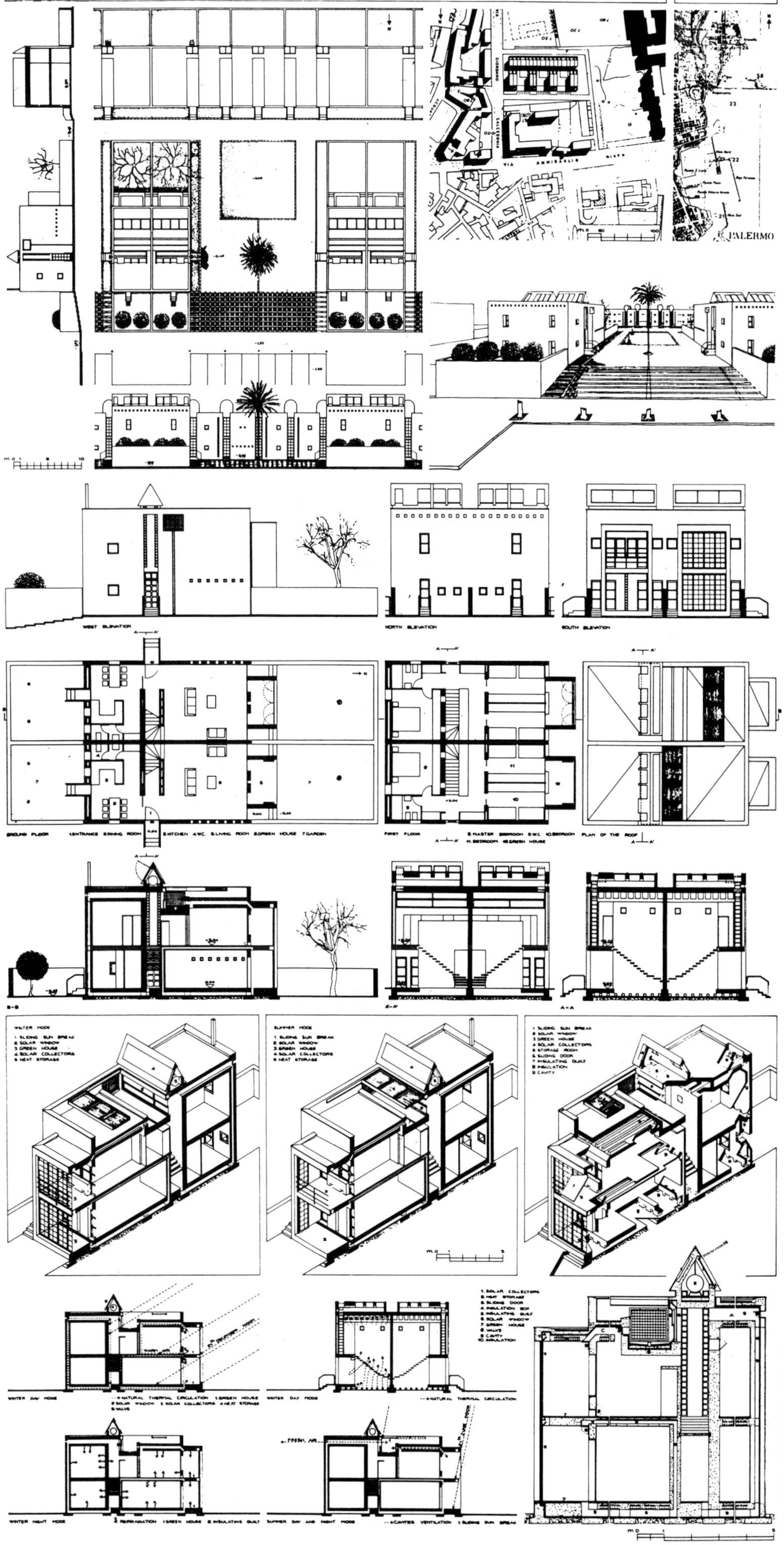

COMMENDATION
CATEGORY A

Our intention is to transform these designs into architecture, lived in by real people. These people, when questioned, reveal (alas) concepts deeply rooted in the functionality and in the social functional aspect of the object house. They also reveal ideas which have arisen from the dreariness of modern suburbs which are, to them, labelled 'Modern Architecture' and about the beauty of the 'Ancient Style', which embraces all the rich architecture of history up to the fake rustic style of 'Vecchia Maremma'.

In order to avoid aesthetic judgement of one single building, the performance of which will depend very much upon its disposition and the poor weather of the province, we have decided to propose detailed plans for a complete urban development which is geared to the ordinary pedestrian. There are squares on three distinct levels which centralize the public services and leisure facilities: in this way the entire complex maintains its panoramic and bioclimatic characteristics and prompts the proper use of the historic areas rather than the new suburbs. We proceeded to break up the existing network of roads and to plan new districts in sufficient detail to cover all the various requirements.

The dominant house-type assessed in the calculations is a duplex building with two facades, situated above accommodation on the ground level and set out in two rows. Access to the apartments is be a glass-covered gallery which passes between and serves both the ground and first floors and which provides a buffer zone and a semi-covered private area where children can play. In the centre, above the communal services, are dwellings on one level and the two fronted duplexes built in an oblique tower. At the side of the main square there are three small villas with patios which are covered in summer.

Three different passive solar systems are used. These are very simple in both concept and execution and form part of the structure:-

System A — double windows with direct solar gains. Night insulation is provided by curtains made of heavy material with velcro fastenings. In summer these windows allow cross ventilation.

System B — double windows with direct gains from sunlight as in system A, with space

DESIGN TEAM

Antonio Bastreghi
Giorgio Esposito
Paulo Puccetti
Antonio Cambiotti
Gianni Mannocci

Studio di Architettura
via Delle Belle Donne 13
50123 Firenze
Italy

LOCATION
Pomarance
Italy

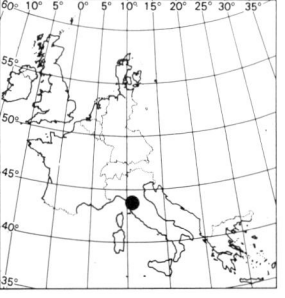

between the glass windows. The large glass window remains open during the summer while the overhang screens the inner window which opens in winter by means of a sash device. The inner window also regulates the passage of hot air flowing through the intermediary space. Night insulation is as in system A.

System C — solar air collector built into the wall. This works by natural convection, with an absorber of low thermal inertia fixed between the glass wall and insulation.

Heat is stored in the ceilings and floors which are constructed of concrete blocks in which iron pipes are embedded. Hollow concrete blocks rather than the usual red bricks span between the supporting beams.

The thermosyphon affect of the collector is obtained by hot air passing through the ducts until it emerges at the air vents in the ceiling of the north room. It re-enters the inlet ducts via the air vents in the door.

Reverse flow at night is prevented by plastic automatic non-return valves. A manual valve for summer and winter permits hot air to be directed either into the canals or to the outside — thus creating internal ventilation. This system has been studied by Prof O. A. Barra and the Civil Engineer, T. Costantini (cf. 1,2,3).

JUDGES' COMMENTS
We commend A Bastreghi, G Esposito, P Puccetti, A Cambiotti and G Mannocci for an autonomous, well worked out, elegantly presented and stylish block near Pisa in Italy. As shown, the scheme seems to have no visible context but for the stylishly complete world that it achieves within its own interlocking self, and for its high technical performance we are happy to commend it.

TECHNICAL ASSESSORS' COMMENTS
A low-rise high density scheme utilizing direct gains — with night insulation — and a modified Barra Costantini wall. An interesting and nicely presented scheme.

The calculations are correct.

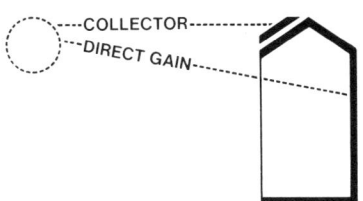

─COLLECTOR──────
─DIRECT GAIN──────

TECHNICAL DATA

For explanation of data see page 16.

Latitude: 42° 25'N
Altitude: 250 m
Data Point: Pisa

DWELLING DESCRIPTION (Typical Unit)
Heated Volume: 373 m³

APERTURE	A	B	C	D
System Type	DG	DG	C	
Net Area m²	7.9	8.1	4.3	
Glazing Layers	2	2	2	
Night Insulation	Yes	Yes	No	
τ	0.65	0.65	0.65	
Comment				

Aperture/Heated Volume: 0.055 m²/m³
Primary Mass/
     Related Aperture: 105.3 Wh/m²°C
Remote Mass/
     Related Aperture: 783.5 Wh/m²°C
Air Change Rate: 0.75 ac/h
Building Loss Coeff.: 4.40 kWh/DD
                   : 182.20 W/°C

DWELLING PERFORMANCE (Typical Unit)
% Internal Gains: 38.0
% Auxiliary Heating: 22.0
% Useful Solar Gains: 40.0
Annual Solar Gains Fraction: 0.64
Figure of Merit: 0.002 kWh/DDm²
Useful Solar Gains/
     m² of Aperture: 145.0 kWh/m²yr
Min. Temp. without Heating: 5.8°C
Min. Outdoor Temperature: −3.0°C

ENERGY CHARACTERISTICS

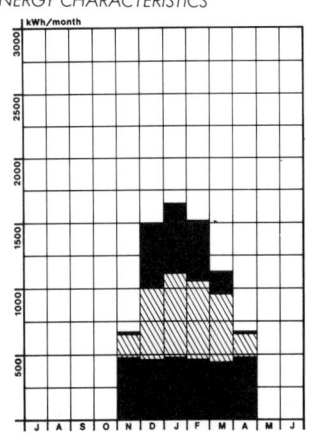

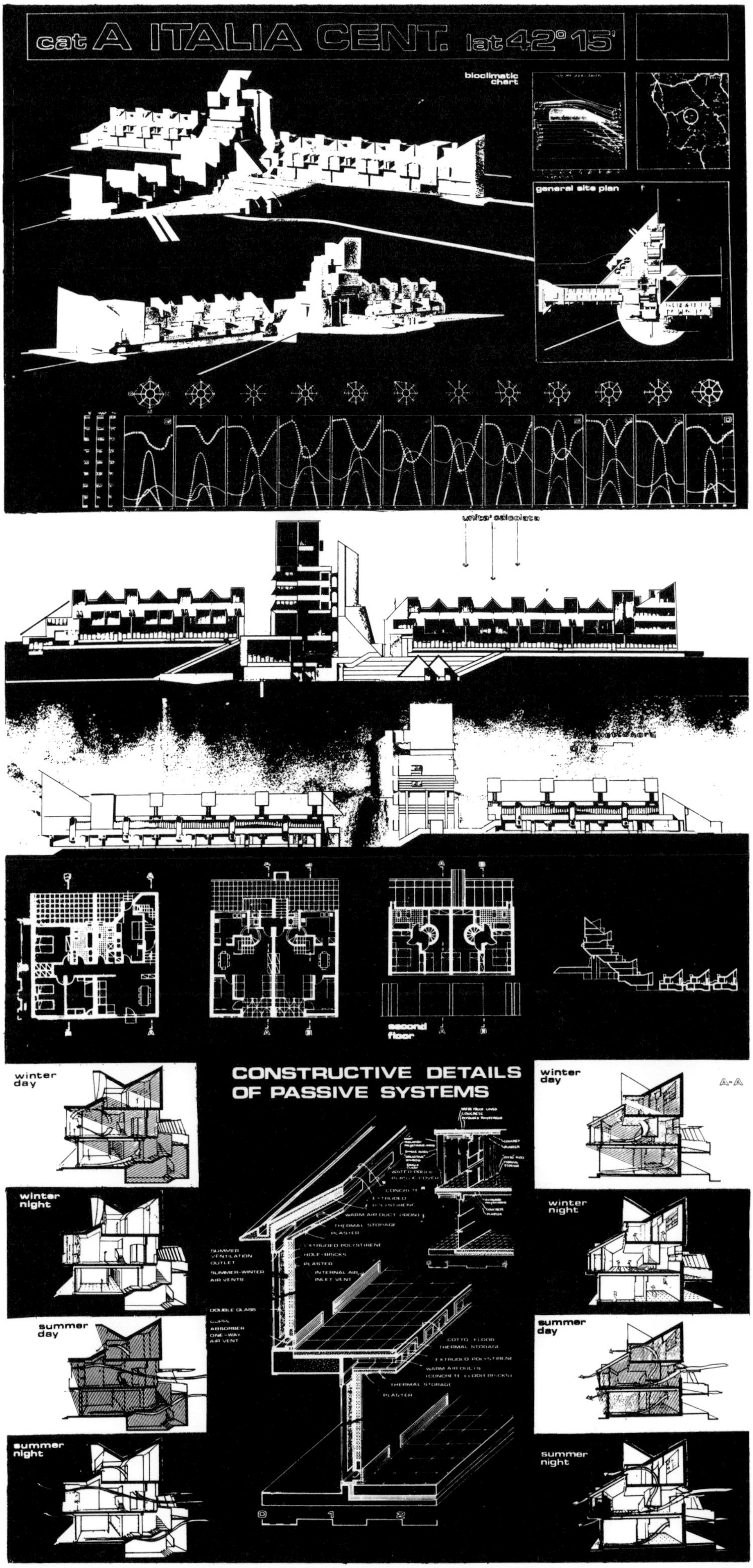

COMMENDATION
CATEGORY A

We propose a socio-ecological development plan for Herfølge, a small town near Copenhagen, based on ecological, social and climate-responsive buildings. The town will offer new facilities for alternative energy production, industrial production and the study of social-ecology, as well as solar residential communities for a population of up to 2,500 people.

The plan calls for the development of three major areas, which are as follows:-

1. *A Solar Community* — this will provide a variety of low-energy dwellings for up to 2,500 inhabitants, as well as work places, schools, social facilities and recreation areas.

2. *A Socio-Ecological Centre* — for the investigation of the interrelationship between energy, lifestyle and the environment. This will function as an information, education and research centre for the town.

3. *A Solar Technology Research Area* — this will include areas for energy and resource production, industrial production, agricultural production and general research.

These proposals will ensure that the town is self-sufficient in energy whilst providing new jobs and dwellings for a growing population. In addition, extensive energy-conservation techniques will be employed in order to reduce the energy usage of housing, industry and transportation.

The Solar Communities are designed in response to the local energy, environmental and social conditions. The *family-group*, which consists of less than thirty dwellings and a communal building, is the basic unit from which the site plan has been generated. It expresses the notion of the *village as solar ecology*. The family group is derived from a

DESIGN TEAM

David Coleman
Ernst G Brodersen

Schulenburger Landstr 276
3000 Hannover
F R Germany

balance between social factors and the economies of scale of energy-producing and waste-processing equipment.

The energy production cycle for a family-group includes systems for wind generation, co-generation, biological waste processing and bio-fuel production, earth-heat extraction via heat pumps and various active and passive sun collection systems. These systems are located in or around each communal building. The common house also contains work shops and social/recreational facilities and represents a total of ten per cent of the built area of each family-group. In addition, all of the dwellings feature independent energy conservation, ventilation and passive solar systems.

JUDGES' COMMENTS

Finally, we would like to commend David E Coleman and Ernst G Brodersen for their farm-like scheme of clustered housing, fifty kilometres from Copenhagen. Passive solar energy in northern climates can be shown to play its part in a total package of energy retention which includes other forms of generation such as wind and water and the recycling of materials; a total ecological approach. This scheme illustrates most elegantly, by means of very pretty drawings, the possibility of including passive solar houses in such an arrangement.

TECHNICAL ASSESSORS' COMMENTS

A clustered housing scheme with the emphasis on ecological issues and utilising direct and sun space gains together with high levels of insulation. The systems involved are not illustrated.

The calculations were correct apart from the over estimation of internal gains.

LOCATION
Herfølge
Denmark

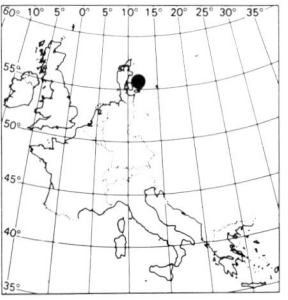

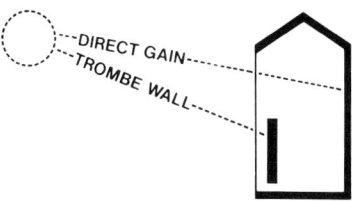

DIRECT GAIN
TROMBE WALL

TECHNICAL DATA

This data has been recalculated.
For explanation of data see page 16.

Latitude: 55° 25'N
Altitude: 10m
Data Point: Copenhagen

DWELLING DESCRIPTION (Typical Unit)

Heated Volume: 200 m³

APERTURE	A	B	C	D
System Type	DG	DG	DG	TW
Net Area m²	1.5	2.5	3.6	2.6
Glazing Layers	3	3	4	2
Night Insulation	Yes	Yes	Yes	Yes
τ	0.70	0.70	0.62	0.62
Comment				

Aperture/Heated Volume: 0.051 m²/m³
Primary Mass/
    Related Aperture: 222.1 Wh/m²°C
Remote Mass/
    Related Aperture: —Wh/m²°C
Air Change Rate: 0.75 ac/h
Building Loss Coeff.: 2.36 kWh/DD
                    : 98.5 W/°C

DWELLING PERFORMANCE (Typical Unit)

% Internal Gains: 46.0
% Auxiliary Heating: 39.2
% Useful Solar Gains: 14.8
Annual Solar Gains Fraction: 0.27
Figure of Merit: 0.004 kWh/DDm²
Useful Solar Gains/
    m² of Aperture: 105.4 kWh/m²yr
Min. Temp. without Heating: 4.4°C
Min. Outdoor Temperature: −6.5°C

ENERGY CHARACTERISTICS

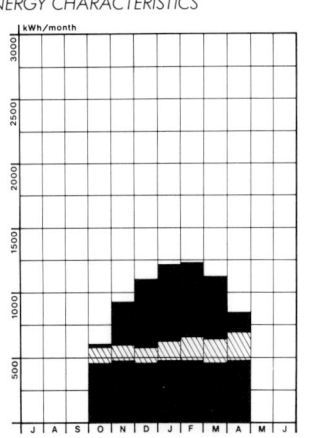

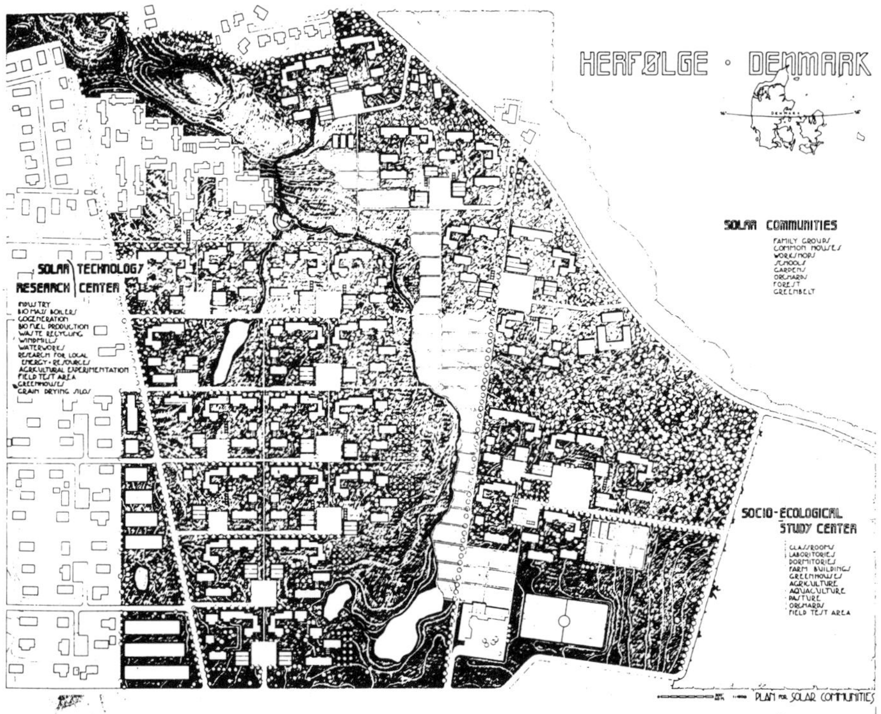

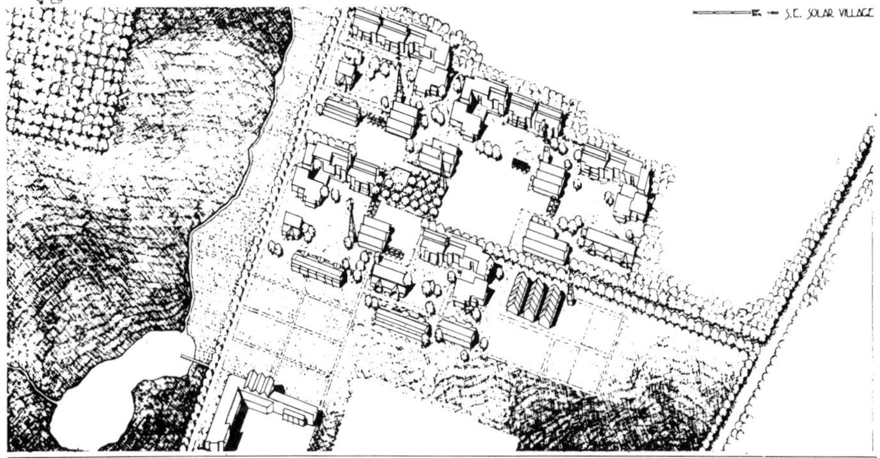

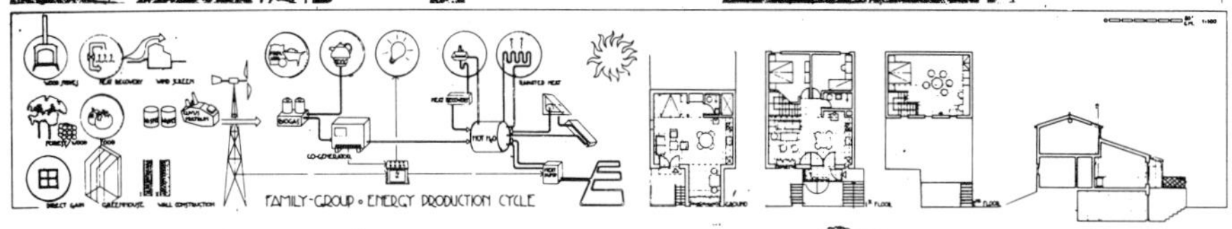

HERFØLGE · DENMARK

SOLAR COMMUNITIES

SOLAR TECHNOLOGY RESEARCH CENTER

SOCIO-ECOLOGICAL STUDY CENTER

PLAN FOR SOLAR COMMUNITIES

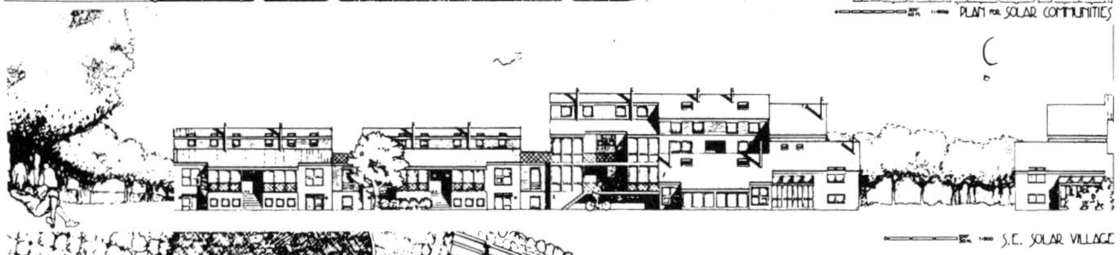

S.C. SOLAR VILLAGE

FAMILY-GROUP · ENERGY PRODUCTION CYCLE

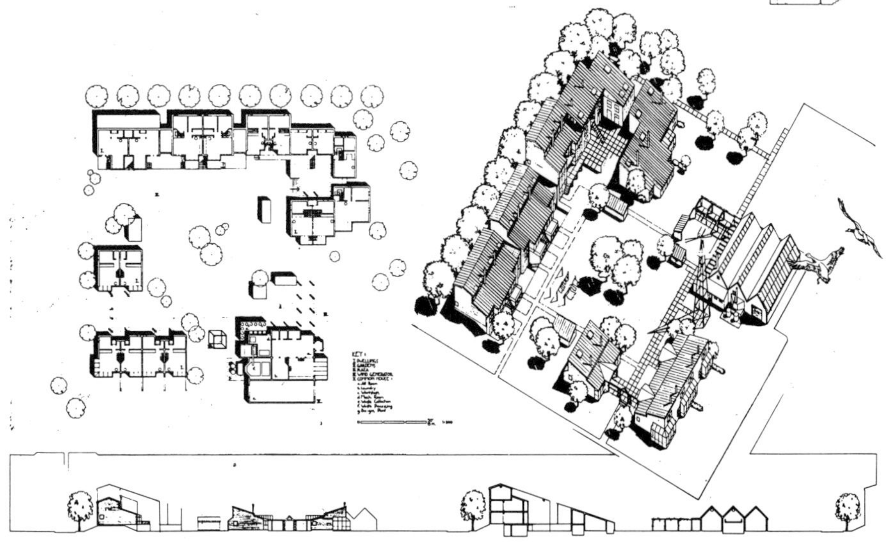

OTHER DETAILS OF INTEREST
CATEGORY A

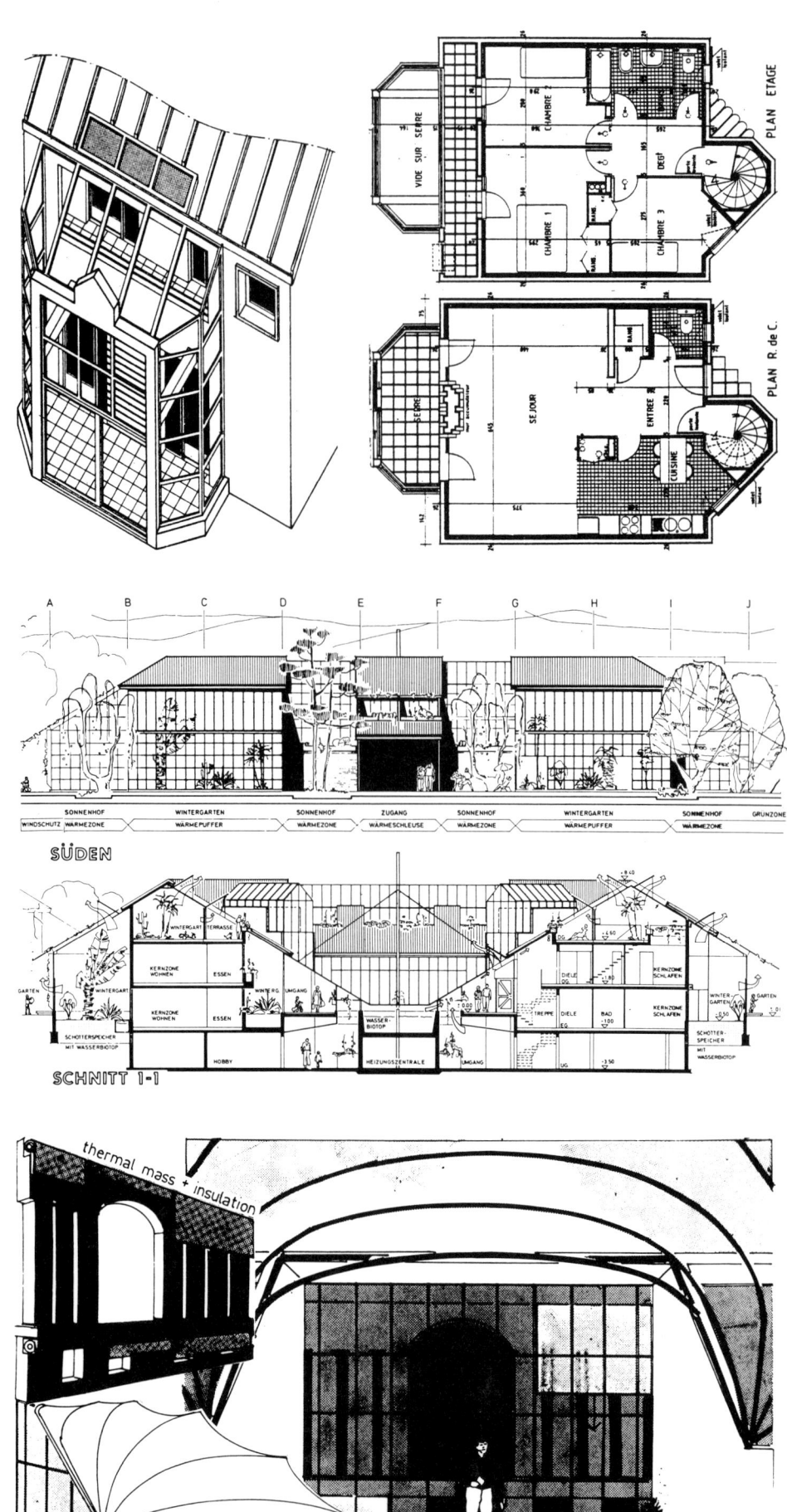

DESIGN TEAM

Richard Senpau Roca
Alain Eble
Gilles Vayssiere

48 Rue Richard Lenoir
75011 Paris
FRANCE

LOCATION
St Quentin en Yvelines,
France

Latitude 48°49'N Altitude 50m

DESIGN TEAM

Joachim Budack
Egon Karp
Elisabeth Gertz

Podbielskistrasse 99
3000 Hannover
F R Germany

LOCATION
Hannover,
West Germany

Latitude 52°27'N Altitude 53m

DESIGN TEAM

John Olie
Eric Vastert

Wilhelminastraat 18
6921 ZM Duiven
The Netherlands

LOCATION
Westervoort,
The Netherlands

Latitude 51°57'N Altitude 10m

OTHER DETAILS
OF INTEREST
CATEGORY A

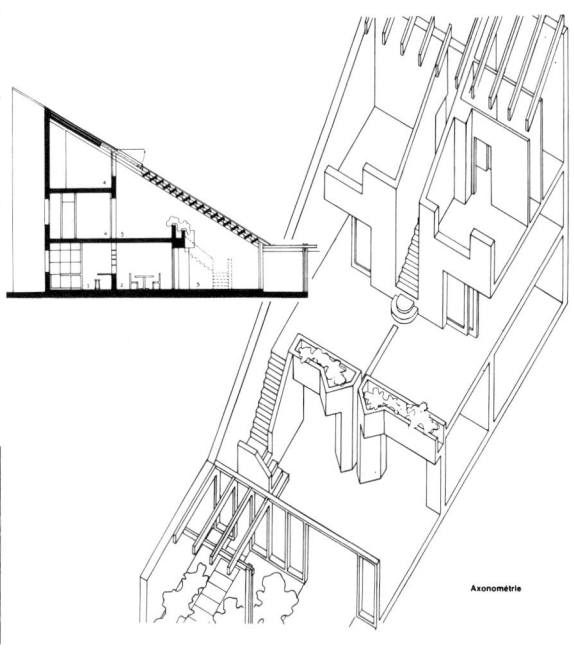

Axonométrie

DESIGN TEAM

Luc Schuiten
Pierre Gonay
Luc Deleuze
Stephane Vervaecke
Johan Nerman

21 Kaalheidestraat
1990 Overijse
Belgium

LOCATION
Namur,
Belgium

Latitude 50°45′N Altitude 100m

DESIGNER

Jean Bouillot

3 Rue de L'Agent Bailly
75009 Paris
France

LOCATION
Nuits Saint Georges,
France

Latitude 47°9′N Altitude   m

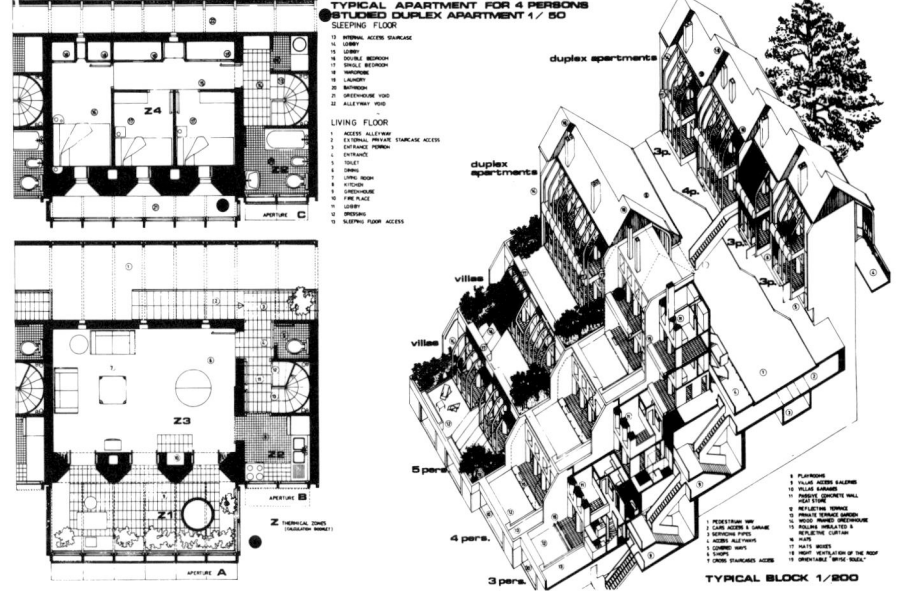

TYPICAL APARTMENT FOR 4 PERSONS
STUDIED DUPLEX APARTMENT 1/50
SLEEPING FLOOR

13 INTERNAL ACCESS STAIRCASE
14 LOBBY
15 LOBBY
16 DOUBLE BEDROOM
17 SINGLE BEDROOM
18 WARDROBE
19 LAUNDRY
20 BATHROOM
21 GREENHOUSE VOID
22 ALLEYWAY VOID

LIVING FLOOR

1 ACCESS ALLEYWAY
2 EXTERNAL PRIVATE STAIRCASE ACCESS
3 SEPARATION PYPES
4 ENTRANCE
5 ACCESS ALLEYWAYS
6 TOILET
7 COMBINED WAYS
8 KITCHEN
9 GREENHOUSE
10 FIRE PLACE
11 LOBBY
12 DRESSING
13 SLEEPING FLOOR ACCESS

Z THERMAL ZONES
(HAUSGARTEN BASKET)

duplex apartments
duplex apartments
villas
villas
5 pers.
4 pers.
3 pers.

APERTURE C
APERTURE B
APERTURE A

1 PLAYROOMS
2 VILLAS ACCESS GALERIES
3 VILLAS GARAGE
4 PASSIVE CONCRETE WALL HEAT STORE
5 REFLECTING TERRACE
6 PRIVATE TERRACE GARDEN
7 POLLIBE INSULATED & REFLECTIVE CURTAIN
8 FLATS
9 MAITS BOXES
10 NIGHT VENTILATION OF THE ROOF
11 ORIENTABLE "BRISE SOLEIL"

TYPICAL BLOCK 1/200

CATEGORY B
RETROFIT AND REHABILITATION
OF DWELLINGS

PRIZE WINNERS

FIRST PRIZE
CATEGORY B

12,000 Dutch Gilders

Many of the high rise blocks which were built in the 1950-1965 period are the result of a very one-sided approach — the main object of which was to use simple building techniques at a minimum cost. These buildings do not reflect the image of the town and through their lack of flexibility determine the lifestyle of their inhabitants. Furthermore, the original low building costs have now given rise to high maintenance and energy costs.

The three high rise blocks shown here are on the banks of the 'Niewemaas', at the edge of Rotterdam town centre, and are fairly typical examples of this type of building.

With our proposed additions the blocks of flats can be transformed into a technical and architectonic complex. These new additions have functions other than purely energy/technological ones. The buildings will no longer be an accumulation of small units but will become a complete building with a new identity. The dimensions of the partitions and interconnections of the various elements are determined by the chosen example but our principle can be adapted to other types of tower blocks.

The solar system is basically passive in operation. It is a central system (since it is connected to the existing central heating and ventilation plant) but it may be adjusted to suit in each dwelling. Our additions will solve the basic energy problems by:-

1. Improving the insulation of the building.
2. Creating a better distribution of heat.
3. Improving the heat storage capacity of the building.

The total system consists of:-

A second facade — constructed on the south facade and covering 60% of the surface areas. Glazing between the existing balconies forms a flat surface to the facade, which partly serves as a greenhouse and partly as a passive (thermosyphon) air collector. The warm air rises to the roof where a large warm air reservoir will be created. From here the air will be distributed to the cooler, northern zones via the former refuse lift shaft.

DESIGN TEAM

Helena Jiskrova
Zdenek Zavrel
Els Sonemans

Breitnerstraat 31a
3015 XA Rotterdam
The Netherlands

LOCATION
Rotterdam
The Netherlands

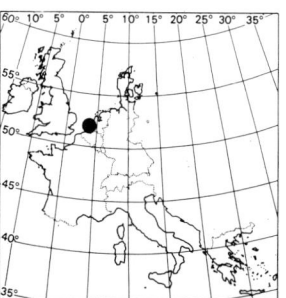

Alterations to the roof — the greater part of the roof is to be re-built in a light twin-walled construction which will function as a collector and as a buffer zone, like the roof of a traditional building. Covered water troughs roughly 250mm deep, through which hot air will be blown are to be placed on the roof. The heat stored in this way will later be given up to cooler air. Air ducts, fans and other technical plant are also situated here — as is some of the storage space which was formerly located on the first floor. There is also a central area on the roof allocated for the use of tenants as, say, a crèche linked to the roof terraces.

Other additions — these occur at the front of the block and have been provided more for architectonic than for energy-saving reasons: they release space on the first floor for accommodation which can then be linked to the surroundings. There is also the possibility of providing a bridge from the mezzanine level to the Maasboulevard. The rebuilding of the car parking area will result in better links with the landscape, protection of the lower part of the building and more space. Greenhouses in front of each block of flats can be used for cultivation during the winter months. The heat collected in these will be distributed via the new circuit.

For the calculations a four-roomed central dwelling has been chosen — a typical, if rather larger than usual, example. Its characteristic feature is the wide living room with an inset balcony offering panoramic views over the city and the Niewemaas. To the rear of the living room is a central service zone. The bedrooms, kitchen and a small loggia are located on the northern side. Hot air is blown into the northern side of this dwelling in winter and is extracted via the existing ductwork in the central zone. A portion of the facade is now being used for air collection purposes whilst the glazing of the second facade, near the balcony, can be adjusted to take climatic changes into account. The second facade will also attenuate the noise from the very busy Maasboulevard.

category **B** country **NETHERLANDS** sector **WEST** latitude **51°54'**

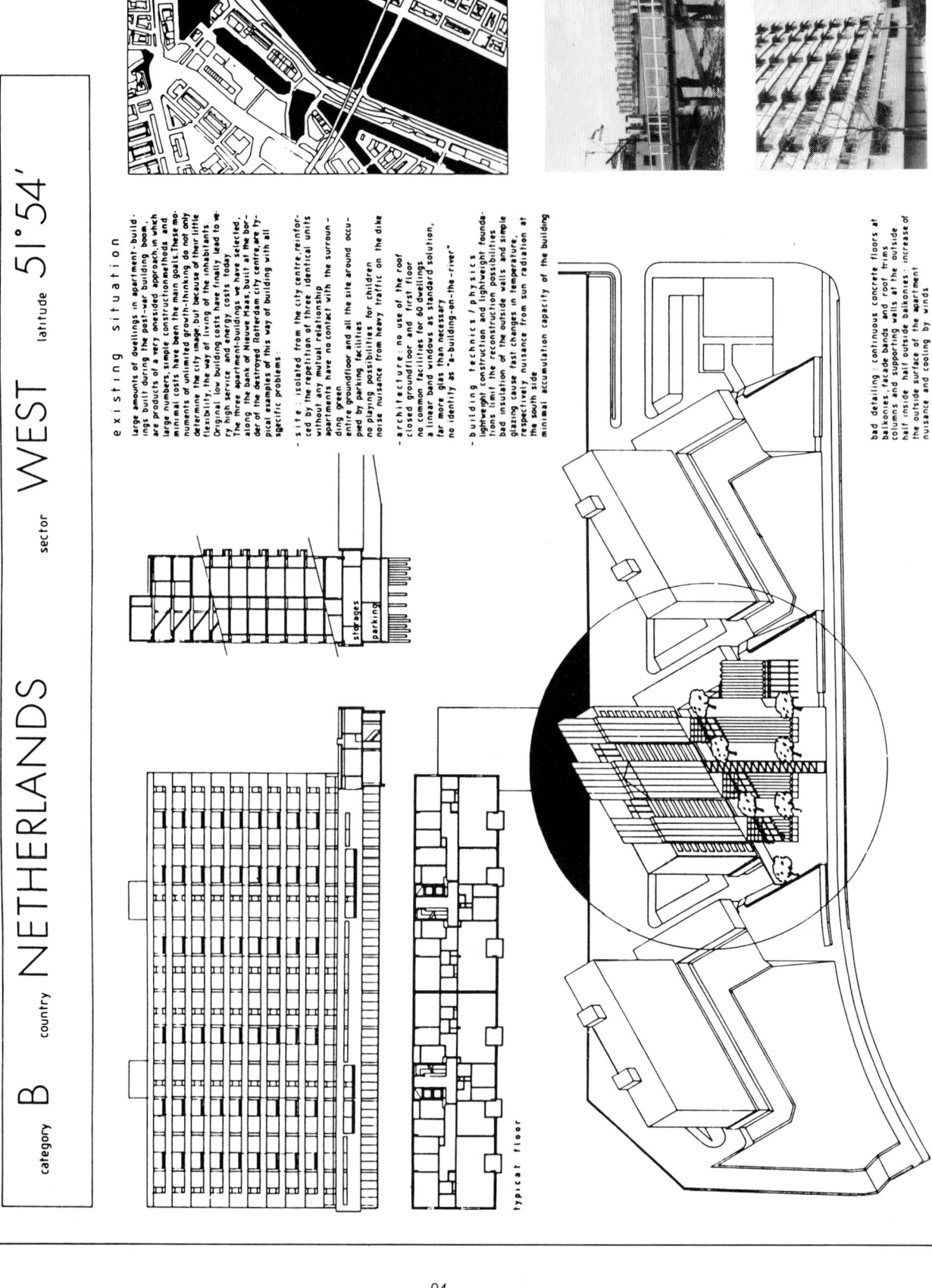

rotterdam

existing situation

large amounts of dwellings in apartment-buildings built during the post-war building boom, are products of a very onesided approach, in which large numbers, simple constructionmethods and minimal costs have been the main goals. These monuments of unlimited growth-thinking do not only determine the city image, but because of their little flexibility, the way of living of the inhabitants. Original low building costs have finally lead to very high service and energy costs today

The three apartment-buildings we have selected, along the bank of Nieuwe Maas, built at the border of the destroyed Rotterdam city centre, are typical examples of this way of building with all specific problems:

- **site** : isolated from the city centre, reinforced by the repetition of three identical units without any mutual relationship. the surrounding green the surrounding green entire groundfloor and all the site around occupied by parking facilities no playing possibilities for children noise nuisance from heavy traffic on the dike

- **architecture** : no use of the roof closed groundfloor and first floor no common facilities for 60 dwellings a linear band windows as standard solution, far more glas than necessary no identity as "a-building-on-the-river"

- **building technics / physics** lightweight construction and lightweight foundations limit the reconstruction possibilities bad insulation of the outside walls and simple glazing cause fast changes in temperature, respectively nuisance from sun radiation at the south side minimal accumulation capacity of the building

bad detailing : continuous concrete floors at balkonies, facade bands and roof trims columns and supporting walls at the outside half inside half outside balkonies : increase of the outside surface of the apartment nuisance and cooling by winds

storages

parking

typical floor

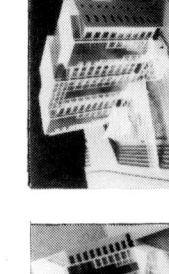
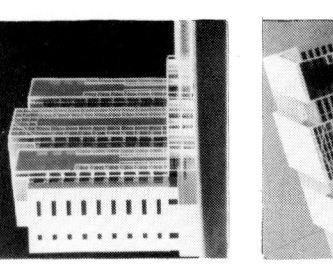
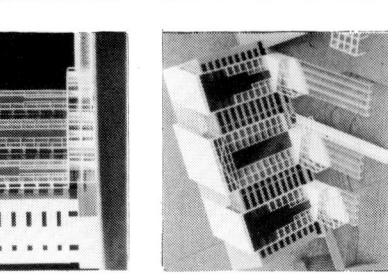

proposal

By means of new additions the apartment-building will be transformed into an-other technical and architectural entity. All newly added elements will get besides theirs energetical functions also clear use-functions and/or a role in the architecture. The image of an appartment building as a compilation of small units is changed into one of a building-as-an-entity, with a new identity. The measures, partitions and mutual connections of the different elements have been determined strongly by this chosen example, but the principple is can very well be adapted to other types of apartment-buildings.

The designed solar system functions mainly as a passive one, only for the circulation of warm air at the north side a fan will be built in. The system adjoined to the existing hand as of central heating and ventilation and on the other hand individually per apartment. The part which belongs to the apartment can be operated from there.

Technically this proposal aims at solving basic energetic problems as far as possible within the lightweight structure.

1/ improvement of the insulation by means of:
- reduction of the cooled outside surface
- addition of light insulation (fixed and mobil)
- double glazing
- elimination of cold transmission
- protection of the facade against cooling by winds

2/ beter distribution of the collected solar heat by means of an air circuit, whis has to carry off the superfluous heat from the south facade to an accumulator and/or cooler spaces. During hot weather the circuit can be used for cooling ventilation. The circuit is coupled on the roof, to the existing ventilat system by means of a heat exchanger.

3/ improvement of the accumulating capacity of the building by means of watercontainers with little depth in the added roof floor, according to the carrying capacity of the roof. Addition of more mass for the accumulation of warmth is impossible, because of the sparingly calculated platfoundations. Hot air is used trough this water mass, which slows down the fluctuation of temperature.

The total system consists of:
- a second facade, mounted to the south side over ±60% surface, in three strips. Glazing between the existing balkonies forms a flat zone functioning partly as a protecting green-house, resp glazed verandah, and partly as an air collector with passive (thermosyphon) functioning. The hot air rises up to the roof floor; from there the warm air is distributed to the cooler spaces on north side via the shaft of the unused dustbin elevator

- a roof floor, built up in lightweight double wall construction; this space is functioning as a collector as well as warmth-buffer, just like in traditional buildings. In the roof floor covered containers have been placed with depth of aprox. 15 cm, the warm air is blown through these. The roof floor contains more over air ducts, fans, and possible other installations (sun boilers), and a part of first floor storages. Besides this technical equipment could be in the middle part a room for common use of inhabitants placed, such as for instance a creche, in connection to roof terraces.

- an annexe, in the area in front of the building; this has more an architectural than an energetical function. Living can be extended down to the first floor; a connection with the green area in front of the building possible from the high entrance-passage hall to the Maasboulevard. Building over the parking street brings extra space; connection to the green an protection of this part of the building. Greenhouses in this area provide an additional green; also in the wintertime extra profit in heat will be as well be carried off by the air circuit

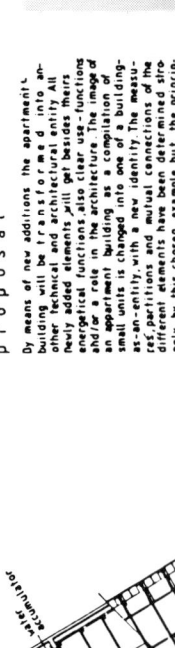

south facade

N

calculated residence

roof floor
residential floor

0 5 10 15 20 25M

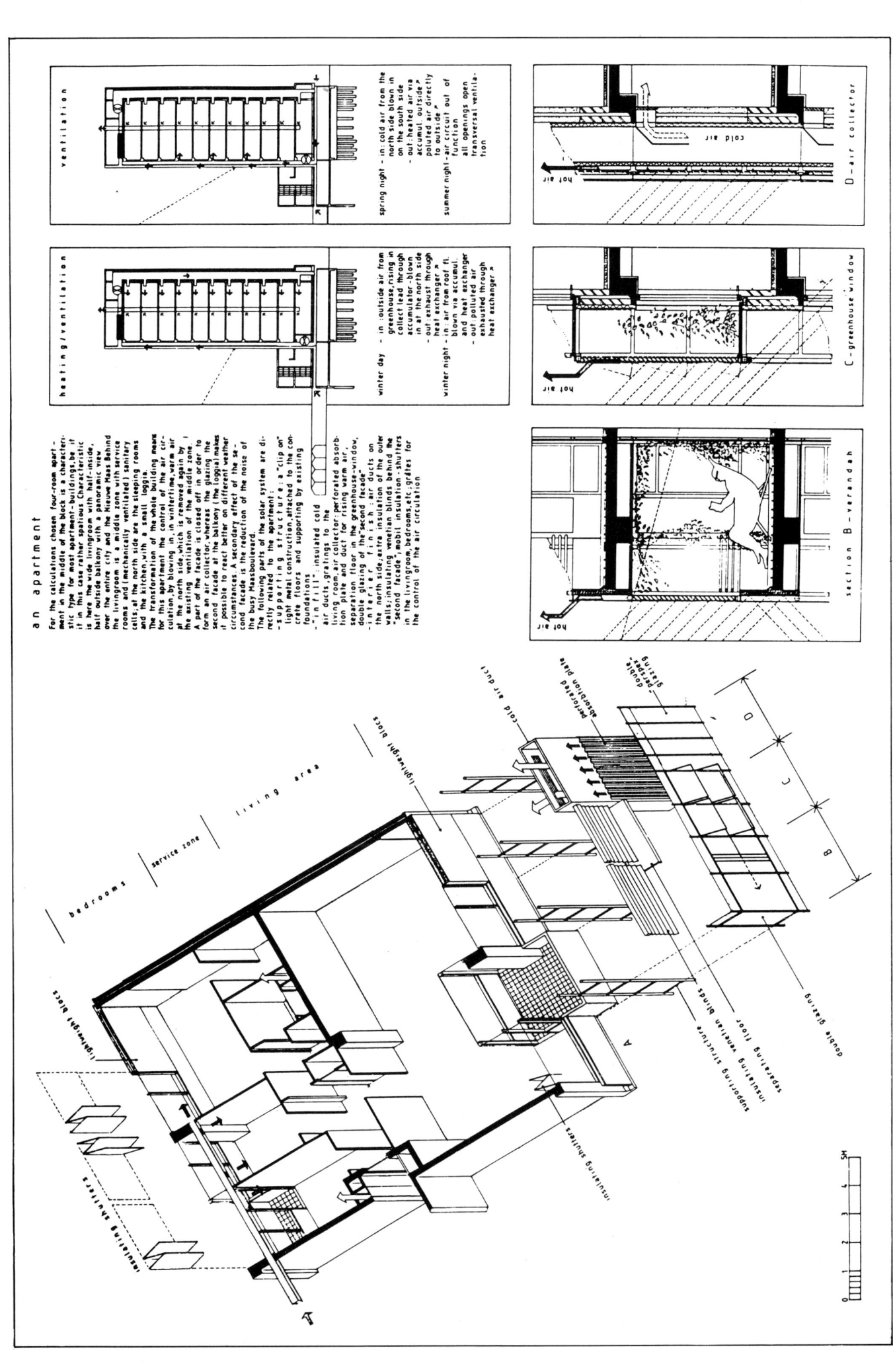

an apartment

For the calculations chosen four-room apartment in the middle of the block is a characteristic type for most apartment-buildings, be it in this case rather spacious. Characteristic is here the sub living room with half-inside, half outside balcony with a panoramic view over the entire city and the Nieuwe Maas. Behind the livingroom is a middle zone with service rooms and (mechanically ventilated) sanitary cells, at the north side are the sleeping rooms and the kitchen, with a small loggia.

The transformation of the whole building means for this apartment the control of the air circulation, by blowing in, in wintertime warm air at the north side, which is removed again by the existing ventilation of the middle zone.

A part of the facade is closed off in order to form an air collector, whereas the glazing the second facade at the balcony (the loggia) makes it possible to react better on different weather circumstances. A secondary effect of the second facade is the reduction of the noise of the busy Maasboulevard.

The following parts of the solar system are directly related to the apartment:
- supporting structure: a "clip on" light metal construction, attached to the concrete floors and supporting by existing foundations
- "in fill": insulated cold air ducts, gratings to the living room, air collector: perforated absorbtion plate and duct for rising warm air, separation floor of the greenhouse-window, double glazing of the "second facade"
- interior finish: air ducts on the north side; extra insulation of the outer walls; insulating venetian blinds behind the "second facade", mobil insulation-shutters in the livingroom, bedrooms, etc; grates for the control of the air circulation

ventilation

spring night - in : cold air from the north side blown in on the south side
- out: heated air via accumul. outside ↗
- poluted air directly to outside ↗

summer night - air circuit out of function; all openings open transversal ventilation

heating/ventilation

winter day - in : outside air from greenhouse, rising in collect lead through accumulator - blown in at the north side
- out: exhaust through heat exchanger ↗

winter night - in : air from roof fl. blown via accumul. and heat exchanger
- out: poluted air exhausted through heat exchanger ↗

D - air collector

C - greenhouse window

section B - verandeh

bedrooms | service zone | living area

cold air duct

double glazing

perforated absorbtion plate

supporting structure

existing blocs

insulating shutters

lightweight blocs

air ducts, gratings to the

0 1 2 3 4 5M

JUDGES' COMMENTS

Both on technical and aesthetic grounds we thought that Helena Jiskrova and Zdenek Zavrel were clear winners of the First prize of 12,000 Dutch Gilders. Their scheme for the transformation of a ten storey slab block in Rotterdam uses a twin wall polyskin to pre-heat fresh air and to achieve a high degree of insulation. They use this skin in conjunction with an added atrium entrance and foothills of greenhouses to transform the 1960's block from a kind of gridded universality to one that on the inside provides the flats with an additional protective layer of greenhouse and balcony and, on the outside, re-organises the composition of the facade to read as an entity and to count in the composition of the city and riverscape. It was not hard to choose a winner which dealt so thoroughly and gracefully with the knotty problem offered by the post-war slab block.

TECHNICAL ASSESSORS' COMMENTS

By the addition of a twin-wall plastic skin to the facade, this rehabilitation of a large apartment block incorporates a fresh air preheating system. This is an efficient scheme which appears to be practicable.

Some minor errors were discovered in the calculations.

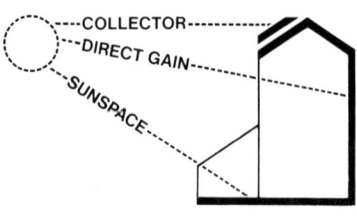

TECHNICAL DATA

This data has been recalculated.
For explanation of data see page 16.

Latitude: 51° 54'N
Altitude: 3 m
Data Point: De Bilt

DWELLING DESCRIPTION (Typical Unit)
Heated Volume: 408 m³

APERTURE	A	B	C	D
System Type	DG	SS	SS	C
Net Area m²	4.0	6.2	5.5	4.8
Glazing Layers	2	3	3	2
Night Insulation	Yes	Yes	Yes	
τ	0.40	0.50	0.50	0.50
Comment	SE +O or SW +O	SE +O or SW +O	SE +O or SW +O	SE +O or SW +O

Aperture/Heated Volume: 0.043 m²/m³
Primary Mass/
   Related Aperture: 110.0 Wh/m²°C
Remote Mass/
   Related Aperture: 130.0 Wh/m²°C
Air Change Rate: 0.35 ac/h m.v.
Building Loss Coeff.: 3.00 kWh/DD
         : 127.00 W/°C

DWELLING PERFORMANCE (Typical Unit)
% Internal Gains: 45.0
% Auxiliary Heating: 35.0
% Useful Solar Gains: 20.0
Annual Solar Gains Fraction: 0.37
Figure of Merit: 0.0023 kWh/DDm²
Useful Solar Gains/
   m² of Aperture: 82.0 kWh/m²yr
Min. Temp. without Heating: 5.7°C
Min. Outdoor Temperature: −9.3°C

ENERGY CHARACTERISTICS

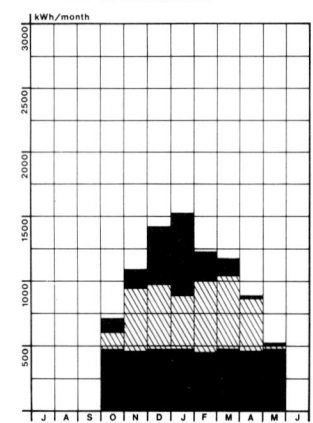

Existing building.

SECOND PRIZE
CATEGORY B

22,000 French Francs

From Lille's political and geographical viewpoint, this building, which is the subject of our rehabilitation proposals, poses problems of such a nature that no one feels able to find a satisfactory solution.

This masterpiece was 'bequeathed to the citizens of Lille at great expense' by the philanthropist, Charles Rameau, at the end of the nineteenth century. This ageing 'palace' is expensive to maintain, is underused and is rather a cumbersome curio in this residential suburb.

Three major aims influenced our project:-

— to preserve the architecture of the building's conservatory

— to demonstrate the potential for the re-conversion of this type of architecture which represents the era of great metal constructions

— to demonstrate clearly the possible uses of thermal resources linked with the use of fenestration.

DESIGN TEAM

Michel H Ripoll
Hubert Maes
Elisabeth Romand-Monnier
Olivier Ronat

58 rue de Lattre de Tassigny
59290 Wasequehal
France

LOCATION
Lille
France

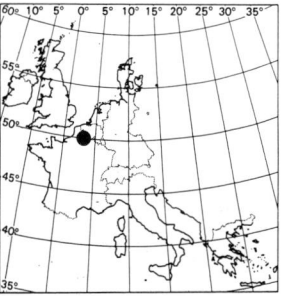

Our proposals are based upon three main criteria:

— to make the maximum use of the bioclimatic potential of this construction.

— to create a structured residential unit which opens up the building to its immediate surroundings.

— to acquire an architectural terminology that has the scope for confronting the 'neo classical mauresque' eclecticism of this old horticultural temple.

In our endeavour to maximise distribution of the passive solar gain, we have formed a plan for the distribution and organisation of duplex residences with a two directional orientation which will amalgamate bioclimatic qualities and also reduce the heating requirement of each dwelling.

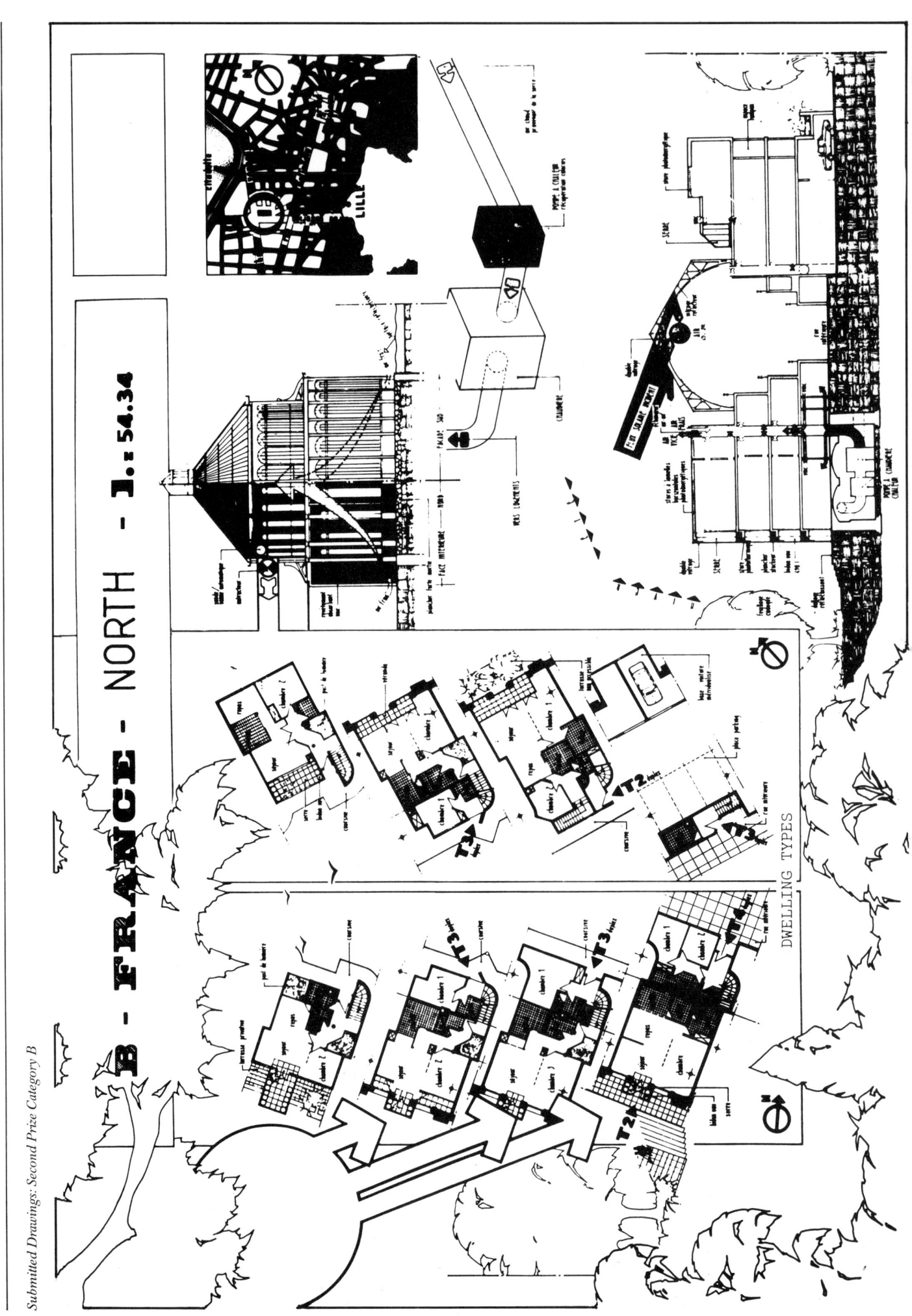

B - FRANCE - NORTH - 1 : 54.34

DWELLING TYPES

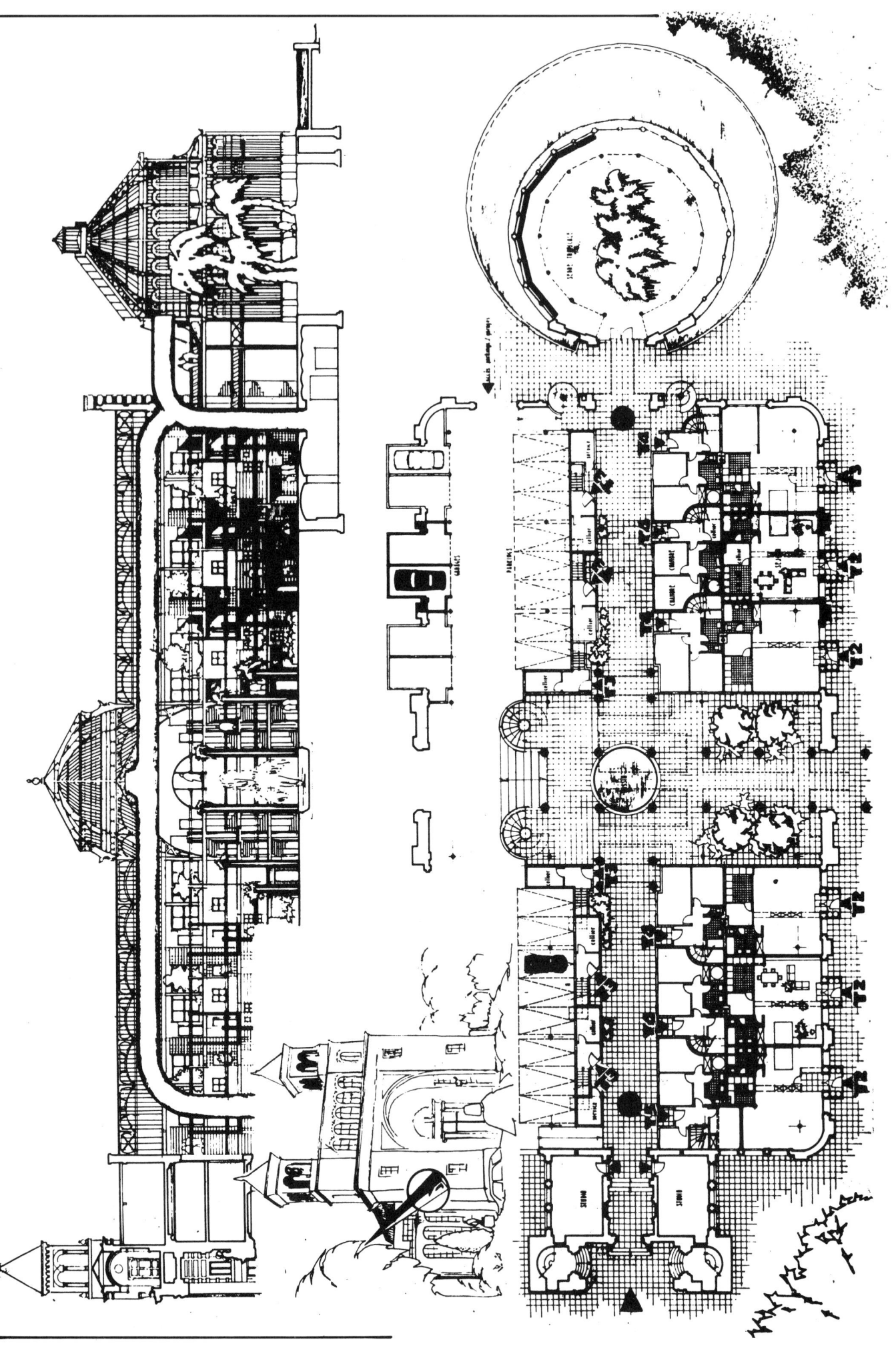

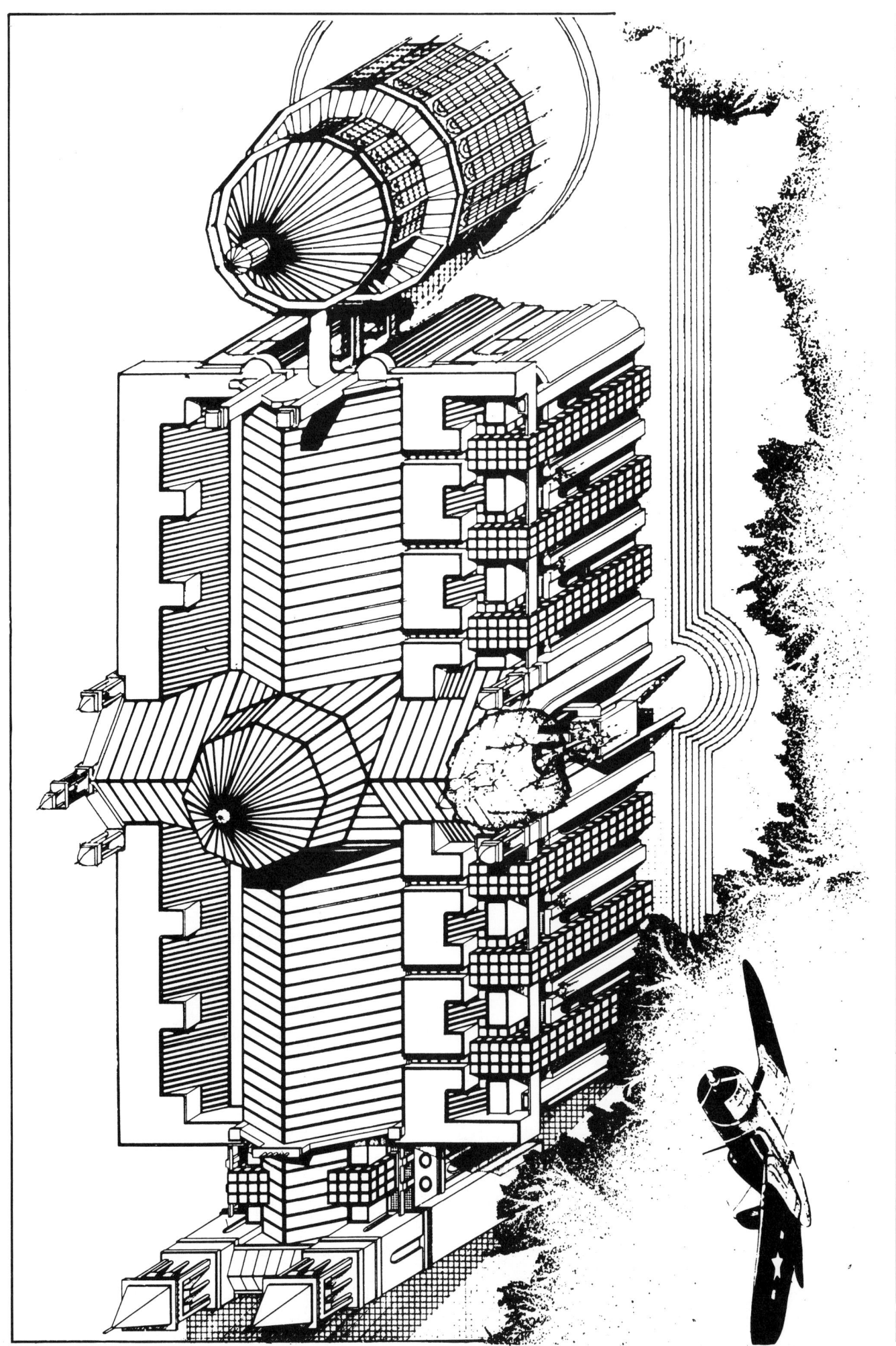

JUDGES' COMMENTS

The Second prize of 22,000 French Francs goes to Michel H Ripoll, Hubert Maes, Elisabeth Romand-Monnier and Olivier Ronat for the best of the schemes which used housing as a means to restore historic buildings. The 85 year old Palais Rameau glasshouse in Lille is adapted with great energy to serve as a large number of solar heated houses and apartments. After working out the plans of the upper levels (which are unclearly shown on the first sheet), we were able to see the great clarity of the main section and plan, and most especially the skilful handling of the exterior of the building. The new elements that contribute to solar heating are vigorously combined in a balanced way with the existing doorways, buttresses, cornice towers and base: they enhance the existing building and at no point detract from it by the polite "in keepingness" that is more common today. This is reclamation without pastiche.

TECHNICAL ASSESSORS' COMMENTS

This is a complex scheme and some features have not been taken into account in the calculations. Both the northern and southern units make use of direct and sunspace gains. The scheme also makes use of a glazed atrium and a large existing glass house to pre-heat the ventilation air. However, the technical descriptions of the air handling systems are inadequate.

The entrant had claimed 82% solar contribution but the ventilation heat losses had been calculated for only one dwelling.

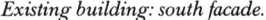

TECHNICAL DATA

This data has been recalculated.
For explanation of data see page 16.

Latitude: 50° 34'N
Altitude: 44 m
Data Point: Lille

DWELLING DESCRIPTION (Typical Unit)
Heated Volume: 167 m³

APERTURE	A	B	C	D
System Type	DG	SS	WW	
Net Area m²	5.0	2.5	2.5	
Glazing Layers	1	1	2	
Night Insulation	Yes	Yes	Yes	
τ	0.40	0.40	0.40	
Comment	O	O	O	

Aperture/Heated Volume: 0.06 m²/m³
Primary Mass/
   Related Aperture: 1740.0 Wh/m²°C
Remote Mass/
   Related Aperture: —Wh/m²°C
Air Change Rate: 0.75 ac/h
Building Loss Coeff.: 2.48 kWh/DD
  : 103.25 W/°C

DWELLING PERFORMANCE (Typical Unit)
% Internal Gains: 53.0
% Auxiliary Heating: 29.0
% Useful Solar Gains: 18.0
Annual Solar Gains Fraction: 0.38
Figure of Merit: 0.004 kWh/DDm²
Useful Solar Gains/
   m² of Aperture: 110.8 kWh/m²yr
Min. Temp. without Heating: 8.5°C
Min. Outdoor Temperature: —7.6°C

ENERGY CHARACTERISTICS

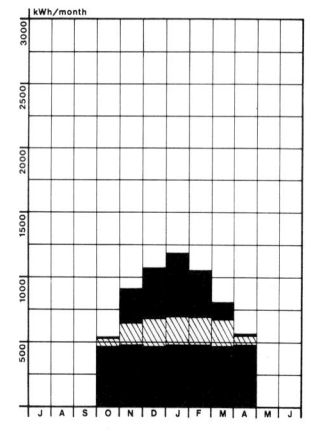

Existing building: south facade.

Most cities in Europe are surrounded by dull residential housing. These grey zones can be one result of bad planning with which one is reluctant to deal. One is tempted to be concerned with new development projects, but energy wastage also ought to encourage an ecological reassessment. Instead of widening the distance between town and country, the interdependency between the two could supplement the understanding of the respective lifestyles. Even if the introduction of, say, animal husbandry and kitchen gardens does not lead to a self-sufficient suburb it will, at least, increase the understanding of our natural origins.

The following positive features of our chosen site should be mentioned. Generally the buildings are of sound construction and materials. The area is ideally situated with respect to public transport (trains and buses) and is also well within cycling distance to the community services such as schools and libraries. A large proportion of the buildings in this area are sound and usable but an improvement of the energy performance of these 1950's houses need not lead to the poorly designed concrete buildings so common today.

This typical fifties multi-storey housing, situated on a north facing slope, is well suited for passive solar heating due to the orientation of the houses — which are of a yellow brick, 300mm non-insulated cavity wall construction. The saddleback roofs are clad with black asbestos cement slates and are pitched at twenty five degrees. The buildings are sound and well ventilated.

The site vegetation consists of a coniferous shelter belt to the north and deciduous trees giving shade in front of large glazed areas. The deciduous trees are generally of the fruit, berry or nut-bearing type. The site vegetation helps to counteract the formation of turbulent winds.

External insulation will be applied to utilize the heat storage capabilities of the

DESIGN TEAM

Ulla Falck
Dorthe Henriksen
Anne Marie Nielsen

Finsensvej 118
2000 Kobenhavn F
Denmark

existing brick and concrete. The existing window areas are retained for economic and ecological reasons. On the north facade the existing sealed double glazing and internal shutters are retained. On the south facade the existing balconies are enlarged to conservatories incorporating insulating curtains. The other south facing windows are to be fitted with sealed triple glazing units in order to improve the effect of the internal shutters and thereby improve the operation of the passive solar heating system. In addition to the collection of direct solar radiation, the area under the windows is utilized as a solar air collector. About 50% of south facing roof area is taken up with solar collectors which heat the north facing rooms and which acts as the fresh air intake for the building. The solar collector's surplus heat is stored in the stairwell. Existing floor plans of the flats are to be improved with regard to function, energy and season so that everybody will have the choice of using either north facing or south facing rooms. The existing central oil-fired boiler house will give supplementary heat and hot water, but conversion to a renewable energy source such as hydrogen, windpower or earth heat will be possible if desired. Our suggested passive solar heating system can, in the future, be enlarged with solar collectors for hot water in the summer and rock bed storage in the cellar etc.

Passive solar architecture should not be considered as the newest gimmick in our engineering/technical/computer world but is, after all, only a question of the application of common sense and sound building materials to ecological issues. There has always been — long before there were any engineers and architects — an ecological style of building, but the rapid rise in our technological capabilities over the last century has meant that we have tended to lose our roots and have come to evaluate dwellings in purely financial terms.

LOCATION
Kildeparken
Denmark

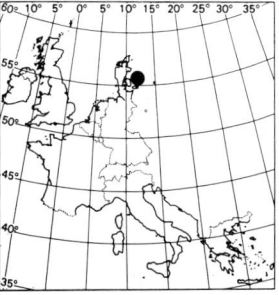

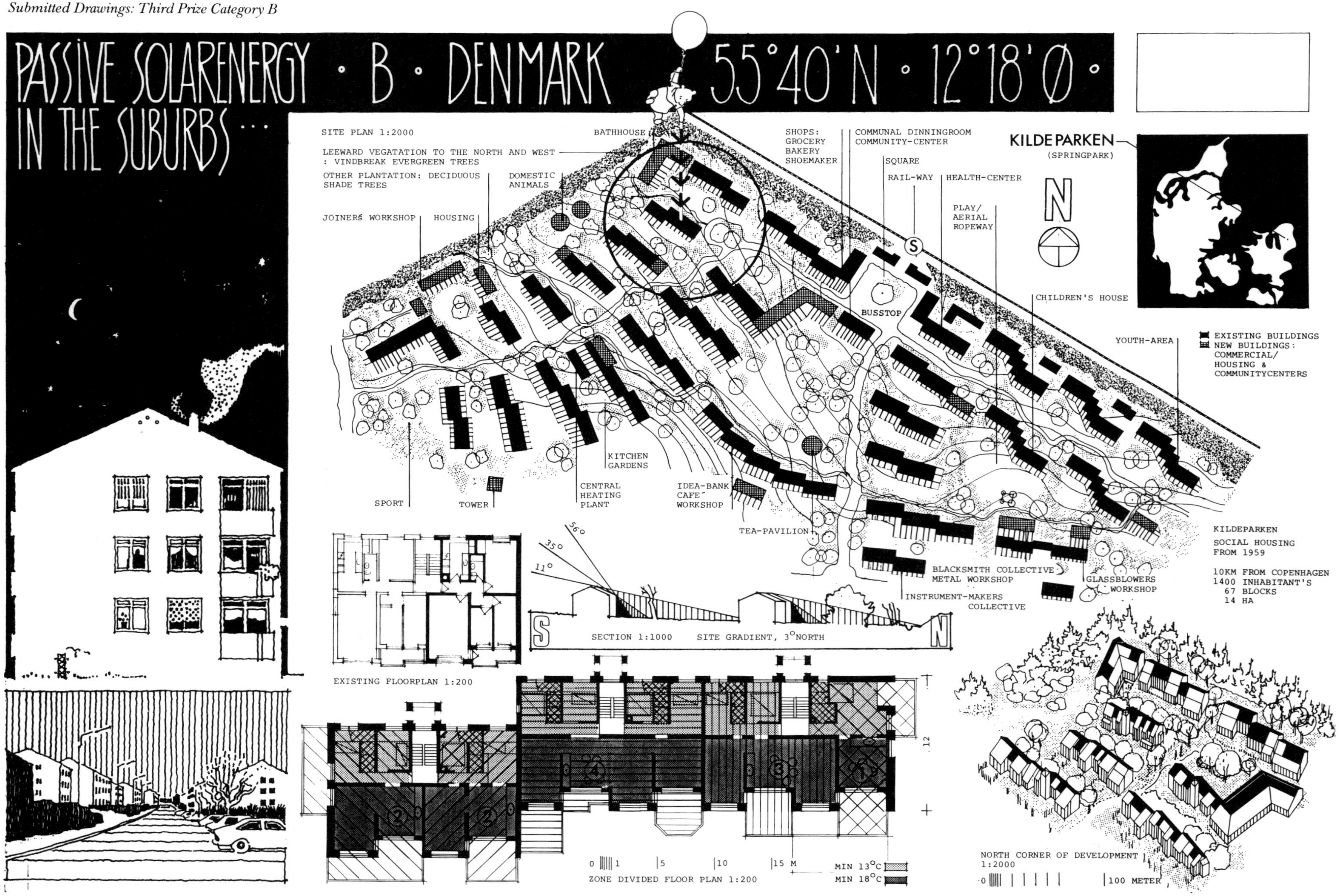
PASSIVE SOLARENERGY • B • DENMARK 55°40'N • 12°18'Ø •
IN THE SUBURBS...
SITE PLAN 1:2000
LEEWARD VEGATATION TO THE NORTH AND WEST : VINDBREAK EVERGREEN TREES
OTHER PLANTATION: DECIDUOUS SHADE TREES
DOMESTIC ANIMALS
JOINERS WORKSHOP
HOUSING
BATHHOUSE
SHOPS: GROCERY BAKERY SHOEMAKER
COMMUNAL DINNINGROOM COMMUNITY-CENTER
SQUARE
RAIL-WAY
HEALTH-CENTER
PLAY/ AERIAL ROPEWAY
BUSSTOP
CHILDREN'S HOUSE
YOUTH-AREA
KILDEPARKEN
(SPRINGPARK)
N
EXISTING BUILDINGS
NEW BUILDINGS: COMMERCIAL/ HOUSING & COMMUNITYCENTERS
SPORT
TOWER
KITCHEN GARDENS
CENTRAL HEATING PLANT
IDEA-BANK CAFE´ WORKSHOP
TEA-PAVILION
BLACKSMITH COLLECTIVE METAL WORKSHOP
INSTRUMENT-MAKERS COLLECTIVE
GLASSBLOWERS WORKSHOP
KILDEPARKEN
SOCIAL HOUSING FROM 1959
10KM FROM COPENHAGEN
1400 INHABITANT'S
67 BLOCKS
14 HA
56°
35°
11°
S
SECTION 1:1000 SITE GRADIENT, 3°NORTH
N
EXISTING FLOORPLAN 1:200
0 1 5 10 15 M
ZONE DIVIDED FLOOR PLAN 1:200
MIN 13°C
MIN 18°C
12
NORTH CORNER OF DEVELOPMENT 1:2000
0 100 METER

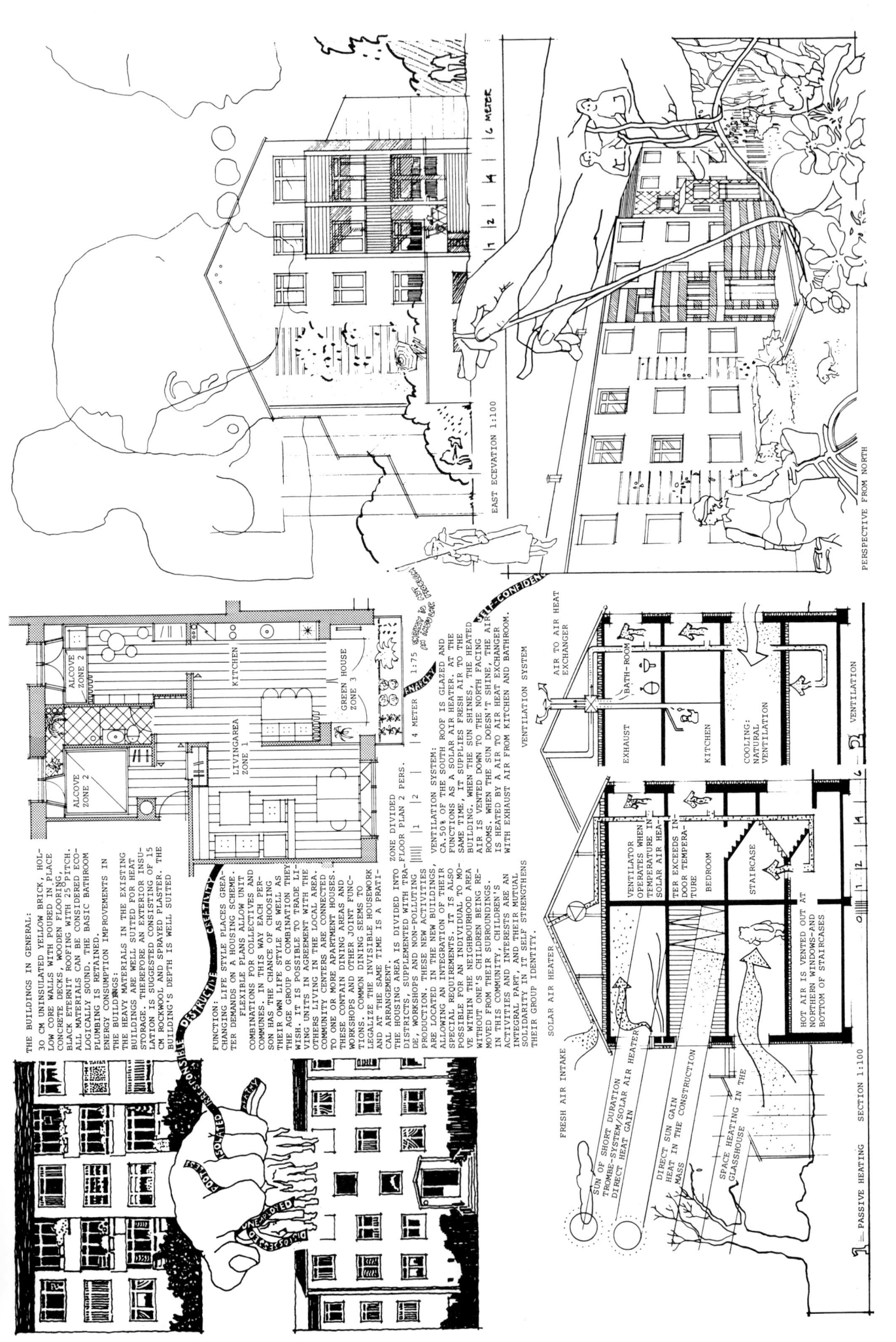

THE BUILDINGS IN GENERAL:
30 CM UNINSULATED YELLOW BRICK, HOL-
LOW CORE WALLS WITH POURED IN PLACE
CONCRETE DECKS, WOODEN FLOORING.
BLACK ETERNIT ROOFING WITH 25° PITCH.
ALL MATERIALS CAN BE CONSIDERED ECO-
LOGICALLY SOUND. THE BASIC BATHROOM
PLUMBING IS RETAINED.
ENERGY CONSUMPTION IMPROVEMENTS IN
THE BUILDINGS:
THE HEAVY MATERIALS IN THE EXISTING
BUILDINGS ARE WELL SUITED FOR HEAT
STORAGE. THEREFORE AN EXTERIOR INSU-
LATION IS SUGGESTED CONSISTING OF 15
CM ROCKWOOL AND SPRAYED PLASTER. THE
BUILDING'S DEPTH IS WELL SUITED

FUNCTION: LIFE STYLE PLACES GREA-
TER DEMANDS ON A HOUSING SCHEME.
FLEXIBLE PLANS ALLOW UNIT
COMBINATIONS FOR COLLECTIVES AND
COMMUNES. IN THIS WAY EACH PER-
SON HAS THE CHANCE OF CHOOSING
THEIR OWN LIFE STYLE AS WELL AS
THE AGE GROUP OR COMBINATION THEY
WISH. IT IS POSSIBLE TO TRADE LI-
VING UNITS IN AGREEMENT WITH THE
OTHERS LIVING IN THE LOCAL AREA.
COMMUNITY CENTERS ARE CONNECTED
TO ONE OR MORE APARTMENT HOUSES.
THESE CONTAIN DINING AREAS AND
WORKSHOPS AND OTHER JOINT FUNC-
TIONS. COMMON DINING SEEMS TO
LEGALIZE THE INVISIBLE HOUSEWORK
AND AT THE SAME TIME IS A PRAI-
CE ARRANGEMENT.
THE HOUSING AREA IS DIVIDED INTO
DISTRICTS, SUPPLEMENTED WITH TRA-
DE WORKSHOPS AND NON-POLLUTING
PRODUCTION. THESE NEW ACTIVITIES
ARE LOCATED IN THE NEW BUILDINGS,
ALLOWING AN INTEGRATION OF THEIR
SPECIAL REQUIREMENTS. IT IS ALSO
POSSIBLE FOR AN INDIVIDUAL TO MO-
VE WITHIN THE NEIGHBOURHOOD AREA
WITHOUT ONE'S CHILDREN BEING RE-
MOVED FROM THEIR SURROUNDINGS.
IN THIS COMMUNITY, CHILDREN'S
ACTIVITIES AND INTERESTS ARE AN
INTEGRAL PART, AND THEIR MUTUAL
SOLIDARITY IN IT SELF STRENGTHENS
THEIR GROUP IDENTITY.

ALCOVE ZONE 2
ALCOVE ZONE 2
KITCHEN
LIVINGAREA ZONE 1
GREEN HOUSE ZONE 3

FLOOR PLAN 2 PERS.
ZONE DIVIDED

VENTILATION SYSTEM:
CA. 50% OF THE SOUTH ROOF IS GLAZED AND
FUNCTIONS AS A SOLAR AIR HEATER. AT THE
SAME TIME, IT SUPPLIES FRESH AIR TO THE
BUILDING. WHEN THE SUN SHINES, THE HEATED
AIR IS VENTED DOWN TO THE NORTH FACING
ROOMS. WHEN THE SUN DOESN'T SHINE, THE AIR
IS HEATED BY A AIR TO AIR HEAT EXCHANGER
WITH EXHAUST AIR FROM KITCHEN AND BATHROOM.

EAST ELEVATION 1:100

PERSPECTIVE FROM NORTH

FRESH AIR INTAKE
SOLAR AIR HEATER
SUN OF SHORT DURATION
TROMBE-SYSTEM/SOLAR AIR HEATER
DIRECT HEAT GAIN
DIRECT SUN GAIN HEAT IN THE CONSTRUCTION
SPACE HEATING IN THE GLASSHOUSE
HOT AIR IS VENTED OUT AT NORTHERN WINDOWS AND BOTTOM OF STAIRCASES
VENTILATOR OPERATES WHEN TEMPERATURE IN SOLAR AIR HEA-TER EXCEEDS IN-DOOR TEMPERA-TURE
BEDROOM
STAIRCASE
PASSIVE HEATING   SECTION 1:100

AIR TO AIR HEAT EXCHANGER
EXHAUST
BATH-ROOM
KITCHEN
COOLING: NATURAL VENTILATION
VENTILATION SYSTEM
VENTILATION

ENERGY 1:75
METER

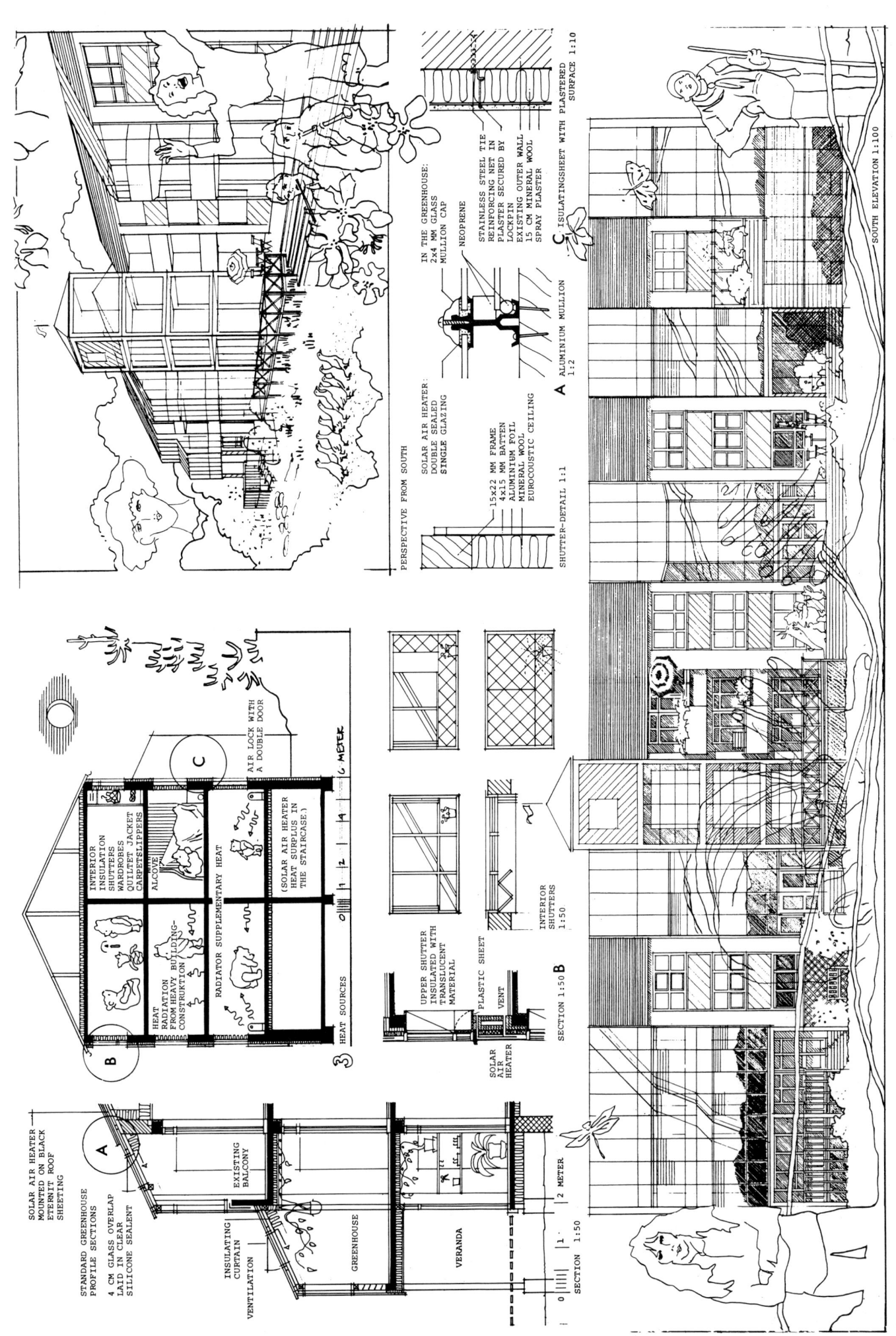

PERSPECTIVE FROM SOUTH

IN THE GREENHOUSE:
2x4 MM GLASS
MULLION CAP

NEOPRENE

STAINLESS STEEL TIE
REINFORCING NET IN
PLASTER SECURED BY
LOCKPIN
EXISTING OUTER WALL
15 CM MINERAL WOOL
SPRAY PLASTER

SOLAR AIR HEATER:
DOUBLE SEALED
SINGLE GLAZING

15x22 MM FRAME
4x15 MM BATTEN
ALUMINIUM FOIL
MINERAL WOOL
EUROCOUSTIC CEILING

SHUTTER-DETAIL 1:1

A ALUMINIUM MULLION
   1:2

C ISULATINGSHEET WITH PLASTERED
   SURFACE 1:10

SOUTH ELEVATION 1:100

STANDARD GREENHOUSE
PROFILE SECTIONS

4 CM GLASS OVERLAP
LAID IN CLEAR
SILICONE SEALENT

SOLAR AIR HEATER
MOUNTED ON BLACK
ETERNIT ROOF
SHEETING

INSULATING
CURTAIN

VENTILATION

EXISTING
BALCONY

GREENHOUSE

VERANDA

SECTION 1:50

0   1   2 METER

INTERIOR
INSULATION
SHUTTERS
WARDROBES
QUILTET JACKET
CARPETSLIPPERS

ALCOVE

HEAT
RADIATION
FROM HEAVY BUILDING-
CONSTRUKTION

RADIATOR SUPPLEMENTARY HEAT

(SOLAR AIR HEATER
HEAT SURPLUS IN
THE STAIRCASE.)

AIR LOCK WITH
A DOUBLE DOOR

6 METER

3 HEAT SOURCES

UPPER SHUTTER
INSULATED WITH
TRANSLUCENT
MATERIAL

PLASTIC SHEET

VENT

SOLAR
AIR
HEATER

SECTION 1:50 B

INTERIOR
SHUTTERS
1:50

JUDGES' COMMENTS

7,000 Danish Krona goes to Ulla Falk, Dorthe Henriksen and Anne Marie Nielsen for their remodelling of four storey rows of apartments in Denmark. The interiors of the apartments are well reorganised, though we had some doubts about the northern half being used as a 13°C buffer zone. We thought that the additions of verandas and glasshouses on the south side were simple and effective and would add greatly to the quality of the interior and exterior.

Existing building: south facade.

TECHNICAL ASSESSORS' COMMENTS

This retrofit of existing 4 storey middle-income housing utilises direct and sunspace gains. A thermosyphon air collector and a roof mounted air collector are used to preheat ventilation air. External insulation and the double and triple glazing of all apertures are the other main features of the scheme.

In the calculations the northern zone of the house was assumed to be a buffer zone with an internal temperature of 13°C. This temperature was thought to be unrealistically low for zones separated by apparently uninsulated partitions.

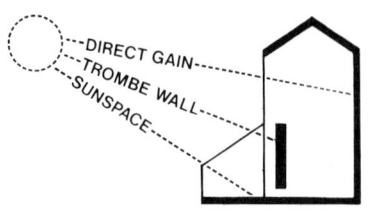

TECHNICAL DATA

For explanation of data see page 16.

Latitude: 55° 40'N
Altitude: 0 m
Data Point: Copenhagen

DWELLING DESCRIPTION (Typical Unit)
Heated Volume: 100 m³

APERTURE	A	B	C	D
System Type	DG	TW	SS	
Net Area m²	3.8	2.9	12.0	
Glazing Layers	2	2	1	
Night Insulation	Yes	Yes	Yes	
τ	0.70	0.70	0.60	
Comment	R	R	R	
	+	+	+	
	O	O	O	

Aperture/Heated Volume: 0.187 m²/m³
Primary Mass/
　　Related Aperture: 84.0 Wh/m²°C
Remote Mass/
　　Related Aperture: — Wh/m²°C
Air Change Rate: 0.75 ac/h
Building Loss Coeff.: 1.69 kWh/DD
　　　　　　　　　: 70.51 W/°C

DWELLING PERFORMANCE (Typical Unit)
% Internal Gains: 40.0
% Auxiliary Heating: 21.0
% Useful Solar Gains: 39.0
Annual Solar Gains Fraction: 0.64
Figure of Merit: 0.003 kWh/DDm²
Useful Solar Gains/
　　m² of Aperture: 112.3 kWh/m²yr
Min. Temp. without Heating: 15.0°C
Min. Outdoor Temperature: —6.5°C

ENERGY CHARACTERISTICS

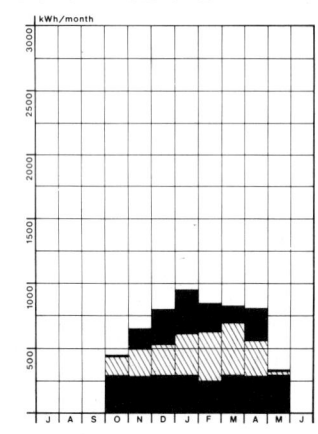

SHARED
THIRD PRIZE
CATEGORY B

2,000 Deutsch Marks

The climate of Esslingen am Neckar is influenced by the western winds which in the densely industrialized Neckar valley carry dust and noxious fumes into the town. The existing blocks, although they increase the air flow, do nothing to reduce the air pollution and do not provide sufficient fresh air and ventilation.

The Urbanstr/Blumenstr block originated at the end of the nineteenth century and was enlarged in the 1950s and 60s without due regard to the block structure. Today it is characterised by dark backyards, partly disused storage sheds and a garage.

The construction of new buildings and the restoration of old ones results in a combination of small, nuisance-free business premises (at the centre of the development block and in the basements) and dwellings (on the periphery of the blocks). The existing vegetation functions as a wind break as well as providing fresh air and stabilising the moisture balance. The new and old buildings are to be linked by glazed connections which are set back from the road and so do not interfere with the detached-house appearance. Minor constructional alterations to the existing timber framed building fabric will re-orientate the rooms with respect to energy considerations. (At the moment the living rooms face north and the bathroom, toilet, larder and bedroom face south).

Conservatories are to be added for use as additional living space. The glazed links between the buildings will enlarge the living area, create a sun lounge, act as a buffer zone and reduce the external surface area.

Building materials are chosen and produced ecologically. Locally obtained and manufactured materials and simple construction methods will lower the building costs. It is even possible that the materials will be obtained and partially worked by the

DESIGN TEAM

Michael Muller
Dieter Berreth
Willi Kruppa

Egerlanderstr 21
D 7140 Ludwigsburg
F R Germany

LOCATION
Esslingen am Neckar
F R Germany

dwelling owner himself.

The conservatories will become energy traps — they are of simple steel construction with sand filled concrete trough heat stores. Alternatively these troughs may be used for growing plants.

The existing timber frame and brick infill construction will be partially widened by constructing outer walls of solid brick, so that warm air may circulate in the 600mm gap thus created. The clinker filling between the timber framework will be replaced by a brick slag filling with a heat retaining ceramic lining. This will form the heat store. Clay pipes will be placed inside the filling forming air ducts connecting the glass house and storage walls.

In the summer the vegetation of the region tends naturally to cool and balance the air moisture and leafy trees will provide shade in open ground. By cultivating his greenhouse, the inhabitant will complete the passive system.

Moveable insulation (heat retaining roller blinds) is provided behind the windows and sliding doors. The north and east walls are constructed of lightweight fibre board panels with rough-cast insulating render.

The south facing wall is constructed of a whitewashed lightweight fibreboard building panel. The south wall has a low insulation value, since in winter the wall will also collect solar heat passively during day time. During the night the heat loss is lower than that of the north and east facing walls because of the stored heat and the phased emission of heat. In summer the south facing wall will act as a 'cooler' since the temperature of the wall is reduced by the vegetation on the wall which shades it and cools it by evaporation. Furthermore the wall absorbs relatively little energy because of its steep angle to the sun.

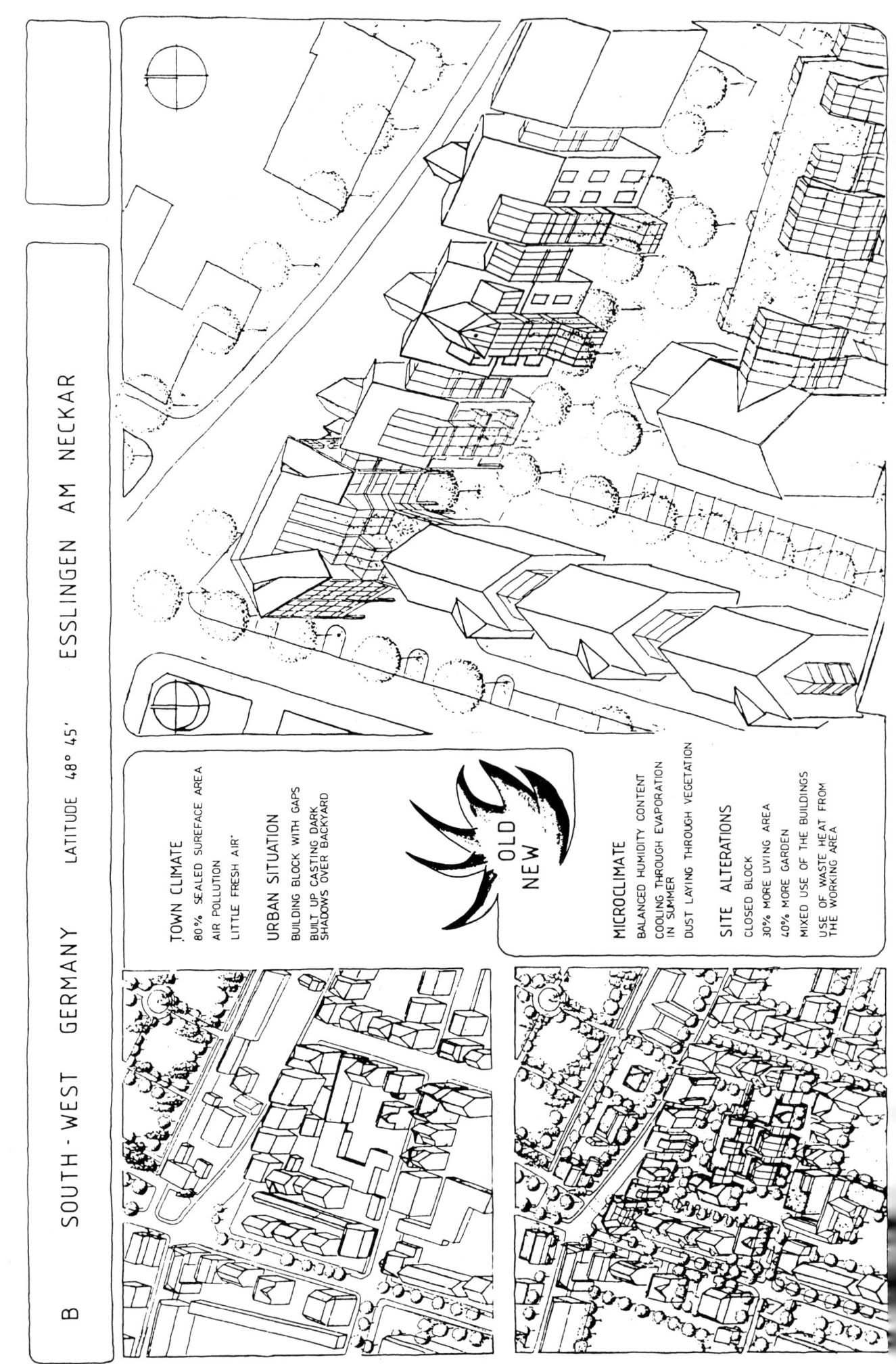

B   SOUTH-WEST   GERMANY   LATITUDE 48° 45'   ESSLINGEN AM NECKAR

TOWN CLIMATE
80% SEALED SUREFACE AREA
AIR POLLUTION
LITTLE FRESH AIR'

URBAN SITUATION
BUILDING BLOCK WITH GAPS
BUILT UP CASTING DARK
SHADOWS OVER BACKYARD

OLD
NEW

MICROCLIMATE
BALANCED HUMIDITY CONTENT
COOLING THROUGH EVAPORATION
IN SUMMER
DUST LAYING THROUGH VEGETATION

SITE ALTERATIONS
CLOSED BLOCK
30% MORE LIVING AREA
40% MORE GARDEN
MIXED USE OF THE BUILDINGS
USE OF WASTE HEAT FROM
THE WORKING AREA

JUDGES' COMMENTS

2,000 Deutsch Marks goes to Michael Muller, Dieter Berreth and Willi Kruppa for their simple and logical scheme for remodelling a group of 45-year old walk-up apartment buildings in Esslingen. The apartments are sensibly replanned in order to get the main rooms on to the south side and this also achieves a better plan for its own sake. Sunspaces are then added, both between the small blocks of apartments and as extensions to the new living rooms on the south side. In addition to this the corner block is further extended to give it a corner-like character for the benefit of the surroundings. There is a very clear understanding of the scale of the problem in both the economical and the aesthetic sense.

TECHNICAL ASSESSORS' COMMENTS

This is the rehabilitation of a group of multi-storey houses in Esslingen. The proposed solar apertures may be subject to over shadowing problems. The blocks have been replanned in order to provide a more favourable orientation to the living areas. Sunspaces have been added to the facade and between the blocks. The interaction between direct gain and remote storage will cause difficulty and there is doubt concerning the efficacy of the proposals for charging the underfloor storage.

The night-time U-values are rather optimistic and the internal gains have been over estimated — the calculations were therefore unreliable.

Existing building: north facade.

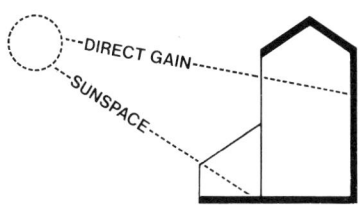

TECHNICAL DATA

This data has been recalculated.
For explanation of data see page 16.

Latitude: 48° 45'N
Altitude: 240 m
Data Point: Wurzburg

DWELLING DESCRIPTION (Typical Unit)
Heated Volume: 637 m³

APERTURE	A	B	C	D
System Type	SS	DG		
Net Area m²	105.6			
Glazing Layers	2	2		
Night Insulation	Yes	Yes		
τ	0.60	0.55		
Comment	T	T		
	+	+		
	SSE	SSE		

Aperture/Heated Volume: 0.18 m²/m³
Primary Mass/
    Related Aperture: 53.0 Wh/m²°C
Remote Mass/
    Related Aperture: 820.0 Wh/m²°C
Air Change Rate: 0.80 ac/h
Building Loss Coeff.: 16.84 kWh/DD
             : 701.58 W/°C

DWELLING PERFORMANCE (Typical Unit)
% Internal Gains: 9.0
% Auxiliary Heating: 29.0
% Useful Solar Gains: 62.0
Annual Solar Gains Fraction: 0.68
Figure of Merit: 0.007 kWh/DDm²
Useful Solar Gains/
    m² of Aperture: 261.8 kWh/m²yr
Min. Temp. without Heating: −9.6°C
Min. Outdoor Temperature: −12.8°C

ENERGY CHARACTERISTICS

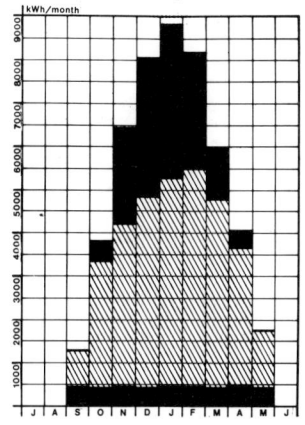

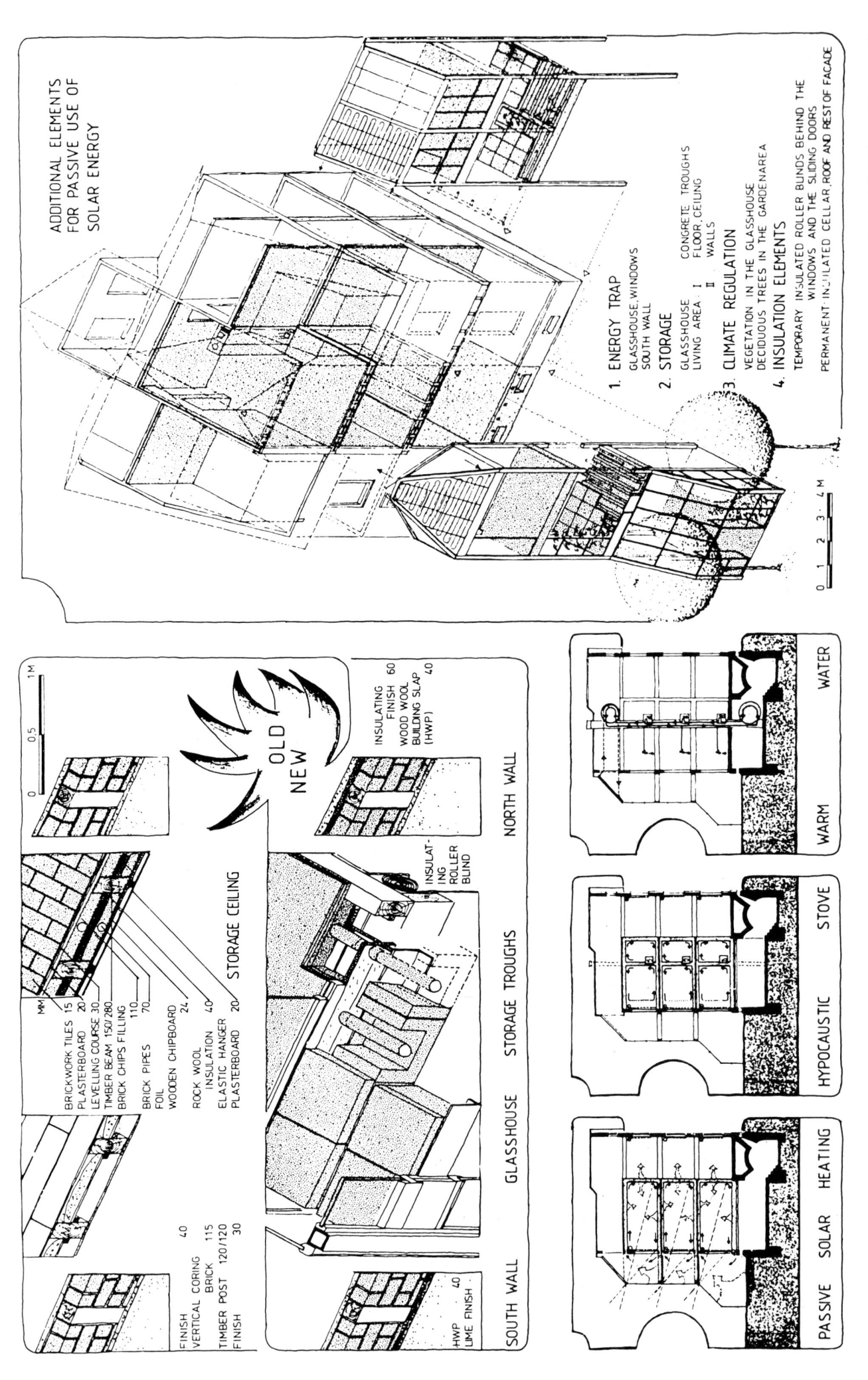

ADDITIONAL ELEMENTS FOR PASSIVE USE OF SOLAR ENERGY

1. ENERGY TRAP
   GLASSHOUSE, WINDOWS
   SOUTH WALL

2. STORAGE
   GLASSHOUSE   CONCRETE TROUGHS
   LIVING AREA I   FLOOR, CEILING
              II   WALLS

3. CLIMATE REGULATION
   VEGETATION IN THE GLASSHOUSE
   DECIDUOUS TREES IN THE GARDEN AREA

4. INSULATION ELEMENTS
   TEMPORARY INSULATED ROLLER BLINDS BEHIND THE
   WINDOWS AND THE SLIDING DOORS
   PERMANENT INSULATED CELLAR, ROOF AND REST OF FACADE

0 1 2 3 4 M

MM
BRICKWORK TILES 15
PLASTERBOARD 20
LEVELLING COURSE 30
TIMBER BEAM 150/280
BRICK CHIPS FILLING 110

BRICK PIPES 70
FOIL
WOODEN CHIPBOARD 24

ROCK WOOL 40
INSULATION
ELASTIC HANGER
PLASTERBOARD 20

STORAGE CEILING

INSULATING
FINISH 60
WOOD WOOL
BUILDING SLAP 40
(HWP)

NORTH WALL

GLASSHOUSE

STORAGE TROUGHS

INSULAT-
ING
ROLLER
BLIND

OLD
NEW

FINISH 40
VERTICAL CORING
BRICK 115
TIMBER POST 120/120
FINISH 30

HWP 40
LIME FINISH

SOUTH WALL

WATER

WARM

STOVE

HYPOCAUSTIC

PASSIVE   SOLAR   HEATING

0   0.5   1M

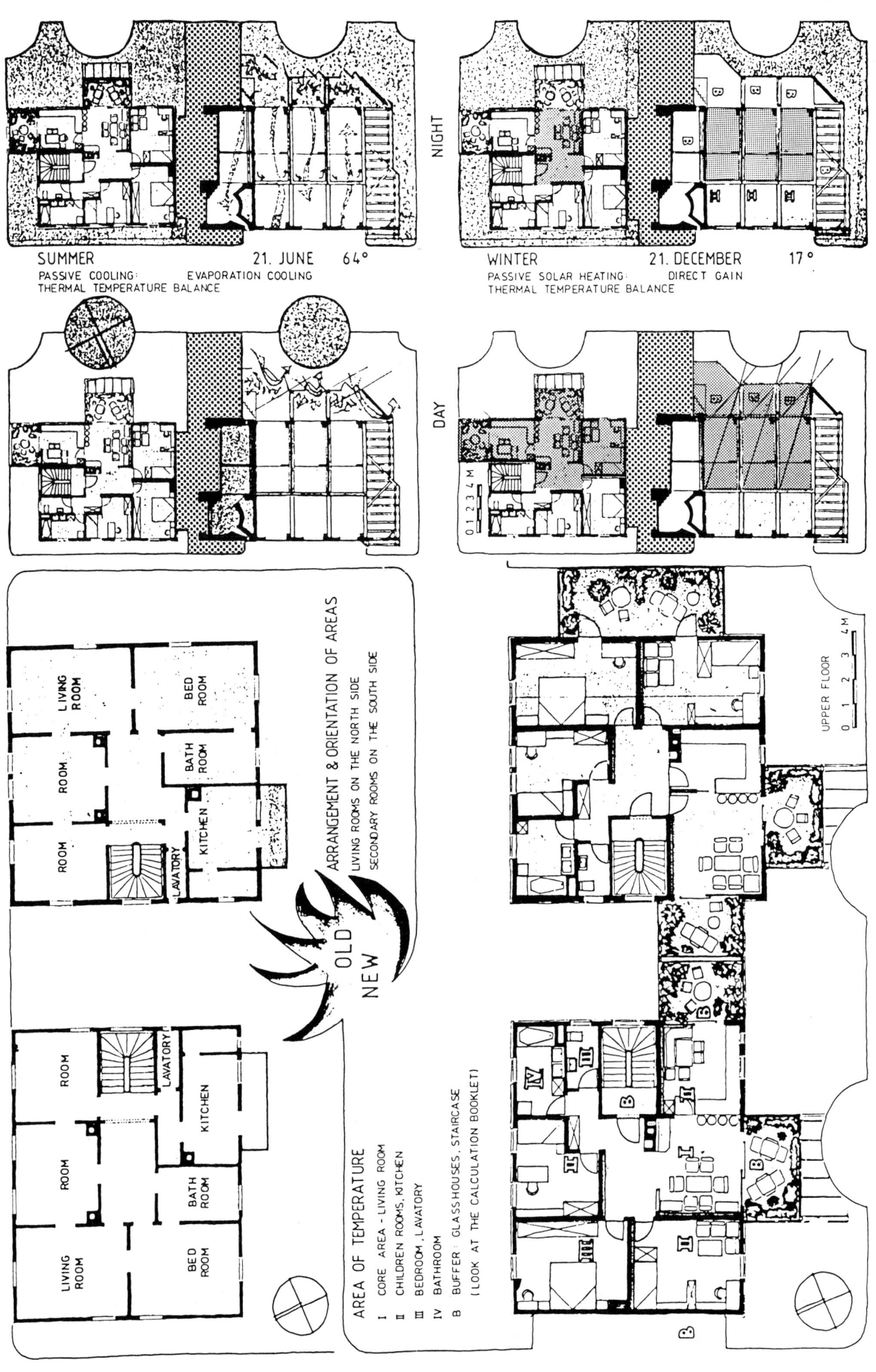

SUMMER   21. JUNE   64°
PASSIVE COOLING: EVAPORATION COOLING
THERMAL TEMPERATURE BALANCE

WINTER   21. DECEMBER   17°
PASSIVE SOLAR HEATING: DIRECT GAIN
THERMAL TEMPERATURE BALANCE

NIGHT

DAY

0 1 2 3 4 M

LIVING ROOM
ROOM
ROOM
BED ROOM
BATH ROOM
KITCHEN
LAVATORY

OLD
NEW

ARRANGEMENT & ORIENTATION OF AREAS
LIVING ROOMS ON THE NORTH SIDE
SECONDARY ROOMS ON THE SOUTH SIDE

AREA OF TEMPERATURE
I   CORE AREA - LIVING ROOM
II   CHILDREN ROOMS, KITCHEN
III   BEDROOM, LAVATORY
IV   BATHROOM
B   BUFFER: GLASSHOUSES, STAIRCASE
(LOOK AT THE CALCULATION BOOKLET)

ROOM
ROOM
LIVING ROOM
BED ROOM
BATH ROOM
LAVATORY
KITCHEN

UPPER FLOOR

0 1 2 3 4 M

CATEGORY B
RETROFIT AND REHABILITATION
OF DWELLINGS

COMMENDATIONS

SPECIAL MENTIONS

OTHER DETAILS
OF INTEREST

COMMENDATION
CATEGORY B

Our aim is not to adapt a solar collector to fit on to any sort of architecture, but to create an architecture that has developed from its relation to the sun.

From an urban point of view we have tried to provide large exterior areas to reduce overshading and afford protection from prevailing winds.

From an architectural view we have created a determinedly modern solar urban architecture symbolizing a response to solar problems in local design, and playing on the opposition between the 'cold' facade — with enclosed staircases — and the 'hot' facade — with greenhouses over opened dwellings.

The Facade is ... Queen!

The problem of the facade is an inherent one for architecture. The facade is the visible and therefore the public part of a building. It constitutes an urban cultural artefact. Since an architectural work is the expression of a volume enclosing several dwelling funtions, the facade — particularly in towns — has the role of giving appearance to this volume.

The Free Facade and the Pleasure of Composition

The architectural project presented here has tried to make the facade play its true role and take on an appearance that gives formal expression to the relationship between the inner and outer aspects of the architectural volume. The facade here isn't just a face but reflects the use associated with physical effects of opaque and transparent elements: a thermic typology of facade elements that produces a rich and diverse urban bioclimatic architecture.

The 'cold' facade: the roof, brick elevations, balcony and staircases all give relations of form between inside and outside.

The 'hot' facade: greenhouses used as living areas give rhythm to the hot facade.

Internal layout: the spaces are simple but rich.

Solar heat is collected by direct gains to the south windows, and to the greenhouses which heat the recirculation air during heating periods. Automatic vents distribute the solar energy to the other rooms. The energy is stored in the existing concrete floors and massive walls. The application of external rockwool insulation, double glazing with PVC frames and extra PVC shutters helps to retain the heat.

In the day-time warm air leaves the

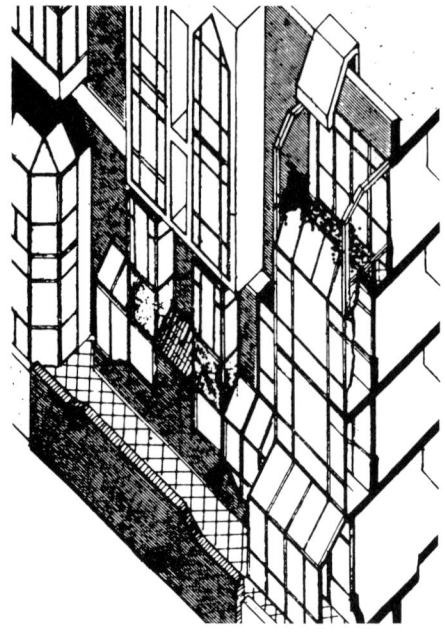

DESIGN TEAM

Dominique Pilate
and
Atelier du Soleil
(Association 1901)

23 rue Gosselet
59000 Lille
France

LOCATION
Lille
France

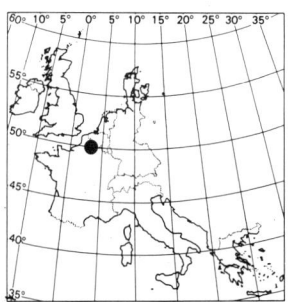

greenhouses and goes to the living and bedrooms and from there to the other rooms before being extracted through the kitchen and bathroom. At night-time the principle is the same. The heat contribution now comes from the energy being released from the concrete floors and massive brickwalls in the greenhouses and dwellings.

The passive solutions are adopted because they are more satisfactory from an architectural point of view since they create additional spaces and interest whilst providing the heating needs of the dwelling. Solar collectors may be mounted on the roof for water heating purposes.

Our system is very simple for the tenants to operate. In winter, the only operations required are the opening and closing of shutters to the greenhouse and window. In the summer, the tenants will need to open the cellar grilles and the greenhouse sashes, reversing the system and providing summer cooling. Solar gains are controlled by the naturally occuring solar reflection and by movable shutters and mechanical ventillation etc.

JUDGES' COMMENTS

First among the Commendations, we wish to congratulate Dominique Pilate for taking the most boring and boorish block of flats in Lille and transforming it by means of well-scaled and enjoyable solar devices. Although there was no indication of shading systems which are as important as collection systems, the judges thought that these additions could only further improve the elevations and that it need not detract from the commendation.

TECHNICAL ASSESSORS' COMMENTS

This rehabilitation of a group of 4 storey low cost housing blocks features the addition of sunspaces on the south facade and extra insulation applied externally. Mechanical ventilation is included in the scheme, but in general the ventilation is poorly considered. Active domestic hot water collectors are mounted on the roof. There appears to be no shading incorporated in the design. An appartment was used as a basis for the calculations which, having practically no external surfaces, was not a typical unit and does not give realistic values for the buildings performance.

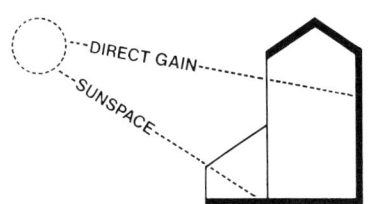

—DIRECT GAIN
—SUNSPACE

TECHNICAL DATA

This data has been recalculated.
For explanation of data see page 16.

Latitude: 50° 38'N
Altitude: 25 m
Data Point: Paris

DWELLING DESCRIPTION (Typical Unit)

Heated Volume: 112 m³

APERTURE	A	B	C	D
System Type	SS	SS	DG	
Net Area m²	7	3.3	1.4	
Glazing Layers	2	2	2	
Night Insulation	Yes	Yes	Yes	
τ	0.7	0.7	0.7	
Comment				

Aperture/Heated Volume: 0.104 m2/m³
Primary Mass/
   Related Aperture: 422.0 Wh/m²°C
Remote Mass/
   Related Aperture: 564.0 Wh/m²°C
Air Change Rate: 0.75 ac/h
Building Loss Coeff.: 1.72 kWh/DD
          : 71.80 W/°C

DWELLING PERFORMANCE (Typical Unit)

% Internal Gains: 48.0
% Auxiliary Heating: 22.0
% Useful Solar Gains: 30.0
Annual Solar Gains Fraction: 0.58
Figure of Merit: 0.003 kWh/DDm2
Useful Solar Gains/
   m² of Aperture: 101.0 kWh/m²yr
Min. Temp. without Heating: 24°C
Min. Outdoor Temperature: −5.1°C

ENERGY CHARACTERISTICS

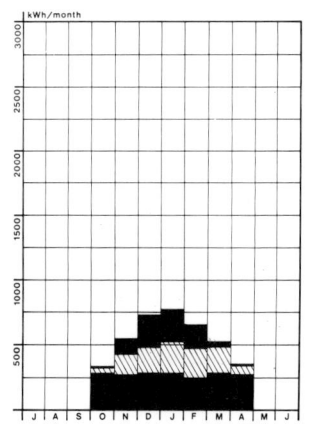

cat. B FRANCE   N. 50°38

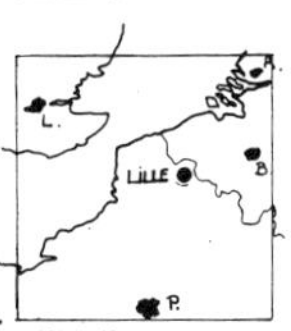

Context: A large existing building stock of high-density high-rise housing built between 1956 and 1960: the social housing "Concorde".
The site localited on the South arterial road of Lille near the motor-way Paris-Dunkerque.
It's composed eighteen tenement buildings with variable height (4 to 15 floors).

This housing estate groups 2000 social housings low cost rent. A partiel rehabilitation forecasted specially in thermic (plastic windows with double glazing) equipement of kitchen and bathroom ...
We propose a most important rehabilitation and a bioclimatic solution to adapt in this retrofit.

NORTH - FAÇADES - SOUTH

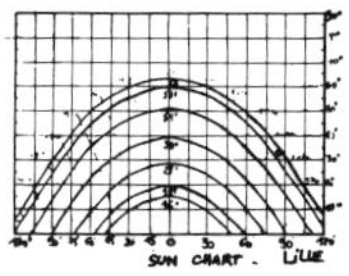

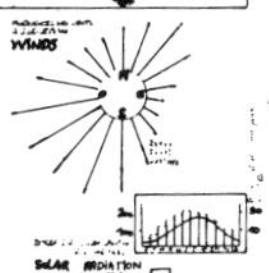

Axonometric view from South
scale : 1:2000

S.1:125   Façades ...
HOT SIDE

S.
1:100
COLD SIDE

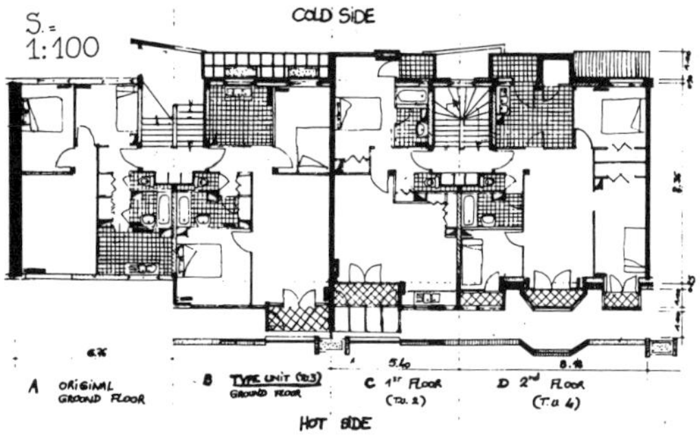

A ORIGINAL GROUND FLOOR
B TYPE UNIT (T3) GROUND FLOOR
C 1st FLOOR (T4 : 1)
D 2nd FLOOR (T4 4)
HOT SIDE

Main principles: From point of architectural view, at first sity:
1. ENERGY SAVING : outside insulation (CF. 0.10), plastic windows with double glazing in hot side, and double glazing in cold side, outside PVC shutters, inside curtains ... . "double skin" hot and cold → "buffer-areas". . Stock solar energy in dwelling inertia (Concrete floor, massive brick wall...)
2. TO COLLECT SOLAR HEAT by passive solution:
. direct gains by the south window.
. Greenhouse elements and window collectors heat the renewal air in heating periods (Tu 3 to 5t in greenhouses). Autoregulating airing grilles distribute solar energy in the other rooms (Combles to be used with natural thermocirculation, air-regulation systeme VMC....)
This system is very simple use: - In winter the only intervention are daily opening-closing shutters in greenhouses and windows. - In summer, they are natural: opening grilles of cellar and greenhouses sashs, inversing the system and giving summer cooling Control of overheating with natural solar reflection, and shutters - curtains' systems ...).

Thermic zones

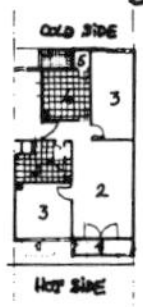

① Greenhouse. Hot transition area.
② Day living area. 19°C.
③ Bedrooms. 17-18°C.
④ Serving areas
⑤ Accessary calorific production. 20t.

COLD SIDE
HOT SIDE

...COLD SIDE   S.= 1:125

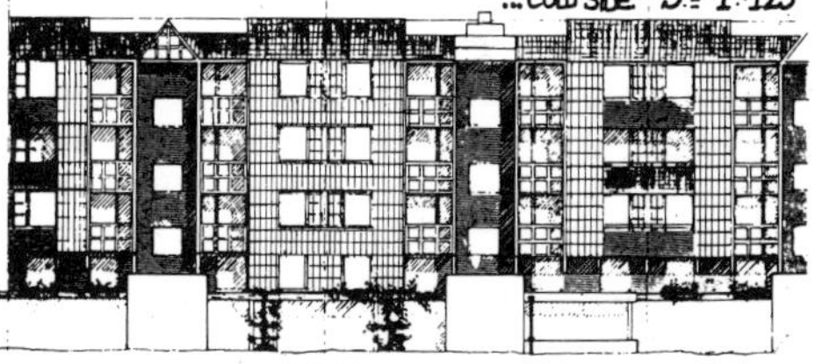

Beyond the bioclimatic system advantage the recourse of hot and cold buffer-areas allow to produce a new architectural modelage of façades and most advantageous organisation of rooms (kitchen and bathroom to north, with natural light, ...).
Instead of repeated and cheary architecture we substitute a typology of façade éléments diversificated and architectural ...   SUN SAVE the FAÇADES...!

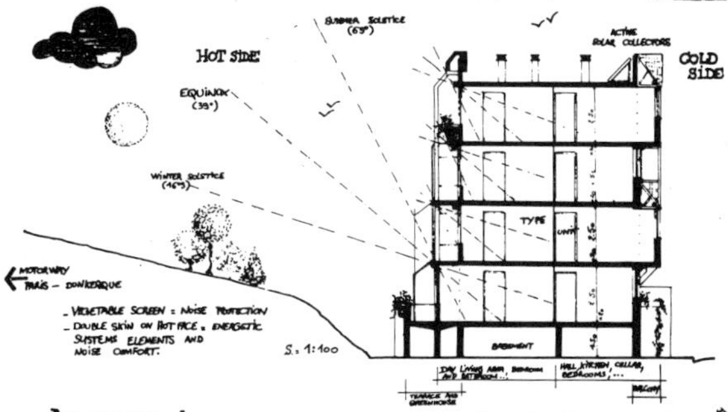

Axonometric view from South
S. 1: 100

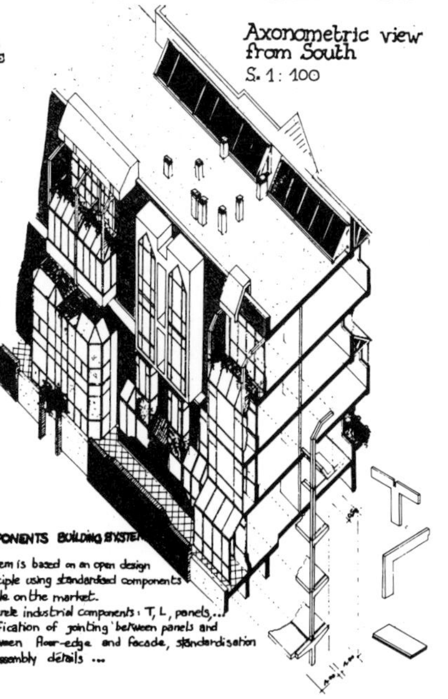

Air movements
S. = 1:100
Air heating/cooling control

WINTER
HOT SIDE
SUMMER

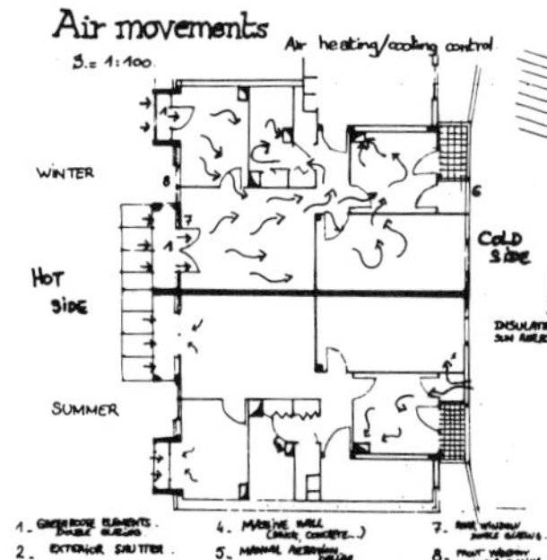

ABSORPTION - DIGESTION - ELIMINATION
SYSTEM

DAY WINTER

NIGHT

DAY SUMMER

NIGHT

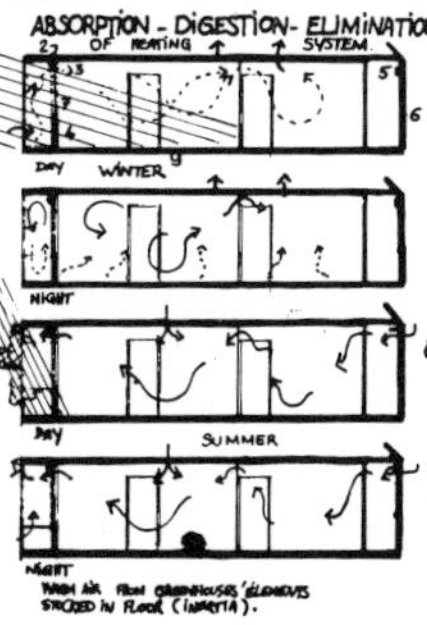

COMPONENTS BUILDING SYSTEM
System is based on an open design principle using standardised components avaible on the market.
Concrete industrial components : T, L, panels...
Unification of jointing between panels and between floor-edge and façade, standardisation of assembly details ...

COMMENDATION
CATEGORY B

Since participating in the First European Passive Solar Competition the author has considered the possibility of 'solarizing' his own dwelling thereby improving the accommodation and devising a system which could be adapted to the bulk of commercial housing in the Irish context.

The gable fronted layout of the dwelling imposed considerable restrictions:-

A. Minimum exposed frontage
B. Long elevations entirely shaded

However, the existing plan form and structural system proved to be readily adaptable:-

A. Large area of roof exposed
B. Low roof pitch 22° with open truss structure
C. Freedom to alter internal partitions
D. Large area of unused space fronting the garage
E. Large underfloor void with concrete base

SOLUTION

The living area with sunken seating becomes the 'hearth' of the house with all associated functions enveloping it. This space contains all the circulation and auxiliary heat sources and can be expanded for summer living.

The principle openings, partitions, water services and the bathroom are maintained; the entrance is considerably improved and the little-used garage is replaced by a car port.

To cater for the variety of orientations a range of solar collection areas is proposed:-

(see drawings)

1. Solar furnace A for morning insolation

2. Direct gain to living 'hearth'

3. Gable solar furnace B, direct gain from windows and thermo-syphon, for afternoon insolation

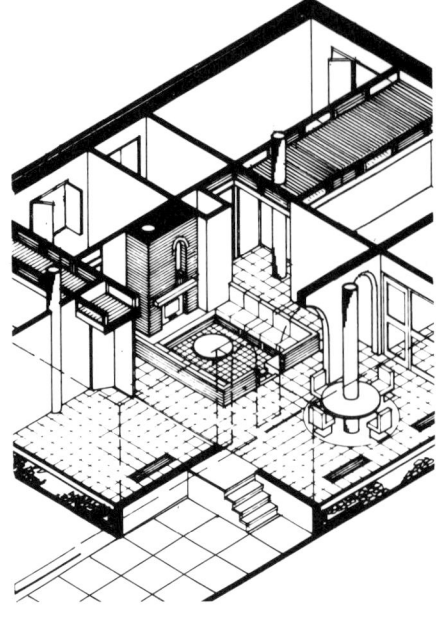

DESIGN TEAM

James F McManus
Mark O'Reilly
Hugh Durham

McManus Architects
56 Railpark
Maynooth
Co Kildare
Ireland

4. Pyramid solar furnace C for all-day insolation.

5. Reversible ducts to underfloor rock store are strategically placed to maintain an even balance.

We consider that this system can be adapted to a range of circumstances, even for two stories, by the adjustment of the available areas for collection.

JUDGES' COMMENTS

For achievement in adversity we wish to commend James F McManus, Mark O'Reilly and Hugh Durham for a scheme that reorganises an amazingly crass estate of bungalows in Maynooth, in Ireland.

The bungalows themselves are replanned and extended towards one another so that the living room becomes a heart to the surrounding bedrooms. This is well combined with the section in which the extended roofs, combined with the existing ones, become the solar devices. The scheme is a good example of the real possibility of reclaiming such estates to civilised living. Nevertheless, the scheme was clearly an overkill in technical terms.

TECHNICAL ASSESSORS' COMMENTS

This rehabilitation of an estate of bungalows involves major replanning and utilizes direct gain and solar air collectors with an under-floor rock bed. This is a hybrid system. It is thought that the transfer of heat to the rock bed would be ineffective. This is an inappropriate development of solar principles.

Errors were discovered in the calculations.

LOCATION
Maynooth
Ireland

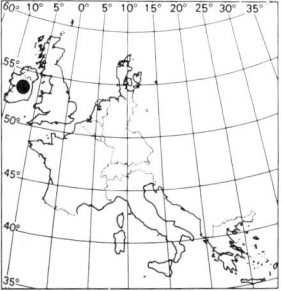

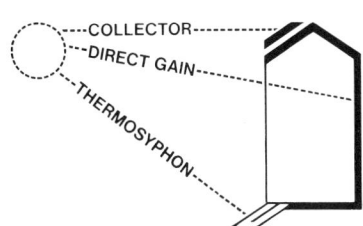

TECHNICAL DATA

This data has been recalculated.
For explanation of data see page 16.

Latitude: 53° 22'N
Altitude: 60 m
Data Point: Valentia

DWELLING DESCRIPTION (Typical Unit)
Heated Volume: 361 m³

APERTURE	A	B	C	D
System Type	C	C	DG	TS
Net Area m²	3.6	3.6	8.3	12.2
Glazing Layers	2	2	2	2
Night Insulation	Yes	Yes	Yes	Yes
τ	0.80	0.80	0.80	0.80
Comment	T+R	T+R	T+R	T+R

Aperture/Heated Volume: 0.077 m²/m³
Primary Mass/
 Related Aperture: 134.0 Wh/m²°C
Remote Mass/
 Related Aperture: 375.0 Wh/m²°C
Air Change Rate: 1.00 ac/h
Building Loss Coeff.: 7.59 kWh/DD
 : 316.25 W/°C

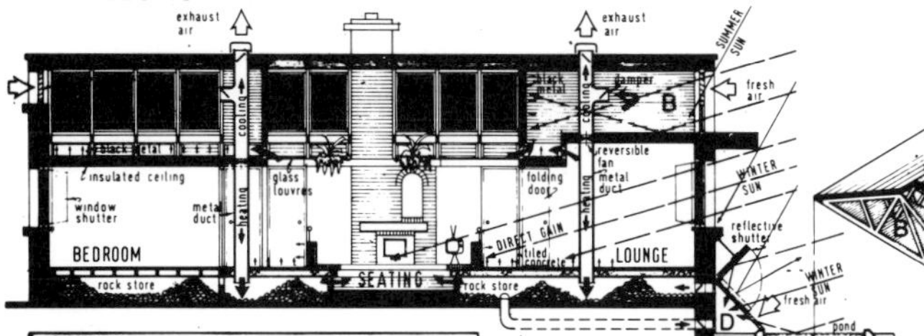

DWELLING PERFORMANCE (Typical Unit)
% Internal Gains: 28.0
% Auxiliary Heating: 44.0
% Useful Solar Gains: 28.0
Annual Solar Gains Fraction: 0.39
Figure of Merit: 0.007 kWh/DDm²
Useful Solar Gains/
 m² of Aperture: 201.0 kWh/m²yr
Min. Temp. without Heating: −1.5°C
Min. Outdoor Temperature: −7.1°C

ENERGY CHARACTERISTICS

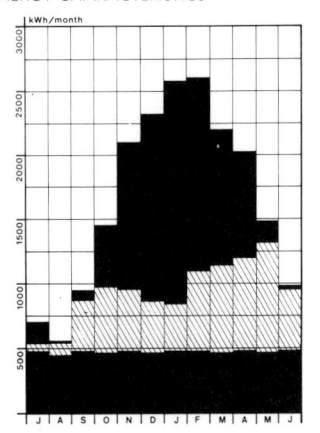

kWh/month

J A S O N D J F M A M J

IRELAND EAST 53·4°N - 6·36°W

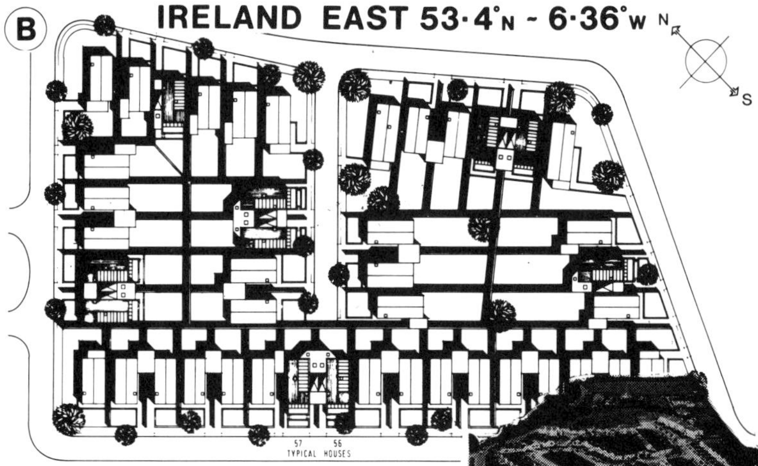

SITE PLAN 1:500

LOCATION 1:10560

EXISTING ELEVATION

SOLAR ELEVATION

EXISTING PLAN

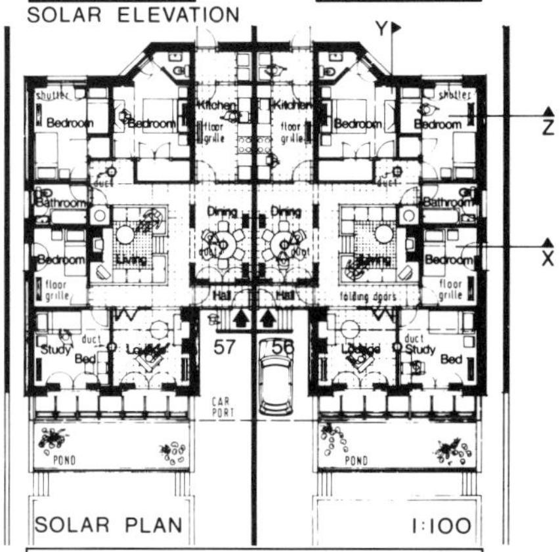

SOLAR PLAN 1:100

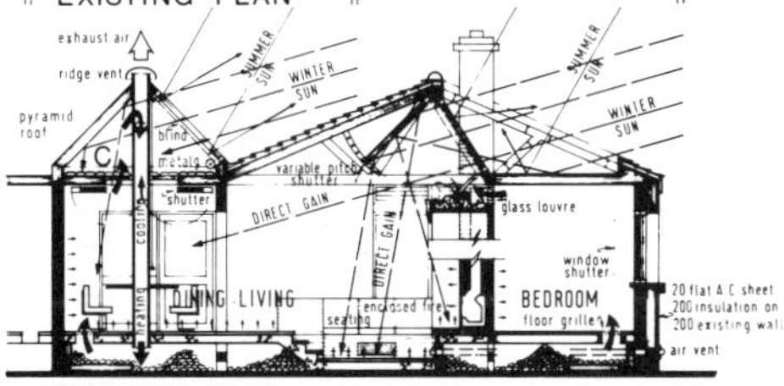

SECTION AT X

SECTION AT Y 1:50

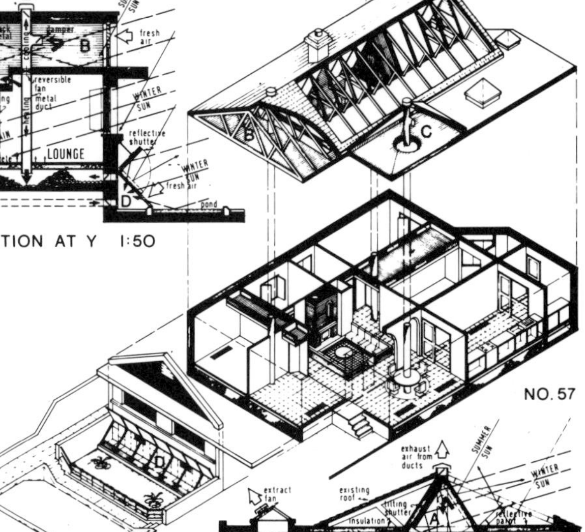

NO. 57

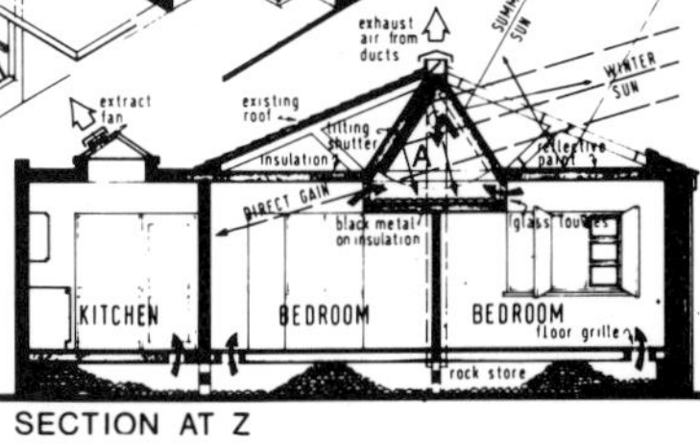

SECTION AT Z

COMMENDATION
CATEGORY B

The aim of our proposal is to open up these east/west orientated buildings towards the south, in order to optimise solar energy input and thereby maximise solar heat collection. Conservatories provide the new openings with buffer zones to reduce heat losses. Heat storage bins in the conservatory and in the house, storage floors, Glauber's salt storage and rock storage result in the spaced emission of heat thus minimizing the additional heat requirements. The houses have been provided with additional thermal insulation. Movable insulation is also provided for the conservatories and all vents. The building will be protected against overheating by providing shade and air vents.

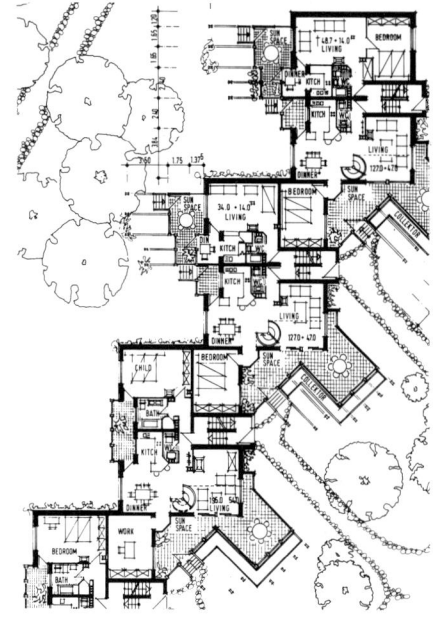

DESIGN TEAM

Jurgen Rauer
Rolf Beele

Cherusker Str 23
D 1000 Berlin 62
F R Germany

LOCATION
Berlin
F R Germany

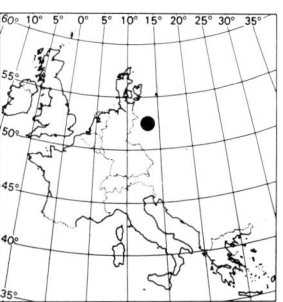

JUDGES' COMMENTS

Our commendation goes to Jurgen Rauer and Rolf Beele for their reclamation of an echelon of recent four storey apartments in Berlin. The original buildings are a lot more attractive than those that were tackled by the first two commended schemes and the alterations are on a more luxurious level: we commend the scheme for the high quality of the alterations to the plans and their extension outwards (usually diagonally) to provide a far more comfortable living space within.

TECHNICAL ASSESSORS' COMMENTS

A rehabilitation of a 4 storey block of flats by the addition of sunspaces. Air from the sunspace is blown through floor ducts containing phase change thermal storage material. On one floor both the northern and southern flats are served by the same sunspace.

The calculations are correct.

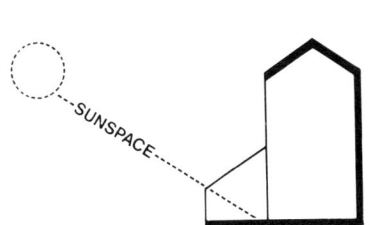

SUNSPACE

TECHNICAL DATA

For explanation of data see page 16.

Latitude: 52° 30'N
Altitude: 100 m
Data Point: Berlin

DWELLING DESCRIPTION (Typical Unit)
Heated Volume: 245 m³

APERTURE	A	B	C	D
System Type	SS	SS	SS	
Net Area m²	10.7	7.0	4.8	
Glazing Layers	2	2	2	
Night Insulation	Yes	Yes	Yes	
τ	0.80	0.70	0.30	
Comment	T+R	T+R	SE+R +O	

Aperture/Heated Volume: 0.092 m²/m³
Primary Mass/
    Related Aperture: 87.1 Wh/m²°C
Remote Mass/
    Related Aperture: 145.7 Wh/m²°C
Air Change Rate: 0.75 ac/h
Building Loss Coeff.: 3.5 kWh/DD
           : 147.0 W/°C

DWELLING PERFORMANCE (Typical Unit)
% Internal Gains: 31.0
% Auxiliary Heating: 44.0
% Useful Solar Gains: 25.0
Annual Solar Gains Fraction: 0.361
Figure of Merit: 0.006 kWh/DDm²
Useful Solar Gains/
    m² of Aperture: 132.8 kWh/m²yr
Min. Temp. without Heating: −0.7°C
Min. Outdoor Temperature: −12.15°C

ENERGY CHARACTERISTICS

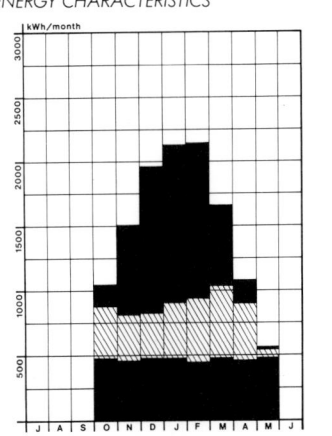

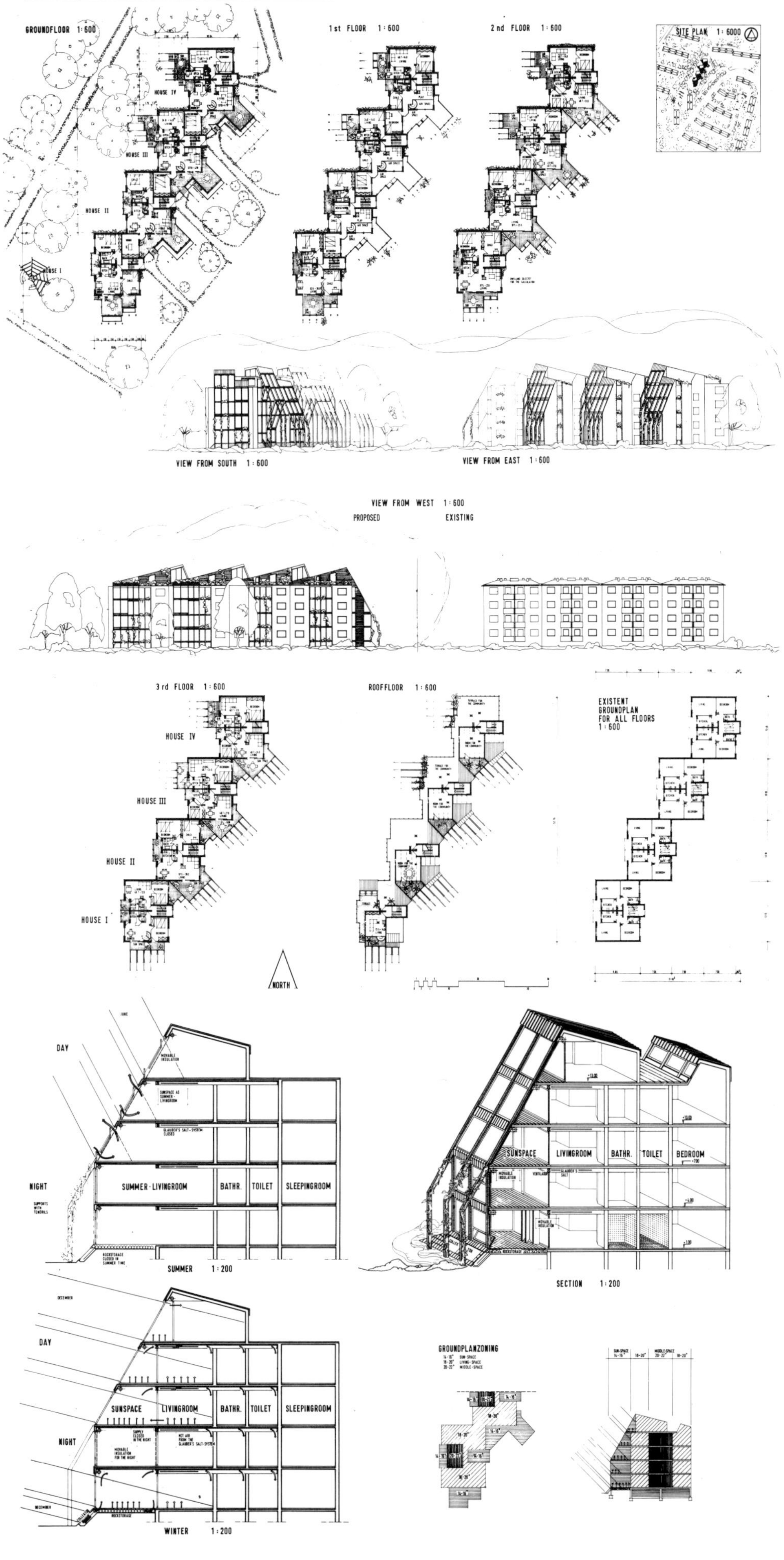

GROUNDFLOOR 1:600

1st FLOOR 1:600

2nd FLOOR 1:600

SITE PLAN 1:6000

HOUSE IV

HOUSE III

HOUSE II

HOUSE I

VIEW FROM SOUTH 1:600

VIEW FROM EAST 1:600

VIEW FROM WEST 1:600
PROPOSED   EXISTING

3rd FLOOR 1:600

ROOFFLOOR 1:600

EXISTENT GROUNDPLAN FOR ALL FLOORS 1:600

HOUSE IV

HOUSE III

HOUSE II

HOUSE I

NORTH

DAY

NIGHT

SUMMER 1:200

SUNSPACE LIVINGROOM BATHR. TOILET BEDROOM

SECTION 1:200

DAY

NIGHT

SUNSPACE LIVINGROOM BATHR. TOILET SLEEPINGROOM

WINTER 1:200

SUMMER-LIVINGROOM BATHR. TOILET SLEEPINGROOM

GROUNDPLANZONING

COMMENDATION
CATEGORY B

The site on which the building to be renovated stands is situated at the beginning of 'rue Colbert' in the old 'quartier de la Bourse'.

This district is regarded as being 'run down' and since 1892 it has been the subject of many renovation projects. Demolition work began around 1915 but the building concerned, which was erected in 1892 and which stands on the edge of the older district on rue Colbert, was not touched. The rue Neive Saint Martin as extended as far as 'Cours Belsunce' (rue Francois Mireur). During this initial operation the building adjacent to 3 rue Colbert was demolished forming a gable wall to the premises with which we are concerned.

Since then several development schemes have been considered from time to time — one of these projects suggested the incorporation of 'our' building within a new urban web.

Work on the 'Bourse' shopping centre, which is now nearing completion, did not begin until the early seventies. Our building should have been pulled down in a later stage of the renovation work.

SEE DRAWINGS

— The internal layout of each flat is altered as little as possible because of the cost of renovation work.

— Apartment B has almost no solar gains except in the afternoon on the west side. Apartments A and C benefit from the communal greenhouse. As it is impossible to apply passive solar systems to apartment B this apartment is insulated from the adjoining flats A and C and a conventional heating system is employed.

— All the windows (apart from those that face south) are to be double glazed. To help retain the architectural quality of the building and to reduce the renovation costs the original shutters are retained.

PROCEDURE

1. The formation of new window openings in the gable wall.

DESIGN TEAM

Jean Louis Izard
Daniel Verger
Philippe Reby

Groupe ABC
Ecole d'Architecture de Luminy
13288 Marseille
France

LOCATION
Marseille
France

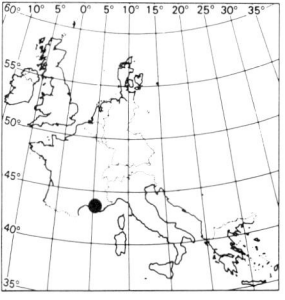

2. The addition of a new facade to incorporate the solar systems (direct gain, solar air panels and bow windows) and external insulation. The existing wall is to be used for thermal inertia.

3. The inner yard of the building is to be converted into a communal greenhouse.

4. Since regulations required that the uppermost floor was to be set back, two individual greenhouses are created at that level.

5. The four other facades are not to be changed. External insulation is not used because of the architectural interest of the facades. The internally applied insulation does not however increase the thermal resistance of the 500mm thick existing wall.

6. The existing function of the ground floor is not to be changed. A commercial gallery is planned in front of the new shopping centre.

JUDGES' COMMENTS

We commend Jean Louis Izard, Daniel Verger and Philippe Reby for their alteration of a 97-year-old block of apartments in Marseille. This is a much earlier apartment building than the ones so far discussed. At some time in history it was cut in half, leaving an exposed gable wall and half a lightwell on view from the street.

We enjoyed the way in which the lightwell was enclosed as a collector and a new elevation was added to the gable wall which, though clearly lightweight and partly translucent, referred fairly elegantly to the more ponderous masonry facades which abutted it.

TECHNICAL ASSESSORS' COMMENTS

A rehabilitation a of 7 storey apartment block in Marseille incorporating sunspaces along the facade, recessed bay windows to each apartment and wall collectors (the operation of which is misconceived).

The calculation results were found to be optimistic: the internal gains were excessive by a factor of 3 and thus the performance predictions were unreliable.

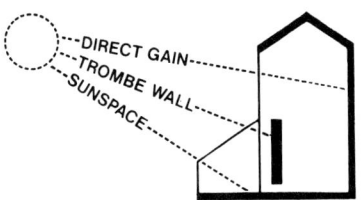

DIRECT GAIN
TROMBE WALL
SUNSPACE

TECHNICAL DATA

This data has been recalculated.
For explanation of data see page 16.

Latitude: 43° 18'N
Altitude: 3 m
Data Point: Marigane

DWELLING DESCRIPTION (Typical Unit)
Heated Volume: 348 m³

APERTURE	A	B	C	D
System Type	DG	TW	DG	SS
Net Area m²	10.8	4.3	13.0	7.0
Glazing Layers	1	1	2	1
Night Insulation	Yes	Yes	Yes	Yes
τ		0.70	0.75	0.60	0.75
Comment				

Aperture/Heated Volume: 0.101 m²/m³
Primary Mass/
    Related Aperture: 213 Wh/m²°C
Remote Mass/
    Related Aperture: — Wh/m²°C
Air Change Rate: 0.75 ac/h
Building Loss Coeff.: 4.83 kWh/DD
    : 201.4 W/°C

DWELLING PERFORMANCE (Typical Unit)
% Internal Gains: 37.0
% Auxiliary Heating: 9.0
% Useful Solar Gains: 54.0
Annual Solar Gains Fraction: 0.85
Figure of Merit: 0.001 kWh/DDm²
Useful Solar Gains/
    m² of Aperture: 90.8 kWh/m²yr
Min. Temp. without Heating: 4.2°C
Min. Outdoor Temperature: —3.0°C

ENERGY CHARACTERISTICS

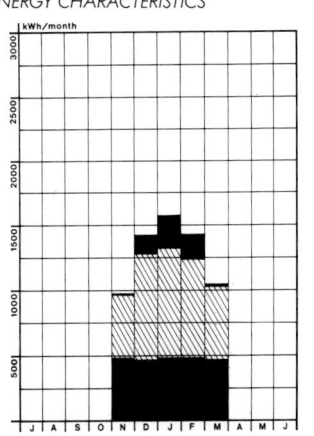

B/ FRANCE MARSEILLE /43°37'N

HISTORICAL EVOLUTION

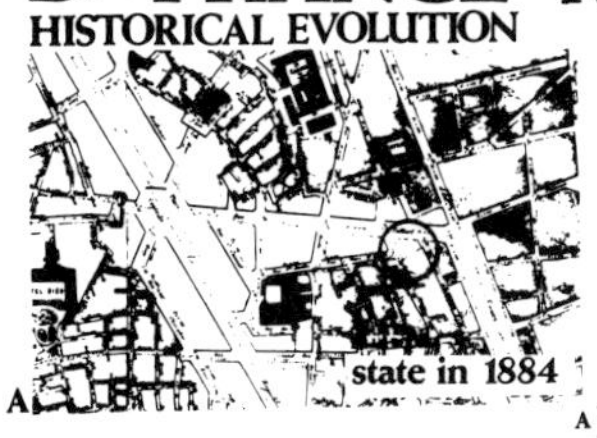

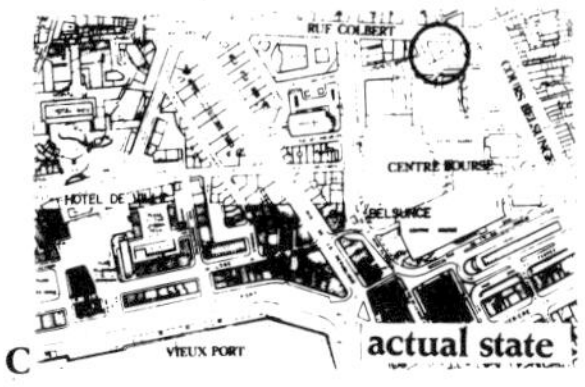

A — state in 1884
B — projet 1932
C — actual state

A The plan of Marseille centre town in 1884

The site on which the building to be renovated stands at the opening of "rue Colbert" in the old
district called "quartier de la Bourse".
This district regarded as unhealthy and as a shame for a city like Marseille has been the object
of many projects of total renovation since 1892.
The pulling down work began around 1915, but the building put up in 1892 on "rue Colbert" at the
edge of the older district were not touched. "Rue Neuve Saint Martin" was extended as far as
"cours Belsunce" (Rue François Mireur).
The next building being pulled down during that opening operation, the adjacent wall of "3 rue
Colbert" became a "blind wall"(gable).

B Several projects of development which hadn't been carried out were suggested at different times.
One of those projects considered inserting "our" building within the new urban web.

C Only since the early seventies did they start putting up on that site the "Bourse" shopping
center now about to be completed.
Our building ought to have been pulled down in a later stage in the renovation work.

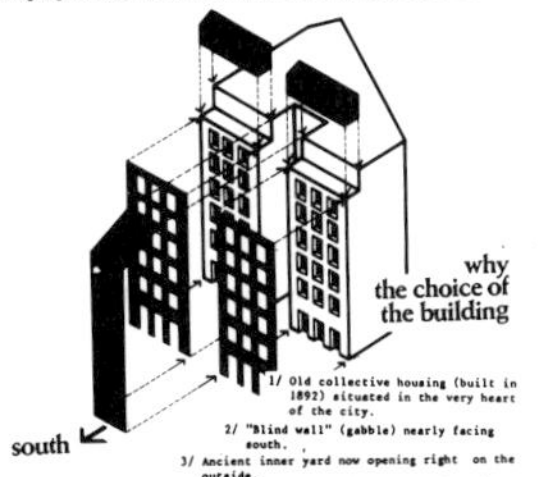

why the choice of the building

south

1/ Old collective housing (built in
1892) situated in the very heart
of the city.
2/ "blind wall" (gable) nearly facing
south.
3/ Ancient inner yard now opening right on the
outside.
By the way of conclusion : the project is
meant to show that renovation using passive
solar systems is possible even in collective
housing in the heart of Marseille.

SUGGESTION

1/ Opening window in the "blind wall"(gable)

2/ Superposition of an extra front with a view to install solar
systems (direct gain, air solar pannels, and bow windows) and
outside insulation. The old wall is used for inertia.

3/ The inner yard of the building is transformed into a collective
greenhouse.

4/ As regulation required the top floor to be set back in the area, two
individual greenhouses will be created at that level.

5/ The four other fronts are not to be changed. The inside insulation
is avoided because of the architectural interest of the housefronts.
Finally, the inner insulation doesn't much improve thermic resistance of the wall (thickness = 20 inches).

6/ Preservation of the present function of the ground floor.
A commercial gallery is planned in front of the new shopping center
"Centre Bourse".

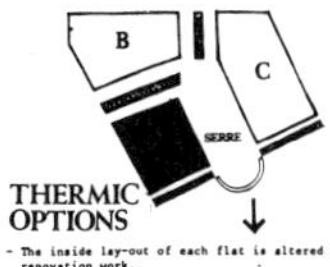

THERMIC OPTIONS

- The inside lay-out of each flat is altered as little as possible because of an inexpensive
renovation work.
- Apartment "B" has almost no solar gains except in the afternoon on the west side. Moreover,
apartment "A" and "C" benefit the collective greenhouse.
As the renovation with passive solar systems is impossible for apartment "B", thermical insulation is placed between apartment "A", "C" and "B". So for apartment "B" a casual heating system
is used.
- For the other windows except those facing south 25, thermical resistance is improved by double
panes.
Fer the insulation of the windows, the original shutters are kept so as not to change the
architectural aspect of the building and also in order to reduce the renovation coast.

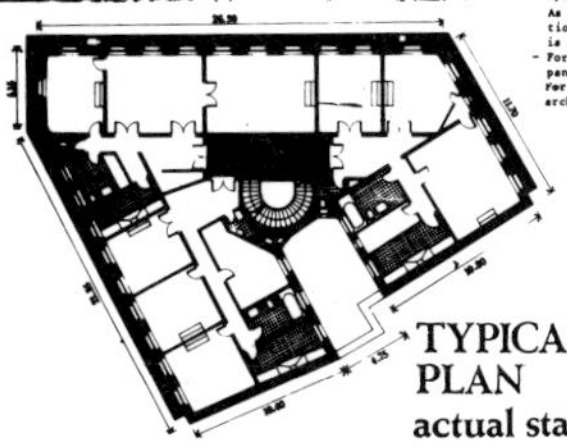

SERRE
SUD
VENTIL.
MECA.
CONTROLEE
FORME POUR
MIEUX CAPTER
HIVER
ETE

SECTION H·H

TYPICAL PLAN
actual state

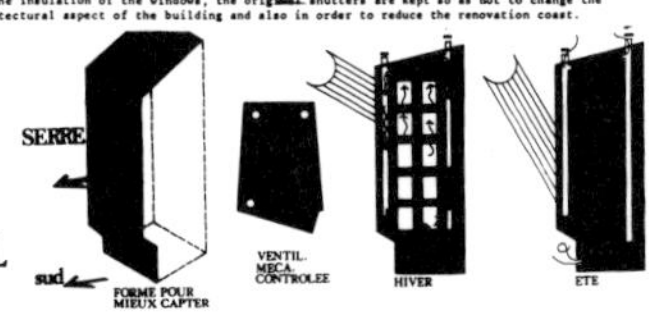

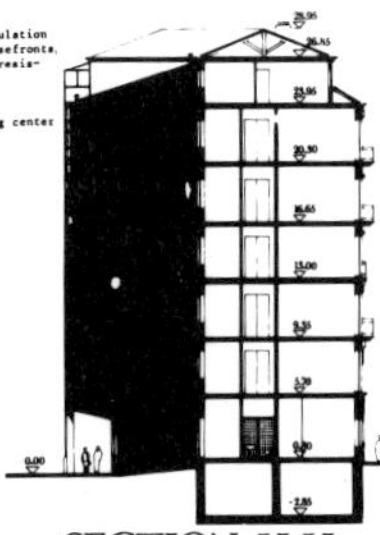

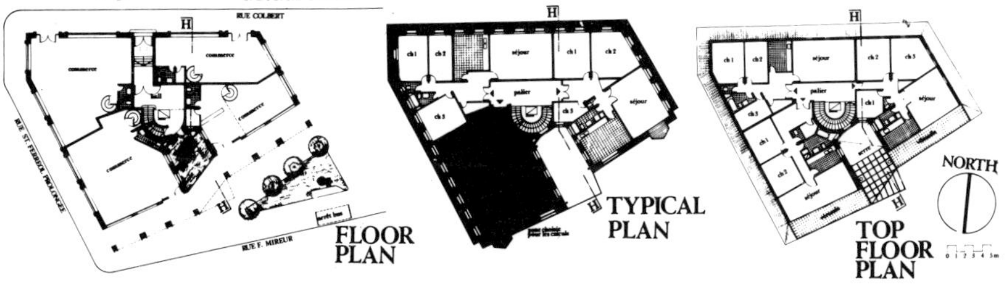

FLOOR PLAN

TYPICAL PLAN

TOP FLOOR PLAN

NORTH

NORTH -4° WEST -5° WEST -25° SOUTH -25° NORTH-55°

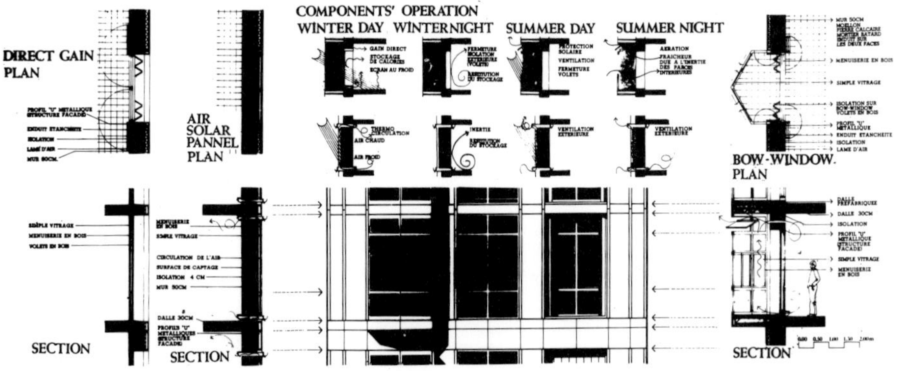

COMPONENTS' OPERATION
WINTER DAY WINTER NIGHT SUMMER DAY SUMMER NIGHT

DIRECT GAIN PLAN

AIR SOLAR PANNEL PLAN

BOW-WINDOW. PLAN

SECTION SECTION SECTION

COMMENDATION
CATEGORY B

As a military town Dendermonde had several fortresses with which to defend the city and the barracks, situated along the northern avenue, are a silent witness to this. The town has an indefinable ghost value with which many generations of Dendermonde have grown up — whilst the old barracks also have material values; 1,200mm thick brick walls carry brick arches with a north-south orientation.

The building is well positioned. It is light and sunny and affords a degree of privacy even though it is only a short walk from the local market. The ground level flooring will be retained in those small scale spaces which are to be used for commercial purposes and by means of a small entrance (say the continuation of the spiral staircase) an additional dwelling could be added. These trading areas, together with the duplex dwellings above are in direct contact with, and approachable from, the conservatory thus creating a blend of both these functions.

A membrane of glass surrounds the entire building which then becomes a heat store owing to its enormous mass of masonry. It will be necessary to remove a twelve metre wide strip of brick wall and arches in order to let in daylight and sun. The three-cornered bay will also benefit from this light and sun.

SYSTEM (numbers refer to transverse section A.B.)

At the northern facade are the garages, situated under a cultivated inclined plane which, together with the evergreen trees, forms a wind-break. The new roof covering consists of glass domes which continue over the entire building, descending vertically to form the southern facade. Supports, 1,200mm wide, hold up these domes and act as flower boxes from which climbing plants will grow to screen the glass during the summer months. The indoor-gardens which will act to intercept visitors and promote communication between the various dwellings also supply supplementary heating, limit the heat losses and create a lot of flexible internal space which is not subject to changes in weather conditions. The heat above the 'Trombe ceiling', originating from under the roof conservatory, is distributed along the ventilator (2). The space between the floor of

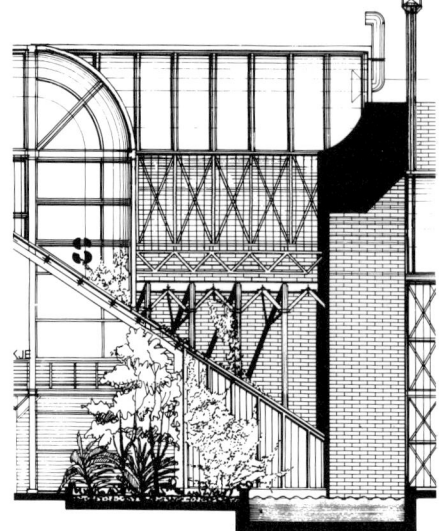

DESIGNER

Luk Van Neste

Oude Molenstraat 21
8400 Oostende
Belgium

the dwelling and the ceiling of the shop (7) enables cold air to be supplied in warm periods to the hottest parts of the building and then, via the ventilator (2) in the double glazed ceiling, to be distributed via the 'chimney' (1).

Horizontal moving plates, covered in polyurethane, can insulate the ceiling and thus limit any loss of heat.

1. 'solar' chimney (with valve and radial ventilator)
2. ventilator (air current turn-table)
3. double glazing
4. solar protection
5. night insulation — lamellae
6. night insulation — roller blinds
7. ventilation room
8. deciduous climbing plant

JUDGES' COMMENTS

For the very well presented conversion of the military barracks in Dendermonde in Belgium, we commend Luk Van Neste. We found the erosion of the central space and its extension into an east-west atrium to be very elegant, both spatially and for solar gain, and despite some doubts about detailed elevational treatment we thought that the scheme honoured and respected the historic building.

TECHNICAL ASSESSORS' COMMENTS

This rehabilitation of a military barracks uses a sunspace system by the partial removal and glazing of the existing barrel vaulted roof. Horizontal roof slabs are used for heat storage. The assessors are concerned about the excessive areas of horizontal glazing at this latitude which will contribute little in winter and cause overheating in summer. However it is likely that these problems could be solved. The assessors are impressed with the potential of the scheme.

The difficulties in calculating the effect of buffer spaces with the competition method were apparent with this scheme and errors in the calculations led to generally unreliable results.

LOCATION
Dendermonde
Belgium

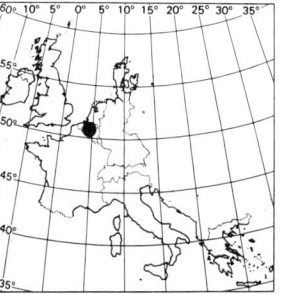

B. BELGIE . N . 51
VERBOUWING VAN KAZERNE IN HET STADSCENTRUM — DENDERMONDE

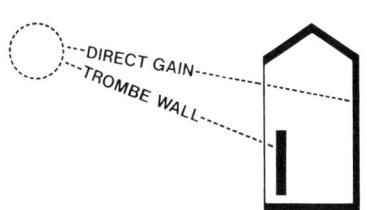

DIRECT GAIN
TROMBE WALL

TECHNICAL DATA
This data has been recalculated.
For explanation of data see page 16.

Latitude: 51° 2'N
Altitude: 4 m
Data Point: Brussels

DWELLING DESCRIPTION (Typical Unit)
Heated Volume: 301 m³

APERTURE	A	B	C	D
System Type	TW	DG	DG	DG
Net Area m²	56.5	22.0	14.3	14.13
Glazing Layers	1	2	2	2
Night Insulation	No	Yes	Yes	Yes
τ	0.6	0.3	0.3	0.7
Comment		O	O	

Aperture/Heated Volume: 0.355 m²/m³
Primary Mass/
    Related Aperture: 145.0 Wh/m²°C
Remote Mass/
    Related Aperture: 21.0 Wh/m²°C
Air Change Rate: 0.75 ac/h
Building Loss Coeff.: 6.43 kWh/DD
    : 267.9 W/°C

DWELLING PERFORMANCE (Typical Unit)
% Internal Gains: 24.0
% Auxiliary Heating: 21.0
% Useful Solar Gains: 55.0
Annual Solar Gains Fraction: 0.72
Figure of Merit: 0.004 kWh/DDm²
Useful Solar Gains/
    m² of Aperture: 94.5 kWh/m²yr
Min. Temp. without Heating: 0.0°C
Min. Outdoor Temperature: −7.6°C

ENERGY CHARACTERISTICS

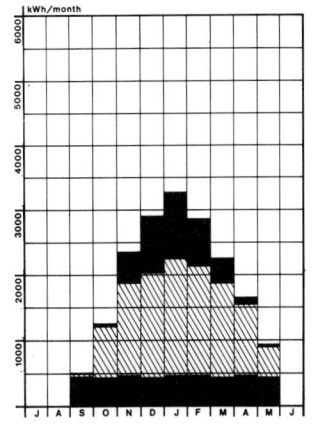

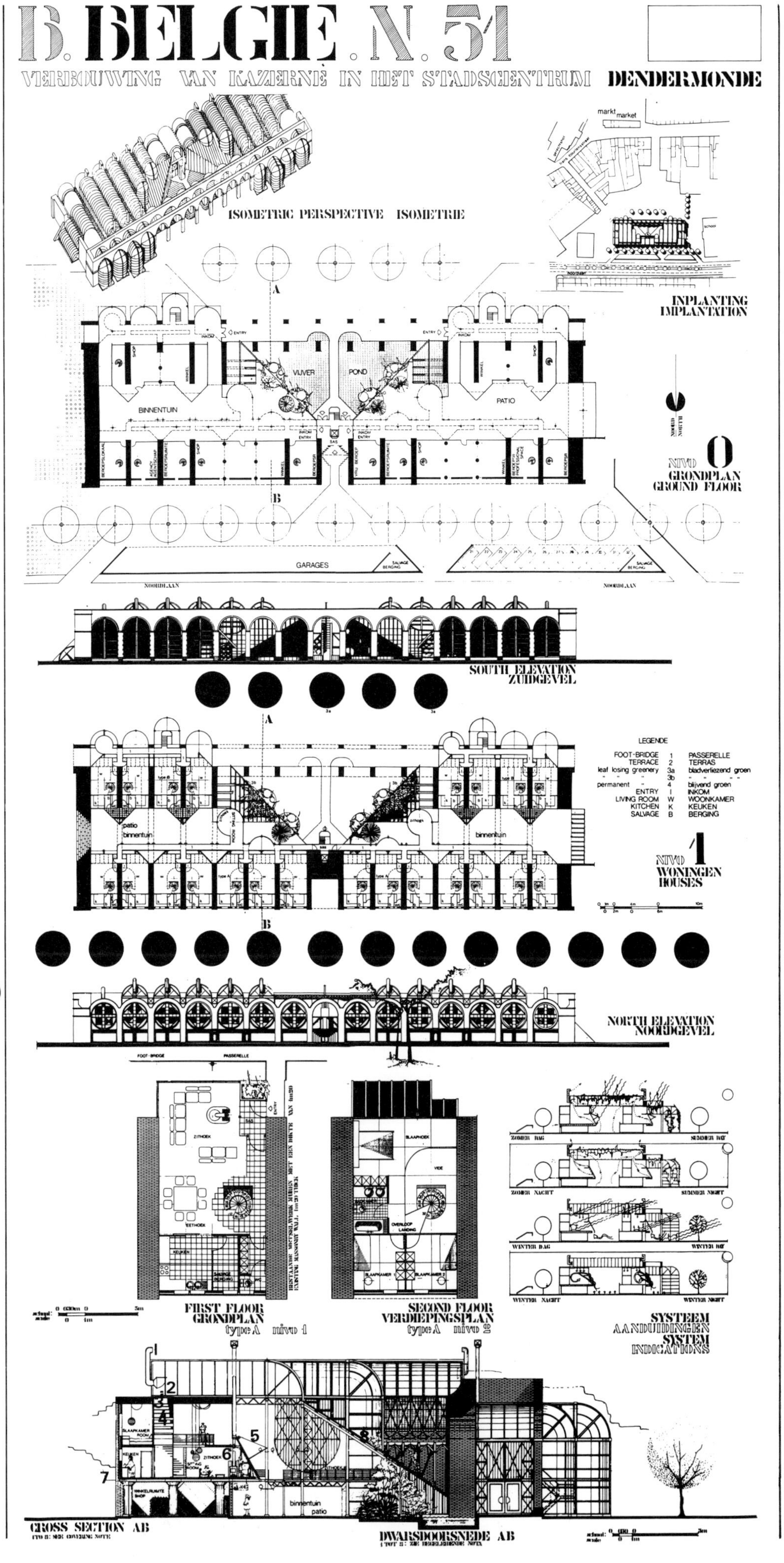

kWh/month

J A S O N D J F M A M J

ISOMETRIC PERSPECTIVE ISOMETRIE

market
markt

INPLANTING
IMPLANTATION

VIJVER POND

BINNENTUIN

PATIO

ENTRY ENTRY

GARAGES SALVAGE BERGING

NOORDLAAN NOORDLAAN

0
NIVO
GRONDPLAN
GROUND FLOOR

SOUTH ELEVATION
ZUIDGEVEL

LEGENDE
FOOT-BRIDGE	1	PASSERELLE
TERRACE	2	TERRAS
leaf losing greenery	3a	bladverliezend groen
permanent	3b	blijvend groen
ENTRY	I	INKOM
LIVING ROOM	W	WOONKAMER
KITCHEN	K	KEUKEN
SALVAGE	B	BERGING

patio binnentuin

binnentuin

1
NIVO
WONINGEN
HOUSES

NORTH ELEVATION
NOORDGEVEL

FOOT-BRIDGE PASSERELLE

FIRST FLOOR
GRONDPLAN
type A nivo 1

SECOND FLOOR
VERDIEPINGSPLAN
type A nivo 2

ZOMER DAG SUMMER DAY
ZOMER NACHT SUMMER NIGHT
WINTER DAG WINTER DAY
WINTER NACHT WINTER NIGHT

SYSTEEM
AANDUIDINGEN
SYSTEM
INDICATIONS

CROSS SECTION AB
DWARSDOORSNEDE AB

COMMENDATION
CATEGORY B

The house was constructed in 1919 and is situated between two taller buildings in the centre of Brussels. The owner, who is married and has four children, wants to live there with two other families each of three persons. The central, period skylight and the beautiful staircase are to be retained.

The southern facade is constructed of a double plexiglass skin, the cavity of which is filled with THERMO-PLUS gas. 100mm away from the structural wall there are venetian blinds of COPPERTON material, acting on one side as an absorber and on the other as a reflectant. The solar heating is thus directly absorbed and reflected into the house. This set-up gives air temperatures of between 22°C and 23°C in overcast weather. In the summer the inversion of the venetian blinds makes it possible to reject the radiation. With an external night temperature of -8°C an internal temperature of 9°C will be maintained in the greenhouse during the night.

There are 15m² of window area in the gaming room. The rest of the roof is made of the same prefabricated plexiglass skin as the Maison Rouge. The commercial diameter of plexiglass, at 3,000mm, is half the width of the house itself. The heated air absorbed by the COPPERTON blinds is forced by a fan through a ventilator in the fireplace constructed of magnesium bricks.

High prisms in the light well throw light on to the central skylight.

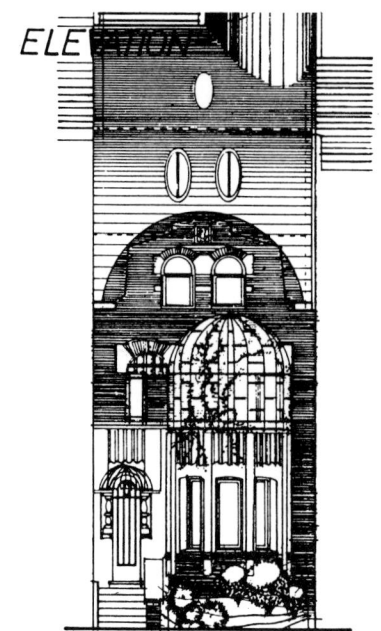

DESIGN TEAM

Michel Duvivier
Andre de Wind

313 Avenue Moliere
1060 Brussels
Belgium

Heat storage takes place in the following places:-
1. the fire-place with magnesium bricks.
2. the chemical heat stores.
3. the pool of water in the greenhouse.
4. near the pool, in acetophenone tubes.

JUDGES' COMMENTS
And finally we commend Michel Duvivier for his elegant conversion of a very gracious 63-year-old house in Brussels. Though we were primarily looking for groups of houses and their relationship to the surrounding patterns of occupation, we include this house for its stylish understanding of the original and its panache in using the language of that original in its development of a solar contribution. The section through the 5 storey sunspace, that rises out of the stairwell and descends down the back of the house, is a case in point.

TECHNICAL ASSESSORS' COMMENTS
This rehabilitation of an elegant house in Brussels is interestingly detailed and utilizes phase change material for thermal storage. Collection occurs in a five storey high sun space which is attached to the back of the building.

The calculations were generally unreliable — the losses were conservative, the gains optimistic and the thermal storage had been over-sized.

LOCATION
Brussels
Belgium

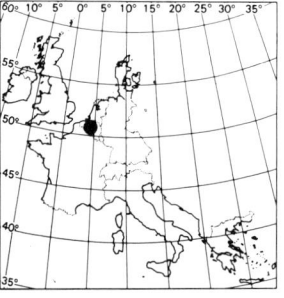

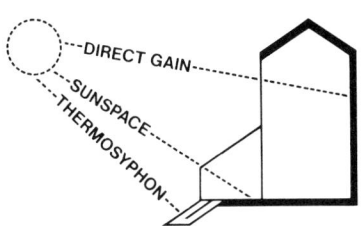

DIRECT GAIN
SUNSPACE
THERMOSYPHON

TECHNICAL DATA

This data has been recalculated.
For explanation of data see page 16.

Latitude: 50° 48'N
Altitude: 100 m
Data Point: Brussels

DWELLING DESCRIPTION (Typical Unit)
Heated Volume: 287 m³

APERTURE	A	B	C	D
System Type	SS	TS	DG	
Net Area m²	26.0	15.3	3.3	
Glazing Layers	2	1	3	
Night Insulation	Yes	Yes	Yes	
τ	0.60	0.90	0.90	
Comment	T+O	T	T	

Aperture/Heated Volume: 0.262 m²/m³
Primary Mass/
   Related Aperture: 210.0 Wh/m²°C
Remote Mass/
   Related Aperture: 1920.0 Wh/m²°C
Air Change Rate: 0.75 ac/h
Building Loss Coeff.: 6.92 kWh/DD
           : 288.33 W/°C

DWELLING PERFORMANCE (Typical Unit)
% Internal Gains: 22.0
% Auxiliary Heating: 44.0
% Useful Solar Gains: 34.0
Annual Solar Gains Fraction: 0.44
Figure of Merit: 0.007 kWh/DDm²
Useful Solar Gains/
   m² of Aperture: 148.9 kWh/m²yr
Min. Temp. without Heating: − 2.7°C
Min. Outdoor Temperature: − 7.9°C

ENERGY CHARACTERISTICS

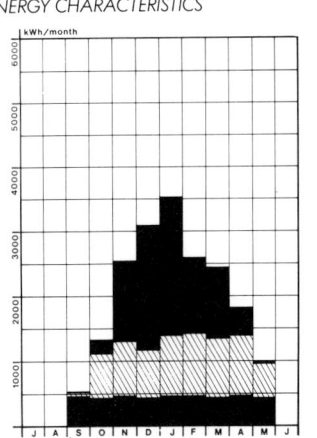

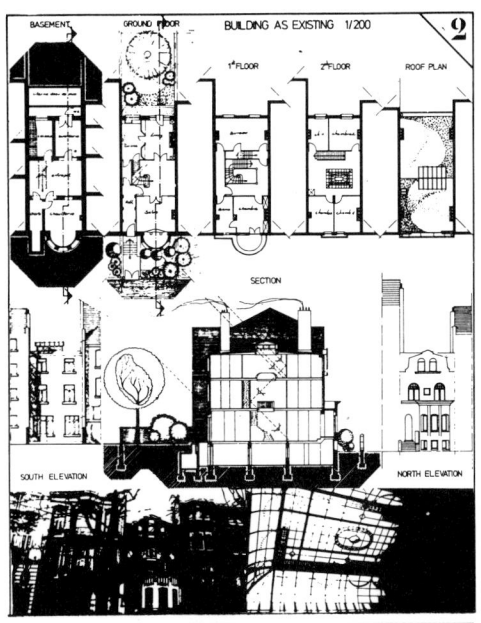

BUILDING AS EXISTING 1/200

BASEMENT · GROUND FLOOR · 1ˢᵗ FLOOR · 2ⁿᵈ FLOOR · ROOF PLAN

SECTION

SOUTH ELEVATION · NORTH ELEVATION

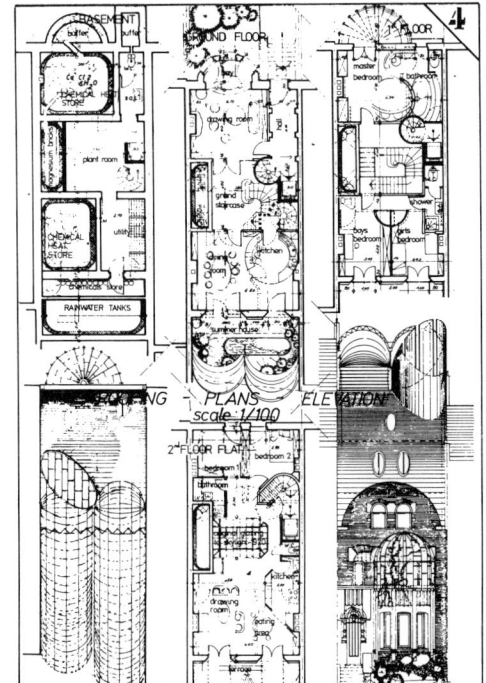

PLANS — ELEVATION
scale 1/100

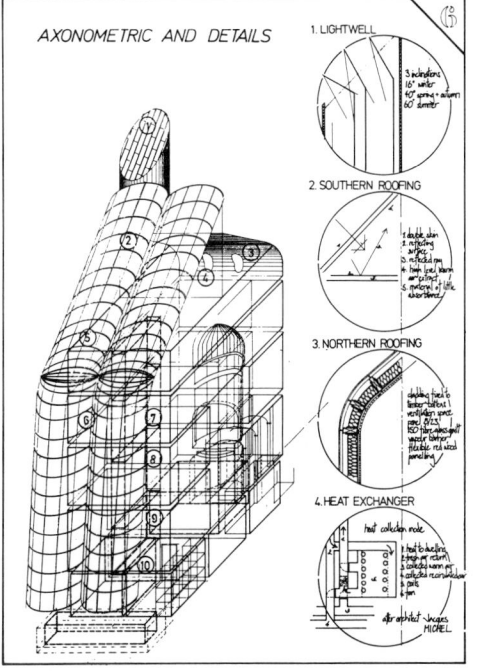

AXONOMETRIC AND DETAILS

1. LIGHTWELL
2. SOUTHERN ROOFING
3. NORTHERN ROOFING
4. HEAT EXCHANGER

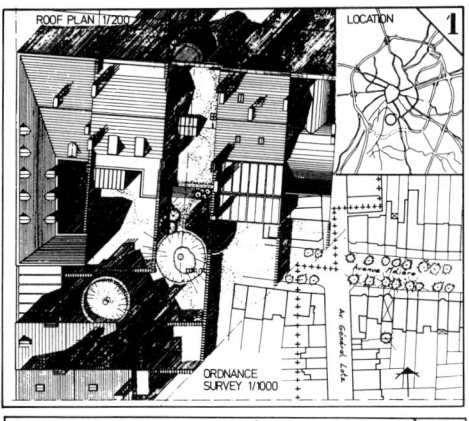

ROOF PLAN 1/200 · LOCATION

ORDNANCE SURVEY 1/1000

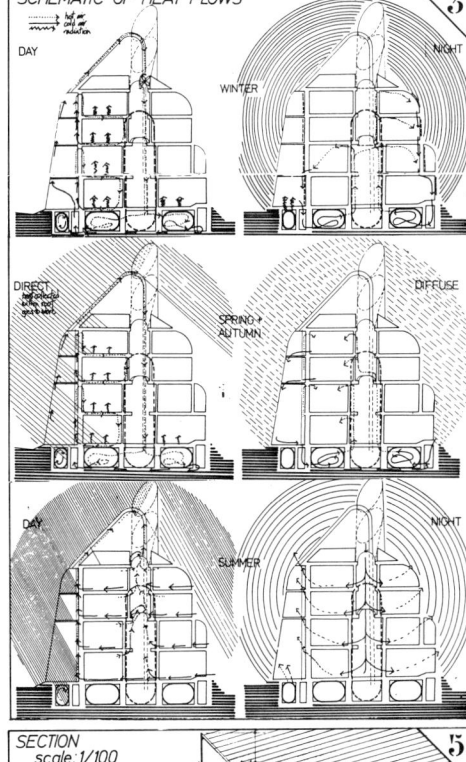

SCHEMATIC OF HEAT FLOWS

DAY · NIGHT
WINTER

DIRECT · DIFFUSE
SPRING + AUTUMN

DAY · NIGHT
SUMMER

SECTION
scale: 1/100

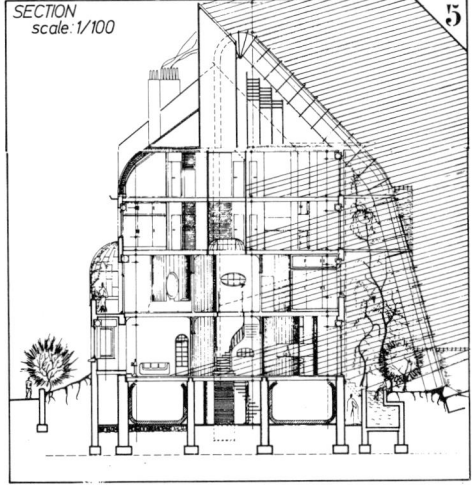

SECTION
scale: 1/100

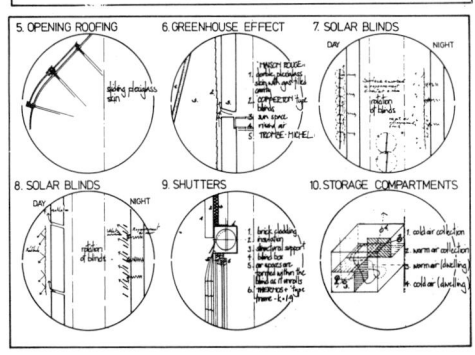

5. OPENING ROOFING · 6. GREENHOUSE EFFECT · 7. SOLAR BLINDS
8. SOLAR BLINDS · 9. SHUTTERS · 10. STORAGE COMPARTMENTS

SPECIAL MENTION
CATEGORY B

The 'M' system can be applied to any existing type of residential units.

On the drawings, various possibilities for system 'M' are illustrated. For example, sheets 1 and 2 concern houses built after 1930, whereas sheet 3, which represents our dwelling as a reference guide for the calculations, shows a house built before 1900.

We have chosen an old house for three reasons:-

1. The housing crisis
2. The economic crisis
3. The environmental problem

Our dwelling is situated in the Haute Marne — a region that has an especially high number of villages — the houses are built of stone and have two or three storeys (although, in general, only one floor is used).

In order to cope with the housing crisis it is necessary to create new extensions which conform architecturally to environmental and urban regulations. However, in spite of these regulations, these extensions are often ill suited to the environment.

The existing houses often undergo restoration. Most of them possess vaulted cellars which are partially underground and which are obviously the most interesting part of the construction with regard to energy conservation. There are at least one hundred cellars in each village and these were formerly used for the storage of the wine that the families produced locally. Because this era is nearly over — we propose maximum energy conservation using system 'M'.

By using system 'M', most of the disadvantages of the conservatory are eliminated:-

— rotating insulation (moved either manually or automatically) allows the system to perform variable functions

— rotating insulation controls excessive radiation during the summer

— a round conservatory is heated rapidly and the volume of unused air is minimized

— the shape of the heat store facilitates heat gain and the radiation and transmission of heat by conduction

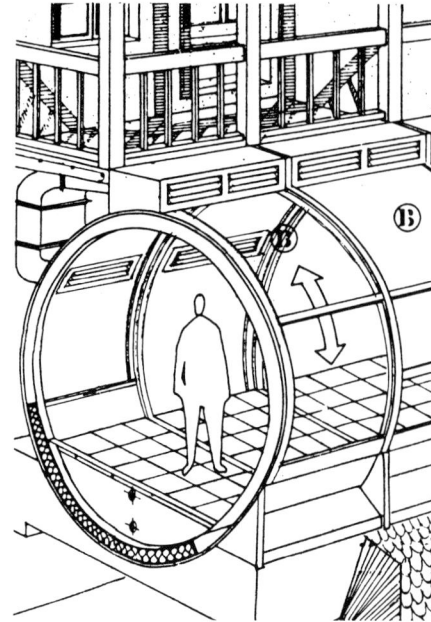

DESIGN TEAM

Resat Gecit
Gerboud Pierre
Marie Helene Gecit
Benedicte Chatel

52210 Dancevoir
France

LOCATION
Dancevoir
France

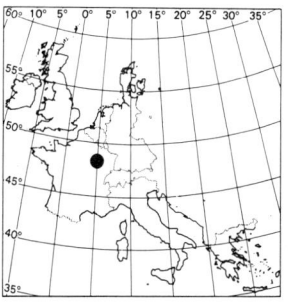

— the interior of the rotating part reflects all the rays on to the heat store, this system being identical to a concentrated receiver

— the storage of warm air does not require a thick wall between the conservatory and the house or between the conservatory and the exterior

— in front of the existing openings (door with 2 leaves: 1,500mm wide) we have decided to create a prefabricated system with a module of 1,500mm. The length of the conservatory may vary according to whether one uses components A, B or C (see sheet 2)

An economic study based on calculations made by our research department showed that:-

— each component costs approximately £480 ... a conservatory with 7 modules costs about £3340

— heating a house with fuel or electricity costs roughly £960

— our conservatory makes a 30% saving and therefore will become cost effective within approximately ten years.

JUDGES' COMMENTS

For sheer ingenuity, we wish to make special mention of Resat Gecit, Gerboud Pierre, Marie Helene Gecit and Benedicte Chatel for their prefabricated addition to the south front of an existing house at Chaumont in France.

TECHNICAL ASSESSORS' COMMENTS

This solar extension to an existing house is technically innovative and intended for prefabricated construction. The cylindrical sunspace features movable insulation, heat storage in water, external shutters and air circulation to the house. Some cost projections are included.

Major errors were discovered in the thermal calculations.

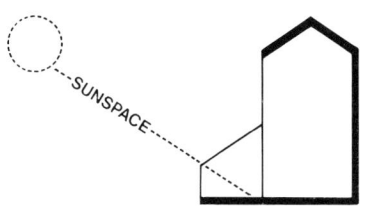

SUNSPACE

TECHNICAL DATA

This data has been recalculated.
For explanation of data see page 16.

Latitude: 48° 00'N
Altitude: 300 m
Data Point: Paris

DWELLING DESCRIPTION (Typical Unit)
Heated Volume: 230 m³

APERTURE	A	B	C	D
System Type	SS			
Net Area m²	51.0			
Glazing Layers	2			
Night Insulation	No			
τ	0.74			
Comment	T			

Aperture/Heated Volume: 0.221 m²/m³
Primary Mass/
    Related Aperture: 273.0 Wh/m²°C
Remote Mass/
    Related Aperture: —Wh/m²°C
Air Change Rate: 0.75 ac/h
Building Loss Coeff.: 10.10 kWh/DD
    : 419.00 W/°C

DWELLING PERFORMANCE (Typical Unit)
% Internal Gains: 16.0
% Auxiliary Heating: 36.0
% Useful Solar Gains: 48.0
Annual Solar Gains Fraction: 0.57
Figure of Merit: 0.015 kWh/DDm²
Useful Solar Gains/
    m² of Aperture: 229.3 kWh/m²yr
Min. Temp. without Heating: —1.0°C
Min. Outdoor Temperature: —5.1°C

ENERGY CHARACTERISTICS

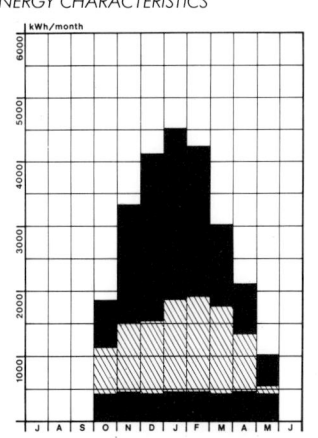

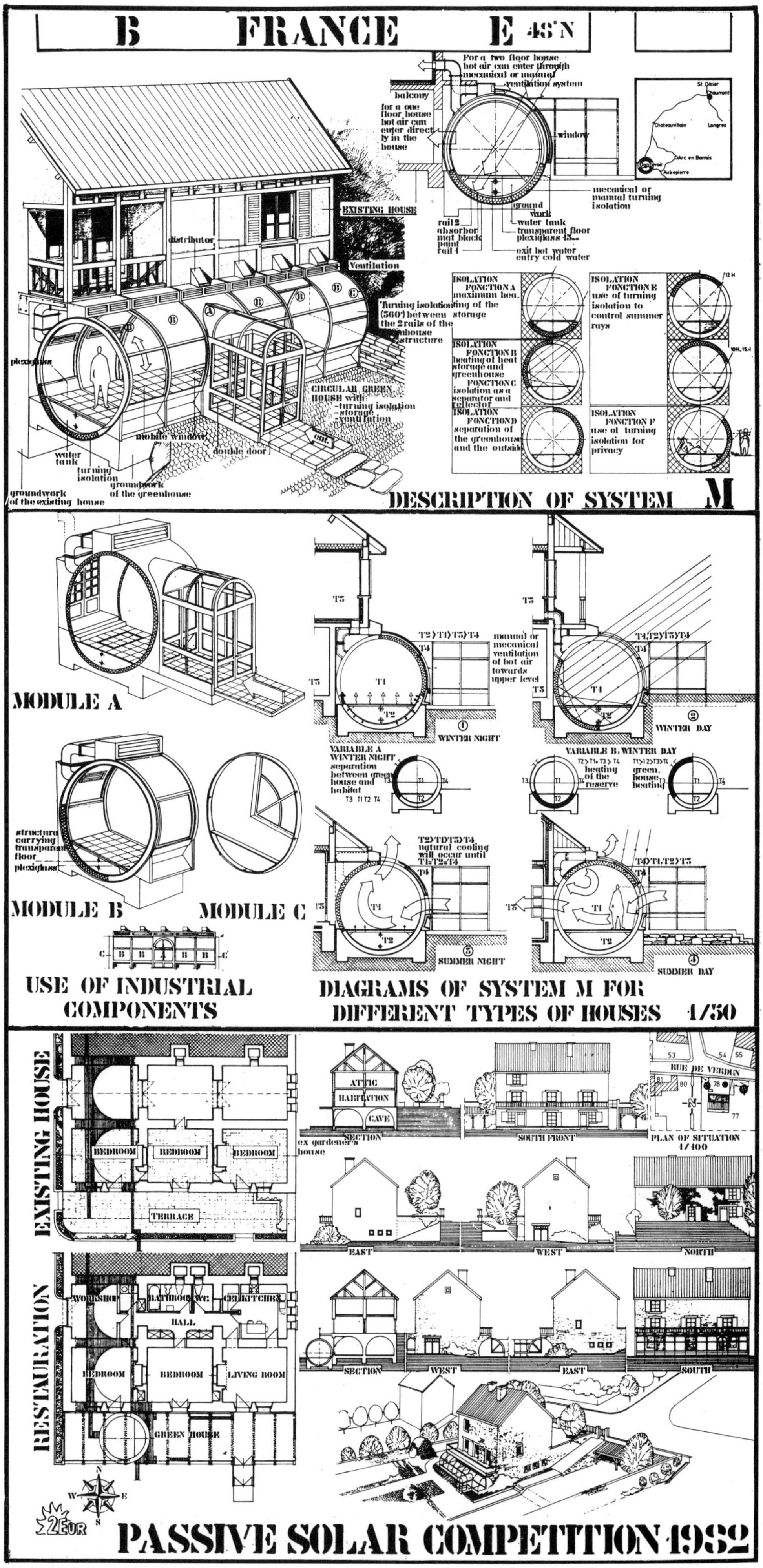

kWh/month

J A S O N D J F M A M J

B FRANCE E 48'N

EXISTING HOUSE

DESCRIPTION OF SYSTEM M

MODULE A

MODULE B   MODULE C

USE OF INDUSTRIAL COMPONENTS

DIAGRAMS OF SYSTEM M FOR DIFFERENT TYPES OF HOUSES 1/50

WINTER NIGHT   WINTER DAY

VARIABLE A WINTER NIGHT
separation between green house and habitat

VARIABLE B WINTER DAY
heating of the reserve

SUMMER NIGHT   SUMMER DAY

EXISTING HOUSE

RESTAURATION

BEDROOM BEDROOM BEDROOM
TERRACE

WORKSHOP BATHROOM WC KITCHEN
HALL
BEDROOM BEDROOM LIVING ROOM
GREEN HOUSE

ATTIC HABITATION
CAVE
SECTION   SOUTH FRONT

EAST   WEST   NORTH

SECTION   WEST   EAST   SOUTH

RUE DE VERDUN
PLAN OF SITUATION 1/100

PASSIVE SOLAR COMPETITION 1982

SPECIAL MENTION
CATEGORY B

There are several troglodytic dwellings built of ashlar stone on this site.

Their natural constant temperature and orientation facilitates the installation of passive solar heating.

The caves are ventilated by inducing differential temperatures with thermal masses placed on the inside of the caves.

Heating, by means of under-floor storage, reduces the upward capillary movement in the tuffaceous stone and in this way avoids excess humidity in the caves.

Air, preheated in underground caves ('the cafforts'), is drawn into the solar collectors and/or sunspace by natural convection.

It is envisaged that there will be no problems of over heating in summer but it may sometimes be necessary to provide back-up heating.

The masonry and tuffaceous stone structure of the conservatories provides stability for the facade.

In our calculations we ignored the losses through the partition walls of the cave dwelling (since these are at a constant temperature).

DESIGN TEAM

Roland Kwiatowski
Sylvere Gougeon

29 rue Alphonse Bertillon
75015 Paris
France

LOCATION
Troo
France

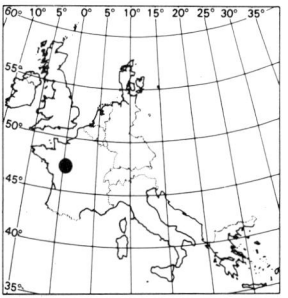

JUDGES' COMMENTS

We wish to make special mention of Roland Kwiatkowski and Sylvere Gougeon for thier inventive rehabilitation of cave dwellings in the Loire region of France. The rehabilitation includes anti-condensation devices and lightwells in addition to the solar devices.

TECHNICAL ASSESSORS' COMMENTS

A rehabilitation of cave dwellings utilizing a sun space with a pebble bed and mechanical ventilation which draws air from underground caves to avoid condensation in winter.

The calculations were not wholly relevant to this particular approach.

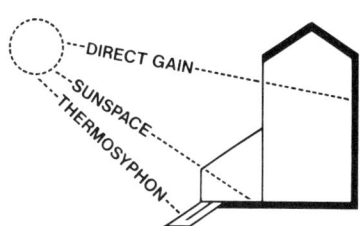

DIRECT GAIN
SUNSPACE
THERMOSYPHON

TECHNICAL DATA

This data has been recalculated.
For explanation of data see page 16.

Latitude: 47° 25'N
Altitude: 100 m
Data Point: Tours

DWELLING DESCRIPTION (Typical Unit)
Heated Volume: 295 m^3

APERTURE	A	B	C	D
System Type	DG	SS	TS	
Net Area m^2	7.7	30.4	18.5	
Glazing Layers	2	2	1	
Night Insulation	Yes	No	No	
τ	0.70	0.75	0.90	
Comment	T	T+R		

Aperture/Heated Volume: 0.192 m^2/m^3
Primary Mass/
Related Aperture: 1158.0 $Wh/m^2{}^\circ C$
Remote Mass/
Related Aperture: 324.7 $Wh/m^2{}^\circ C$
Air Change Rate: 0.80 ac/h
Building Loss Coeff.: 10.10 kWh/DD
: 420.80 W/°C

DWELLING PERFORMANCE (Typical Unit)
% Internal Gains: 17.0
% Auxiliary Heating: 37.0
% Useful Solar Gains: 46.0
Annual Solar Gains Fraction: 0.56
Figure of Merit: 0.015 kWh/DDm^2
Useful Solar Gains/
m^2 of Aperture: 209.3 kWh/m^2yr
Min. Temp. without Heating: 8.3°C
Min. Outdoor Temperature: −6.1°C

ENERGY CHARACTERISTICS

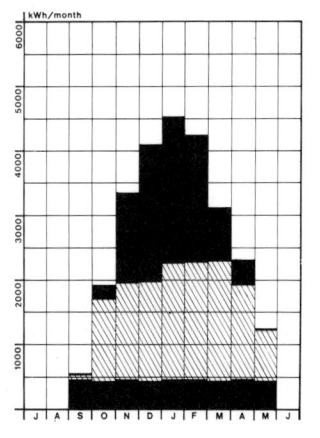

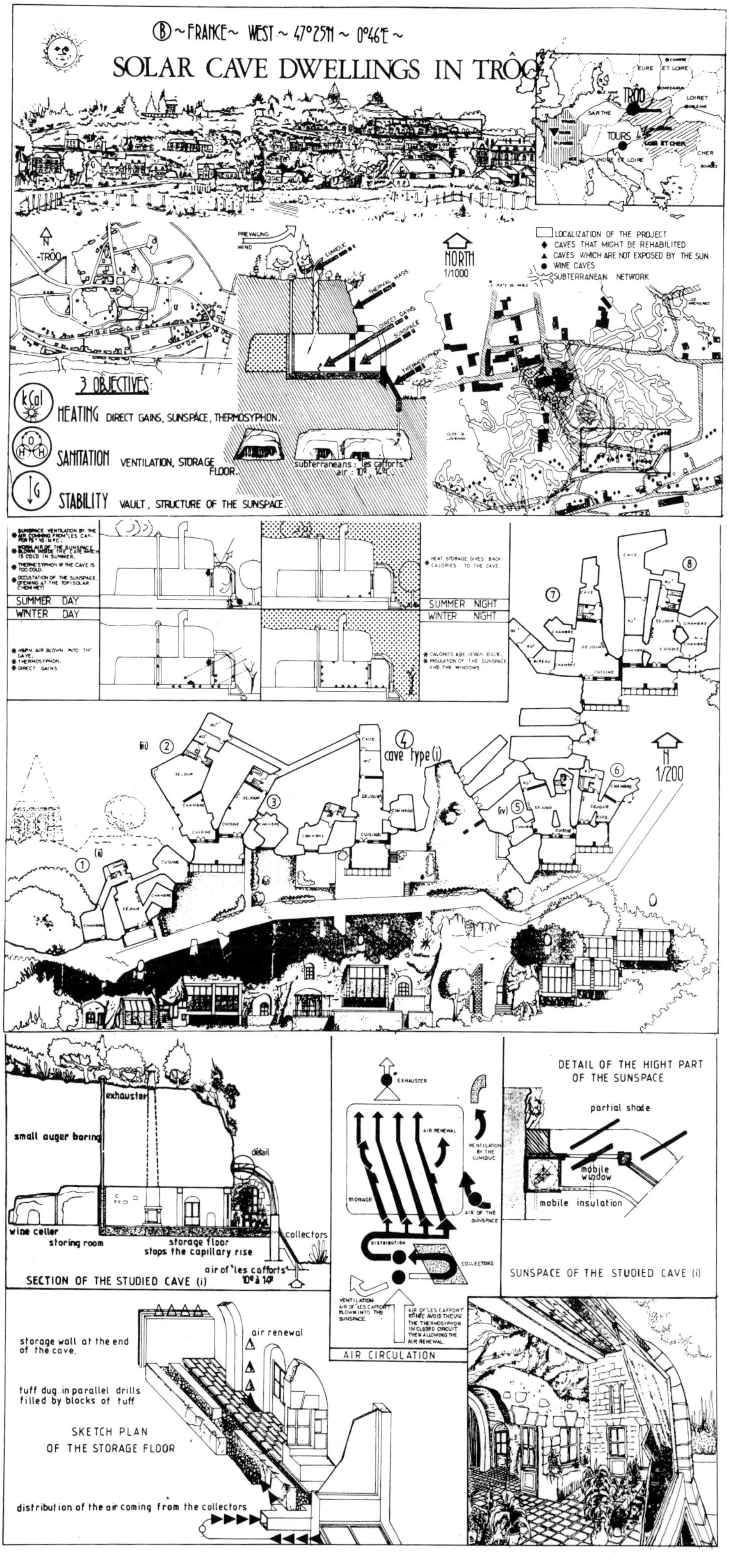

kWh/month
6000
5000
4000
3000
2000
1000
J A S O N D J F M A M J

B ~ FRANCE ~ WEST ~ 47°25'N ~ 0°46'E ~
SOLAR CAVE DWELLINGS IN TRÔO
TRÔO
TOURS
SARTHE
LOIRET
LOIR ET CHER
CHER
INDRE ET LOIRE
EURE ET LOIRE
N
NORTH
1/1000
PREVAILING WIND
LUMIDUC
THERMAL MASS
DIRECT GAINS
SUNSPACE
THERMOSYPHON
LOCALIZATION OF THE PROJECT
CAVES THAT MIGHT BE REHABILITED
CAVES WHICH ARE NOT EXPOSED BY THE SUN
WINE CAVES
SUBTERRANEAN NETWORK
3 OBJECTIVES:
kCal
HEATING DIRECT GAINS, SUNSPACE, THERMOSYPHON.
SANITATION VENTILATION, STORAGE FLOOR.
STABILITY VAULT, STRUCTURE OF THE SUNSPACE.
subterraneans: les caffort's air: 10°, 14°C.
SUMMER DAY
WINTER DAY
SUMMER NIGHT
WINTER NIGHT
HEAT STORAGE GIVES BACK CALORIES TO THE CAVE.
WARM AIR BLOWN INTO THE CAVE.
THERMOSYPHON.
DIRECT GAINS.
CALORIES ARE GIVEN BACK.
INSULATION OF THE SUNSPACE AND THE WINDOWS.
cave type (i)
N
1/200
SEJOUR
CHAMBRE
CUISINE
CAVE
small auger boring
exhauster
détail
wine celler
storing room
storage floor
stops the capillary rise
collectors
air of 'les cafforts' 10° à 14°
SECTION OF THE STUDIED CAVE (i)
EXHAUSTER
AIR RENEWAL
VENTILATION BY THE LUMIDUC
STORAGE
AIR OF THE SUNSPACE
DISTRIBUTION
COLLECTORS
AIR CIRCULATION
DETAIL OF THE HIGHT PART OF THE SUNSPACE
partial shade
mobile window
mobile insulation
SUNSPACE OF THE STUDIED CAVE (i)
storage wall at the end of the cave.
air renewal
tuff dug in parallel drills filled by blocks of tuff
SKETCH PLAN OF THE STORAGE FLOOR
distribution of the air coming from the collectors

SPECIAL MENTION
CATEGORY B

The project is concerned with the renovation of a group of cave dwellings which have been inhabited since the end of the last century.

This region has many dwellings of this type which have been formed simply by the extraction of the tuffaceous stone.

It seemed to us to be profitable to incorporate a passive collection system into this type of dwelling.

During the summer months, the internal temperature of the caves (at 9-15°C) is too cool and it is therefore necessary to introduce the maximum amount of heat from the outside (traditional heating methods will solve this problem during the winter months).
We decided upon the use of a trickle system together with added sun spaces for the passive solar collection system.

Construction of a conservatory in front of a space is beneficial: in the winter months it creates a buffer zone which prevents unwanted thermal loss between the inside air and the outside. In the summer months it collects the energy necessary for heating the surrounding air by means of its solar collection function.

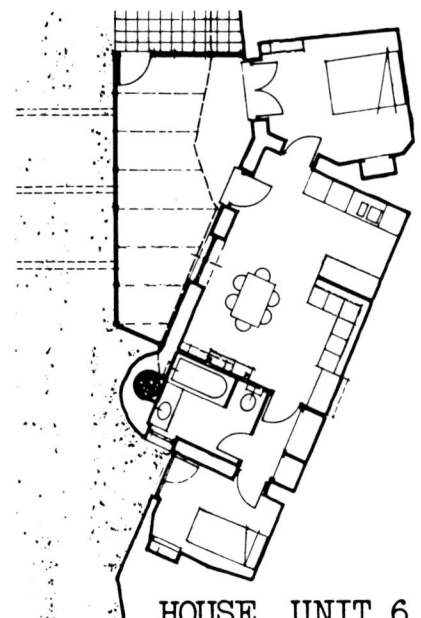

HOUSE UNIT 6

DESIGN TEAM

Gilbert Chamblay
Vincent Courbowlay

8 rue Gwillawme Bertrand
75011 Paris
France

LOCATION
Genille
France

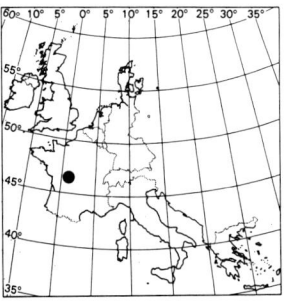

JUDGES' COMMENTS

We also wish to make special mention of Gilbert Chamblay and Vincent Courbowlay for their remodelling of a different set of Loire region caves. This scheme does much less to the caves than the previous one and the sunspace wall is simpler, more continuous and rather more elegant. This led the judges to feel that caves should probably not be improved. However we want to give these schemes a special mention for their inventiveness and their elegant presentation.

TECHNICAL ASSESSORS' COMMENTS

This rehabilitation of cave dwellings in the Loire features added sun space and mass storage walls. The rock store under the sun space is probably redundant. This is a simple system which is flawed in execution.

No calculations were submitted.

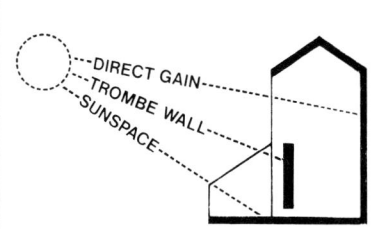

DIRECT GAIN
TROMBE WALL
SUNSPACE

TECHNICAL DATA

This data has been recalculated.
For explanation of data see page 16.

Latitude: 47° 10'N
Altitude: 100 m
Data Point: Tours

DWELLING DESCRIPTION (Typical Unit)
Heated Volume: 130 m³

APERTURE	A	B	C	D
System Type	DG	TW	SS	
Net Area m²	1.5	14.5	21.0	
Glazing Layers	2	2	2	
Night Insulation	Yes	Yes	Yes	
τ	0.70	0.70	0.70	
Comment				

Aperture/Heated Volume: 0.28 m²/m³
Primary Mass/
    Related Aperture: 130 Wh/m²°C
Remote Mass/
    Related Aperture: —Wh/m²°C
Air Change Rate: 0.75 ac/h
Building Loss Coeff.: 5.81 kWh/DD
            : 242.20 W/°C

DWELLING PERFORMANCE (Typical Unit)
% Internal Gains: 27.0
% Auxiliary Heating: 27.0
% Useful Solar Gains: 46.0
Annual Solar Gains Fraction: 0.63
Figure of Merit: 0.012 kWh/DDm²
Useful Solar Gains/
    m² of Aperture: 180.0 kWh/m²yr
Min. Temp. without Heating: —1.7°C
Min. Outdoor Temperature: —7.4°C

ENERGY CHARACTERISTICS

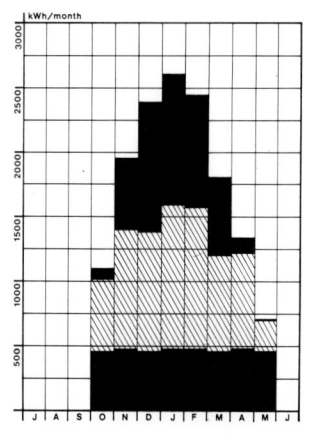

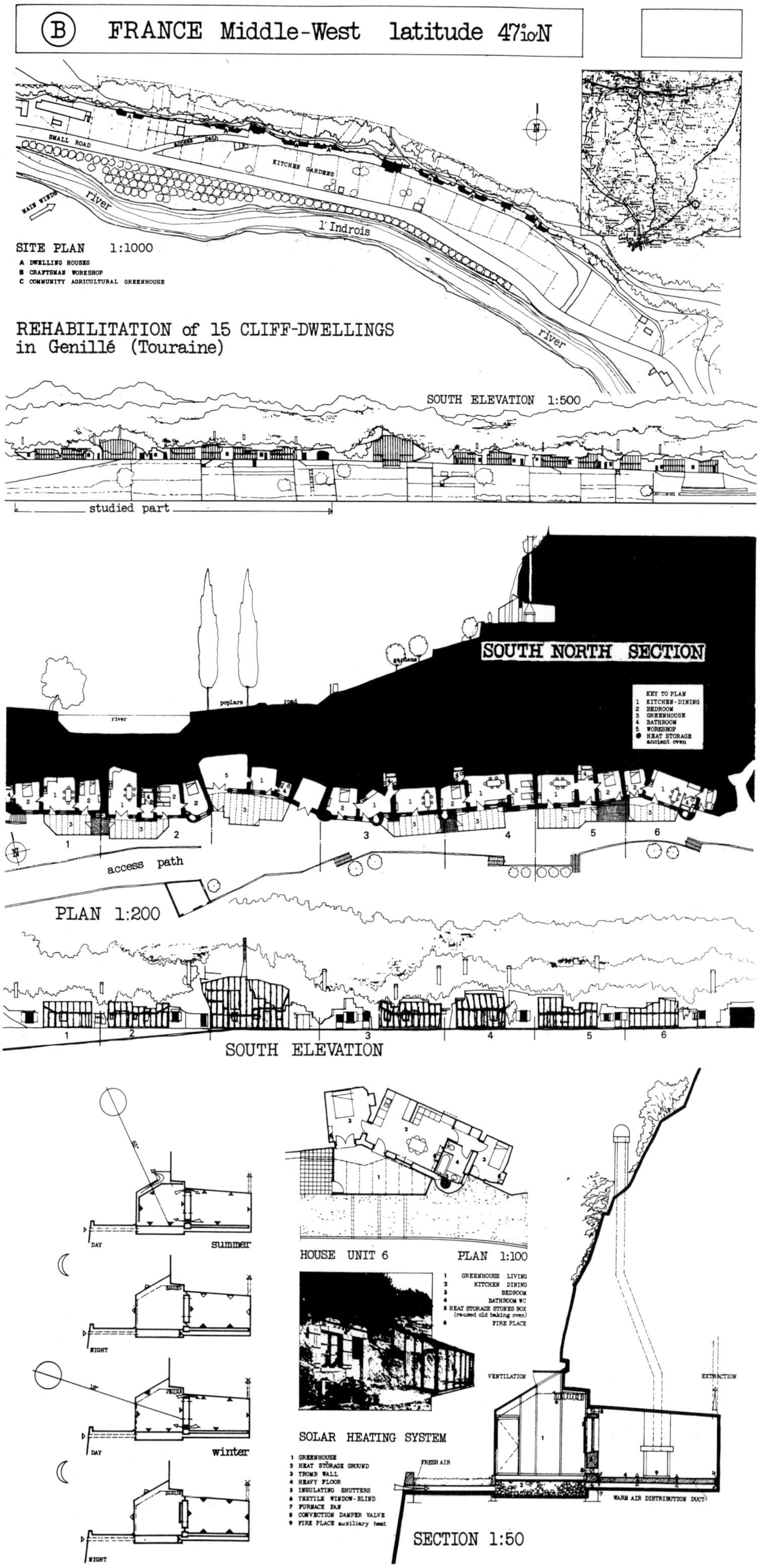

kWh/month

J A S O N D J F M A M J

SITE PLAN 1:1000

A DWELLING HOUSES
B CRAFTSMAN WORKSHOP
C COMMUNITY AGRICULTURAL GREENHOUSE

l' Indrois

REHABILITATION of 15 CLIFF-DWELLINGS in Genillé (Touraine)

SOUTH ELEVATION 1:500

studied part

SOUTH NORTH SECTION

KEY TO PLAN
1 KITCHEN-DINING
2 BEDROOM
3 GREENHOUSE
4 BATHROOM
5 WORKSHOP
● HEAT STORAGE ancient oven

river

poplars
road
gardens

access path

PLAN 1:200

SOUTH ELEVATION

DAY   summer

NIGHT

DAY   winter

NIGHT

HOUSE UNIT 6   PLAN 1:100

1 GREENHOUSE LIVING
2 KITCHEN DINING
3 BEDROOM
4 BATHROOM WC
5 HEAT STORAGE STONES BOX (re-used old baking oven)
6 FIRE PLACE

SOLAR HEATING SYSTEM

1 GREENHOUSE
2 HEAT STORAGE GROUND
3 TROMB WALL
4 HEAVY FLOOR
5 INSULATING SHUTTERS
6 TEXTILE WINDOW-BLIND
7 FURNACE FAN
8 CONVECTION DAMPER VALVE
9 FIRE PLACE auxiliary heat

VENTILATION

FRESH AIR

EXTRACTION

WARM AIR DISTRIBUTION DUCT

SECTION 1:50

OTHER DETAILS OF INTEREST
CATEGORY B

DESIGN TEAM

Barbara Schelling
Manfred Niemann

Rostädferstr 14
D 6072 Sprendlingen-Dreieich
F R Germany

LOCATION
Darmstadt,
West Germany

Latitude 50°N Altitude 200m

DESIGN TEAM

Johannes Dell
Jürgen Neuberger
Kosta Mathey

Fachbereich 15
Technische Hochschule
Darmstadt
F R Germany

LOCATION
Mazzarino,
Italy

Latitude 37°20′N Altitude 573m

DESIGNER

Gerhard Meerphol

Dieckstrasse 3
44 Munster
F R Germany

LOCATION
Munster,
West Germany

Latitude 52°N Altitude 62m

CATEGORY LETTER B FEDERAL REPUBLIC OF GERMANY SOUTH-WEST / LATITUDE 50°

SHEET·1

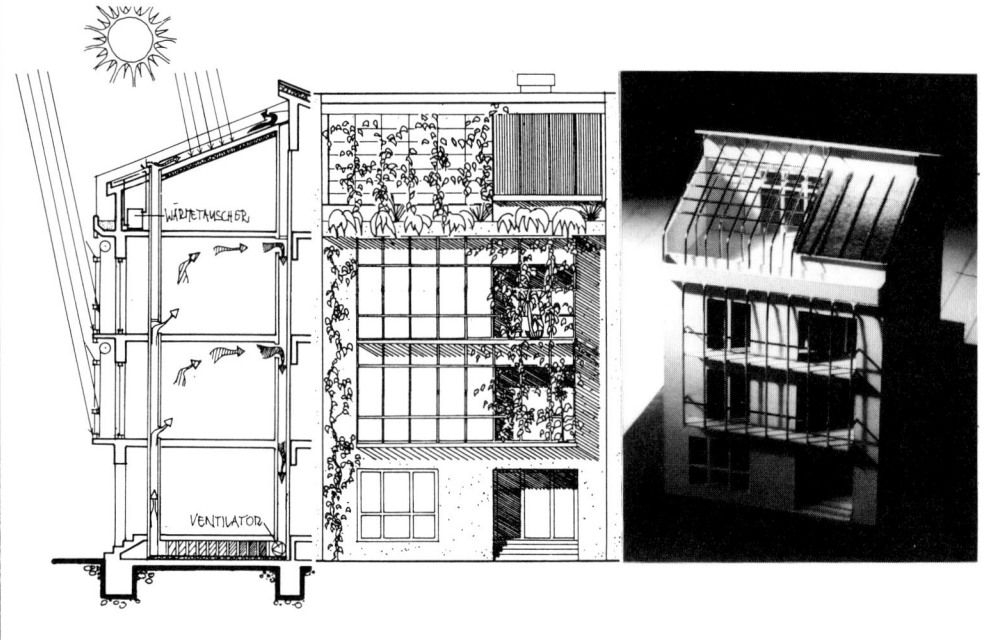

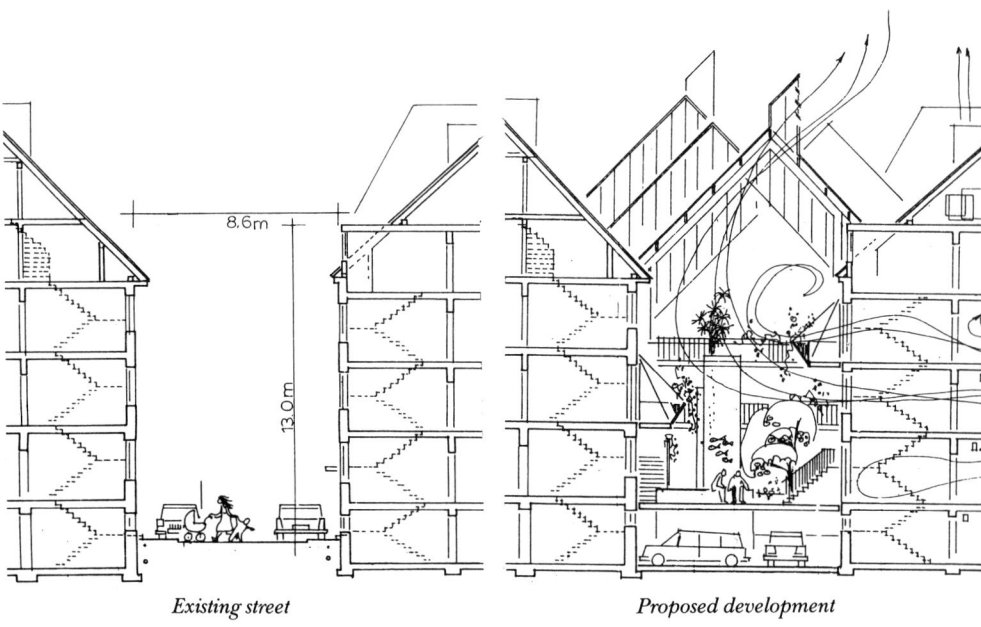

Existing street *Proposed development*

136

OTHER DETAILS OF INTEREST
CATEGORY B

DESIGN TEAM

Heidemarie Dymek
Heinz Dieter Wolff

Marienstrasse 18
404 Neuss 1
F R Germany

LOCATION
Brittany,
France

Latitude 47°36′N Altitude 2m

DESIGNER

Hans Peter Long

Buchenweg A
5500 Trier-Ehrang
F R Germany

LOCATION
Trier,
West Germany

Latitude 50°N Altitude 271m

APPENDIX
CALCULATIONS BOOKLET

The Commission of the European Communities Directorate General XII for Science Research & Development

Second European Passive Solar Competition 1982

CALCULATIONS BOOKLET

1 CATEGORY:

A. High Density, Low-rise Housing:————————————————————— ☐

Proposed Site Density:.————————————— ▢ bed-spaces per hectare

B. Retrofit and Rehabilitation of Dwellings:—————————————— ☐

Age of Building:————————————————————————— ▢ years

2 SITE DATA:

Address: ....

Latitude —— ▢ ◆**1**   Longitude —— ▢   Altitude —— ▢ m ◆**2**

Location: ▢ km (distance) —— ▢ (direction) from .... (nearest city)

▢ km (distance) —— ▢ (direction) from .... (data point)

Nature of surrounding landscape (Open Fields, Urban etc.): ....

Slope of site:———————— ▢   Direction of slope:——————— ▢ facing

	Winter	Summer
Direction of Major Winds		
Associated Weather (Rain, Snow, Dry, etc.)		
Wind Temperature (Hot, Warm or Cold)		
Ave. Relative Humidity (Low, Medium or High)		
Ave. Monthly Precipitation		

Annual Degree Days (Base 18.3°C): ————————————————— ▢ ◆**3**

From Data Booklet or local sources.

3 DESIGN AIMS:

4 SUN PATH:

For each aperture, photocopy the Sun Chart for the closest latitude (Figs. 1-6 from the Data Booklet) and plot the frame formed by the building (edges of the solar aperture, overhangs etc.) and the site skyline using orientation and altitude angle (from the centre of the aperture) of buildings, evergreen trees, hills etc. Paste in boxes below.

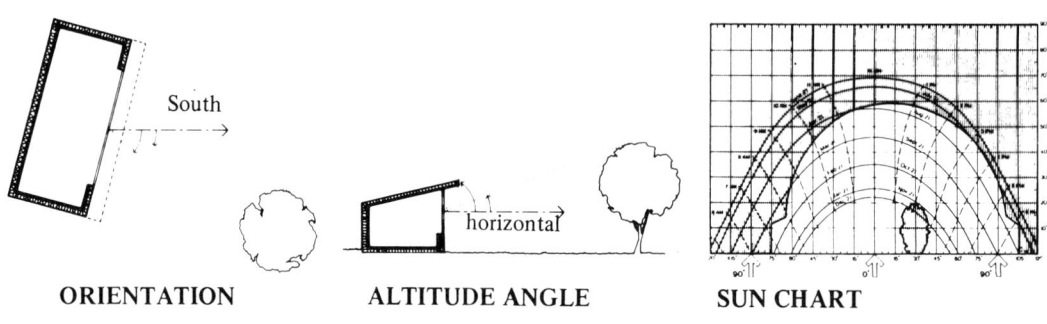

ORIENTATION　　　**ALTITUDE ANGLE**　　　**SUN CHART**

APERTURE A　　　**APERTURE B**

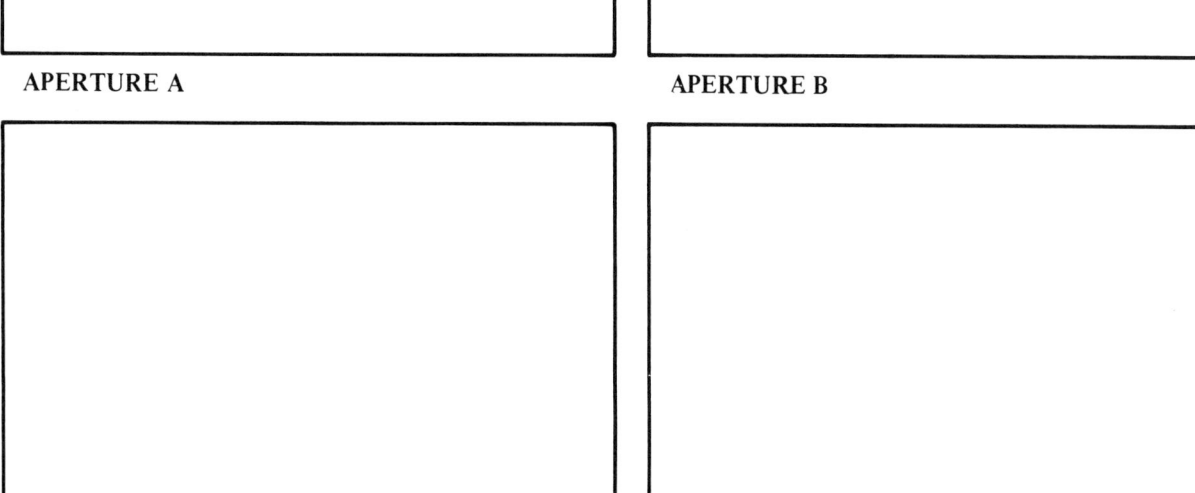

APERTURE C　　　**APERTURE D**

The following Site and Building Proposals sections are designed to encourage the entrant to consider some important aspects of Passive design. For this reason, specific values of, for example, zone temperatures may be approximations rather than based on additional and possibly complex calculations.

5 SITE PROPOSALS:

Entrance locations with respect to wind: ....

....

Pedestrian route locations with respect to wind: ....

....

Vegetation: Shading: ....

Wind-Breaks: ....

Earth-berming _ _ _ _ _ ☐   Underground building _ _ ☐   Ponds, Swimming Pools, etc. _ _ ☐

Natural Ventilation: ....

Other: ....

....

6 BUILDING PROPOSALS:

Number of Dwelling Units: _ ☐

Typical Units:

Type	No. of Occupants	Total Area (m²)	Heated Area (m²)	Heated Volume (m³)	No. of Unit Type
(i)				◆4	
(ii)					
(iii)					
(iv)					

Unit (i) used for Passive Calculations.

Thermal Zoning:

Zone	Area (m²)	Volume (m³)	Summer Day Max. Temp. (°C)	Summer Night Ave. Temp. (°C)	Winter Day Ave. Temp. (°C)	Winter Night Min. Temp. (°C)

Temperatures may be estimated, rather than calculated.

Thermal Storage:

Primary Thermal Capacity can be defined as the capacity of that part of the Storage Element which is directly insolated at noon in mid-Winter. Secondary Thermal Capacity is all thermal storage within view of the Primary Store. Remote Thermal Capacity is that storage which receives energy by convection only and not re-radiation from the Primary Store: ie. Rock-bed, Hypocaust or any other storage not within sight of the Primary Store.

Primary and Secondary Storage:

Storage Element (Floor, Wall, etc.)	Material	**6.1** Density (kg/m³)	**6.2** Thickness (m)	**6.3** Surface Area (m²)	**6.4** Fraction of Surface Insolated at Noon in Mid-Winter	**6.5** Exposed Mass (kg)	**6.6** Specific Heat (Wh/kg°C)	**6.7** Primary Thermal Capacity (Wh/°C)	**6.8** Secondary Thermal Capacity (Wh/°C)
								◆ 5	◆ 6

$$\boxed{6.5} = \boxed{6.1} \times \boxed{6.2} \times \boxed{6.3} \times \boxed{6.4}$$

$$\boxed{6.7} = \boxed{6.5} \times \boxed{6.6}$$

$$\boxed{6.8} = \boxed{6.1} \times \boxed{6.2} \times \boxed{6.3} \times (1 - \boxed{6.4}) \times \boxed{6.6}$$

See Data Booklet for typical values of Density and Specific Heat.

Remote Storage:

Storage Element (Floor, Wall, Rockbed etc)	Material	**6.9** Volume (m³)	**6.10** Density (kg/m³)	**6.11** Specific Heat (Wh/kg°C)	**6.12** Thermal Capacity (Wh/°C)
					◆ 7

$$\boxed{6.12} = \boxed{6.9} \times \boxed{6.10} \times \boxed{6.11}$$

4

Auxiliary Heating Systems:

Type	Fuel	Control Method	Capacity (kW)

Total Auxiliary Heating Capacity:

Method and Frequency of Actions
required for Thermal Control of the Building (Manual or Automatic):

Winter: ....

....

Summer: ....

....

Appliances and Equipment Required: ....

....

Fans:

Location	Use	Volume Flow (m³/h)	Power (W)	Hours Use per Year	Annual Consumption (kWh/yr)

Calculations of air handling performance are beyond the scope of this booklet. Sensible approximations should be made.

Space Cooling

Night-Sky Radiation____ ☐   Evaporative Cooling___ ☐   Earth Cooling_____ ☐

Induced Ventilation ___ ☐   Natural Ventilation___ ☐   Dehumidification____ ☐

Description: ....

....

....

Where cooling is a major factor in the design, supporting calculations should be included as an Appendix.

5

7   BUILDING HEAT LOSS:

Step 7.1   The ventilation loss is calculated, as the product of the building volume (or the heated zone volume if the building is temperature zoned), the heat capacity of air at sea level (0.34 Wh/$^\circ$Cm^3), the Air Density Ratio (obtained from Fig. 7 to allow for different site altitudes) and the design air change rate. 3/4-1 AC/h is recommended for a well insulated building.

Design Air Change Rate: _   ▨ AC/h **8**

If the building is totally mechanically ventilated with a heat exchanger, **8** should be the adjusted air change rate for calculation purposes.

In this case the actual air change rate would be: _ _ _ _ _ _ _ _ _ _ _ _ ▨ AC/h

Heat Exchanger _ _ _ ▨

Extent of ventilation system: ....

....

Cost of ventilation system: _ _ _ _ _ _ _ _ _ _ _ _ _ _ _ _ _ ▨

Heat Exchanger Manufacturer (name and address): ....

....

$$\frac{\text{Ventilation}}{\text{Loss}} = \text{Volume} \times \frac{\text{Specific}}{\text{Heat}} \times \frac{\text{Air}}{\text{Density}} \times \frac{\text{Air}}{\text{Change}}$$
$$\text{Ratio} \qquad \text{Rate}$$

$$= \qquad \times \ 0.34 \ \times \qquad \times \qquad = \boxed{\quad} \ \text{W}/^\circ\text{C} \ \blacklozenge\textbf{9}$$

$$\blacklozenge\textbf{9} = \blacklozenge\textbf{4} \times 0.34 \times \boxed{\frac{\text{Fig.7}}{\blacklozenge\textbf{2}}} \times \blacklozenge\textbf{8}$$

For altitudes below 500m the Air Density Ratio can be taken as 1.

Step 7.2   For all external elements of the building, work out the area of each window, wall section, door, roof etc. and list below. List the appropriate U-value (W/$^\circ$Cm^2). The area multiplied by the U-value gives the Fabric Loss through each element.

Where an element is insulated at night, work out two U-values, one for the element without and one with insulation. Then calculate an average assuming that during the heating season the night insulation is in use for 15 hours per day.

Where the heated space is protected by a buffer zone of intermediate temperature, between that of the heated zone and the outside, the Fabric Loss through the connecting element is obtained by multiplying the product of the area and the U-value by a Buffer Space Factor which is given by:

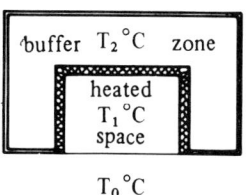

$$\frac{(T_1 - T_2)}{(T_1 - T_0)}$$

where: T_0 = the outside temperature

T_1 = the heated space temperature

T_2 = the buffer zone temperature

6

If the building is temperature zoned in this way, heat losses should be calculated for the heated zone only.

T_2 can be calculated from the steady state heat loss equation for the buffer space:

$$(T_1 - T_2) \times U_{1,2} \times A_{1,2} = (T_2 - T_0) \times \left((U_{2,0} \times A_{2,0}) + \left(\begin{array}{c} \text{Buffer} \\ \text{Space} \\ \text{Volume} \end{array} \times 0.34 \times \begin{array}{c} \text{Air} \\ \text{Density} \\ \text{Ratio} \end{array} \times \begin{array}{c} \text{Air} \\ \text{Change} \\ \text{Rate} \end{array} \right) \right)$$

where $U_{1,2}, A_{1,2}$ = the U-value and area of the element between the heated zone and the buffer zone.

$U_{2,0}, A_{2,0}$ = the U-value and area of the element between the buffer zone and the outside.

The Buffer Space Factor is a property of the building and is constant: it can be calculated for any values of T_0, T_1. If there is no buffer space, the factor is 1.

If the buffer space is insulated at night, two Factors must be calculated, one for day and one for night.

For two or more buffer spaces, similar steady state heat loss equations can be constructed to calculate temperatures.

The Fabric Loss for Non-Solar and Solar elements are tabulated separately, where Solar elements are any glazed areas designed to provide solar gains.

Non-Solar elements:

Building Element	Material	Thickness (m)	**7.1** Area (m²)	**7.2** Daytime U-value (W/°Cm²)	**7.3** Daytime Buffer Factor	**7.4** Daytime Fabric Loss (W/°C)	**7.5** Night Time U-value (W/°Cm²)	**7.6** Night Time Buffer Factor	**7.7** Night Time Fabric Loss (W/°C)

7.4 = **7.1** × **7.2** × **7.3**

7.7 = **7.1** × **7.5** × **7.6**

⬥10⬥   ⬥11⬥

Non-Solar Element Fabric Conductance: _   W/°C ⬥12⬥

$$⬥12⬥ = \frac{(9 \times ⬥10⬥) + (15 \times ⬥11⬥)}{24}$$

For the Passive Solar elements, the U-value of a double-glazed Trombe Wall, for example, would be calculated as

$$\frac{1}{R_1 + R_2 + R_3 + R_4 + R_5}$$

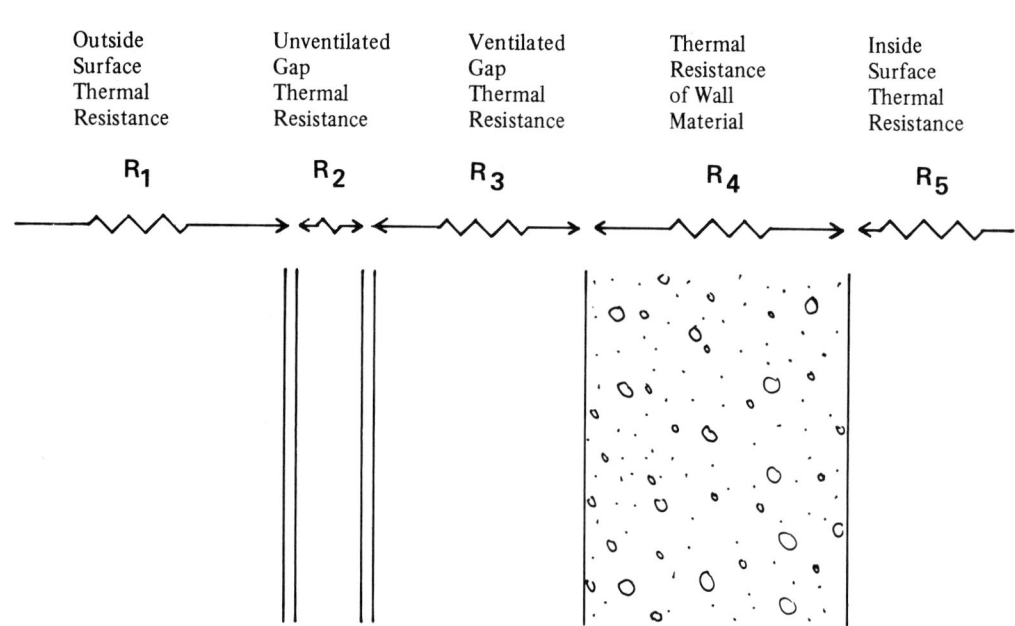

Outside Surface Thermal Resistance	Unventilated Gap Thermal Resistance	Ventilated Gap Thermal Resistance	Thermal Resistance of Wall Material	Inside Surface Thermal Resistance
R_1	R_2	R_3	R_4	R_5

Ventilated Gap Thermal Resistance can be assumed equal to that for the Unventilated Gap.

Passive Solar Elements:

Passive Element (Conservatory) Trombe Wall, Window, etc.)	**7.8** Area (m²)	No. of Glazings	**7.9** Daytime U-value (W/°Cm²)	**7.10** Daytime Buffer Space Factor	**7.11** Daytime Fabric Loss (W/°C)	**7.12** Night Time U-value (W/°Cm²)	**7.13** Night Time Buffer Factor	**7.14** Night Time Fabric Loss (W/°C)	% of Surface Shaded at Mid-summer Noon
A									
B									
C									
D									

7.11 = **7.8** × **7.9** × **7.10**

7.14 = **7.8** × **7.12** × **7.13**

⬥13

⬥14

Passive Solar Element Fabric Conductance:_   W/°C ◆15

◆15 $\dfrac{(9 \times ⬥13) + (15 \times ⬥14)}{24}$

8

Step 7.3 Total Building Loss = Non-solar Element Fabric Conductance + Passive Solar Element Fabric Conductance + Ventilation Loss

$$= \quad + \quad + \quad = \boxed{ \text{W/}^\circ\text{C} \;\; \blacklozenge 16}$$

Building Loss Coefficient $= \dfrac{24}{1000}$ x Total Building Loss $= \dfrac{24}{1000}$ x $\quad = \boxed{ \text{kWh/DD} \;\; \blacklozenge 17}$

$$\blacklozenge 16 = (\;\blacklozenge 12 + \blacklozenge 15 + \blacklozenge 9\;) \qquad\qquad \blacklozenge 17 = \dfrac{24}{1000} \times \blacklozenge 16$$

Step 7.4 Non-Solar Building Loss Coefficient $= \dfrac{24}{1000}$ x $\left(\text{Non-Solar Element Fabric Conductance} + \text{Ventilation Loss} \right)$

$$= \dfrac{24}{1000} \times (\quad + \quad) = \boxed{ \text{kWh/DD} \;\; \blacklozenge 18}$$

$$\blacklozenge 18 = \dfrac{24}{1000} \times (\;\blacklozenge 12 + \blacklozenge 9\;)$$

The difference between these two coefficients and their importance is explained in the following paragraphs.

Step 7.5 Night-Time Building Loss Coefficient $= \dfrac{24}{1000}$ x $\left(\text{Total Non-Solar Night-time Fabric Loss} + \text{Total Passive Solar Night-time Fabric Loss} + \text{Ventilation Loss} \right)$

$$= \dfrac{24}{1000} \times (\quad + \quad + \quad) = \boxed{ \text{kWh/DD} \;\; \blacklozenge 19}$$

$$\blacklozenge 19 = \dfrac{24}{1000} \times (\;\blacklozenge 11 + \blacklozenge 14 + \blacklozenge 9\;)$$

Step 7.6 Window frames, mullions etc. can account for up to 20% of the total element area and so the aperture is calculated as the total glazed area, not the total element area.

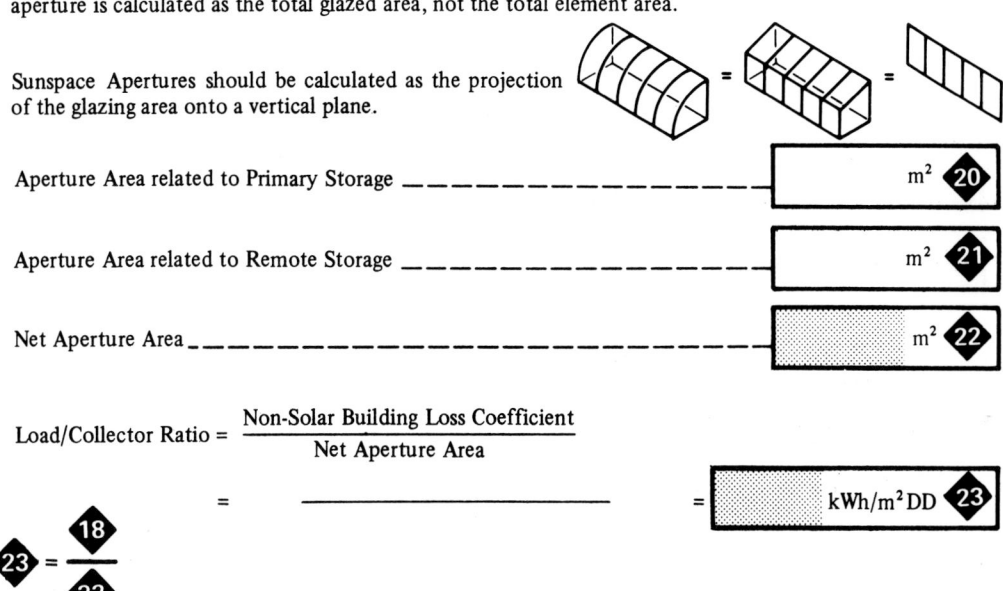

Sunspace Apertures should be calculated as the projection of the glazing area onto a vertical plane.

Aperture Area related to Primary Storage _____ $\boxed{ \text{m}^2 \;\; \blacklozenge 20}$

Aperture Area related to Remote Storage _____ $\boxed{ \text{m}^2 \;\; \blacklozenge 21}$

Net Aperture Area _____ $\boxed{ \text{m}^2 \;\; \blacklozenge 22}$

Load/Collector Ratio $= \dfrac{\text{Non-Solar Building Loss Coefficient}}{\text{Net Aperture Area}}$

$$= \dfrac{}{} = \boxed{ \text{kWh/m}^2\text{DD} \;\; \blacklozenge 23}$$

$$\blacklozenge 23 = \dfrac{\blacklozenge 18}{\blacklozenge 22}$$

Direct gains through glazing in the back wall of the sunspace are assumed to be included in the gains from the sunspace and should not be calculated separately.

9

The estimation technique represented here is based on a procedure devised at the Los Alamos Scientific Laboratory, New Mexico (ref. "Passive Solar Design Handbook, Volume 2", Balcomb, J.D., U.S. Dept. of Energy, 1980). The method was developed by means of computer simulation of the different variables which combine the most important factors of a particular site climate and building construction: absorbed solar radiation, monthly Degree Days, building heat loss coefficient and solar aperture area. These factors are obtained from readily available data sources and simple calculations. Other computer simulation graphs allow complex building properties such as overhang or tilt to be included without attendant complexity of calculations.

The performance graphs were plotted for two variations — with and without night-time insulation — on each of three Passive Solar types: Direct Gain, Trombe Wall and Water Wall. For the sake of this calculation, Attached Sunspaces can be assumed to behave as Trombe Walls; the aperture is thus calculated as the projection of the sunspace glazing onto the back wall. Direct gains through the back wall of the sunspace are assumed to be included in this calculation. No simple technique exists for performance evaluation of Thermosyphonic Passive Systems: they should also be assumed to behave as Trombe Walls.

The technique consists of seven basic stages:

i)   Firstly the Building Loss Coefficient is calculated. This is the total heat loss from the building per day per °C temperature difference between the inside and outside environments. It is determined from the outside areas of all the external building elements (including the passive solar elements) and their U-values, and the ventilation losses.

ii)   The Building Loss Coefficient is used to find the temperature rise in the building caused by the Internal Gains from lighting, cooking, people etc. This temperature rise is subtracted from the minimum acceptable internal temperature (the Thermostat Setting for the Auxiliary Heating System) to give the Base Temperature for the calculation of Monthly Degree Days. Different buildings on the same site could thus have different Base Temperatures and so have different Degree Day values; the Data Book includes Annual Degree Day values to a base of 18.3°C for climate comparison of the data points.

iii)   The monthly Solar Zenith angles are calculated for the site: these are the Latitude less the solar Declination at noon in mid-month (90° minus the Solar Altitude). The Solar Zenith Angle is the geometrical function which is used to describe the movement of the sun in relation to the building to give (from graphs) the increase or reduction in the absorbed solar gain, due to orientation, collector tilt, ground reflectance etc. The average monthly total Solar Radiation, incident on a vertical, south-facing plane, per square metre can be obtained from the Data Booklet for a number of EEC locations. Applicants may use locally available information for other locations and apply the monthly vertical/horizontal ratio from Fig. 8 to convert Solar Radiation on a Horizontal Surface to Solar Radiation on a Vertical South Face. This is multiplied by all the above property factors (orientation etc.) to calculate the actual Absorbed Solar Radiation (per month per m²) for each Solar Aperture.

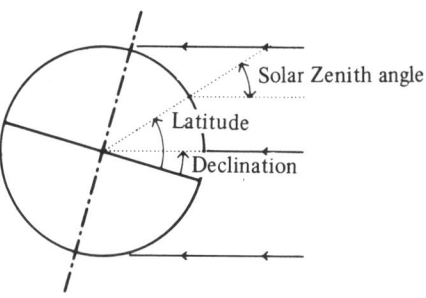

iv)   The Load/Collector Ratio 23 of the Passive System is a measure of the potential effectiveness of the system: if the aperture is small in relation to the building heat loss (i.e. the Load/Collector Ratio is high) the solar gain is less able to make a significant contribution to the total heat requirement. The Los Alamos calculation method assumes that as the Solar Aperture gains more energy for the system than it loses, the heat loss through the solar elements should be seen as not contributing to the overall building load. For this reason the Load/Collector Ratio for the computer simulations was calculated as the *Non-Solar* Building Loss Coefficient divided by the total Aperture Area: to obtain correct results from the performance graphs, this Ratio is calculated in the same way for the building under consideration.

v)   The Radiation Absorbed per Degree Day and the Load/Collector Ratio relate the necessary aspects of the climate and building skin, for determining (from graphs) the Monthly Savings Fraction of the particular Passive System. The graphs are plotted for two conditions: with and without night-time insulation. To interpolate for the actual value of night insulation, the Night Insulation Factor (from graphs) is applied to the Monthly Savings Fraction to obtain an Adjusted Monthly Savings Fraction.

vi)   The Adjusted Monthly Savings Fractions are calculated for all the Solar Apertures and then combined to provide an overall Savings Fraction weighted for the areas of solar aperture. From this the monthly Solar Gains and Auxiliary Heating Requirement can be calculated.

vii) The annual Solar Savings Fraction is calculated from the ratio of the Annual Auxiliary Heating Requirement to the Annual Net Thermal Load. This Fraction is not exactly the same as that proposed in the Los Alamos method, which compares the Auxiliary Heating Requirement with that of a similar building with an adiabatic (thermally neutral) wall replacing the solar aperture. The Solar Savings Fraction calculated here effectively compares the Auxiliary Requirement with that of the same building with no solar gains.

The organisers apologise for the length and apparent complexity of this calculations booklet. Passive systems may be simple in concept but they are complex to analyse thermally, because of the large number of influencing variables. To include the most important of these variables it was necessary to make the calculations booklet this long, but the method is in fact more simple than it appears at first.

The method selected for this booklet is an updated version of the one distributed for the First European Passive Solar Competition in 1980. The method has several limitations of which the user should be aware:

thermal comfort is not assessed and therefore, as a tool for correct distribution of thermal mass, this method is poor. Calculations for condensation and overheating are omitted from this booklet not for lack of importance but for lack of space; use of the methods listed in the "Guidelines for Passive Solar Heating Design" booklet is recommended.

the performance graphs were produced assuming particular typical values for the components of the passive systems — thermal storage capacity, thickness of the collector wall, range of acceptable internal temperatures, number of hours of night-time insulation etc. These reference values can be found on page 40 of the "Passive Solar Design Handbook, Volume 2". If the design varies far from these reference cases, the calculation will be less valid.

the conversion graph included in the Handbook for horizontal to vertical insolation may be accurate for U.S. climates where there are few overcast days and therefore radiation is mostly direct. Northern Europe however has far more diffuse radiation and the graph is unacceptable. There is very little comparative data from which to construct a graph for Europe, but using the data which is available we have produced an approximate graph.

the method assumes that the building is a single zone, i.e. that all the air in the building is being continually mixed. This is not usually the case in practice.

degree day data for different base temperatures does not exist for the European sites listed in the data booklet and therefore we have to use average monthly temperatures to calculate degree days to different bases. This is rather inaccurate, especially at both ends of the heating season.

It is important to consider the probable annual consumption of fans and other control devices and to set this against the solar gains calculated in this booklet.

Once the absorbed radiation has been calculated in this booklet (Columns **8.10** - **8.21**) it is possible to work backwards through the calculation method to determine, from the performance graphs, approximate values for the Load/Collector Ratio, Aperture and Building Loss Coefficient required to give a desired Adjusted Monthly Savings Fraction for the building (i.e. to achieve 40% solar heating in January or 80% in March).

The Balcomb calculation method is designed for the calculation of annual auxiliary heating requirements. Limited validation tests of this adapted version of the method have been undertaken by the authors of this booklet for two sites in Europe. These have produced conservative results for annual auxiliary heating requirements and exaggerated results for useful solar gain against comparative empirical results. When the measured building data was used as input to the calculation, however, good agreement was found.

Entrants who wish to use alternative calculation methods must also complete the following tables for comparison.

11

Month	8.1 Thermostat Setting (°C)	8.2 Internal Gains (kWh/day)	8.3 Base Temp. (°C)	8.4 Monthly Ave. Air Temp. (°C)	8.4½ No. of Days	8.5 Monthly Degree Days	8.6 Net Thermal Load (kWh/mo)	8.7 Monthly Internal Gains (kWh/mo)	8.8 Gross Monthly Heat Loss (kWh/mo)	Month	8.8½ Monthly Solar Declination (°)	8.9 Solar Zenith Angle (°)
			$8.1 - \dfrac{8.2}{◆17}$			$8.4\tfrac12 \times (8.3 - 8.4)$	$8.5 \times ◆17$	$8.2 \times 8.4\tfrac12$	$8.6 + 8.7$			$1 - 8.8\tfrac12$
J					31					J	21.4	
A					31					A	14.0	
S					30					S	2.8	
O					31					O	−9.1	
N					30					N	−18.6	
D					31					D	−23.1	
J					31					J	−21.4	
F					28					F	−14.0	
M					31					M	−2.8	
A					30					A	9.1	
M					31					M	18.6	
J					30					J	23.1	
							◆24	◆25	◆26			

Step 8.1 List Minimum Acceptable Internal Temperatures under Column 8.1, Thermostat Setting.

18°C is suggested as a comfortable minimum.

Step 8.2 List daily heating from internal sources, such as lights, cooking etc., in Column 8.2.

See Guidelines for average levels.

Step 8.3 Calculate Degree Day Base Temperatures as follows, and list under Column 8.3 :

$$\text{Base Temperature} = \text{Thermostat Setting} - \frac{\text{Internal gains}}{\text{Building Loss Coefficient}}$$

Step 8.4 Tabulate Monthly Average Air Temperature in Column 8.4 .

Temperatures from Data Booklet or local sources.

Step 8.5 Calculate Monthly Degree Days as follows, and list in Column 8.5 :

$$\begin{array}{c}\text{Monthly}\\\text{Degree}\\\text{Days}\end{array} = \begin{array}{c}\text{No. of}\\\text{Days in}\\\text{Month}\end{array} \times \left(\begin{array}{c}\text{Base}\\\text{Temperature}\end{array} - \begin{array}{c}\text{Monthly}\\\text{Ave. Air}\\\text{Temperature}\end{array}\right)$$

List data for positive values only.

Step 8.6 Multiply Monthly Degree Days by the Building Loss Coefficient and List under Column 8.6 Net Thermal Load.

Step 8.7 Multiply number of days in month by Internal Gains and list in Column 8.7, Monthly Internal Gains.

Step 8.8 Add Monthly Internal Gains to Net Thermal Load and list in Column 8.8 , Gross Monthly Heat Loss.

Step 8.9 In Column 8.9 list Solar Zenith Angle = Latitude − Monthly Solar Declination.

APERTURE ☐ (A, B, C .....)	8.10	×	8.11	×	8.12	×	8.13	×	8.14	×	8.15	×	8.16	=	8.17

Solar Collector Type:...........................
(Trombe Wall, Direct Gain etc.)

Factors affecting the amount of Solar Radiation incident on the solar aperture

Product of all Factors

Area of Collector:. [m²]

Net Glazed Area:
(Collector Area Less Framing, Mullions etc.) [m²] ◆27

No. of Glazings: [ ]

Night-time U-value: (including glazing, insulation etc.) [W/m² °C] ◆28

Orientation: (Measured from South = 0°: West = East = 90°) [°]

Tilt: (Measured from Horizontal = 0°: Vertical = 90°) [°]

Ground Reflectance: [ ]

8.10	Fig. 9	8.11	Figs. 10–13	8.12	Fig. 14	8.13	Figs. 15–17	8.14	Figs. 18–21	8.15	Figs. 1–6	8.16	Figs. 22–25
8.9		8.9		8.9		8.9		8.9				8.9	

X Overhang: [m] ◆29

Y Separation: [m] ◆30

Z Solar Wall Height: [m] ◆31

Overhang Ratio: ◆32 = ◆29 / ◆31

Separation Ratio: ◆33 = ◆30 / ◆31

For all solar Apertures (A, B, C ....) fill in the separate double-page blocks as follows (if there is only one aperture then only one double page block should be filled in and so on. Columns **8.26 A–D** should be used as necessary):
Only months with positive Degree Days should be calculated.

Record all Collector Information in the left hand column of the table above.

Step 8.10 Obtain the orientation factor from Fig. 9, with the monthly Solar Zenith angle from Column **8.9** and interpolating for intermediate orientations. List in Column **8.10**.

Step 8.11 Obtain the tilt factors from Figs. 10-13, with the monthly Solar Zenith angle and interpolating for intermediate orientations and tilts. List in Column **8.11**.

Step 8.12 If the ground reflectance is other than 0.3, obtain the Ground Reflectance Factor from Fig. 14 and the Solar Zenith angle. List in Column **8.12**. The monthly Ground Reflectance can vary, for example, due to snow.

See Data Booklet for typical values.

Step 8.13 If there is an horizontal specular (ie. mirrored or non-diffusing) reflector in front of the solar aperture, record the Reflection Correction Factor in Column **8.13**. The factor varies with Solar Zenith Angle, Reflector Length, Aspect Ratio and Reflectance: values for typical geometries and reflectances can be obtained from Figs. 15-17.

If there is no specular reflector, the factor is 1.

Step 8.14 Obtain Transmittance Factors from Figs. 18-21 and the Solar Zenith angle, interpolating for intermediate orientations and tilts. List in Column **8.14**.

Step 8.15 For each month, measure from the completed Sun Chart the length of the Sun-path within the frame created by the building and the length of the Sun-path unobstructed by trees etc. within the frame. Divide the unobstructed length by the total length to give the monthly Site Shading Factor. List under Column **8.15**.

Step 8.16 Calculate the Overhang Ratio = Overhang / Solar Wall Height and the Separation Ratio = Separation / Solar Wall Height and record in ◆32, ◆33.

Obtain the Overhang Shadowing Factor from Figs. 21-25 and the Solar Zenith angle, interpolating for intermediate Overhang and Separation Ratios. List in Column **8.16**.

Step 8.17 Calculate the Product of all the above Factors, Columns **8.10** – **8.16** and list in Column **8.17**.

13

	8.18 Solar Radiation (S-facing Surface) (kWh/m²mo)	8.19 Net Solar Radiation (kWh/mo)	8.20 Incident Radiation (kWh/m²mo)	8.21 Solar Radiation Absorbed (kWh/m²mo)	8.22 Radiation Absorbed per Degree Day	8.23 Monthly Savings Fraction (No night Insulation)	8.24 Monthly Savings Fraction (With night Insulation)	8.25 Adjusted Monthly Savings Fraction	
Month		$8.18 \times \langle27\rangle$	8.18×8.17	$8.20 \times \langle34\rangle$	$\dfrac{8.21}{8.5}$	Figs. 27 to 29 $\downarrow$ 8.22 $\langle23\rangle$	Figs. 30 to 32 $\downarrow$ 8.22 $\langle23\rangle$	$(\langle35\rangle \times 8.24) + (1-\langle35\rangle) \times 8.23$	**Month**
J									J
A									A
S									S
O									O
N									N
D									D
J									J
F									F
M									M
A									A
M									M
J									J

Absorptance	$\langle34\rangle$

Night Insulation Factor	$\langle35\rangle$ ◄ Fig.26 $\langle28\rangle$

Step 8.18 Tabulate the Monthly Solar Radiation on a South-facing, Vertical Surface in Column 8.18.

From Data Booklet or Local Sources. If local solar data is only available in the form of Radiation on a Horizontal Surface, multiply this by the monthly Vertical/Horizontal Ratio, obtained from Fig.8.

Step 8.19 Multiply the Solar Radiation by the Net Glazed Area to obtain the Net Solar Radiation. List in Column 8.19.

Step 8.20 Multiply the Monthly Solar Radiation by the Product of all Factors to obtain the Incident Solar Radiation. List in Column 8.20

Step 8.21 Record Absorptance of the Solar collector in ◄34►.

See Data Booklet for Typical values. For direct Gain systems the absorptance is assumed to be 0.9.

Multiply the Incident Solar Radiation by the Absorptance to obtain the Absorbed Solar Radiation. List in Column 8.21.

Step 8.22 To obtain the Radiation absorbed per Degree Day, divide the Absorbed solar Radiation by the Monthly Degree Days, and list in Column 8.22.

Step 8.23 From the Radiation Absorbed per Degree Day, the Load/Collector Ratio (◄23►) and Figs. 27-29, obtain the Monthly Savings Fraction for the relevant Collector Type, without night-time insulation. List under Column 8.23.

Step 8.24 From the Radiation Absorbed per Degree Day, the Load/Collector Ratio (◄23►) and Figs. 30-32, obtain the Monthly Savings Fraction for the relevant Collector Type, with night-time insulation. List under Column 8.24.

Step 8.25 Obtain the Night Insulation Factor from Fig. 26 and the Night-time U-value (◄28►) and record in ◄35►.

Calculate the Adjusted Monthly Savings Fraction, as below, and list in Column 8.25.

$$\text{Adjusted Monthly Savings Fraction} = \left(\text{Night Insulation Factor} \times \text{Column } 8.24\right) + \left(\left(1 - \text{Night Insulation Factor}\right) \times \text{Column } 8.23\right)$$

Step 8.26 For a single solar aperture, the adjusted monthly Savings Fraction (Column 8.25) should be copied directly into Column 8.27 and the calculation continued from Step 8.28.

Where there are two or more solar apertures, multiply the Adjusted Monthly Savings Fraction for each by its Aperture Area, divided by the Total Aperture Area.

List under Columns 8.26 A-D.

14

152

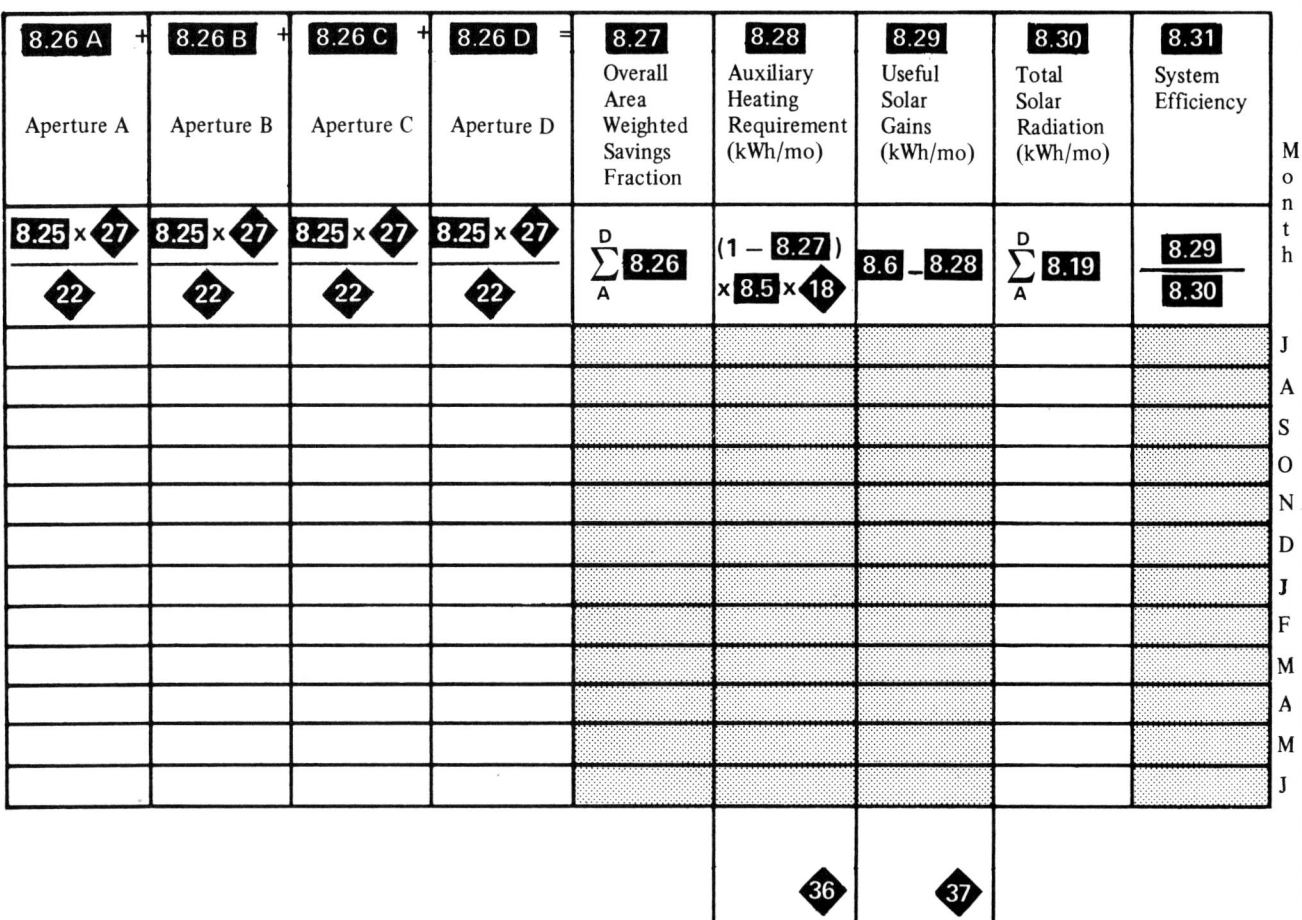

Step 8.27 Add Columns `8.26 A–D` to give the Overall Area-Weighted Savings Fractions and list these in Column `8.27`.

Step 8.28 Calculate the Auxiliary Heating Requirement as follows and list under Column `8.28`:

$$\begin{array}{c}\text{Auxiliary}\\\text{Heating}\\\text{Requirement}\end{array} = \left(1 - \begin{array}{c}\text{Overall}\\\text{Area-weighted}\\\text{Savings Fraction}\end{array}\right) \times \begin{array}{c}\text{Monthly}\\\text{Degree}\\\text{Days}\end{array} \times \begin{array}{c}\text{Non-Solar}\\\text{Building Loss}\\\text{Coefficient}\end{array}$$

Step 8.29 Subtract Auxiliary Heating Requirement from the Net Thermal Load and List in Column `8.29`, Useful Solar Gains.

Step 8.30 For each month, calculate the sum of the Net Solar Radiation on all the Solar Apertures and list in Column `8.30`, Total Solar Radiation.

Step 8.31 Divide Useful Solar Gains by the Total Solar Radiation to obtain the System Efficiency, Column `8.31`.

Step 8.32 Total up each of Columns `8.6`, `8.7`, `8.8`, `8.28`, `8.29`.

Count rows only where monthly DD positive.

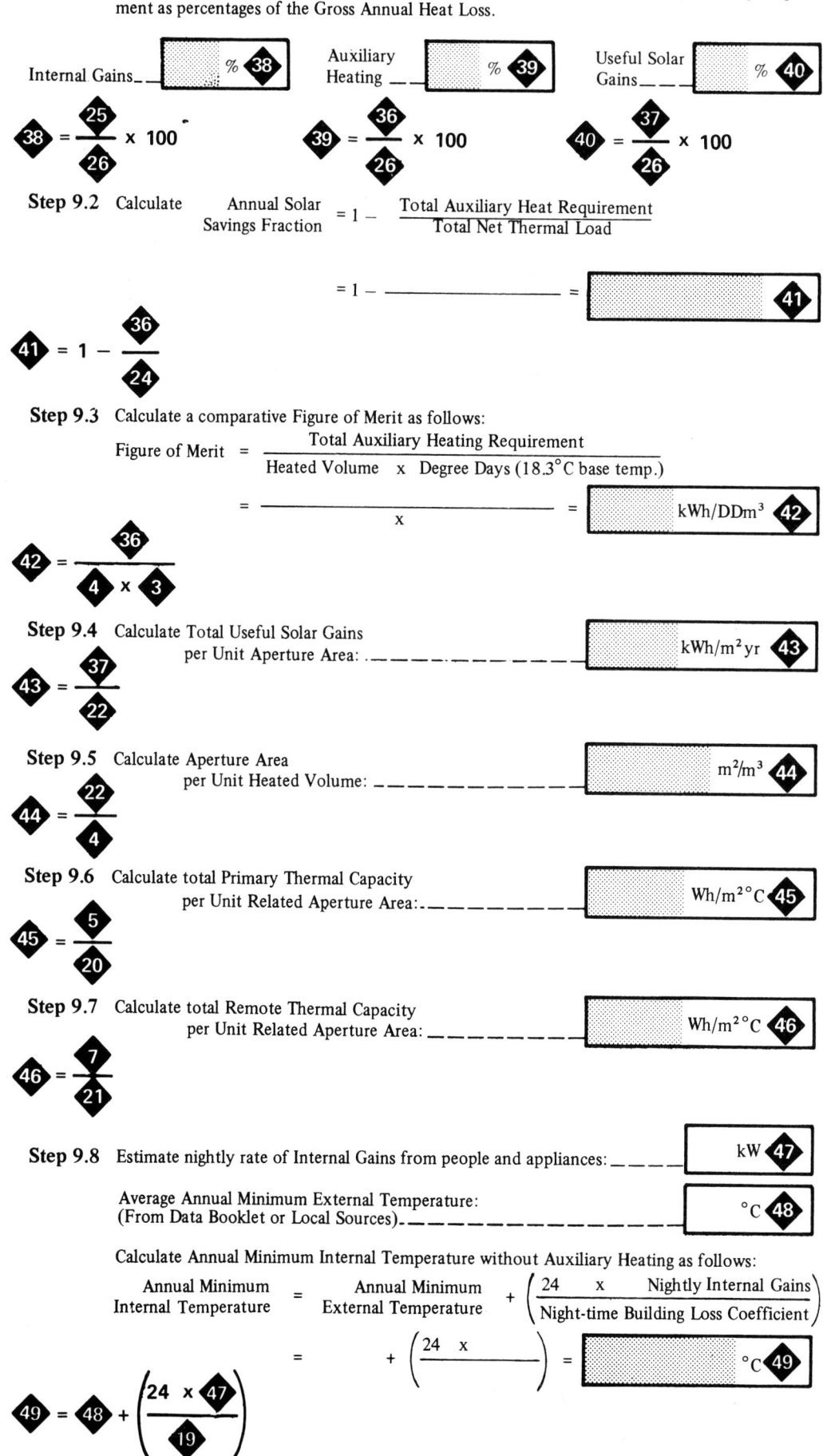

9 COMPARATIVE PERFORMANCE CRITERIA:

Step 9.1 Calculate Total Internal Gains, Total Useful Solar Gains and Total Auxiliary Heating Requirement as percentages of the Gross Annual Heat Loss.

Internal Gains ____ [% ◆38]   Auxiliary Heating ____ [% ◆39]   Useful Solar Gains ____ [% ◆40]

$$\boxed{38} = \frac{\boxed{25}}{\boxed{26}} \times 100 \qquad \boxed{39} = \frac{\boxed{36}}{\boxed{26}} \times 100 \qquad \boxed{40} = \frac{\boxed{37}}{\boxed{26}} \times 100$$

Step 9.2 Calculate $\dfrac{\text{Annual Solar}}{\text{Savings Fraction}} = 1 - \dfrac{\text{Total Auxiliary Heat Requirement}}{\text{Total Net Thermal Load}}$

$$= 1 - \frac{}{} = \boxed{\qquad\qquad \blacklozenge 41}$$

$$\boxed{41} = 1 - \frac{\boxed{36}}{\boxed{24}}$$

Step 9.3 Calculate a comparative Figure of Merit as follows:

$$\text{Figure of Merit} = \frac{\text{Total Auxiliary Heating Requirement}}{\text{Heated Volume} \ \times \ \text{Degree Days (18.3°C base temp.)}}$$

$$= \frac{}{\times} = \boxed{\qquad \text{kWh/DDm}^3 \ \blacklozenge 42}$$

$$\boxed{42} = \frac{\boxed{36}}{\boxed{4} \times \boxed{3}}$$

Step 9.4 Calculate Total Useful Solar Gains per Unit Aperture Area: ____ [kWh/m² yr ◆43]

$$\boxed{43} = \frac{\boxed{37}}{\boxed{22}}$$

Step 9.5 Calculate Aperture Area per Unit Heated Volume: ____ [m²/m³ ◆44]

$$\boxed{44} = \frac{\boxed{22}}{\boxed{4}}$$

Step 9.6 Calculate total Primary Thermal Capacity per Unit Related Aperture Area: ____ [Wh/m²°C ◆45]

$$\boxed{45} = \frac{\boxed{5}}{\boxed{20}}$$

Step 9.7 Calculate total Remote Thermal Capacity per Unit Related Aperture Area: ____ [Wh/m²°C ◆46]

$$\boxed{46} = \frac{\boxed{7}}{\boxed{21}}$$

Step 9.8 Estimate nightly rate of Internal Gains from people and appliances: ____ [kW ◆47]

Average Annual Minimum External Temperature:
(From Data Booklet or Local Sources) ____ [°C ◆48]

Calculate Annual Minimum Internal Temperature without Auxiliary Heating as follows:

$$\frac{\text{Annual Minimum}}{\text{Internal Temperature}} = \frac{\text{Annual Minimum}}{\text{External Temperature}} + \left(\frac{24 \ \times \ \text{Nightly Internal Gains}}{\text{Night-time Building Loss Coefficient}} \right)$$

$$= + \left(\frac{24 \ \times }{} \right) = \boxed{\qquad \text{°C} \ \blacklozenge 49}$$

$$\boxed{49} = \boxed{48} + \left(\frac{24 \times \boxed{47}}{\boxed{19}} \right)$$

16

154

10   GRAPH:

Plot a histogram (Fig. 33) of Gross Heat Loss, showing the proportions of Internal Gains, Useful Solar Gains and Auxiliary Heating Requirement for each month.

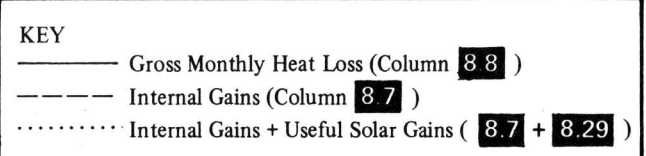

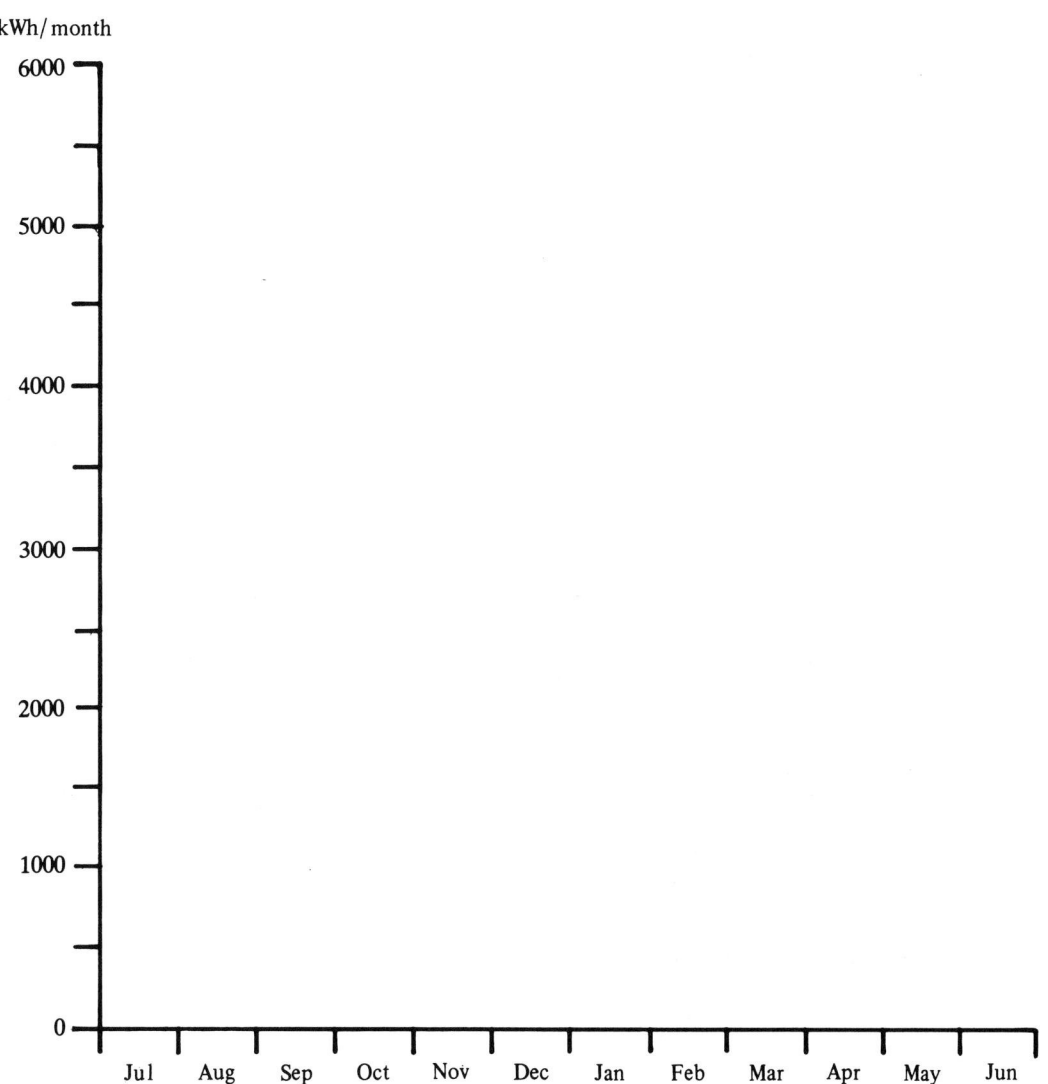

Fig. 33

17

ENTRIES WHICH SATISFIED THE TECHNICAL ASSESSORS' CRITERIA

CATEGORY A

Christian Blachot and Bernard Cogne	FRANCE
Vincenzo Bacigalupi, Cristina Benedetti, Giancarlo Cavallera and Vitangelo Pugliese	ITALY
Steve Tompkins	U.K.
Johannes Brucker, Angelica Fellhaver, Reinhard A Langner and Manfred Vietz	F R GERMANY
Jørgen Andersen and Ove Jørgensen	DENMARK
Anne-Marie Adenis, Gerard Baldet, Mimi Tjoyas, Ch. Marzo, Bernard Cabanne, Clean Energy and Isomobile	FRANCE
Bernard F M Andral	FRANCE
Jean Pierre Franca and Brigitte Ferrand	FRANCE
Ernst G Brodersen and David Coleman	F R GERMANY
Hans-Peter Hebensperger and Werner Sporrer	F R GERMANY
Michael Stosslein, Karin Warthmann and Bernd Sinning	F R GERMANY
David McHugh, Eoin O'Cofaigh and Flemming Rasmussen	IRELAND
A Bastreghi, G Esposito, P Puccetti, A Cambiotti and G Mannocci	ITALY
Alessandro Gioli, Marco Sala, Andrea Corsi, Branka Jankovich and Adriana Toti	ITALY
Aldo Lauritano, Anna Maria Cuccia and Antonino Caleca	ITALY
Vittorio Zanfagnini, Pierluigi de Col Impiantista, Roberto Verzegnassi and Magda Ferreghini	ITALY
Jon Kristinsson, Godfried Augenbroe and Edward Tumbuan	THE NETHERLANDS
Michel de la Hoye	BELGIUM
Luc Schuiten, Pierre Gonay, Luc Deleuze, Stephanie Vervaecke and Johan Herman	BELGIUM
Peter Hald, Flemming Jensen, Jørgen Schultz and Mads Rønne	DENMARK

Poul Qvist Hansen, Søren Qvist Hansen	DENMARK
Jens Hornung and Miomir-Bata Zivkovic	DENMARK
Bjarne Pedersen	DENMARK
Jean Bouillot	FRANCE
Jean Claude Croize, Loic Hamayon and Nicole Haumont	FRANCE
Nave Henri	FRANCE
Frederic Langlois, Franck Dallemagne, Yves Dubois, Alain Gendreau and Nicolas Vincent	FRANCE
Alain le Masson and Thierry De Dinechin	FRANCE
Dominique Petry Amiel, and Gerard Saurel	FRANCE
Messrs Robert, Hannigsberg, Coatanroch and Mesdames Garoche and Gourdon	FRANCE
Richard Senpau Roca, Alain Eble and Gilles Vayssiere	FRANCE
Joachim Budack, Egon Karp and Elisabeth Gertz	F R GERMANY
Claus Centner and Kosta Mathey	F R GERMANY
Hans Ulrich Gunter	F R GERMANY
Winfried Klimesch and Karl Miller	F R GERMANY
Dietmar Kobiella, Jakob Lehrecke and Harald Becker	F R GERMANY
Joanna Kotowski	F R GERMANY
Hans Peter Long	F R GERMANY
Horst Mallmann	F R GERMANY
Uwe Strobel	F R GERMANY
Sean O'Laoire, Hugh A Murray, Brian Thompson, Harry Kennedy and Roderick Mannion	IRELAND
Colin Shaw	IRELAND
Michele M Lepore, Giorgi Caizzi, Loredana Spro and Rosella Silverio	ITALY
Guiseppe Riano, Guido Riano, Nicola Varriale and Bartolomeo Tagliaferri	ITALY
John Olie and Eric Vastert	THE NETHERLANDS
Robert J Gooderham	U.K.

CATEGORY B

Helena Jiskrova, Zdenek Zavrel and Els Sonemans	THE NETHERLANDS
Michel Ripoll, Hubert Maes, Elisabeth Romand-Monnier and Olivier Ronat	FRANCE
Ulla Falck, Dorthe Henriksen and Anne Marie Nielsen	DENMARK
Michael Muller, Dieter Berreth and Willi Kruppa	F R GERMANY
Michel Duvivier and Andre de Wind	BELGIUM
Luk Van Neste	BELGIUM
Jean Louis Izard, Daniel Verger and Philippe Reby	FRANCE
Domique Pilate and Atelier du Soleil (Association 1901)	FRANCE
Jurgen Rauer and Rolf Beele	F R GERMANY
James F McManus, Mark O'Reilly and Hugh Durham	IRELAND

Gilbert Chamblay and Vincent Courbowlay	FRANCE
Resat Gecit, Gerboud Pierre, Marie Helene Gecit and Benedicte Chatel	FRANCE
Roland Kwiatowski and Sylvere Gougeon	FRANCE
Daniel Varrault	FRANCE
Johannes Dell, Jürgen Neuberger and Kosta Mathey	F R GERMANY
Heidemarie Dymek and Heinz Dieter Wolff	F R GERMANY
Gerhard Meerpohl	F R GERMANY
Barbara Schelling and Manfred Niemann	F R GERMANY
F F Holvast and D E van Woerden	THE NETHERLANDS
Messrs Lion, Bakhuizen and van Kuijk	THE NETHERLANDS